Dancing the Politics of Pleasure at the New Orleans Second Line

Dancing the Politics of Pleasure at the New Orleans Second Line

RACHEL CARRICO

UNIVERSITY OF ILLINOIS PRESS
Urbana, Chicago, and Springfield

© 2024 by the Board of Trustees
of the University of Illinois
All rights reserved
1 2 3 4 5 C P 5 4 3 2 1
♾ This book is printed on acid-free paper.

This publication was supported in part by the
University of Florida Center for the Humanities
and the Public Sphere (Rothman Endowment).

Library of Congress Cataloging-in-Publication Data

Names: Carrico, Rachel, 1979– author.
Title: Dancing the politics of pleasure at the New Orleans
    second line / Rachel Carrico.
Description: Urbana : University of Illinois Press, [2024] |
    Includes bibliographical references and index.
Identifiers: LCCN 2024012562 (print) | LCCN 2024012563
    (ebook) | ISBN 9780252045974 (cloth ; acid-free paper) |
    ISBN 9780252088070 (paperback ; acid-free paper) | ISBN
    9780252047152 (ebook)
Subjects: LCSH: Parades—Social aspects—Louisiana—New
    Orleans. | Brass bands—Social aspects—Louisiana—New
    Orleans. | Bands (Music)—Louisiana—New Orleans. |
    Funeral rites and ceremonies—Louisiana—New Orleans.
    | Dixieland music—History and criticism. | Arts—
    Louisiana—New Orleans. | Carnival—Louisiana—New
    Orleans. | African Americans—Lousiana—New Orleans—
    Social life and customs. | New Orleans (La.)—Social life
    and customs. | New Orleans (La.)—Civilization.
Classification: LCC GT4011.N6 C37 2024 (print) | LCC
    GT4011.N6 (ebook) | DDC 791.6—dc23/eng/20240509
LC record available at https://lccn.loc.gov/2024012562
LC ebook record available at https://lccn.loc.gov/2024012563

For Derek and Ellis

Contents

Acknowledgments ix
Author's Note: Online Material xv

CHAPTER 1 Coming Out the Door 1
    INTERLUDE Barbara Lacen Keller 27
CHAPTER 2 Community.. 31
    INTERLUDE Rodrick "Scubble" Davis 55
CHAPTER 3 Spirit.. 59
    INTERLUDE Gerald Platenburg............................. 85
CHAPTER 4 Freedom 89
    INTERLUDE Terrylyn Dorsey 115
CHAPTER 5 Do Whatcha Wanna 119
    INTERLUDE Nicole Lazard................................. 143
CHAPTER 6 Home 147
    INTERLUDE Joe Stern 173

Epilogue: Social Aid and Pleasure in a Pandemic 179
Notes 191
Bibliography.. 229
Index 249

Acknowledgments

Dancing the Politics of Pleasure at the New Orleans Second Line began in the Critical Dance Studies program at the University of California–Riverside, guided by a dream team of mentors: Marta E. Savigliano, whose "Choreographies of Writing" course incubated my first published piece of writing about New Orleans; Anthea Kraut, who watched the project evolve over the years and had crucial insight to offer with each iteration; and Priya Srinivasan, who delivered support and accountability on many levels, often from half a world away. Thanks also go to Jayna Brown, Rickerby Hinds, and Linda Tomko. I am very proud to be a Riverside graduate. This project wouldn't look the way it does without the education I received from every professor there. I would never have gotten to Riverside without André Lepecki and Barbara Browning, who introduced me to this thing called dance studies when I was an MA student in performance studies at New York University. I still pick up your writing when I crave inspiration.

Beyond UCR and NYU, many networks of support helped bring this book into being. I received valuable feedback, especially from Nadine George-Graves, on an early version at the Mellon Dance Studies in/and the Humanities Summer Fellows Program. I remain grateful to Susan Manning, Rebecca Schneider, and Janice Ross for establishing that infrastructure, which sustained me through graduate school and beyond. Special thanks to Janice Ross for bringing me to Stanford University as a Mellon postdoctoral fellow in Dance Studies in/and the Humanities, which afforded time to imagine the formation of this book, and for her dedicated mentorship during that time and after. I also extend deep gratitude to those who established the Collegium for African Diaspora Dance, especially Thomas F. DeFrantz and Tara Aisha Willis, for painstaking editorial labor on my first published article about the Second Line. Thank you for creating another tremendous mechanism of support for dance research, and for welcoming me as a visitor in the circle of African diaspora dance. The generous editorial attention of Jennifer Atkins, Melissa Blanco Borelli, Ana Tamayo-Duque, and Sherril Dodds helped me think more deeply about dance and the Second Line as I prepared versions of chapters for publication. Additional thanks go to Imani Kai Johnson for reading a draft of my essay in the *Oxford Handbook of Dance and Competition* and offering crucial insight. I am grateful to Shawn Womack for the invitation to join the dance faculty of Colorado College for a semester, which allowed me the time and space to experiment with moving this research onto the stage with the incredible students there. Thank you to my University of Oregon colleagues, especially Maria Fernanda Escallón, Sarah Ebert, and Shannon Mockli, for your companionship while I drafted and redrafted the book proposal. While a visiting assistant professor at Reed College, I was delighted to connect with Mark Burford and Oluyinka Akinjiola around our shared research into New Orleans's music and dance cultures. I extend a heartfelt thanks to my Reed colleagues—Jack Pryor, Kate Bredeson, Victoria Fortuna, and Catherine Ming T'ien Duffly—who read exploratory writing on the Glass House and covered my classes when I was off doing fieldwork, supported by a grant from the Stillman Drake Fund for Faculty Development.

I am indebted to many people in New Orleans whose mentorship and generosity made this research possible and pleasurable. I am grateful to the city's many librarians and archivists for their stewardship of materials that document second lining's pasts. A fellowship from the New Orleans Jazz and Heritage Foundation Archive allowed me to collect the oral histories that serve as interludes between the chapters. Thanks to Dolores Hooper, Kia Robinson, and most of all to Rachel Lyons, whose assistance and support have gone far beyond the call of duty. Thanks to the staff at the Amistad Research Center, including Lisa Moore and especially Phillip Cunningham, whose tireless searching and scanning was the only reason I was able to keep research going during the COVID-19 pandemic. Thanks also go to the many librarians at the New Orleans Public Library who have assisted over the years at the Louisiana Division/City Archives and Special Collections and the African American Resource Center; the librarians at the University of New Orleans's Earl K. Long Library, who led me to 1980s issues of the music journal *Wavelengths*; Siva Black at the New Orleans Notarial Archives, whose savvy in navigating the dizzying system of New Orleans property documentation was indispensable; and Bruce Raeburn at the Hogan Jazz Archives, whose comment about period-specific understandings of pleasure was so important. For trusting me as a documentarian with their oral history projects, I am thankful to

Susan Tucker at Tulane University's Newcomb Archive and to Esàilama G. A. Diouf, creator of Nfungotah, Inc., and the Dance for Life Oral History Project. Big thanks are owed to the staff at the Historic New Orleans Collection, especially Molly Cleaver, Jessica Dorman, Siobhán McKiernan, and Rebecca Smith, for research assistance, swift paperwork, and especially for granting permission to reprint portions of material previously published as an essay, "The Dancing," in *Dancing in the Streets: Social Aid and Pleasure Clubs on the Streets of New Orleans* (Historic New Orleans Collection, 2021), which appear throughout these chapters.

My deep gratitude goes to Rachel Breunlin (whose work with the Neighborhood Story Project remains a beacon for me, showing me what ethnography can and should do: the NSP's books provided a guide for how to organize the interludes in this book); Helen A. Regis (who, beyond publishing her foundational Second Line scholarship, offered up her casita and shared wisdom over coffee); Matt Sakakeeny (whose question about my research, "Where's the love?" cracked open a necessary new direction as I crafted the book); Greer Mendy (for casting me, teaching me, reading my writing, and publishing hers); and Kim Vaz-Deville (for her tough questions and sincere encouragement). A conversation with Morgan Clevenger sent me running back to the manuscript to revise its chapter structure. For inviting me to contribute dance scholarship to their important volumes on New Orleans's Black parading traditions, I am grateful to Karen Celestan, Judy Cooper, and Kim Vaz-Deville. Additional thanks go to Edwin Buggage for giving me an outlet to tell second liners' stories in the *Data News Weekly*, portions of which are reprinted in this book. Thank you to Pableaux Johnson, Freddye Hill, MJ Mastrogiovanni, and Judy Cooper for documenting the Second Line tradition with such love and care, and for your permission to publish your images. Jawole Zollar and the whole Urban Bush Women Summer Leadership Institute net-that-works: You have impacted this book in more ways than you know. I may never have come to New Orleans if it hadn't been for Jan Gilbert's magical ways and may never have known the beauty of second lining if not for Cynthia Garza's invitation. Thank you both for everything.

The bulk of this book was written while in my current post as assistant professor of dance studies at the University of Florida, where I have been lucky enough to work under Peter Carpenter as director of the School of Theatre and Dance and to receive crucial support through his generosity. At UF, I have also had the good fortune to work closely with the leadership of the College of the Arts (COTA), namely Dean Onye Ozuzu and Associate Deans Tony Kolenic, Sophia Krys Acord, and Jennifer Setlow. Each time I talked with one of them about my research, I walked away with a grander vision *and* the resources to support it. The same goes for Oṣubi Craig, director of the college's Center for Arts, Migration, and Entrepreneurship (CAME), where I am privileged to be an affiliate faculty member. The UF Center for Humanities in the Public Sphere lent support through multiple grants and much-needed writing retreats. A COTA Works in Process grant, along with funding from CAME, allowed me to conduct a manuscript workshop. Huge thanks to workshop reviewers Stephanie McKee, Thomas F. DeFrantz, and Jillian Hernandez (thanks also to Jill for the welcome company during coffee shop writing sessions); to Barbara Mennel for facilitating; and to School of Theatre and Dance respondents Rujeko Dumbutshena, Noesha Noel, Sabrina Blakney, Peter Carpenter, Colleen Rua, and Jeni Lomnick-Higgins. My colleagues in the COTA humanities writing group—Sarah Politz (organizer extraordinaire!), Laura Dallman, Imani Mosely, Jashodara Sen, Colleen Rua, and Alvaro Lima—carried me through drafts of most chapters. While writing, I enjoyed the gift of working alongside supportive dance colleagues: Melissa Brenner, Xan Burley, Rujeko Dumbutshena, Meredith Farnum, Joan Frosch, Isa García Rose, Elizabeth Johnson, Mellissa Montilla, Augusto Soledade, Alex Springer, Brianna Taylor, and Trent D. Williams Jr. Thanks also to my colleagues in the Center for Arts in Medicine and the Department of Gender, Sexuality, and Women's Studies. I am particularly grateful for Alana Jackson, Colleen Rua, and Jillian Hernandez, who have been become thought partners, co-conspirators, and friends. Vicki Masters and Jeni Lomnick-Higgins: Nothing happens without you. Thank you a million times over. These people and infrastructures, along with my students, have made UF the absolute best place to be while bringing this decade-long project to a close.

The team at the University of Illinois Press has made a wonderful home for this book and its companion website. Thanks to Marika Christofides for contacting me and offering initial guidance on the proposal; to Mariah Mendes Schaefer and Gary Smith for acing all things logistical; and especially to Laurie Matheson for her encouragement, support, and patience with my litany of first-time-author questions and fretting. She always knew, much better than I did, what I would need in order to complete this project during the upheaval of moving my family across the country, starting a new job, the onset of the pandemic, and much more. Thank you, Laurie, for selecting two anonymous readers who, at the height of COVID disruptions, poured tremendous thoughtfulness and attention into their reviews. I was overwhelmed by their generosity, and the book is better for it. UIP's production team did a magnificent job turning a folder of files into a book. Special thanks go to Tad Ringo, and to Jane Zanichkowsky for her careful copyediting. Megan Pugh, an excellent dance scholar in her own right, was the developmental editor for this book; her keen eyes and capacious vision improved the final text beyond measure. Hats off to Sabrina

Blakney and Justine Veras for research assistance, and to Matthew Neil and Kelly Bowker for copyediting assistance. Thanks are also owed to the team at Ideas on Fire for producing an index that charts the book's terrain so insightfully; UF librarian Melissa Jerome for hunting down newspaper citations at the eleventh hour; and to Jess Pinkham, Beth McLaughlin, and everyone at Adept Word Management for taking such care to develop oral history transcripts that communicate clearly while honoring each speaker's voice. It's an art.

My heart swells when I recount the writing groups and partners that sustained me throughout many phases of this project, starting with my UCR pals, J. Dellecave Michelle Timmons Summers, Anusha Kedhar, and Hannah Schwadron (Hannah, how lucky I am that you are also in North Florida). During fieldwork in New Orleans, the NOWFREE collective—Catherine Michna, Heidi Hoechst, and Kate Kokontis—clarified for me the political and ethical stakes of the work. Days of writing in Philadelphia were buoyed by the company of Julie Johnson, Colleen Hooper, Joanna Dee Das, Saroya Corbett, and Charmy Wells. I am grateful for Latanya d. Tigner, whose "yes" to co-authoring an essay in 2020 eased my isolation throughout the pandemic. Thank you, Shukrani Gray, for swapping drafts, doing tarot readings, dancing with me, conducting interviews side-by-side, and much more; and to Daniella Santoro for a decade-plus of research companionship and treasured friendship. I couldn't imagine doing any of this without you. Thanks also to Dasha Chapman and Ann Mazzocca, whose company I have enjoyed throughout, from conferences to Second Lines. Getting to the finish line was nourished by the virtual comradery and WhatsApp lifeline of my Zoom writing crew—Joanna Dee Das, Saroya Corbett, Elizabeth Craft, Adanna Kai Jones, and Esther Kurtz—who were on my screen even as I wrote these words.

An author is supported by her intellectual communities, but books cannot get written without the inner circles of family and family-like. The entire staff at Persimmon Early Learning Academy let me rest easy while my child was in their care, even when that meant navigating the perilous terrain of preschool in a pandemic. This book would not exist without your labor. The baristas at Curia on the Drag kept me caffeinated at my outdoor home-office-away-from-home-office during many long writing sessions. My Goat in the Road family, ever growing, once upon a time tolerated my late arrival to Sunday rehearsals because I couldn't pull myself away from the Second Line and cheered me on as this book neared completion. I'm very proud to be a part of this organization. Thank you for letting me hang on as the eternal board member. Thank you, Vanessa Pierson, for the stream of postcard pep talks that kept me going in the eleventh hour. Thank you, Cassandra Erb, for always providing a soft place for me to land when I return to New Orleans, and for the weekly phone calls that keep me sane, connected, and open-hearted during the darkest days. The Nucleus—you know who you are and how much you mean to me. You were there when it all began.

I had the good sense to marry someone who loves to Second Line as much as I do. I can't imagine asking anyone but you, Derek Burdette, to make the kinds of sacrifices you've made to feed my footwork obsession and to bring this book into the world (all while writing a book of your own). To Ellis: You started second lining in my womb and now carry your own fan. You keep me grounded and honest; you remind me of the magic that is this world; you cure me of my delusions about myself and help me just say it plain. I sent the proposal for this book on the day you were due; years later, I am a better writer and better a human because I am your mother. My own mother first enrolled me in dance class and now she and my father fly around the country to celebrate career milestones, to see the New Orleans I love, provide free childcare so I can do what I love, and support in so many ways that I could never completely list them. My siblings and grandparents remain curious and celebratory about the work and for that I am also grateful. Thank you to my family for everything.

My participation in the Second Line community began long before this book was even an idea and will continue long after its publication. Words cannot express my gratitude for those who have invited me into the culture, including Catina Braxton Robertson, one of the most creative, big-hearted, hardest-working people I'll ever know. To my fellow Ice Divas, especially Kristy Magner, Arielle Guice, and Wynoka Boudreaux, I love you all. Thank you for allowing me to share a part of our story in print. Edward Buckner, I hold deep admiration for your fierce vision, your hustle, and your heart. Thank you for reading every word I give you, for setting me straight when I get off-track, and for always picking up the phone. There would be no book without the generosity of these individuals and the others whose stories it tells. I am honored that Joe Stern and Barbara Lacen Keller (may they rest in peace), Barbara's daughter Kelly Dixon, Rodrick Davis, Terrylyn Dorsey, Nicole Lazard, and Gerald Platenburg granted generous permission to share excerpts of their oral histories as the chapter interludes in this book. For agreeing to share full recordings and transcripts on the companion website, I thank those six individuals as well as Wellington Ratcliff Jr., Catina Braxton Robertson, Don Robertson, Tamara Jackson Snowden, and Tyree Smith. Thank you also to everyone else who sat for the interviews, listed in the bibliography, which inform and enrich the chapters. This book exists because of the generosity, intelligence, and support of everyone listed here, and so many more that their names could fill a tome of its own. Any and all limitations of the book are wholly my own.

Author's Note: Online Material

Supplemental online material that will enrich readers' engagement with *Dancing the Politics of Pleasure at the New Orleans Second Line* can be found at the University of Illinois Press website and accessed through the web page for this book. There you will find videos of dancing at the Second Line that accompany specific descriptions in the text. You will also find complete oral histories that I conducted with eleven individuals whose voices appear throughout the book (some videos, some audio files, all with accompanying transcripts). Some of these oral history recordings are also paired with videos of the individual dancing or other related media. Additional oral history interviews, drawn from other sources, are also included. Five of the oral histories appear first on the web page, and callouts are noted in multiple chapters, since excerpts from these interviews appear throughout the book. The rest of the material is segmented into chapters to make it easier to move through book and website sequentially and to assign specific chapters for classroom use. Finally, I have compiled a list of supplemental links to point interested students and other researchers to other online repositories of Second Line knowledge.

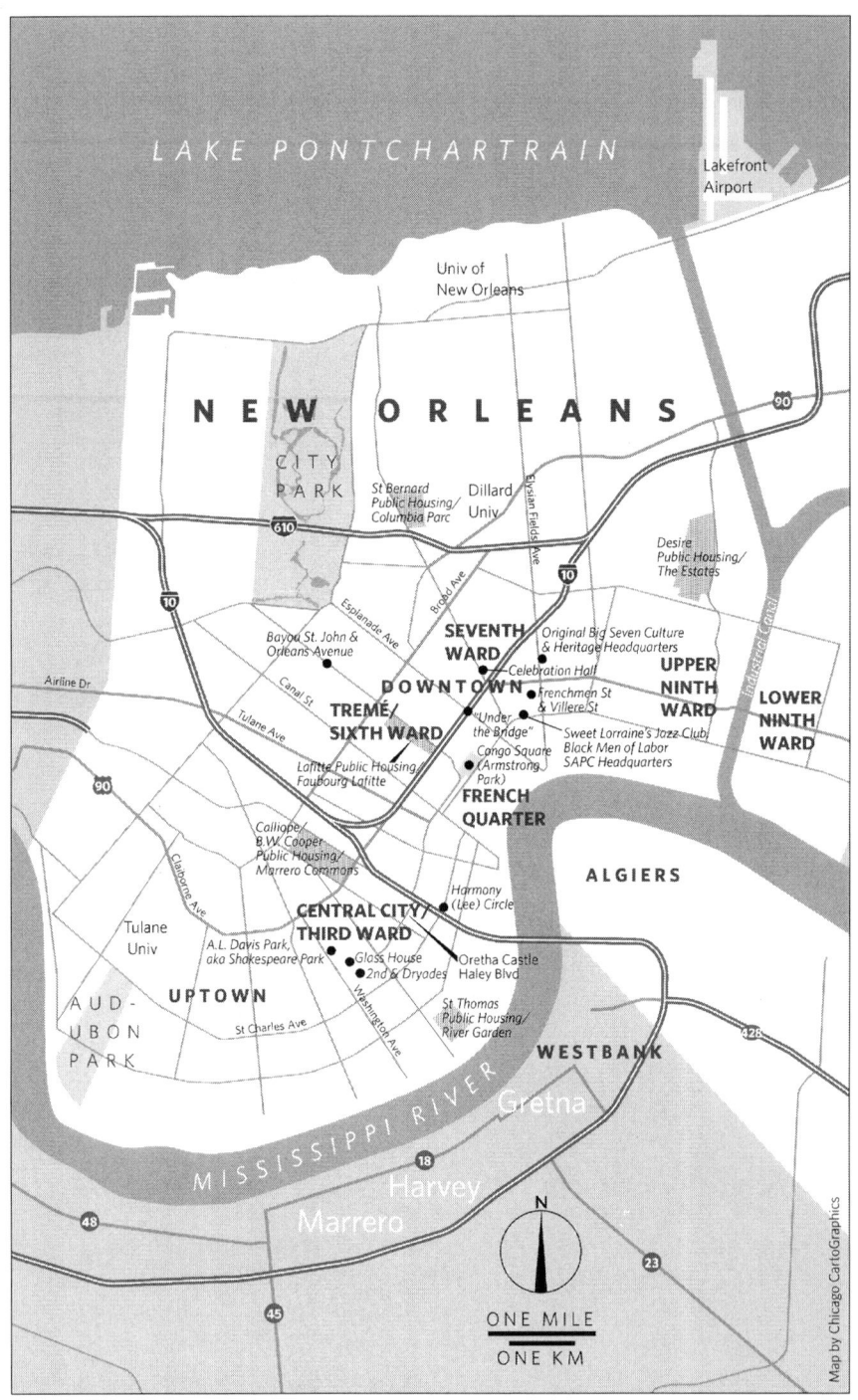

Second Line geographies in New Orleans, Louisiana. (Map by Dennis McClendon.)

CHAPTER 1

Coming Out the Door

The sun glistened on the water as I joined a large crowd gathered between the banks of Bayou St. John and the gas station on Orleans Avenue in New Orleans. It was a Sunday in March 2014, and we eagerly awaited Keep-N-It Real Social & Pleasure Club's annual anniversary parade. People greeted each other with strong hugs, wide smiles, and expressions of gratitude for the cool breeze. This kind of gorgeous day—low seventies, a few wispy clouds in the sky—could not be taken for granted in New Orleans, where heat, humidity, and serious storms could threaten any springtime activity. But on this Sunday, the mild weather seemed to welcome the first Second Line parade in weeks, since they had been suspended during Mardi Gras. Those unfamiliar with the city's complex parading cultures may associate parades with Mardi Gras exclusively, but in fact, a large contingent of New Orleanians anxiously awaits the *end* of Carnival season so they can get back to parading—back to second lining, that is.

Since the late nineteenth century, Afro-Creole and African American New Orleanians have organized brass band processions, known as "Second Lines," that take hold of public spaces with rhythm and forward motion.[1] Today, hundreds or thousands of paraders pack into neighborhood streets, showcasing a distinctive form of improvised footwork that moves them along a multi-mile processional route. Second liners call these parades "church for dancers," and they happen, appropriately enough, every Sunday. The calendar is only interrupted during the hottest summer months and when the city devotes its infrastructural resources to the major tourist events, Mardi Gras and Jazz Fest. But if it were up to second liners, they'd parade all year long.

Second Line parades are thrown in New Orleans for all sorts of occasions: weddings, conventions, holidays, festivals, family parties, and, very important, funerals, but when New Orleanians today talk about *the* Second Line, they are most likely referring to the parades hosted each Sunday by the dues-paying members of a parading organization. Each group spends a year designing suits and coordinating accessories to wear and carry as they lead a sonic-kinetic journey. They plan and advertise the route, secure a parading permit from the city, and hire the police escorts and the band. When it's finally their day, the group presents a unique kaleidoscope of rhythm, motion, and color that processes through the city, featuring elaborate regalia; food and drink; theatrical ceremony; spoken, written, and visual rhetoric; live music (the ambulatory brass bands) and recorded music (New Orleans's homegrown brand of hip hop, called bounce, booming from speakers mounted on truck-pulled floats); and dancing—lots and lots of dancing. "Second lining" refers to all participatory parade activity, such as walking, strutting, and chanting, but the term also names a distinct dance form showcased during the parade: improvised, percussive, footwork-heavy, individually executed yet collectively experienced. The choreographic structure of a Second Line parade is simple. The hosting organization and brass band form the first line, or main line, and the trumpet's blare invites all within earshot to form a second line around them, giving the event its name. The fact that the entire phenomenon and its music's signature Second Line beat are named after the joiners insists that the peripheral action is of central importance.

Each Second Line begins when the brass band strikes up at 1:00 p.m. sharp (noon during the winter months' daylight savings time). One by one, each member of the organization hosting that Sunday's parade "comes out the door," dramatically revealing him- or herself to the waiting public. Groups usually come out the door of someone's house or a neighborhood bar, but other locations include the high school that members once attended or a fancy hotel in the central business district. Some clubs pride themselves on staging dramatic entrances such as emerging from the back of a U-Haul truck parked inconspicuously on the street (as the Lady Buckjumpers did in 2013) or a streetcar that rolled up near the crowd (the Divine Ladies in 2014).

When a club comes out the door, it unveils that year's design scheme. Members dress identically in brightly colored suits and brandish matching accessories such as feathered fans, decorated umbrellas, or bejeweled canes. For example, Keep-N-It Real's 2014 color scheme featured cotton-candy-pink blazers and slacks with maroon accessories. Since each club's

Tremé Sidewalk Steppers lead a large crowd down North Claiborne Avenue on February 2, 2014. (Photo by Judy Cooper.)

membership numbers can range from two people to one hundred (with ages in the same spread), coming out the door can take a little or a long time. As members emerge, they are expected to show out—dropping low, jumping high, spinning, and working their feet so fast that their shoes hover just above the pavement. Some club members plan clever performances for their moments in the spotlight; some simply let the spirit or intuition guide them. Some choreograph a sequence of new or trademarked steps (see video 1.1 on this book's web page). The crowd momentarily plays the roles of spectator, documentarian, and critic, vocally assessing color scheme, apparel choices, and dance ability while capturing the moment on smartphones. Four men unfurl lengths of yellow industrial rope to create an aisle from the door to the middle of the street, slicing through the tight knot of supporters. Very often, they have to cajole the crowd to "open it up!" After all club members have come out the door they move into the street, with ropes on either side. The band walks immediately behind the club. Everyone else—family, friends, members of other Second Line groups, neighbors, weekly die-hards, the casually curious, ambulatory vendors, professional photographers, and more—all fall in behind the band, alongside the ropes, or even in front of the club, circumscribed by police escorts who block traffic with squad cars and motorcycles. The

Kobin Wright coming out the door during the Keep-N-It Real SAPC's Second Line parade on March 9, 2014. (Photo by Judy Cooper.)

whole procession moves through the streets as a dancing collective for four straight hours, the maximum time allotted by the city's parading permit, making several planned stops along a predetermined route.

On that Sunday in March 2014, the Second Line community's anticipation seemed evident by the large number of people that showed up. That day I touched base with many second liners whom I had met during the past years and months, people whose stories beat at the heart of this book. I had been attending Second Lines as often as my schedule allowed since I had moved to New Orleans six years earlier, in 2008. At the time, I was one of many white outsiders pulled to New Orleans by the post-Katrina recovery economy, and I quickly learned that Second Lines were chief among the artistic and cultural practices crucial to grassroots recovery from that disaster and many forms of ongoing disasters. By the time I arrived at Keep-N-It Real's 2014 parade I had been faithfully joining Second Lines every Sunday for about a year. I was ready to get back to second lining after the Mardi Gras break, and based on the numbers, it seemed I wasn't alone. Certainly, some portion of the large crowd came because this was a special parade for Keep-N-It Real. It was their tenth anniversary, proclaimed on their fan designs, which featured a monogrammed car with "10th Anniversary" printed in the center. Others also came to support the two newer clubs that joined Keep-N-It Real, the Chosen Few Social & Pleasure Club (established 2011) and the Ice Divas Social & Pleasure Club (established 2013). These three organizations totaled about twenty-five people, but I estimated several thousand in attendance. With three bands, the crowd could spread out and find plenty of room to dance. The community's eagerness to return to the streets was also evident in people's joyful movement. Inside the ropes, children imitated the adults, matching high-knee steps and prone pauses on the pavement. A rope carrier leaned back, counterbalancing with his partner on the other end of the nylon cable and freeing his feet to really work. Outside the ropes, a few intrepid dancers scaled structures along the route to groove above the crowd, including one woman who improvised footwork on the elevated porch of a Baptist church. She concluded her solo with a sign of the cross (a Catholic gesture of reverence for a Baptist site of worship, suggesting the city's overlapping Christian communities) before dashing down the stairs and back into the procession.

    Keep-N-It Real's 2014 Second Line continued to be blessed by sunshine and mild breezes throughout its four-hour duration, but paraders simultaneously moved through a different, much more hostile kind of weather. The Black studies scholar Christina Sharpe defines *weather* as "the totality of our environments; the weather is the total climate; and that climate is antiblack."[2] Antiblackness is as characteristic of New Orleans's weather as its humidity. The environment that surrounded Keep-N-It Real's 2014 Second Line evidenced Sharpe's insistence that, even if the country tries to forget, the total climate of antiblackness persists: "Slave law transformed into lynch law, into Jim and Jane Crow, and other administrative logics that remember the brutal conditions of enslavement after the event of slavery has supposedly come to an end."[3] About halfway through their parade Keep-N-It Real turned off St. Charles Avenue and onto Esplanade Avenue. We moved away from the French Quarter, our backs to the site of antebellum slave pens just a few blocks behind us. A historical marker erected in the center of Esplanade Avenue lets tourists know that "more enslaved people were sold here . . . than anywhere else in the U.S."[4] Even further behind us, at the end of Esplanade, flowed the Mississippi River, the reason for the city's existence. The river has played a major role in shifting economies of trade, first of flesh and cotton, then of oil and gas, now of cruise ship passengers. For a long stretch of the twentieth century, jobs at the port supported a Black middle class. But following the 1986 oil bust, the economic impact of the port waned and Black New Orleanians suffered disproportionately high rates of unemployment. In order to alleviate the economic crisis the city turned almost exclusively to tourism, but the low-wage service jobs it generated did nothing to lift its residents out of poverty, a fact worsened by an under-resourced public school system.[5]

As we danced up Esplanade, the Iberville public housing development was visible in the near distance. It held the distinction of being the last public housing complex left standing after the Katrina disaster in 2005, but bulldozers had already arrived to demolish it. Though most public housing structures fared well in the storm and floods, the city tore them down, contributing to the prolonged, and in many cases permanent, displacement of the tens of thousands of African American New Orleanians who resided in them.[6] The short walk between the historical marker of the slave trade and the bulldozers parked outside the Iberville illuminated Sharpe's claim that Black people live in slavery's wake, since "the means and modes of Black subjection may have changed, but the fact and structure of that subjection remain."[7] In light of this fact, she looks to literature, visual culture, performance, and Black expressive culture as instances of "wake work," observing and mediating Black un/survival.[8]

The entire Second Line tradition could be considered wake work, but its power comes into vibrant focus in particular moments, as when parades move "under the bridge." As we strutted up Esplanade we approached one of the most anticipated moments of downtown Second Lines: flowing underneath a portion of Interstate 10 that sits above North Claiborne Avenue. Here, paraders pause to revel in the exhilarating sensations created by the concrete enclosure. In this temporally intimate space, acoustics amplify horns and chants to peak volume. Dancers turn up, too.[9] Under the bridge, the collective reaches the zenith of energy, showmanship, and joy. The bridge's central role in generating pleasure during downtown parades is all the more remarkable given the painful circumstances of its origins. Interstate 10 slices directly through Tremé, one of the country's oldest African American neighborhoods. The construction of the highway in the 1960s destroyed twelve blocks of historic homes and obliterated North Claiborne Avenue's wide neutral ground (or grassy median), the nerve center for Black commerce and performance traditions.[10] While many have lamented the interstate's detrimental impact on Black culture and commerce, one community leader remained less pessimistic about it. Before her death in 2009, Antoinette Dorsey Kador Fox, known to most as Antoinette K-Doe or Miss Antoinette, ran a nightclub on this avenue called the Mother In Law Lounge (which still stands today). Each Mardi Gras day starting in 2004, she second lined with her Baby Dolls, a century-old Black Carnival masking tradition, and in rainy years her group found shelter under the bridge. A reporter once asked her about the I-10, and she replied, "Keep in mind what you had, don't lose that, but think about what you got now. If it rains on Mardi Gras day, that's a big umbrella."[11] Miss Antoinette's comment articulates a way to maneuver through meteorological and ontological weather. Like her Baby Dolls, second liners repurpose the ground of antiblackness into a space of Black joy.

• • •

Dancing the Politics of Pleasure at the New Orleans Second Line explores how dancing bodies articulate and experience the Second Line's politics of pleasure within a critical framework of race and its intersections with gender, culture, and class. To be sure, second lining is, now more than ever, enjoyed by people of many races, nationalities, and places of origin (including me). Second liners' articulations and experiences of pleasure are not predetermined by race, gender, or geography but, rather, the meanings and effects of those pleasures must be understood in context. In order to comprehend the ways in which dancing bodies negotiate state power, social scripts, and gaps left by capitalism, we must conceive of pleasure as an experience enmeshed within lived realities and histories of oppression. This enmeshment is what endows pleasure with power.[12] As stated by the Afrofuturist Ingrid LaFleur, "For oppressed people to intentionally cultivate pleasure is an act of resistance."[13]

Pleasure's central place in the Second Line tradition can be found in the names of the groups that organize each parade. Most call themselves social aid and pleasure clubs (SAPCs), proclaiming their dual purpose of providing social or mutual aid *and* pleasure for themselves and their communities. The Prince of Wales SAPC, one of the oldest organizations parading today, was incorporated in 1929 with both aspects of its mission written into the charter: "The object and purpose of the Corporation is to aid one another when in distress; to give entertainments and other functions for the amusement of the members, and perform all that a corporation of the kind is permitted to do by law."[14] Clubs such as the Prince of Wales belong to a constellation of Black voluntary organizations that have, since the late eighteenth century, created alternative means of access to resources and social networks in response to the institutional racism that has consistently barred people of color from full admittance to mainstream politics, economics, and social life. These collectives were initially organized to provide social services such as access to medical treatment and small loans.[15] They ministered not only to the body but also to the spirit by ensuring a proper burial for their members and by providing collective enjoyment through organized social events such as parades. As the writer Rebecca Solnit summarizes, New Orleans's Black voluntary associations "provided tangible necessities (social aid) when things went wrong but intangible ones (social pleasure) when they went right."[16] Today, the aiding arm of SAPCs often takes the form of philanthropic efforts such as coat and backpack drives, nursing home visits, and feeding the unhoused. Even clubs that call themselves "social and pleasure clubs" (S&PCs, dropping the "aid"), like Keep-N-It Real, often adhere to the Second Line's mutual aid spirit. Black voluntary associations' activities have shifted over the centuries but have consistently responded to need and provided occasions for pleasure.

These organizations' brass band–led processions blossomed at the dawn of the twentieth century, playing a crucial role in the development of a music and dance form we now call jazz. Earlier than dancers in northern cities did, New Orleanians demanded "hot" rhythms to support their "ratty" dancing.[17] Ratty dancing made its way out of nightclubs and into the streets as paraders improvised forward-moving footwork to incorporate popular dances of the time (and still do today).[18] With such dances as the belly rub, the strut, and the Funky Butt, a new generation expressed notions of autonomy and sexuality that emerged in the Progressive Era.[19] Libidinal pleasure was (and is) a component of the "P" in SAPC but pleasure is not limited to sex. To be sure, sexual connotations attended notions of pleasure in the nineteenth and early twentieth-century United States ("women of pleasure" was a euphemism for sex workers), but "social pleasures" were also understood to be part of a wholesome, genteel life. A search in New Orleans newspapers in the 1860s and 1870s turns up editorial praise for those who "prefer[red] social pleasures to trivial pastimes" and were "content to mingle in the purity of social pleasure."[20] Social pleasures enabled one's fluid movement through society, so much so that some sought lessons in pleasure. In 1875 the *New Orleans Republican* advertised the services of a man offering tutorials in the art of conversation, "most essential to social pleasures."[21] When the Prince of Wales SAPC was incorporated in 1929, it joined a multitude of similar organizations formed by Black New Orleanians—such as the Ladies' Charity, Aid, and

Pleasure Club, the Leisure Hour Pleasure and Embroidery Club, and the Zion City Sick and Friendship Club—for the express purpose of providing these kinds of social pleasures.[22] Today's social aid and pleasure clubs continue the tradition by giving, as the Prince of Wales's charter details, "entertainments and other functions" such as parades and dances "for the amusement of the members" and their communities. As with life in general, the Second Line's pleasures have, from its beginnings, encompassed a wide array of delights.

Still today, second lining brings different kinds of pleasures, such as stress relief and community pride, to different people. For Terrinika Smith, an avid second liner in her twenties, the sound of the brass band commands her to drop her responsibilities and respond with her most spectacular footwork. "[There's] something about the beat," she said. "I don't care if they're going *dat dat dat!* Or the cymbals warming up or the trumpet. Something about the music just get to you and be like, 'It's time to show.'" The drums and trumpets ease her frustrations, which mount each week as a hard-working single mom.

> To me, second lining is part of my culture, second lining is who I am. It was something I was brought up on, something I was taught, and I'm teaching it now to my son, so he can love it. . . . Second lining is me, where I can be me—free, do whatever I want, don't got to worry about nothing. Second lining is who I am. I *am* second lining.[23]

For Tamara Jackson Snowden, a veteran leader in the Second Line community, the collective pride generated by the dancing crowd drives her to organize the VIP Ladies & Kids SAPC parade every year. She reflected,

> The community depends on you. For those four hours, they depend on having that parade. They take ownership and pride when they know that the parade is happening in their neighborhood, passing in front of their door, by their houses, and their bars—they [the paraders] coming to their bars—so they take [it], they invest in it, and then that investment creates a sense of harmony and pride that just transcends from the front of the parade to the back.[24]

Jackson Snowden's emphasis on the pride of a neighborhood that invests in itself as a site of prosperity and harmony is important given histories of destruction and disinvestment in the working-class African American neighborhoods where Second Lines roll. Taken together, Smith's and Jackson Snowden's reflections testify to a range of sensory and psychological joys generated by dancing through the streets with their families and neighbors in time to an ambulatory brass band. As these women make choices about how, where, when, and with whom to dance, they reclaim self and city through motion and rhythm. They, along with their fellow second liners, enjoy the parade's pleasurable effects: the ecstasy of freeing oneself in time with others and the pride of collectively owning a place and a history. All of this, and more, constitutes the Second Line's politics of pleasure.

Smith and Jackson Snowden also suggest ways in which the body is the primary site of enjoying the Second Line. Paraders might exchange smiles; gaze on the club's colorful suits, polished shoes, and decorated floats; smell grilled sausage prepared by food vendors; taste an ice-cold beer pulled from a cooler on wheels; and feel the satisfying slap of a tambourine against the palm. The following chapters consider how and why generations of Black New Orleanians have generated bodily pleasure, by collective dancing in public spaces, to playfully maneuver within and against spatial, social, and structural systems of oppression. In other words, this book argues that bodily pleasure, including but not limited to dance, is central to the Second Line's political force.

Dancing the Politics of Pleasure at the New Orleans Second Line pays close attention to bodies in motion in order to understand movement as a mode of negotiating power. Following dance scholar Randy Martin's influential 1998 work on dance and politics, *Critical Moves: Dance Studies in Theory and Politics*, I look to dance as one of many social realms in which power is negotiated. Once expanded beyond the actions of elected officials, voters, and activists, Martin argues, politics become recognizable in virtually all aspects of social life where everyday negotiations of power occur. Martin's focus on political action, rather than ideas, makes room for dance in discussions of politics. Put simply, bodies are central to making politics *work*. As he urges, "Politics goes nowhere without movement."[25] This may be obvious when protestors put their bodies on the line, but I argue that it can also be true of pleasurable marches such as Second Line parades.[26] Bodily movement and politics are not mirrors of one another, Martin argues, nor are they reducible to each other, but one cannot exist without the other.[27] Second lining cannot, by itself, automatically cause change in other social arenas, but it has the power to, in Martin's words, "enlarge the sense of what is possible" in social life.[28] These parades enlarge the sense of what is possible in terms of kinship, economic circulation, property ownership, and more. Its power is located in its imaginings of a possible future—but second liners do not wait on the state to enact changes. They make the life they want in each moment of creating and experiencing pleasure.

My analysis joins recent studies of dance, theater, film, and culture that employ the politics of pleasure as an epistemological and theoretical lens through which to consider performances, especially those by women of color and LGBTQ performers.[29] Like many of these scholars, I draw on an intellectual tradition in African American studies and Black feminist thought. In the words of the novelist and theorist Ishmael Reed, "There's so much more to black pleasure than merely fun."[30] One may look at a Second Line and see nothing but a party going on, a distraction from "real" political work. In contrast, Joan Morgan's project "Pleasure Politics" argues that pleasure is not only a "desirable goal and a social and political imperative" but also an "under-theorized resistance strategy for black women in the United States and Caribbean."[31] The African American studies scholar Imani Perry echoes Morgan's assertions when she claims that "Blackness is an immense and defiant joy." Black music, dance, and language, she says, are no less than a testimony to the grace of living as protest, a refusal of the terms of antiblackness. In "Racism Is Terrible. Blackness Is Not," written in the wake of George Floyd's murder in 2020, Perry instructed white and other non-Black readers in how to understand the singing, dancing, and chanting at Black Lives Matter protests that swept the United States and the world: "Do not misunderstand. This is not an absence of grief or rage, or a distraction. It is insistence."[32] Perry's manifesto appeared in the *Atlantic* at a cultural moment in the English-speaking world when "Black joy" and "Black excellence" had entered the zeitgeist, with advocates insisting on the need to supplant recurrent tropes of Black suffering and death with resplendent representations of and opportunities for a wider spectrum of Black humanity, including pleasure and brilliance.[33] As podcasts, museum programs, dedicated Instagram feeds, and editorials celebrated the resistive and healing properties of Black joy, activist and thinker adrienne maree brown's 2019 book *Pleasure Activism: The Politics of Feeling Good* became a *New York Times* bestseller. By centering the experiences of Black women, including many Black queer women, brown shows that pursuits of pleasure through sex, drugs, fashion, cooking, and more can generate justice and liberation.[34]

Second lining invites a consideration of the serious work of Black joy, excellence, and pleasure in many realms of social life, including labor, history, and commodity exchange. For example, the labors of pleasurable dancing and music making at the Second Line resist the objectification of Black bodies under racial capitalism.[35] Second lines' relation to racial capitalism dates to the antebellum period, when enslaved and free Africans and people of African descent gathered to drum and dance on Sundays in a designated field now known as Congo Square. Congo Square's legacy animates today's paraders, whose unproductive labor reworks the legacies of slavery that continue to mark Black bodies as instruments of manual labor in service of capitalist production. At the same time, Second Line choreographies keep buried histories alive. Each step crystallizes centuries of rhythmic play and bodily movement that have been passed down in backyards, kitchens, and neighborhood streets. Owing to its grassroots modes of transmission, second lining can serve as an important form of communication and record keeping, especially since its practitioners historically have been barred from traditional platforms for speech and omitted from the archive.[36]

Like those Sunday gatherings in Congo Square, Second Lines have also attracted an audience, and this complicates the work that pleasure can do. As bell hooks has convincingly argued, Black music and dance have been commodified and consumed worldwide—a phenomenon that hooks famously called "eating the other"—in ways that can neutralize their subversive potential.[37] Second Lines are vulnerable to commodification, put to use by the city's tourism campaigns and appearing in global popular culture (Beyoncé Knowles Carter's 2016 sensation *Formation*, to give one notable example). Yet in contrast to New Orleans's hip hop performance genre, bounce, which has been made popular by the stardom of Big Freedia, second lining has either eluded or just not yet been launched into the mainstream. Reasons for this might include the tradition's deep attachment to place and its participatory structure.[38] Whatever the reasons, SAPC parades remain the provenance of locals in Black neighborhoods, not to be confused with the processions that visitors can purchase to accompany the city's many destination weddings and conventions. The public nature of SAPC Second Lines means that they are accessible to anyone eager to experience this unique New Orleans phenomenon, but even if an audience is present, these parades exist, in the words of E. Patrick Johnson, "not *for* but *despite* display."[39] Writing about Second Lines in the 1990s, the anthropologist Helen A. Regis claimed that, because second lining requires participation, not spectatorship, it resists objectification. The fence that separated white onlookers from the dancers at Congo Square invited the audience to "eat the other," and so can the invisible fence between buskers who perform for tourists' tips in the French Quarter. But if the tourist joins the parade on second liners' home turf, Regis concluded, "it is the tourist who is transformed and appropriated by the Second Line rather than the reverse."[40] Regis's assessment largely holds in the 2020s but is complicated by the ways in which the internet and social media have opened new kinds of "turf" and new modes of appropriation. For example, increasing access to parade routes has made it easier for those outside the community to join. The clubs advertise their itineraries on a route sheet, a single-page photocopied flier that also lists other information such as the parade's theme and suit colors or names of the club members, royal court, and individuals who merit special thanks. Until the early twenty-first century route sheets were distributed in hard copy via informal networks, but since then, parade information has become widely available online.[41]

Changes wrought by Katrina, locally known as "the storm," have also impacted local-outsider dynamics at Sunday Second Lines. Post-Katrina tourism narratives, promoted by voluntourism, disaster tours, and the authenticity-seeking devotees of the HBO series *Treme*, have steadily expanded the tourist track into areas previously deemed unworthy of sightseeing.[42] As a result, it seems, more and more visitors, newcomers, and other curious travelers have made their way to Second Lines in the twenty-first century. I've spoken with many longtime regulars who insist that they used to be able to count the white second liners on one hand. According to Family Ties SAPC secretary Tyree Smith, "Before the storm, they never really did have white folks out there. They really didn't." But when we spoke in 2014, he noted, "They got white folk out there, they got Chinese folk out there, they got all kinds of people out there." Smith was not bothered by the increasing presence of non-Black attendees. "You know, I'm glad that they out there," he said. "I want to show off for them. Let them see what we do."[43] As Smith's words indicate, onlookers are not turned away, but the show is not *for* them: It is for self and community. Second Lines exert performative force despite, not for, outsiders' enjoyment (listen to the full interview on this book's web page).

When Tyree Smith shows off for outsiders, he exemplifies how second liners cultivate a physical knowledge of power through a repertoire of steps and stances that serve as both a metaphor of and training for political consciousness. For example, each forward-moving, rhythmic-kinetic mass of people manifests a value placed on the collective as an alternative to capitalist individualism. Footwork requires physical negotiations with gravity, between succumbing and resisting, that reflect a nimble approach to power. The dance form crystallizes second liners' flexible responses to power that neither submit nor which are on full display, for example, when club presidents negotiate with police escorts about when to start or stall a parade because of inclement weather. In addition, paraders' choreographic uses of the cityscape, which take them not only through the streets but also onto rooftops, articulate a valuation of land as cultural inheritance as opposed to private property. In these ways and more, second liners mobilize footwork as an improvisational, tactical mobility that enables them to constantly maneuver within *and* against spatial, social, and structural terrains of power.[44]

Understanding dance's relation to power along axes of race, class, and gender requires in-depth analysis of the steps themselves, not as objects to be catalogued but as modes of moving through and being in the world. Paraders are usually less concerned with which steps the dancer executes than with how she performs those steps, and, at the heart of it, why she is dancing in the first place. When I first began this research, I was perplexed by a contradiction between the bodily performances that I saw on the street each week and the language that I heard second liners use to talk about their dancing—or, more precisely, to *not* talk about it. I found that many participants insisted that second lining is no more than a personal response to the music, and therefore, there is no right or wrong way to do it. At the same time, the dancing that I witnessed and attempted to emulate was incredibly specific. I came to understand that descriptions of second lining as individual expression represent a core value: Second liners privilege the dancing's function over its form. The Rebirth Brass Band gave voice to this value in their early '90s hit "Do Whatcha Wanna."[45] This attitude indicates second liners' definition of dancing as much more than a list of dos and don'ts. It is, instead, a vehicle for communing with others, catching the spirit, connecting to history, and claiming home. In sum, even though second lining can be described as a specific, coherent, and legible dance form that is historically rooted and aesthetically sophisticated, the fact remains that what it *is* matters less to dancers, and therefore to me, than what it *does*.

That said, some words about practitioners' terminology are in order. In its most capacious definition, second lining requires nothing more than feeling the music and feeling good. As long as one is (usually) moving on the beat and (generally) moving forward with the crowd, then that person is second lining. But when speaking of dance, second liners are more likely to use such terms as stepping, buckjumping, footwork, and rolling. "Stepping" describes a buoyant, high-knee strut. "Buckjumping" refers to what happens when dancers turn up their energetic output, for example, dropping to the ground and leaping in the air. "Footwork" is the art of executing intricate rhythmic patterns with the feet. Unlike stepping and buckjumping, footwork indicates a level of technical virtuosity, and second liners who take their dancing seriously look at each other's footwork to distinguish amateurs from artists. What second liners call "rolling" accurately names a sensation experienced by dancers when they are locked in with the music and moving forward over uneven surfaces as if gliding on ice. To be clear, those who call themselves footwork artists still espouse a do-whatcha-wanna philosophy. Virtuosity is not necessarily at odds with efficacy.

Many factors shape dancers' preferences for varieties of second lining, including their neighborhood allegiances (footwork is generally aligned with downtown and buckjumping with uptown), generation (stepping is more characteristic of pre–civil rights era second lining), respectability politics (buckjumping is sometimes seen as less dignified than stepping), and gender (criteria for excellent footwork and buckjumping are often coded as masculine). Stepping, buckjumping, and footwork are overlapping categories that I separate here only for the sake of discussion. They constantly erupt and dissolve during the procession, and one dancer will often incorporate all three expressions in one musical phrase. Not everyone dances, but those who do often shift from walking to strutting to full-blown footwork—perhaps with an occasional bout of buckjumping thrown in—and then melt back into walking. Second lining-as-pedestrian activity constantly shifts to dancing and back again.

• • •

My own participation, and in many ways this book, testify to Tyree Smith's observation that outsiders' enthusiasm for Second Lines has increased since Katrina. I attended my first Second Line in 2007 while in town volunteering as a production assistant for a performance organized by a local artists' collective.[46] The friend who took me to my first parade was a New Orleans resident, fellow dancer, and performance scholar. I did my best to dance along with her. Much of my dance experience had been in studio settings, centered on Europeanist forms and aesthetics (ballet, modern, and whitewashed versions of tap and jazz). As a white woman raised in a conservative Christian community in the deeply segregated suburbs of St. Louis, Missouri, I was not socialized to respond to the Second Line's invitations to the body. Despite my limitations, my first parade revealed that footwork is only one way to enjoy the experience. Walking with friends, sipping a beer, feeling the drumbeat pulse in my chest, and appreciating sartorial designs (of the first liners and dressed-to-be-seen second liners)—these sensations are crucial to the Second Line's pleasures as well. Many years later, I continue to return to the Second Line, and keep writing about it, because of the immense joy that it brings me.

Shortly after that summer of volunteering, I relocated to New Orleans. I was working for a nonprofit arts organization in New York, wanting to learn more about how artists and culture bearers address structural inequities through their craft and to better understand how to support that work. I chose to move to New Orleans to learn from the artists and culture bearers who were leading community responses to disaster recovery. I arrived in 2008, just as the city was shifting out of the immediate phase of brick-and-mortar rebuilding. I co-founded a theater company and a children's playwriting festival with other transplanted performing artists.

I became a member of a women's Mardi Gras parading group.[47] During the days, I worked as a nonprofit administrator and arts educator, jobs that were becoming available owing to the influx of funding from outside foundations after the storm.

My nonprofit arts work introduced me to Edward Buckner, president of the Original Big Seven SAPC. At the time, he directed a community center in the Seventh Ward called The Porch. I worked with Edward in my role as an administrator with one of the Porch's fiscal agents. Once he found out that I was a performing artist, he drafted me to teach summer theater classes to youth. In between budgets and lesson plans, I spent hours at the Porch listening to the stories, dreams, and frustrations of Edward and other Seventh Ward residents, including my students. I began attending the Big Seven's annual Mother's Day parade, and subsequently, when I began the research for this book, Edward became an important interlocutor. During my fieldwork I volunteered for the youth programming that he conceptualized as part of the Big Seven's social aid mission, no longer at the Porch but in his house. Edward organizes a youth-led tribe of Black Masking Indians, commonly known as Mardi Gras Indians. It is a New Orleans tradition in which men, women, and children walk the streets in elaborately beaded and feathered suits, paying homage to the Indigenous peoples who established maroon communities with self-emancipated people of African descent.[48] In true Black Masking Indian spirit, Edward's group, the Red Flame Hunters, undertakes the painstaking task of sewing their own suits to debut each Mardi Gras. I spent much of the 2013–2014 Carnival season behind a hot glue gun in Edward's front-room-turned-sewing studio. A few months later, I returned to that room to help produce the streamers and fans for the Big Seven's parade. Because of Edward's generosity in inviting me into the Big Seven's year-round activities, he and his organization factor heavily into the stories that this book tells.

My presence at parades also led me to join a Second Line group myself, a prospect that I never entertained until the invitation was extended. The day that I attended Keep-N-It Real's 2014 parade, the same event described in the vignette that opens this chapter, I met Catina Braxton Robertson. Her club, Ice Divas Social & Pleasure Club, paraded that day along with Keep-N-It Real.[49] I was engrossed in some sweaty footwork when Catina walked to the rope's edge and shouted over the band, "I got a spot for you in here next year if you want it." Apparently, my second lining had improved since my first parade. She pulled her cell phone out of her pocket so that I could enter my number. The next day, she called, and I accepted. My choice to pursue an academic career took me away from New Orleans, but every March I fly back to hit the streets with the Ice Divas. For months leading up to that date, I send in my monthly dues, weigh in on decisions about parade day apparel, and ship my suit and shoes back and forth to get the right fit. Although leaving New Orleans has rendered ongoing ethnographic research sporadic in some ways, being a member of the Ice Divas keeps me tied to a small slice of the community year-round.

By sharing these details about my relationships with African American members of the Second Line community, I do not aim to claim insider status. At the same time, to insist on my outsiderness would disrespect people like Edward and Catina who have generously let me into their lives.[50] My multiple investments and agendas as an insider-outsider are often spatially mapped out at the parade. Once a year I am in the main line, suited up with the Ice Divas. Most of the time, I am in the Second Line, dancing alongside the ropes, behind the band, or on the sidewalk with my favorite footwork fanatics. Sometimes I am in the "third line," a term that the white photographer Michael P. Smith penned in 1990 to describe the ethnomusicologists, English professors, and photographers like himself that he saw orbiting Second Line parades.[51] When I'm third lining, I hover on the perimeter to take photos, record audio, type hasty notes into my smart phone (a strategy I adopted when I realized that pulling out a pen and notebook elicited bewildered stares), conduct informal interviews on the spot, and set up formal ones for a future date.

Third liners had been at work long before Smith's term appeared in print. Writing eight years before Smith, the cultural critic and activist Kalamu ya Salaam reflected on the presence of white documentarians at a Second Line that followed a funeral. To him they looked "at best curious, at worst like vultures, always outside this action even when they were in the middle of the happenings." As Salaam watched them leave the procession, toting cameras, microphones, and notebooks, he imagined that they must be going home to wait for another Black man to die so they could come enjoy another parade.[52] Salaam's comment poignantly evokes the social distance that has historically separated white scholars and our appreciation of Black culture from the realities, including the violent realities, of Black life. He suggests that white consumption of Black culture happens without regard for Black people. Because each parade is rooted at least in part in a death ritual, white enjoyment is predicated on the erasure of Black life.

Dance ethnography may, in some instances, complicate the voyeurism of the third line by emphasizing the researcher's participation, even her pleasure. When I'm not observing and capturing the dancing of others, I travel from the third line's perimeter and get in the middle of things, giving myself over to the sweat and rush of improvised footwork. Reflecting on her ethnographic research on West African masquerades, the anthropologist Margaret Drewal insists that meaningful fieldwork concerning performance practices requires the researcher to engage in the moment rather than stand outside it.[53] As Salaam rightly acknowledges, however, getting in the middle of the happenings does not necessarily place one inside the reality. The writer Ta-Nehisi Coates puts it this way: "It is incredibly hard to be a full participant in the world of cultural identity without experiencing the trauma of racial identity."[54] Each time I step into the Second Line, my body acts as a visible sign of the histories of colonization, cultural theft, and intellectual imperialism committed by white people against people of color in New Orleans and beyond. Conducting research during the years after Hurricane Katrina meant that I not only stepped into *histories* of racist cultural exchanges but engaged (and continue to engage) in a very present struggle over who gets to live in New Orleans, adopt its Black cultural practices, and tell its people's stories.[55]

This book and my participation in the Ice Divas are both part of that struggle. The fact that Catina, an African American New Orleanian who has been second lining her entire life, invited me, a white transplant, to join a SAPC was unusual but not unprecedented. The Ice Divas have maintained an interracial roster since their inception in 2013, when a small group of Black and white members splintered off from a larger, older SAPC to form their own club. Some months after Catina's invitation, I invited her to give an interview as part my research. During our conversation, I asked about her choice to recruit white members into a historically Black tradition. "People is people," she responded. "You don't look at people as color or what have you. People is people, we all human. Everybody can enjoy whatever culture they want to, and I love it."[56] Catina explained that she handpicks her members in a variety of ways. Some are family members or friends, as is typical of most clubs. Sometimes, as in my case, she recruits a new member based on her performance. "When I see them dancing, having a real good time, I'm like, 'I could use her! I'm going to ask her!'" (listen to the full interview on this book's web page).[57]

Catina remains resolute in her point of view, knowing full well that not everyone shares it. Some prefer to keep the tradition within its historic networks of African American New Orleanians. During an interview with a community elder, I was assured that there are SAPCs that only admit African Americans. The leaders of these groups hold that anyone is welcome to attend Second Line parades, but joining a group crosses the line. I explained that, though I am a member of a Second Line group, I respect the widespread need to preserve the instruments of Black joy from further exploitation. I have reflected on this conversation many times since. If I see my scholarship as engaged in a fight against oppression, is my choice to belong to an SAPC at odds with that commitment? A researcher's well-intentioned efforts to participate and perform *more* with her interlocutors may enable her to eschew the distanced observer role, as Drewal argues, but it may also lead her to a new, equally (more?) troublesome role: the interloper. According to the dancers Ajara Alghali and Erin Falker-Obichigha, the interloper inserts herself as an authority in Black dance spaces, hastening a tipping point in which Black spaces are no longer Black.[58] For white researchers of Black dance, and for many researchers who seek to gain understanding of dance practices across cultural divides, the way we enter, contribute to, and exit the communities we study is much more complex than a sliding scale of more performance or less performance can measure.[59]

I have stayed with the Ice Divas because I have formed with them the closeness that all performers know. It comes from producing a thing of beauty, soothing pre-performance jitters, adjusting to unforeseen circumstances (a no-show dancer, rain, a broken shoe), sustaining each other's stamina, and later reviewing injuries, highlights, and snapshots. Kristy Magner, another white member of the Ice Divas, has shared with me that she is also motivated to remain in the group because of the bond she has built with her fellow Ice Divas after ten years of parading together, though she knows that some people are unhappy to see her participate. As a white person as well as researcher I value the fact that, by belonging to the Ice Divas and being involved with the Second Line community at large, I have been able to build relationships, both Black-white and researcher-researched, across differences, even if our relationships can never exist *fully* outside of those dynamics. I relate to Helen Regis's observation, written decades ago, that her participation with a SAPC invited repeated negotiations of her identities, encompassing both transcendent moments of "we-ness" and other moments when differences were reinforced.[60] Joining the club has not erased the power differences that divide me from its Black members, but it has rearranged those differences so that conversations, collaborations, and affection can exist despite them. Undoubtedly, my understanding of the year-round, behind-the-scenes operations of the Second Line culture has benefited from being a member of the Ice Divas, but the group does not play a starring role in this book. My writerly choice to keep the Divas in the background creates a space for relationships with these women that, while never exempt from ethnographic inquiry, preserve something for me and us not held up for scrutiny elsewhere.[61]

• • •

Second lining is a collective experience and, in some ways, I've attempted to honor its multivocality in this book. Throughout, I foreground the voices of many different people in order to avoid centering a single narrative voice. First-person accounts of participants who meticulously describe how and why they dance are culled from in-depth interviews that I conducted with more than sixty individuals: SAPC members, dedicated second liners unaffiliated with clubs, brass band musicians, dance artists, cultural advocates, students in Second Line dance classes, and one New Orleans Police Department officer. Six of these interviews appear between the chapters in the form of edited transcripts (full interviews are available on the companion website). Readers are invited to spend time with the words of expert practitioners who represent a range of perspectives and critical reflections drawn from their various gendered, raced, and generational positions.

I combined the voices of participants with detailed descriptions of bodily movement gleaned from my own dance experiences. During my most concentrated period of fieldwork, the 2013–2014 Second Line season, I attended nearly every Sunday parade from start to finish, in addition to funerals and parades occasioned by other events. As exhausting as this was, it took much more discipline to write up field notes each Sunday night, typing out details such as the parade's route, the club's colors, the number of police officers present, and remarkable moments of dance improvisation. Before long, I also became a regular at Celebration Hall on Wednesday nights, where the To Be Continued Brass Band's weekly show offered a midweek respite for dedicated footwork artists. Finally, the core of my fieldwork involved attending SAPC dances, picnics, fundraisers, backyard parties, weddings, and even the occasional dance studio class, following footwork to all the places it travels.

I consulted primary and secondary historical sources in order to contextualize contemporary events. I drew on a range of sources, including print materials such as biographies, maps, magazines, and newspapers from the nineteenth and twentieth centuries; video, oral, and photo documentation of second lining starting in the mid-twentieth century; and the personal papers of relevant individuals such as local writers, activists, and musicians. The outcome of my interdisciplinary research has led me to conclude that dancing is central to the Second Line tradition, not only in aesthetic terms (although this is certainly true) but also in terms of the tradition's ability to cultivate cultural values and political consciousness for individuals and collectivities. Dancing's ability to generate pleasure is at the center of its power.

My conclusions fall in step with existing scholarship on the Second Line. Along with other distinct yet related African diaspora parading practices in New Orleans, the Second Line has been understood by scholars as a form of Black resistance: a site for activating ancestral memories and performing counter-histories,[62] an agent of spatial transformation,[63] a mechanism for building community,[64] an alternative economy,[65] and a training ground for learning survival skills necessary for poor people and people of color.[66] The idea that the Second Line's resistive force must be understood within a framework of pleasure has been argued most directly by music scholars. For example, the musician and historian Michael G. White claims that, at the start of the twentieth century, the Second Line's music and parade structure modeled "the type of democratic society that the black population sought." Playing and dancing to brass band music in this era "became a vehicle in which to express the aspirations, desires, spirit, and needs of black New Orleans."[67] Speaking of the present day, the ethnomusicologist Matt Sakakeeny argues that second liners articulate a "politics of pleasure" by means of "a display of exuberance within a racialized power structure."[68] Writers such as these frequently celebrate the central role of bodily movement within the performance tradition. *Dancing the Politics of Pleasure at the New Orleans Second Line* adds to that celebration a sustained critical analysis of the dance form. It is axiomatic, and for good reason, to say that Second Line music and dance are inextricable from one another, so I do not seek to disentangle dance from music to study it in isolation. However, the act of documenting Second Line dancing honors it as a specific and sophisticated art form worthy of the critical attention that brass band music has received for decades. This book's focus on dance is not meant to detach it from the parade's other performative dimensions, either, but as an invitation to take seriously the historical and political importance of bodily pleasure experienced by and for Black communities.

If this book expands the focus on dance within New Orleans literature, it also expands the city's presence in dance literature. Surveys of African American and African diaspora dance have long argued for New Orleans's crucial role in the development of jazz dance, focusing on Congo Square, Quadroon balls, and turn-of-the-century social dances.[69] Short but rich descriptions of dance at the Second Line appear in writings on African American dance more generally and in cultural histories of New Orleans.[70] This book adds to these studies an extended consideration of second lining as a contemporary dance form with an ongoing history, a lineage of performers, and shifting aesthetics.

A dance-focused study of the Second Line also invites new considerations of gendered performances. Studying the movements of second liners opens aesthetic analysis beyond the predominantly male brass band musicians to consider female as well as male dancers. Nearly every brass band playing parades is and has historically been composed exclusively of men, but the number of women dancing in the first and Second Lines has been growing exponentially during the past half-century.[71] Therefore, on a very practical level, studying bodily movement necessitates documentation of women's contributions within second lining's history. Beyond the gender identities of participants, music and dance themselves contain different sets of gendered discourses. In Europe and the United States, dance has received less scholarly attention than has music, even in instances when the two are nearly inseparable (as with the Second Line). Dance has been historically delegitimized owing to its lack of a common notation system, its attachment to the body, and its associations with femininity. Music, by contrast, produces a text with its near-universal written documentation, boasts a tradition of scientific inquiry, and is often dominated by male artists (and male scholars).[72] By arguing that dance is a crucial yet overlooked component of the Second Line's aesthetic, social, and political ontology, this book complements the music-centric and male-focused literature on New Orleans parading cultures.[73]

The following chapters consider the politics of pleasure from multiple angles. On one hand, I am interested in the choices that second liners make to choreograph a politics of pleasure. How, where, and when do people move together through space in time? On the other hand, I follow pleasure's trajectories. How do participants experience second lining's material, psychological, and affective effects? What are its lessons for ideas of kinship, modes of knowledge transmission, belonging, and land ownership? Dancers' abilities to "enlarge the sense of what is possible," to evoke Randy Martin again, indicate the stakes of pleasure for Black New Orleanians.

Arranged as a series of interconnected essays in a quasi-chronological order, the chapters form critical linkages between pleasure and liberation, self and communal identities, play and dissent, and reclamations of place. Chapters 2 and 3 are dedicated to two of the primary reasons why second liners dance. Chapter 2, "Community," considers how the dance gives shape to a collective ethos in its practice and choreographic structure. The chapter situates second liners' embodied communal values within the early histories of mutual aid societies, then traces two organizations' twenty-first-century approaches to mutual aid. SilenceIsViolence and the Original Big Seven SAPC address contemporary threats to Black life by confronting the systemic and interpersonal violence that impact their communities. Chapter 3, "Spirit," expands on the common refrain, "Second

Lines are church for dancers," by exploring the parades' spiritual aspects. In mini memorials and full-blown funerals, second liners draw on the rituals of West African, Afro-Caribbean, and African American Christian religions. But sacred experiences are not limited to mortuary rites. During concentrated bouts of footwork done at parades and in nightclubs, dancers attain ecstatic, out-of-body experiences. Whether in a miles-long processional route or inside a compact nightclub, footwork carries second liners through the gates of spirit.

Although the entire book considers the politics of pleasure, Chapter 4, "Freedom," takes it on most directly by turning to the intersections of Black parading cultures and Black-led protest in New Orleans during the 1960s. The chapter focuses on two coordinated actions, the Mardi Gras Blackout of 1961 and the Freedom March in 1963, to illuminate how African American New Orleanians mobilized the social infrastructures built in part through parading communities to organize large-scale resistance. These two examples suggest that carnivalesque processions share ground, literally and figuratively, with direct action protests, since both insist on the freedom of Black people to, in the words of Black Men of Labor SAPC president Fred Johnson, "assemble and move through time and space together."[74] Sometimes, as in the case of the blackout, fighting for the freedom to move meant staying still.

Chapter 5, "Do Whatcha Wanna," details the myriad ways in which second liners share their bodily knowledge with each other. By borrowing and styling moves, cultivating mentors and familial role models, and challenging fellow paraders in call-and-response competitions, second liners share not only physical know-how but also the cultural values embedded within the steps, such as communal as opposed to private property, self-expression, respect for elders, and collective creation. By adjudicating a balance between aesthetic continuity and innovation, each generation of second liners simultaneously maintains and adapts cultural values. The chapter considers one period of dramatic aesthetic transformation—the "brass band renaissance" that began in the late 1970s—to consider how a shift in music and dance can function as both a reflection and an agent of social, political, and cultural change.[75]

One of the values embedded in second liners' steps is pride of place, and that value is the focus of Chapter 6, "Home." The chapter follows second liners to rooftops, where dancing asserts the importance of vertical space in a sinking city and considers how women's high-heeled footwork makes equally forceful claims on ownership of body and place. The story then moves indoors to consider how the footwork that evolved inside one nightclub, the Glass House, in the late 1970s through the early 1990s asserted ownership in the face of a "massive resistance in concrete" to the gains of the civil rights movement.[76] Finally, the chapter considers how Second Line cultural practices move in and through participants' dwelling spaces by tracing the Original Big Seven's relationship with the St. Bernard public housing development from the club's founding there in 1995 through St. Bernard's demolition after Hurricane Katrina and up to more recent entanglements with developers. In each location—rooftop, street, nightclub, and residence—second liners assert ownership of place beyond capitalistic logics and forward modes of belonging that exceed U.S. notions of property as an anchor for citizenship.

As I undertook much of the writing that resulted in this book, the COVID-19 pandemic took hold of the globe, claiming unimaginable numbers of lives and livelihoods. In New Orleans, as elsewhere, African Americans suffered disproportionate numbers of infections and deaths, revealing the sustained impact of structural racism in all facets of American life, not the least of which is healthcare. Simultaneously, in the United States and worldwide, a wave of uprisings condemned another pandemic, antiblackness, and demanded police reform following the murders of George Floyd and Breonna Taylor at the hands of police in Minneapolis and Louisville, respectively. By many accounts, that period also marked the longest continuous absence of Second Line parades in New Orleans's history. The epilogue briefly considers the impacts of the overlapping pandemics on the Second Line tradition with an eye toward some ways in which its politics of pleasure had prepared second liners to creatively maneuver through the newest threats to the parades and to Black life more broadly. Using ethnographic accounts, oral histories, theoretical analyses, and historical examples, the following chapters explore how the movements of second liners across time and space can enlarge our sense of what is possible in our political institutions, in our social groups, in our personal relationships, and in our dancing, now and in the future.

Barbara Lacen Keller addresses an audience at the George and Joyce Wein Jazz & Heritage Center for the New Orleans Jazz & Heritage Foundation's 2021 Jazz & Heritage Concert Series, introducing Shannon Powell. (Photo by Eric Simon for the New Orleans Jazz & Heritage Foundation.)

INTERLUDE

Barbara Lacen Keller

September 5, 2017

Barbara Lacen Keller, who died in 2023 at age seventy-six, was part of some major developments in second lining's history throughout the late twentieth and early twenty-first centuries. She was there for the beginnings of two SAPCs in the 1980s that still dominate the scene today: the Lady Money Wasters and the Original New Orleans Lady Buckjumpers. The "Lacen" portion of her name came from her marriage to Anthony "Tuba Fats" Lacen (1950–2004), one of New Orleans's most celebrated musicians. Barbara Lacen Keller was well known within the cultural communities of second liners and Mardi Gras Indians and beyond owing to her lifetime of leadership in education, healthcare, and job equity. She was fondly nicknamed "the Mayor of Central City" for her work in that neighborhood. Her organizing experience primed her to found the Second Line Cultural Tradition Task Force (renamed the Social Aid and Pleasure Club Task Force and subsequently led by Tamara Jackson Snowden), whose post-Katrina advocacy successfully halted proposed astronomical hikes in Second Line permit fees.

We held this interview at New Orleans City Hall, where, at the time, Lacen Keller worked as the Director of Constituent Services for Council District B Councilwoman Stacey Head. Later she worked in Mayor LaToya Cantrell's Office of Cultural Economy. Both roles allowed her to correct local politicians' misinformation about Second Line parades and to intervene when clubs clashed with the city. In the excerpts below, Lacen Keller reflects on several themes that thread throughout the following chapters, including the importance of family roots in New Orleans's Black cultural practices and the central (but sometimes overlooked) history of mutual aid within New Orleans's parading cultures. She also makes an important point regarding class-based stereotypes of Second Lines, refuting assumptions that second lining is a "degrading" preoccupation of the poor and uneducated (explored more in Chapter 4) and emphasizing instead its links to ancestral memory for all African Americans in New Orleans.

Well, let me share with you a brief history about who I am. . . . I was born in New Orleans, but the uniqueness of my life—and I'm so excited that I am truly what we call a culture bearer—I come from the family and mother [Augustine Germaine Lewis] and father [Julius Rankins] where my mother's side was Mardi Gras Indians social aid and pleasure club. In fact, my mother is, to my knowledge, the only existing Mardi Gras Indian spygirl, and she's eighty-nine years old. She's still living, and they cannot find any other female, or know of any other female, that served as a spygirl with the Mardi Gras Indians. And I also was a Mardi Gras Indian, I was what they call a Little Queen [of the Cheyenne tribe], and I started that at the age of three or four with my mother's family. . . . She was involved in a club called the Jolly Bunch [Social and Pleasure Club]. The Jolly Bunch was a strong club, and they had women, Lady Jolly Bunch. . . . And my father's family . . . were musicians and dancers. I had an uncle [Leroy Rankins], he was a world-renowned saxophone player. My grandfather [Lawrence Rankins Sr.] was a musician, so I come from a very strong culture background of the music, Mardi Gras Indians, and Second Line. My mother was a second liner, so as you can see, I'm deeply rooted in the culture.

. . .

And I was also in the Lady Jolly Bunch; in fact, I was its youngest member at the time that I was in the organization. And then later, I, for some reason, I just drifted away from it, and I had my family, whatever. Then I started a female group of the Money Wasters. I am one of the founders of the Lady Money Wasters, that's out of the Tremé [in the late 1970s]. And then, after I migrated uptown, I joined a club called the Original New Orleans Lady Buckjumpers. And they were like a year old when I joined. . . . They were organized in '84, and [in] '85 [or] '86 I joined the club.[1]

We're Not Just About a Parade

People had the misconception that when it comes to social aid and pleasure clubs, that it's a certain class of people, but that is further from the truth. Because at one time, the culture was known as the backstreet culture. It was known as a culture of a certain class, of somewhat of a degrading [thing], and even until today, there are some people within [the] African American community [who] shun and look down on the social aid and pleasure [clubs], but it comes from all walks . . . educated people, common laborers—people from all walks of life. As people become more knowledgeable of its culture, [they understand that] it is something that derives from the motherland, Africa. Because, you know, we started through the churches, and the benevolent societies, and the benevolence is basically that: taking care of your own. . . . Because at one time, it wasn't to be that we would have insurance, and we had to take care of all the nickels and dimes or however. And those things were created where, through the church or whatever, through the benevolent society, they would take care of the sick and the dead. So, as various organizations within the African American community, especially in New Orleans . . . they have government rules that they must abide by, and it must also have a standard and the quality in representing those organizations.

. . .

And, while I was in the Buckjumpers, I was the PR person. I organized our first back-to-school picnic. Buckjumpers was the first ones to do that. The Lady Buckjumpers, where we did the haircuts and the hair braids—it wasn't just a lot of, come in, get school supplies; it was a family thing. And the other clubs started doing the same thing, you know? And at one time, to be honest with you, in the '80s, the clubs would get together and have a picnic, like the Scene Boosters, the Buckjumpers—it was a lot of clubs uptown. And they would get together, and we'd have a family fun day! Have games, and activities, and it was a wonderful thing, you know. So [what] I'm saying is that the culture has so much within its element, that it's not just about a parade. And that's what I, myself as an elder, and as a culture bearer, that's what I really want the world and people to see: that we stand for something. We're not just about a parade.

. . .

I wanted to say, when I was talking about being a culture bearer, and how important it is for the transition: I'm a mother, four children and four grandchildren. What I did with my four children, I afforded the opportunity to be involved in the culture. And my reasons for that was to expose them to the culture, and what happened is that only two of them decided that they wanted to be a part, and that was fine, but that did not mean I didn't expose them, or teach them. And through that, I have four grandchildren, and out of my four grandchildren, only one of my grandchildren decided [to be involved], and he is a musician. In fact, he has his own brass band, his brass band is called Sons of Jazz. He's a tuba player. And—
RACHEL CARRICO: And what is his name?
BARBARA LACEN KELLER: His name is Michael Brooks. Michael Brooks Jr. And to me, I tell him all the time, I say, "You the spirit." He has the spirit of his grandfather. He plays the tuba, and sometimes his

gestures and the way he move, the way he play the instrument, sometimes I really think, you know, I say, "Boy, you got the spirit of Tuba in you!" So what I am saying is that, what I would wish for my African American sisters and brothers and families, that you afford the children the opportunity to make a choice. You know, and for so long, like I said, people thought it was degrading—"Oh, you don't want to do that like the more common people." It's not that. Educated, fine, hardworking, refined people, you know, that just have a deep love for its culture and want to participate.... It is a very treasured culture. It is, and I get emotional, because of the love that people will only know that it is a part of us, that those of us who may not have the opportunity to ever travel to our motherland, it was, it's a part that was brought there, to instill in us. Because if you look at some—you say you're a dance major. You look at some African dance, and compare it to some Second Line. So connected.... The dancing, it's about, it's about the beat of the music, that's tapping and tipping on your heart. It's the beating of the music that's tapping and tipping on your brain. It's the beats that are tapping and tipping on the ambience, on the taste that's in your mouth, of a good dish that you just ate. That's what it's all about. Right?

RC: That's a beautiful note to end on. [*Lacen Keller laughs*] Unless you'd like to say anything else.

BLK: It is hard to know, and my time for transition will come, and I would hope that when I transition, that people will understand that this is true value, not face value, of how I love my culture.

CHAPTER 2

Community

Ask social aid and pleasure club members why they do what they do, and before long, you will likely hear the word *community* in their answer. Many see their annual parades, in and of themselves, as a service to their communities. Edward Buckner, president of the Original Big Seven SAPC, speaks of his group as a community organization engaged in community service and counts its annual parade as chief among its services. "It gives me a major enjoyment to do that for the community," he said, "and to have the responsibility from the community to do that every year. It makes me want to do a better job."[1] Nicole Lazard, a member of several SAPCs, explains that the parades matter to the clubs' networks in part because the community financially invests in the parades' production.

> [When you parade,] you're giving back to the community. [They] get to see all this hard work, because sometimes you do fundraisers and things, and you let the people see where their money is going, what we spent your money on. On some of these things [suits, decorations, the band, floats, and so on]. Yes, we gave you school supplies, we fed the homeless, but we did use a part of this money to hit the streets. So, to show you that we appreciate it, here it is, your day. Because people be mad if they don't have no Second Line, you know that?[2]

Club members such as Lazard often point out that they're about more than parading, appealing to the assistance they provide year-round. Some sponsor drives to collect and distribute school supplies and children's coats. Others visit nursing homes, host Easter egg hunts, or simply lend money to members who need to pay their bills.[3] The Family Ties SAPC donates toys to a daycare where one member's mother works. It also volunteers at local events, for instance, passing out water to runners during a race. In a variety of ways, SAPCs position themselves to help as needs arise—the clubs are organized and visible, and members often see themselves as role models.

Such clubs are also effective service organizations because they often have access to cash. Club members raise money for their activities in the way mutual aid societies have always done it: by collecting dues from members and hosting fundraisers such as dances, raffles, and fish fries, throughout the year. Primarily, these funds offset the cost of parading— the permit from the city, specially designed suits, custom-made shoes, handmade decorations, float construction, musician fees, and more—but can also be put to other uses as needs arise. "We spend thousands [on our parade] and don't think about it," said Tyree Smith, secretary of Family Ties. He was not exaggerating. Each SAPC member pays monthly dues that often amount to between fifty and one hundred dollars (or more) in addition to contributing hundreds more to cover parade costs.[4] Club members and their families and friends regularly make financial sacrifices to put on a parade for their communities, but they find ways to pump cash into the community as well. As Smith reflected, "A lot of people need help—talking, financial. [We] give back in any kind of way we can."[5] Similarly, Gerald Platenburg, a member of the Nine Times SAPC, insists on the importance of giving back. "Yeah, not just the Second Line part. You know?" he said. "Some clubs do [focus only on parading], but we try to reach out to our community, where we from, and just try to give back. We don't have much, but the little bit we do have, we try to give back to the community."[6] Catina Braxton Robertson, chief executive officer of the Ice Divas, agrees: "That's where our focus really is. It's not just about parading that day, it's about giving back to the community."[7]

When Braxton Robertson, Platenburg, and other SAPC members invoke "the community," they might reference their neighborhoods and extended networks of friends and family members. At other times the term points to a group as large and heterogenous as "the African American community" in New Orleans. Both usages reveal second lining's importance to Black New Orleanians in general and its roots in more local, specific allegiances within the city's many Black communities (formed through schools, churches, professional associations, and more).[8] On other occasions, second liners refer to themselves not as part of the Second Line community but part of "the culture." For example, reflecting on her role in organizing multiple SAPCs to work for their common interests, Tamara Jackson Snowden says she works to serve "the best interest of the culture."[9]

Speaking of both "the community" and "the culture" is common among Black New Orleanians who identify as culture bearers, or people dedicated to maintaining the unique cultural practices of the city's African diaspora, such as masking as Black Masking Indians, Baby Dolls, or SAPCs. The ways in which second liners speak of the community and the culture align with the dance scholar Julie Johnson's findings on how people define the community formed through a West African dance class in Philadelphia. Several dancers and musicians explicitly linked their understandings of community to knowledge of and membership in African and African diasporic culture.[10] Albeit in a different context, many second liners similarly link communal identity to knowledge of and participation in African diasporic culture.

A close look at how second liners conceive of community—and, more important, work at creating it—offers nuanced understanding to scholarly discussions of community. The term has come under critical scrutiny for its pervasive and unexamined usage, especially in philanthropic and nonprofit contexts, including the arts. In her study of the community work of the dance company Urban Bush Women, Nadine George-Graves states it bluntly: "'The community' has oddly come to be a euphemism for 'ghetto,' especially as far as the arts are concerned. Teaching artists go out into 'the community' to bring culture to the underprivileged."[11] Scholars point out that, in most colloquial usages, "community" implies a given and monolithic entity, carries overwhelmingly positive connotations, and is positioned as an altruistic other to capitalism.[12] Communities, however, are not things but processes, requiring constant effort by heterogenous groups of people in order to exist. Contrary to romantic associations with the term, many communities are occasioned by decidedly negative circumstances and defined as much by those excluded as by those included. And, in contrast with perceptions of community efforts as an alternative to capitalist modes of production, communal practices are generative for capitalist exchange.[13] The work of scholars to bring some critical attention to the unexamined uses of *community* is important because, in many cases, this powerful concept has become vacuous, left open for interested parties to fill with whatever definitions fit their agendas. In line with George-Graves's comments, the anthropologist Kate Crehan notes that, for corporations, philanthropists, and nonprofit agencies, *community* is shorthand for the marginalized and economically depressed neighborhoods they wish to "help" or "serve."[14] But, as the cultural critic Miranda Joseph concedes, despite intellectual critiques of the *concept* of community, celebratory claims to community robustly persist.[15] Even if funders, politicians, and philanthropists leverage the concept of community in misguided and possibly pernicious ways, many people have a felt sense of what actual communities they belong to and why they matter.

The fact that community is often ill-defined and idealized is not as important, I argue, as the fact that the concept orients groups of people, including dancers, toward a shared purpose and struggle. In her study of improvised dance, Danielle Goldman makes a similar point regarding understandings of freedom.[16] Because community and freedom are not static but always in motion, they are hard to pin down, and that ambiguity leaves them vulnerable to manipulation and exploitation. But rather than dismiss community as a hollow signifier, I seek to learn more about how it works by looking closely at the messy, imperfect, prismatic processes of creating communities such as those undertaken by second liners in New Orleans.

The philosopher Jean-Luc Nancy uses the "graceless expression" of "being-with" to emphasize the action of sharing space with others while avoiding the assumption of shared identity.[17] To riff on Nancy's term, I suggest that "dancing-with" can be a useful lens for seeing the ways in which dancers foster community. Julie Johnson lifts up the notion of "dancing with" to point out that there are different ways to share space with fellow movers. Dancing *alongside* another does not necessarily require connection, collaboration, or support, but dancing *with* each other means nurturing a communal linkage by attending to one another.[18] At the Second Line, dancing-with can reinforce or resist patterns of relationality mapped out by the other ways people encounter each other in the city, whether through institutions (family, church, school, work, SAPCs), geography (neighborhood), or transactions (commerce, service). But, as Johnson outlines, dancing-with does more than reflect pre-existing relationships; it can also create new ones. For the hundreds to thousands of people who attend each Sunday Second Line, dancing-with both reflects *and* brings into being something that participants feel and name as the Second Line community.

• • •

The circular formations of each Second Line parade enact a value placed on the collective rather than the individual.[19] The procession organizes the dancing collective as an imagined, yet narrowed, circle that orbits around the band. Small circles constantly form when the procession pauses: A small group of dancers, either behind the band or stationed peripherally in a parking lot or driveway, often widens into a ring, encouraging and challenging one or two dancers in the middle by clapping, shouting, or even playing cowbells and tambourines. This is often the domain in which children's footwork skills are honed as they step into the center and perform their best moves to the supportive yet demanding comments of family members and friends. During the VIP Ladies and Kids' 2014 parade, the procession paused for a few moments while the band continued to play. On the sidewalk, Tyree Smith engaged in a spontaneous, friendly footwork battle with another man about his age, advancing and retreating while feeding off each other's energy. Before long, a girl who appeared to be about ten years old walked by with another child and their adult companion. Without a word, she jumped in between the dancing duo. The adults bent forward to verbally encourage the young dancer ("You better get it now!", "Ohhhh!") while she playfully punctuated her footwork with pauses, hip pops, and forward scoots. Within a minute, the exchange amicably disbanded, the ring dissolved back into the line, and many mini collectives moved forward once again (see video 2.1 on this book's web page).

Second liners pack into the limited space afforded by streets and sidewalks to get as close as possible to the musicians. Those less interested in dancing might walk far ahead or behind the crowd, where it is quiet enough to have a conversation and there is room to push a stroller or a bicycle. But those who have come to dance usually do so in close proximity to many other dancing bodies. Some dancers, myself included, prefer to position themselves behind the band, especially if they like to feel the vibrations of the bass drum thumping in their chests. I can usually squeeze into the few feet between the vendors pulling wheeled coolers brimming with iced drinks and the collective of self-styled percussionists beating out polyrhythms on tambourines, cowbells, and glass bottles. Others prefer to station themselves directly beside the band. Here the music is even louder, but one risks getting hit in the head by the slide of a trombone. When dancing alongside the ropes on the right side (or "sidewalk side") of the club, paraders constantly wrestle with the rope carriers for space, especially when negotiating narrow streets lined with parked cars. When I'm here, I swerve around protruding side-view mirrors and press against the rope, which sometimes cuts into my ribs, doing my best to keep up with the band's tempo without bumping into others. Occasionally, small groups of us will bail out of our rope-side spots, jogging ahead in search of a dancing location with a bit more elbow room. Once we leave the street, we must squeeze between parked cars, swerve around trash cans, and climb over bushes and protruding oak tree roots to reach the sidewalk, where yet another compressed space contains dancers moving in close quarters.

Those who dance on the sidewalk, known as "sideliners," execute some of the most intricate, athletic, and quickly moving footwork seen at the parade. As Terry "Squillee" Gable, a member of the Original Big Seven SAPC, explains, "The sidewalk is the dance floor." He did not move from the street to the sidewalk until he had been second lining for a few years and felt confident in his footwork. "Once you hit the sidewalk, there ain't no walking on the sidewalk. You gotta dance on the sidewalk." Gable has instructions for tourists and other parade-goers unfamiliar with the sidewalk's rules: "You see all these people coming, swinging their arms, they sliding their feet, they splitting, they spinning, they doing their thing—and you want to walk. You want to be cute. Get in the street if you want to be cute and watch the parade. That's how it goes."[20] The sidewalk's reputation for high dance standards may be shifting with a new generation of second liners who prefer to dance alongside the ropes and refer to the sidewalk as a space reserved for "senior citizens." The senior citizens (who mostly appear to be in their forties and fifties) dance in incredibly close quarters and never step on each other's toes![21] Even though they must navigate cracked sidewalks, fire hydrants, and porch railings; even though they remain tightly packed and must keep moving forward; and even though no two people are executing the exact same steps, sideliners manage to dance inches from each other and barely touch. They come dangerously close—finding spaces in between each other's feet and around the shoulders, stepping in a space that was occupied by another person's foot only a millisecond earlier, crawling under each other's legs, dropping and spinning in front of a forward-moving dancer, swinging a leg over the head of a man on his knees—but they move sensitively and smoothly, almost never disrupting another's footwork. As sideliners demonstrate, the spatial constraints occasioned by second lining's urban environment have impacted the dance's form over time. The arms stay relatively still and close to the body, and footwork remains directly under the hips, so that one can take up as little real estate as possible on the crowded sidewalk, where the most stunning dancing can be witnessed or experienced.

No matter where dancers position themselves in the procession, the band organizes the crowd to move in relation to the music. Each person improvises their own combination of specific and unique movements, but the beat makes the collective cohere, so that it is possible to stand on a porch, overpass, or other elevated structure and see thousands of heads bobbing up and down together, not in perfect unison but unified. The effect is breathtaking, like the rippling of a vast ocean wave. In its collective experience, circular structures, and interconnected improvisations, Second Line choreography expresses and enacts the tradition's communal values.

• • •

Today's self-described Second Line community can be traced back to Black secret societies and voluntary associations, broad terms used by historians to categorize many types of exclusive organizations that were prevalent among people of African descent across the United States, the Caribbean, and Latin America in the eighteenth, nineteenth, and early twentieth centuries. Such organizations included lodges, craftsmen's unions, religious fraternities, mutual aid societies, benevolent associations, burial associations, social and aid clubs, and, later, social aid and pleasure clubs.[22] The earliest Black secret society on record in New Orleans, perhaps the first in the present-day United States, has been traced to the 1780s.[23] The number of Black voluntary organizations in the city expanded continuously throughout the Civil War and Reconstruction eras, and such groups exploded in popularity at the turn of the twentieth century.[24]

These organizations served multiple essential functions, including assistance, civic engagement, and social activity. Mutual aid societies and benevolent associations enabled their members and families to endure health crises when they were shut out from mainstream access to healthcare. They provided ill members with access to doctors and pharmacists, a pension to defray the impact of missed work, and a "relief committee" to routinely visit the home. These services were of chief importance during epidemics of tuberculosis and pneumonia.[25] During the COVID-19 pandemic, many clubs served similar functions. For example, the Big Seven offered vaccines at an outdoor gathering—a twenty-first-century twist on the groups' historic purpose. Then and now, benevolent associations cover members' funeral expenses, including the cost of hiring a brass band, so that the family can avoid financial disaster and still send the deceased off with dignity and style.[26] Beyond mutual aid, nineteenth-century societies sustained an infrastructure for Black self-reliance and political activism, especially important during the Reconstruction era. Lodges and other organizations brought Black men together to debate political issues that affected them, and in some cases, organize protests or campaigns for office. Societies also hosted purely social gatherings such as dances, picnics, and parades.[27]

Through all their activities, early Black voluntary organizations strengthened the bonds of sub-communities within New Orleans's heterogenous Black population and simultaneously provided an arena for them to come together across their differences. Unlike like the rest of the United States and more like its Caribbean neighbors, New Orleans was initially organized according to a three-tiered racial and caste order:

whites, free people of color, and enslaved people from Africa or of African descent (some would argue that colorism allows the hierarchy to persist today). Since the city's colonial era, its diverse Black communities distinguished themselves not only according to enslaved or free status but also along lines of culture and religion. After the end of slavery, those who had been classified as free people of color in antebellum Louisiana used the term "Creole" to distinguish families whose ancestors had enjoyed free status, with limits, since the eighteenth century.[28] They were often (but not always) Catholic, French-speaking, educated, well connected, and politically active. The city's Afro-Creole (or Creole of color) population may be known to dance scholars owing to the infamous quadroon balls, dances held with the explicit purpose of forming *plaçage* matches, or formal concubinage arrangements, between white men and free women of color.[29] Yet Afro-Creole New Orleanians' influence on dance history extends much further. For example, their active role in voluntary organizations laid the foundation for second lining as we know it today.

Creoles of color weren't the only New Orleanians forming benevolent associations in the nineteenth and twentieth centuries. During the Civil War, the city's Black population swelled as individuals recently freed or self-manumitted flocked to the city from neighboring plantations. Newer arrivals were often (but not always) Protestant, English-speaking, had far less access to education, and had been barred from political participation.[30] During Reconstruction, Black politicians from both Afro-Creole and American Black or Anglo-African communities drew on the strength of benevolent societies, which engaged their members in regular political debate and action. For example, in 1863 the Société d'Economie et d'Assisance Mutuelle (Economy Society), an all-male Afro-Creole society founded in 1836, hosted public gatherings to discuss securing their right to vote.[31] During the same time, American Black members of the Prince Hall Masonic Lodge in New Orleans joined up with chapters across the United States to similarly advocate for full citizenship and male suffrage. At times such community organizations as the Economy Society and Prince Hall Masons forged solidarity *within* their respective communities, reflecting and arguably reinforcing differences between them. At other times they transcended cultural, class, and religious differences to build coalitions in pursuit of a common political or social goal.[32] Even after the end of Reconstruction, when Afro-Creole and American Black politicians were ousted from office and the gains made for racial equality suffered a violent backlash, Black voluntary organizations continued to grow, addressing community needs and organizing politically. By the 1890s Black voluntary organizations were approaching their zenith in New Orleans.[33] The dance scholar Jacqui Malone calls the years between 1890 and 1910 the "golden age of Negro secret societies," when groups that had formed before the Civil War blossomed and many new groups emerged.[34]

In addition to political coalition-building, voluntary societies also brought Black New Orleanians together in the pursuit of pleasure. Mutual aid societies and benevolent associations regularly held parades and dances where their members, families, and neighbors danced to brass band music.[35] Their frequent social activities spurred a large demand for Black brass bands, perhaps becoming their principal customers.[36] Therefore, not coincidentally, the golden age of Negro secret societies was also the golden age of the brass band, an epoch cited by jazz historians as the time when a musical revolution, not yet called "jazz," emerged on the streets and in the clubs, dance halls, brothels, parks, public squares, and living rooms of New Orleans.[37] The clarinetist and music historian Michael White suggests that club parades and jazz funerals, along with church parades, were the three types of brass band processions held during this time period.[38] These events not only kept brass band musicians employed but facilitated the exchange of musical knowledge among oft-segregated populations. As the ethnomusicologist Matt Sakakeeny puts it, the interactions between Creoles of color and Black Americans (and even some European immigrants) created "an efflorescence akin to a chemical reaction brought about by the synthesis of multiple elements: jazz."[39] It is significant that this aesthetic revolution happened in public. As Jim Crow laws took hold, the act of marching through the segregated city asserted, with pleasure, Black societies' shared fights for equality. In all their activities—mutual aid efforts, political organizing, and pleasurable events—Black voluntary organizations in New Orleans at the turn of the century worked to create the democratic society promised during Reconstruction.[40]

Voluntary associations used to be a fact of life in nearly every community in the United States, but by the 1930s they had almost disappeared, except among Black New Orleanians.[41] In 1937 the sociologist Harry J. Walker conducted a study to understand why. He concluded that mutual aid remained more needed there than elsewhere, since the death rate among African American New Orleanians remained much higher than elsewhere in the country, and higher than that of white city residents, owing to conditions of poverty and a lack of access to medical care. But he also noted that voluntary organizations had become deeply ingrained in the habits and customs of the people. Because New Orleanians combined social features such as recreational events and elaborate funerals with "the usual practice of affording insurance benefits," voluntary associations attained "an element of permanency." As a result, the city's benevolent societies offered "a common meeting ground for numbers of people whose social activities in the larger white world were, in a sense, restricted."[42] Jacqui Malone adds further a consideration: African Americans of the eighteenth and nineteenth centuries were *"culturally predisposed* to creating and joining mutual aid societies" because of the prevalence of secret societies in Africa.[43] The historian Jeroen Dewulf locates the origins of New Orleans fraternal organizations' parades specifically in the kingdom of Kongo, where European colonization led to syncretic performance traditions long before its inhabitants were forced into slavery in Louisiana and elsewhere in the Americas.[44] Therefore, the popularity and longevity of New Orleans's Black voluntary associations, including SAPCs, is owed to many factors, including economic circumstances, social need, cultural custom, and ancestral memory. Threats to Black life, and the forms of mutual aid forged to protect against them, have necessarily shifted over the years, but second lining's communal values, by and large, remain.

• • •

Tamara Jackson Snowden knows well the present-day needs of Second Line communities and SAPCs' capacities to respond. She leads the VIP Ladies and Kids SAPC as its president, serves as the director of the Social Aid and Pleasure Club Task Force (an advocacy group), and is the executive director of the nonprofit organization SilenceIsViolence. SilenceIsViolence originated as the mutual aid arm of another SAPC she leads, the Bayou Steppers, but grew into a fully fledged 501(c)(3) organization with a dedicated office and staff on payroll. Since most clubs find less formalized ways to address the pressing needs of their members, families, and neighbors, SilenceIsViolence is a unique example of an SAPC's social aid activities.

About a month after the VIP Ladies and Kids 2014 anniversary parade, I arrived at Jackson Snowden's office to conduct an interview (listen to the full interview on this book's web page). I walked into a two-story building on Oretha Castle Haley Boulevard in the Central City neighborhood, which was shared between SilenceIsViolence and the Juvenile Justice Project of Louisiana. Moving down the hallway, I spotted brightly colored, fluffy plumes erupting from steely gray office tables. The feathers adorned small stacks of fans, accessories commonly held by SAPC members on parade day. When I reached Jackson Snowden's office, I was greeted by a commemorative photograph of Dinerral Shavers, a high school band teacher and member of the Hot 8 Brass Band who was murdered in 2006. When Shavers was killed by a bullet meant for his teenage stepson, his death incited SilenceIsViolence's first march against violence.[45] Alongside

Tamara Jackson Snowden, proud as a peacock, during the VIP Ladies and Kids SAPC's Second Line parade on March 30, 2014. (Photo by Judy Cooper.)

Shavers's photograph hung picture collages of the VIP Ladies and Kids on parade day and plaques commemorating the exemplary service provided by SilenceIsViolence.

I asked Jackson Snowden how her roles as a leader among SAPCs and the director of SilenceIsViolence intersect. She spoke of the pleasure of creating stronger communities through Second Line parades. "Second lining gives you strength to begin tomorrow," she said. "It's a passion that drives from within. And that's what keeps the momentum. That's what keeps clubs coming back, and they do it for their communities."[46] For Jackson Snowden, the collective pride generated by the dancing crowd motivates her to organize the VIP Ladies and Kids parade every year. In fact, the parade she had led a month earlier leveraged community pride as a design concept. Turquoise fabric and peacock-feather fans expressed that year's theme: "Proud as a Peacock." The VIP Ladies and Kids strutted confidently in their peacock-inspired ensembles, emanating pride in themselves, their club, and their community.

In reflecting on the connection among her myriad roles, Jackson Snowden expanded beyond the pleasure of her work to reflect on the pain:

> The clubs initially started as benevolent societies ... and then evolved to social aid and pleasure clubs. The idea was to help your community, help your membership, who couldn't afford funerals and other expenses. These clubs were actually aiding each other within the neighborhoods in which they paraded. Now the aiding portion has changed, just because the needs of the community have changed.[47]

She explained that her SAPCs' major social aid effort is to address the effects of gun violence because it constitutes the most vital need among the clubs, musicians, and their families.

> Unfortunately, it's a commonality that we all share. [A] Prince of Wales [SAPC] member was murdered last year. One of they members. Then you have Brandon Franklin, [who] was killed with TBC Brass Band. The Hot 8 [Brass Band] lost three or four of their members due to violence. It's a commonality.... I mean, I could just continue to call names of victims. And it's just senseless acts of violence. The connection is, we're attached to the community, and this is the real side of what happens. It exists. Violence exists. We're in the inner-city communities, we're in the back streets; there's crime. And sometimes those crimes come home and attack our families. So then we share that commonality of losing.... It's not *one club* that haven't lost a member, almost, or the member in the club lost a family member due to violence. And then sometimes it's on multiple levels. It could be two or three people.... That's common.[48]

Gun violence fragments family structures and communal fabrics in New Orleans's poor and predominantly African American neighborhoods, not only by eliminating lives but also by causing further displacement and isolation among survivors through mass incarceration and neighbors' fear-induced seclusion inside their homes. As it is in cities nationwide, gun violence is occasioned by the informal drug economy and the police terror legitimized by the war on drugs. Both are symptomatic of structural violence. The ethnomusicologist Matt Sakakeeny makes this link when examining the lives of brass band musicians in New Orleans today. Within structures of everyday violence (economic marginalization, increased incarceration, dwindling social services), Sakakeeny says, "interpersonal violence flourishes."[49] He explains how, in the late twentieth century, the rise of the prison-industrial complex and the shrinking of social welfare programs, combined with a shift in New Orleans's market economy away from unionized jobs to more precarious work in the service industry, have disproportionately affected young Black men. In this environment SAPCs are not the only, or even the primary, voluntary associations that offer financial support, belonging, and prestige. Drug trafficking gangs also offer these possibilities. The choice to sell drugs is often the most logical, normalized way for young Black men to earn money. In a city where the murder rate is approximately ten times the national average, interpersonal violence presents itself as a viable, even desirable option for young people operating within illegal drug economies as means to establish powerful positions within those economies.[50] Second Lines reclaim city streets not only from structural forces of dispossession but also from the drug economies and subsequent forms of violence that thrive inside them.

The community that gathers each Sunday during a Second Line parade engages intimately with the realities that Jackson Snowden describes, a "commonality of losing." Clubs memorialize loss by stopping at homes of the deceased or sites of violent incidents. Paraders honor fallen loved ones with commemorative T-shirts, scripted and improvised song lyrics, and dedications printed on route sheets. Even as they mourn, footwork moves second liners through a redemptive reclamation of joy. Their choreographies address not only interpersonal violence but also structural violence. For example, second liners remake perceptions of urban density. In sociological studies, population density has often been correlated with poverty and precarity. Because the Second Line brings people physically close together, it shifts traditional geographies of density from markers of poverty and danger to valuable assets for performative fervor.[51] As paraders nimbly negotiate the physically tight places of the street and sidewalk, they also remake figuratively tight places, Houston Baker's term for the multiple forms of lock-up that have shaped Black experience in the United States.[52] Second liners refashion constraints on mobility and agency into conditions of possibility for them.

In order to foster the Second Line's capacity for communal healing from interpersonal and structural violence, SAPCs actively work to maintain parades as protected spaces. Some club presidents walk their routes a day before their parades with a plea: "If anyone has scores to settle, please don't settle them around our parade."[53] Many clubs include a warning on their route sheets directing participants to leave their guns and troubles at home. For example, the VIP Ladies and Kids' 2014 route sheet asked attendees, "Please leave weapons and animals at home. It's a family affair come out and enjoy!" Not unlike churches, Second Lines hold a special place in the social imagination of many New Orleanians as a safe space for communing, healing, and even catching the spirit.[54]

The tenacity and efficacy of SAPCs' community-building and antiviolence activism is admirable and exemplary. However, some approaches reveal that communities are defined not only by who is included but also who is excluded. In their analysis of the Social Aid and Pleasure Club Task Force and SilenceIsViolence, Lewis Watts and Eric Porter acknowledge that some SAPCs' goals and aesthetics can elevate certain members of "the culture" and dismiss others. They write, "There is a way in which the privileging of culture bearers as healers and agents of reform can lead to the abjection of other members of working-class and poor neighborhoods."[55] Sakakeeny reaches a similar conclusion, noting how SAPCs such as the Black Men of Labor that disallow hip hop music, dress, and dance invest in respectable displays of Blackness and permit an aversion to other modes of Blackness deemed transgressive, detrimental, and violent.[56] These intracommunal tensions become especially apparent any time violent conflict erupts on the streets while a Second Line is in motion.

Such was the case in early 2006, just as Second Lines were beginning to roll after Hurricane Katrina. Before the storm, Tamara Jackson Snowden and other leaders of the parading community had formed an advocacy group called the Second Line Cultural Tradition Task Force to collectively negotiate with the city over permitting and policing concerns. After the storm, the group focused its efforts on organizing a homecoming event. As Jackson Snowden explained, "We decided to organize one of the first parades with all the clubs who [would] parade together [for] the first time. It happened for the first time in history in January of 2006. We hosted a parade with at least thirty social aid and pleasure clubs." The parade transcended neighborhood islands to unify the Second Line community, and "for the first time it actually brought us together."[57] The All-Star Second Line, as it was billed, showcased the clubs' solidarity and provided an opportunity for displaced friends and neighbors to come home and reconnect, if only for a weekend. But the large gathering provided an opportunity for enemies to reconnect, too. Not long after the parade ended, shots rang out a block from its final destination, resulting in three wounded victims. Although no one involved had any connection to the participating SAPCs, the incident stoked fears about returning to the city amid rising crime rates, and the New Orleans Police Department (NOPD) responded by dramatically increasing the costs of parade permits; for some clubs they rose by 300 percent.[58] The NOPD's argument in favor of the cost increases in 2006 rested on the assumption that Second Lines were a magnet for violence and placed the burden of responsibility on the clubs.[59]

After the All-Star parade, the task force changed its name to the New Orleans Social Aid and Pleasure Club Task Force. In an April 2006 interview Jackson Snowden explained that the name change was decided by a new slate of board members put in place become some previous members were still displaced. The new name was chosen in part to gain distance from the term *Second Line*, which, the group feared, people had started to associate with street-level violence. It also sought to emphasize the social aid aspect of parading organizations. Overall, the name change was part of the group's efforts to help people understand, in Jackson Snowden's words, "the true spirit of what we bring forth on a Sunday."[60] Later that year, the task force made its argument forcefully when it partnered with the ACLU to sue the city of New Orleans over its choice to dramatically increase permitting fees. The plaintiffs argued that unreasonable costs violated social aid and pleasure clubs' constitutional rights to freedom of speech, as expressed through second lining, and equal protection under the law.[61] After a year the parties reached an agreement setting a price cap for the clubs at around $2,000 per four-hour parade, meant to pay for ten police officers.[62] In the wake of this significant victory the task force did not rest, since the fee agreement did not end all disputes with city government and the NOPD.[63] The group has continued to defend its culture against accusations that community events stoke interpersonal violence. It was called on to mount these defenses again in 2013, seven years after the All-Star parade, following a shooting that occurred during the Original Big Seven SAPC's 2013 parade.

• • •

The Big Seven parades annually on Mother's Day, and so, in addition to celebrating its club and neighborhood, this event honors maternal figures in the members' families and communities. The club came out the door of president Edward Buckner's home, which it calls the headquarters of the Original Big Seven Culture and Heritage. I stood on the neutral ground, the grassy median in the middle of the street, watching the kids' division dance past with their own brass band. The main division followed, strutting in front of the To Be Continued Brass Band, commonly known as TBC. Dancers love TBC's quick-paced, funky beat, and, since Second Lines involve multiple generations, the band's adaptations of pop songs from past decades (such as "Everyday People" by Sly and the Family Stone) are crowd favorites. When I saw Buckner pass by, he was showing off his footwork in fancy shoes that looked, from my vantage point, like alligator skin.

I jumped into the procession not long before the horns began wailing out a brassy version of Whitney Houston's 1987 pop hit "I Wanna Dance with Somebody," and the procession turned the corner, funneling us from the wide boulevard onto narrow, residential Villere Street. When we reached Villere Street's first intersection with Frenchmen Street, two gunmen sprayed bullets into the crowd. Nineteen people were shot, and another was trampled in the chaos. Although no one died that day, three people suffered severe injuries and remained in critical condition for weeks. I was standing under a stop sign when the violence erupted and was lucky to walk away physically unharmed. The incident became known as the "Mother's Day shooting" locally and in what little national media attention it received.[64] In New Orleans, local newspapers plastered the story across their front pages for well over a week. Within days, police arrested two African American men, brothers Shawn Scott and Aekin Scott (ages twenty-four and nineteen, respectively, at the time), and charged them with twenty counts of attempted murder. Authorities maintained that the bullets were intended as revenge against a target in the parading crowd.[65] None of those involved had any formal relationship to the Original Big Seven or TBC.

Second Line advocates such as the task force rightly point out that such episodes as the Mother's Day shooting are not a defining characteristic of the parades themselves; rather, they are a consequence of systemic issues in the neighborhoods where parades take place. Club members often live in the areas where they parade, but owing to numerous factors related to displacement, especially after Katrina, this residential tie is becoming less and less the norm. Even if not currently residing in those neighborhoods, however, club members often are closely connected to them through childhood networks, existing family in the vicinity, or other kinds of community investments. Many clubs, including the Big Seven, understand that they offer one of the few antidotes to violence in their neighborhoods. Following the shooting, the Big Seven issued a statement on its Facebook page:

> Crime and violence in New Orleans is a systemic problem and we strongly believe that safeguarding our cultural heritage helps to address the roots of violence. We are a cross-generational organization, ages 5–70. Our young people grow up in this culture, are fed by it, and feel loved, supported and connected in ways that build real security. That's crime prevention.[66]

The Big Seven's statement demands that its readers acknowledge the organizations' work to address the structural violence at the root of interpersonal violence. When the Facebook post was reprinted in the city's mainstream newspaper, the *Times-Picayune*, it widened the reach of SAPCs' work to disentangle "Second Line" from "violence" in the minds of those outside the cultural community.

The journalist Deborah "Big Red" Cotton was one of the most vocal advocates for changing negative impressions of the Second Line culture. Her "New Orleans Good Good" blog, YouTube channel, and Facebook page acted as real-time, grassroots chronicles of each week's parade.[67] She suffered severe injuries on that Mother's Day. From her hospital bed, Cotton continued to stress the importance of the parading community as a corrective to structural violence, and she refused to demonize the Scott brothers. "We can no longer take the position, 'Lock them up and throw away the key,'" she said. "We have to ask, 'How can we be our brothers' keepers?'"[68] Complications from Cotton's injuries eventually led to her death on May 2, 2017, four years after the shooting. She was the sole casualty. The Second Line community honored her with a large memorial service and Second Line. Mourners, including the TBC musicians who led the procession, wore red T-shirts emblazoned with Cotton's smiling face. Her ashes rode along in a horse-drawn carriage.[69]

The Big Seven embodied Cotton's life-affirming statements just a few weeks after the 2013 Mother's Day shooting when it took to the streets again with a "re-do" parade. This time, the procession departed from Buckner's house at 1:00 p.m., passed through the intersection where the shooting had occurred, and continued on. The procession wound its way to the site of the former St. Bernard public housing development and ended nearby. It answered a call issued to New Orleanians by the local journalist Jarvis DeBerry days after the incident: "What I do know is that our traditions are worth fighting for," he wrote, "that we ought not let them be killed off by gunmen and that the best way we can show our fight and concern for Deborah [Cotton] and others is to absolutely refuse to stop dancing."[70] That is just what the Big Seven did.

The Big Seven's re-do parade was significant for the club and the Second Line culture at large. It was personally significant for me, too. I needed to show up to the re-do parade and every Second Line for the remainder of the season. By avoiding the parades, even temporarily, I could have tacitly written them off as synonymous with danger and effectively underscored reasons given by the city to restrict the tradition rather than support it. It wasn't easy. It meant confronting, along with my contemporaries, my own mortality.[71] It meant surmounting my fear enough to get back out there every Sunday for the ensuing year. The image captured on security cameras and recycled in local media accounts returned me again and again to the

The Original Big Seven reclaims St. Bernard Avenue during their "re-do" parade on June 1, 2013. (Photo by Judy Cooper.)

questions, "What if it happens again? What if I'm not so lucky the next time?" But if I aspired to be an ally, I knew that I needed to stand—and dance—with Buckner, the Big Seven, and my friends and acquaintances who were also on the intersection of Frenchmen and Villere Streets that day, and who had come to form my own version of a Second Line community. Beyond making a statement, I also returned to the Second Line because I trusted its healing capacity, what Imani Perry poetically calls the "spiritual majesty" of creating joy amid suffering.[72] Attending the re-do parade was an important step in my mental and emotional healing, which were required to continue the research that led to this book.

Even as I faced my own fears, I knew that my privilege shielded me from the very real dangers that many second liners face every day. In the shooting's aftermath, I was viscerally reminded of the vast inequalities that not only structure ethnographic encounters but also render drastically uneven the impacts of physical violence on the lives of Black and white people in New Orleans and, as is becoming increasingly visible in the mainstream, in the United States at large.[73] As Second Line researcher

Helen A. Regis notes, death haunts the living in New Orleans, but the particular manifestations of those hauntings depend tremendously on the racialized political and economic space of the city.[74] In other words, physical precarity may be a human condition that I share with African American New Orleanians, but precarity is unequally distributed, and not all lives are considered equally grievable or valuable.[75] Second liners defy historic and contemporary antiblack racism when taking to the streets to celebrate Black life and honor Black death. They remap the inequitable space of the city into an arena for Black joy and dignity.

Thirty hours after the Mother's Day shooting I attended a community meeting that Mayor Mitch Landrieu convened in the middle of the intersection of Frenchmen and Villere Streets. Landrieu presented a united front with the Big Seven and with the city's culture bearers broadly. "Everybody on this street knows what happened yesterday has nothing to do with the cultural beauty of New Orleans," the mayor told us. "It happened during a sacred event. . . . We all came out here to reclaim this spot and say what happened yesterday does not reflect who the people of New Orleans are or what we're about."[76] The mayor's message departed from the previous officials' rhetoric, which had historically framed second lining and violence as inextricable from one another. For example, in 2006, Deputy Police Superintendent John Bryson defended the city's decision to hike parade fees in the wake of the All-Star parade by voicing the assumption explicitly: "Second lines are noted for the violence of the crowd afterwards—shootings, stabbings and fights," he said.[77] Bryson's comment reflected a long-standing view among elites and officials that considered second lining a causal factor in interpersonal violence. Landrieu's administration had begun to change that narrative, positioning the Second Line community as an important asset in his efforts to reduce the city's murder rate. As Landrieu stood at the corner of Frenchmen and Villere Streets that day, he had begun ramping up his reelection campaign. A centerpiece of his platform was his year-old initiative, "NOLA for Life," conceived as a public health approach to ending youth violence, with a focus on prevention and community collaboration instead of increased policing. The effort's architects explicitly named New Orleans's culture as the "backbone" of its resilience and an important partner in addressing the violence epidemic.[78] Landrieu's response, as well as his administration's inclusion of culture bearers as essential partners in addressing the violence epidemic, reflected years of grassroots advocacy work by the task force and others to change the minds of those in power.

I asked Tamara Jackson Snowden about Landrieu's show of support for the Second Line community. She scoffed. "I think their response was nice but then they hit us with an additional two hundred dollars added to the existing fee structure."[79] This increase came in 2014 as part of the NOPD's consent decree with the Department of Justice. Jackson Snowden's shrug recognized that, periodically, the city's interest in defending Black cultural traditions—due in no small part to the fact that these traditions sustain New Orleans's tourism economy—converges with Second Line communities' interests in defending their own traditions. On these occasions, temporary victories for Black cultural communities are possible.[80] But Jackson Snowden has yet to see a lasting change in the way elected officials and business elites view Second Lines. In her estimation, if the city truly respected the culture, then its officials would cease efforts to "tax [them] out of existence."[81]

• • •

Despite constant assaults on their existence, SAPCs and the parades they sponsor offer a crucial mode for surviving antiblack racism in New Orleans. Though that fact must be recognized, New Orleans poet Kalamu ya Salaam warns against totalizing Black cultural expressions as mere forms of survival. "We are more than just twisted responses to slavery," he writes, "more than a limited range of make-do solutions to inhuman social conditions. . . . Our insistence on constantly creating family is ideological, not pathological. We bond with each other because we believe in the beauty of community."[82] In Salaam's estimation, "the family that dances together stays together." Salaam refers to the collectivity forged through second lining as a "spirit family of the streets." He writes, "What is a spirit family? Well, there is a nuclear family of father, mother and their natural issue. There is an extended family of kin and kind, folk related by circumstance and life struggles. And there is the spirit family, an activity-centered sharing of common cultural values."[83] Salaam names the SAPC as the primary folk expression of the spirit family because of the members' pledge to each other to make *collective* dreams become reality.[84] The clubs belong to a constellation of spirit families.[85] Beyond their historical antecedents, outlined above, other spirit families include, but are by no means limited to, Mardi Gras processional groups such as Black Masking Indian tribes, Skull and Bones gangs, and Baby Doll marching groups; community and cultural centers; churches; youth development organizations; Greek organizations; dance and drum companies; brass and marching bands; sports teams; and work-based, school-based, and neighborhood alliances. These networks frequently overlap and coalesce at Second Lines, which many refer to as "family reunions." As people gather together on the streets each Sunday, they are seen and accounted for: "Haven't seen you in a while, how you doing?" And if a regular second liner arrives late or skips a Sunday (or a month of Sundays), people who do not even know her name will inquire after her, to make sure that everything is all right. The Second Line community encompasses many collectives—extended families, classmates, co-workers, neighbors, and club members—united through parading together, or dancing-with.

As an expression of the spirit family, second-line communities broaden kinship beyond bloodlines.[86] When contextualizing the spirit family in history, Salaam echoes the voice of Hortense Spillers, whose influential analysis of the family in African American life during and after slavery reveals that the institution of the nuclear family is not a natural expression of kinship but, rather, a sociopolitical unit. In the United States, as in other parts of the Western world, nuclear families have ensured the vertical transfer of bloodline, titles, property, and wealth from fathers to sons.[87] Spillers writes that, under the "legal arrangements of enslavement," such functions of the nuclear family were unavailable to captive persons, who were forced into "horizontal relatedness" with others "of same and different blood," both near and far, connected "in a common fabric of memory and inspiration." Spillers's term "horizontal relatedness" offers a conceptually spatial alternative to the vertical transfer of wealth and status secured by the nuclear family, affirming other articulations of kinship beyond the ways in which family has functioned for white and economically privileged people for centuries.[88] The spirit family of the streets can be seen as a contemporary expression of horizontal relatedness.

This is not to say that strong nuclear families are ancillary to the Second Line community. Quite the opposite is true. Second liners often begin to attend parades, learn to dance, or play music because a parent, aunt, or grandparent is already involved. Social and pleasure clubs throughout history have been founded within single families, for example, the Dirty Dozen SAPC, which paraded in the mid-to-late twentieth century and parades again today; Family Ties SAPC; and the Ole N Nu Style Fellas.[89] The spirit family of the streets makes room for all kinds of kinship. A newer SAPC calls itself Footwerk Family, which illustrates the concept perfectly: This family is tied together not by bloodlines or legal arrangements but by a shared commitment to dance.

• • •

The spirit family of the streets assembles on the pavement, of course, and in indoor spaces, because each parade requires months of behind-the-scenes preparation. In the weeks leading up to the Original Big Seven's 2014 parade, one year after the shooting and re-do, I spent many hours at

Edward Buckner's house helping create fans and streamers. As is often the case with performance processes, the day before the big event demanded the longest hours. When I arrived at Buckner's house that Saturday, one Big Seven member sat stationed at the sewing machine, stitching together the streamers. The newest initiate hunched over a folding table, hot gluing ribbon to wooden fan handles. I helped two others trim the tails off blue and white pull-bows before attaching seven bows to the top of each fan. Nearby, Buckner measured another club member's streamer to make sure the medallion would fall at the hip. She stood still as he stretched a measuring tape across her torso, peering over his head to scrutinize the fans. "They should have eight bows," she remarked, "not seven." "And it begins," Buckner groaned. At one point, a rotary cutting tool turned up broken, inciting a collective huff about who was to blame. I offered to drive out to the suburbs and buy one, and when I got back, five boxes of pizza covered the kitchen counters. Soon after, other club members and their families arrived with more refreshments: boxes of fried chicken, a cooler full of cold drinks, and frozen cups (a local treat similar to snow cones). Like any family, the Big Seven cooperated, quarreled, fed each other, and laughed. By the time the club emerged the next afternoon, each bow, rhinestone, and feather was in place. A year of weekly meetings plus a few long crafting sessions not only produced an impeccably designed production but also knit their bonds more closely together. The Second Line community is formed through dancing-with, yes, but those four hours of dancing require months of gluing-with, sewing-with, pulling-bows-with (and arguing-with, eating-with, and laughing-with), so that the entire community can enjoy the club's big day.

For its 2014 parade the Big Seven chose the theme "We Wrote the Book of Love." It is typical for a club to choose a theme that guides design decisions or simply sets the tone for the event. The theme might appear on the route sheet or be monogrammed onto apparel and accessories displayed on parade day. Readers might recognize the theme as a reference to the 1958 doo-wop hit by the Monotones, "Who Wrote the Book of Love?" The Big Seven was also making a local reference to the song "Book of Love" by the New Orleans rhythm and blues singer Tucka, who headlined a concert hosted by the Big Seven's 2014 queen two nights before the parade.

Local and global music references aside, it seems that the Big Seven *did* write the book of love in its published response to the 2013 shooting. More precisely, the Big Seven wrote the book of what bell hooks calls "a love ethic," a notion that emboldens love as a political stance.[90] Hooks writes that "loving practice is not aimed at simply giving an individual greater life satisfaction; it is extolled as the primary way we end domination and oppression."[91] According to hooks, all social movements are guided by a love ethic because it refutes individualism in favor of the communal, presupposing that "everyone has the right to be free, to live fully and well."[92] Similarly, Robin D. G. Kelley speaks of social movements as love letters, since true love and freedom fights require one to surrender expectations of reciprocity. "We have a long history of fighting for others—even people we've never seen before," he said. "If we could learn to do that, then we could actually learn to love."[93] Second lining's history and present provide an important example of Black social movements rooted in love. Its origins in antebellum mutual aid societies exemplify a love ethic as an example of communal responses to racist exclusion from municipal services, civic life, and social gatherings. Today's groups, the SAPCs, serve similar functions, but as Tamara Jackson Snowden explains, the aiding portion has changed to meet twenty-first-century threats to Black life. In their myriad functions, SAPCs redress structural violence, which materializes as racialized patterns of healthcare, housing, and criminal justice, limiting the social mobility of the urban poor. The clubs also combat the interpersonal, physical violence propagated by the informal economy of the drug trade, which flourishes within economies weakened by structural violence and further threatens human agency.[94] The Big Seven's assertion that its "young people grow up in this culture, are fed by it, and feel *loved*, supported and connected in ways that build real security" is a love letter in hooks's and Kelley's sense.[95] The group wielded love as a safeguard against the oppressions of structural violence and against the interpersonal violence it generates.

In their participatory and spatially horizontal structure, Second Line choreographies reinforce and reflect SAPCs' love ethics, moving paraders through a physically communal experience. This is apparent in the parades' ability to absorb everyone who wants to join, doing away with categories of performer and audience; in the effect of dancers congregating by the thousands to collectively "own" the streets; and even in the ways dancers share steps between friend and family networks rather than in dance classes. Pleasurable dancing-with one's family, neighbors, and strangers—who form what Salaam calls a spirit family of the streets and Spillers names as horizontal relatedness—creates affective bonds and networks that nurture and sustain community.

Rodrick "Scubble" Davis dancing during Tremé Sidewalk Steppers SAPC's twenty-fifth anniversary parade on February 2, 2019. (Photo by Pableaux Johnson.)

INTERLUDE

Rodrick "Scubble" Davis

March 25, 2017

Rodrick "Scubble" Davis, two-time Footwork Competition champion, is a self-professed "footwork junkie" who has enjoyed success in converting his self-taught skills into an income by offering occasional Second Line dance classes, performing at the New Orleans Jazz and Heritage Festival, leading Second Lines for weddings and other events, and appearing in commercials and music videos. He discusses his enterprise below, but the bulk of these excerpts focus on Davis's family roots in the Second Line culture and his memories of dancing at his mother's funeral procession. His reflection on the dual purposes of mourning and celebrating contained within the jazz funeral, along with his account of the therapeutic release of celebratory second lining, speaks to the strong spiritual functions of the Second Line tradition.

My name is Rodrick Davis, but in the Second Line world, I'm known as Scubble, Footwork King, and all that stuff there. But I'm actually from this area here, which is the Tremé area, and I was born March 14, 1991. Just made twenty-six about a week ago. . . .

Growing up—I'm not the type to complain, but growing up it was kind of rough, losing my father at a young age. Like, three years old, losing him to the violence, but it happens when you live in an environment like this. But I wouldn't change where I come from for nothing. But yeah, so my mama, she had to carry a lot of the load through us growing up and stuff like that. But, you know, she passed while I was still in high school. I was seventeen at the time, so I had to look after my little sister, who was fifteen at the time. I mean, I can't complain, I just had to grow up, I had to become a man early. So, that kind of pushed me away from basketball and everything that I wanted to do, then I had a son at an early age, so I had to focus on that.

When We Laid My Mom to Rest

Through all that, I still was [dancing]. . . . That's where I release anger, that's where I relieve stress, that's where—whatever's going on, it can be all over during dance. When we have a funeral, like when we laid my dad to rest, we had a Second Line afterwards. When we laid my mom to rest, we had a Second Line after. You know, we don't look at it as a sad thing, we look at it like a homegoing celebration. We don't want to remember them being in a casket, so we know this the last time we gonna hang with their body, so we gonna make sure we enjoy and they be right there with us through the whole time. I mean, they say that we absent the body as a present for the lord, but you know, while we still having that body, we feel like we still got some part of someone, that you're [still] here. So we just roll with the casket, and sometimes you see people dancing on top of caskets, sometimes you see us just walking with it during the Second Line and stuff like that, but yeah, we like to make it more of a homegoing celebration.

. . .

My grandmother was into it, like, my grandma [Shelbra Woods] never missed a Second Line. Like how I am today, that's how she was when she was my age. Everybody [knew] who Shelbra was, she was the brightest lady, she had the reddest hair. She was out there. I mean, it was back when the Dirty Dozen [Brass Band] was still rolling, like, she was out there. She wasn't missing a beat.

. . .

My father was Rodney Amos, but everybody called him Scubble. That's where I actually got the name Scubble from. . . . My father, he was into the Second Line; he didn't do no Second Line parading, he actually played a bass drum. I can't play an instrument, me. I'm at a Second Line, but my mother [Sandra Davis], she was actually in a few social and pleasure clubs, like the Dumaine Street Gang. . . . Then she fell back off there as they got older, when she saw me putting so much into it. So she was like, "I'm not worried about me no more, I'm just gonna let him do his thing." She loved watching me second line and stuff like that.

Right before she passed, we had this little talk. She was telling me, "When I go, don't do all that crying for me and stuff like that." I'm like any other guy, I'm like, "Mom, don't anybody want to hear all that stuff right now. I don't want to have that shit." "I'm just letting you know, when I go away, I don't want you to be doing all that crying, just roll for me. Roll for me." So, when it happened, that's the only thing that was in my mind. Like, of course during the funeral, I was down. I was at my mom's funeral, so yes, I was crying, but as the funeral go on, and the band go to come in the funeral home, cause like, we don't wait. We don't wait, that's how we shed everybody's tears, we know there's tears—when that band come, everybody wiping their face, and they know what time of day it is. So all of a sudden, I just [realized], like, "Man, my mama really gone." Then it hit me, when the band come. . . . I thought of her telling me, "When I go, don't leave with all that, just go out." So immediately, I just jumped out of the chair, just started dancing in the funeral home, the whole funeral home jumped up and started joining me, and I gave her another kiss before we went outside. We rolled on outside and we just paraded around the whole neighborhood, like, it was really big. Like, man—when my mama passed, it was more of a concert than a funeral. [*laughs*]

. . .

They played a mixture of everything, "[I'll] Fly Away," they played a little "[Oh, Didn't He] Ramble," they played a little slow tempo, like the dead man walking, stuff like that. We always got to do the dead man walk, that's just to send 'em home. And then we crank it up. We gonna slow it down, bring 'em on out, laugh right through the flowers and stuff like that, get they last little tears out, but after that, it's all straight to business, it's time to work.

My Legs Is Actually How I Eat

I got a family, well, my son just turned seven now. . . . And my daughter who is just like the, oh man, she is like the selfish part of my heart. My daughter break any man down, I don't care who you is. . . . She two now, she be three Christmas Eve.

. . .

My son, he's already into [second lining], my daughter, she's coming along. We actually did this commercial not too long ago, me, Terrylyn [Dorsey], and a few other guys. They [my son and daughter] saw the commercial, and . . . they lost they mind. . . . It was funny, but it made me feel so good, the way my kid was so excited to see me doing something positive on TV, like I ain't in no handcuffs or nothing like that, or being harassed by the police. Like, I'm doing a commercial. I really want to be a role model for my kids, and have my son wanting to be like me, and not like no other basketball player. That's a hell of a feeling.

. . .

My legs is actually how I eat. Like, I didn't see it, I didn't plan for it, but if I can make a living doing what I love doing, that's something I could do forever. . . . I want to say, you got basketball players that make all this kind of money. Then you got some that, you know, you got, you got superstar basketball players. And you got football players that make

this kind of money, then you got superstar football players. And when you look at the superstars, you look at them like, "Ok, they at where they at because that's what they was put here for on this earth." So me, when it come to second lining, I feel like that's what I was put here for. I ain't make it playing basketball, because that wasn't my thing at life. I was sent here to do this. This is why I'm here, because I didn't try to get into nothing, like it's just, everything came to me. I could do this every day. Every day, I could second line every day. If I could second line every day, and make the money that I'm making when I'm working, I wouldn't, then I wouldn't have to worry about it. But until it get like that, I'm gonna have to work. It's getting there, it's getting there, though.
. . .

Second lining has a major role in my life. Like I said, it gets me through whatever sad day I have, whatever bad day I have, anything that's, you know, feel like it's tearing me apart, or it's breaking me down. . . . A thirty-minute set change all that. . . . Whatever happened, happened. Whatever it is, is. Whatever I can't do, I can't do, but this band about to play, I'm about to enjoy this right here. This is how I get through . . . life, how I overcome all obstacles. The Second Line is how I defeat the devil. And it keeps me out the way. I ain't doing nothing wrong, I mean, it's, it's actually taking me places, . . . you know, Jazz Fest and all that extra stuff. I started second lining because I loved to second line. And my love for it and my passion for it I guess started showing, and me showing up here dancing, like, other people just started to see what I felt in my heart. And that's just that. But I'm gonna second line 'til I can't walk.

CHAPTER 3

Spirit

On May 11, 2014, the Original Big Seven Social Aid and Pleasure Club held its eighteenth annual anniversary parade. I stood on the sidewalk outside the home of the club's president, Edward Buckner, where the Big Seven starts its parade each year, waiting for the members to emerge. The light rain began picking up speed. I crouched under an umbrella alongside a modestly growing crowd of the club's family and friends, avid second liners, and photographers. We all knew that a Second Line waits for almost no one and is stalled by very few things, least of all a rain shower. It might be one of the only events in New Orleans to reliably start and finish on time, because of the strict enforcement of the permits imposed by the city, which limit a parade's duration to four hours. Since club members and their families pour vast amounts of money, energy, and time into planning a single parade per year, few clubs are willing to cancel unless faced with dire circumstances. If they do cancel, then they will likely not find an open Sunday on that season's calendar to reschedule, and if they do not parade for more than two years in a row, they risk losing their spot in the annual lineup.[1] So, we waited in the rain.

A tuba began to thump at 1:00 p.m. sharp. One by one, Big Seven members appeared on Buckner's front porch and glided down the four concrete steps, taking advantage of the lack of friction between the wet concrete and the soles of their patent leather shoes to ride the groove in continuous footwork. The Original Big Seven Junior Steppers, a youth division comprised of members between five and fifteen years old, emerged first, accompanied by an equal number of adult chaperones. The main division came out as the closing act, with Buckner appearing last. He stood at the top of the stairs with arms wide open, white handkerchief in one hand. I imagined that he was holding the club, the crowd, and the day in his arms. In a single gesture, it seemed to me, he was receiving praise and recognition, giving thanks for the moment, and welcoming the rain as a kind of baptismal rebirth (see video 3.1 on this book's web page).

As Buckner descended his stairs and moved into the street, police escorts zipped to the front of the procession on motorcycles, blaring sirens that momentarily drowned out the band. I estimated about twenty police officers escorting this parade, twice as many as usual. They blocked traffic as we all filed into the street. I strutted alongside the ropes, watching as club members crawled on the wet ground and stomped in puddles. I kept my little umbrella open, but the rain blew sideways, so it barely mattered. The small but dedicated crowd surrendered, kicking up water, wringing out shirts and putting them back on. Big Seven member Leo Gorman leaned over the rope and declared, "This is one for the memory books." After the parade concluded, Leo's partner Nikki Thanos reflected, "That was cleansing." I felt so, too.

Although any Second Line parade could turn the would-be obstacle of a rainstorm into a purifying ritual, the 2014 Big Seven parade was an especially significant occasion for Mother Nature to aid the procession's healing potential. The previous year, the Big Seven's parade was tragically halted when two gunmen opened fire into the crowd, injuring nineteen, one of whom eventually died as a result.[2] The club staged a re-do parade weeks after the shooting, retracing its intended route and reclaiming the Second Line's power to unite, heal, and generate joy. When it was time for the Big Seven to come out the door again in 2014, the club was undeterred in its commitment to confront structural and interpersonal violence through performance. As it asserted in a public statement issued shortly after the 2013 incident, the club's focus on youth builds real security.[3] Given this context, the rain did not discourage many in the club nor its community to parade in May 2014; they embraced raindrops as baptismal water, healing the community's pain and blessing the parade's spiritual functions. Cultivating spirituality is an important domain of the Second Line's politics of pleasure, tapping into histories of resistance, transcending oppression, and daring to imagine a future unbound by present-day limitations.

Chapter 2 explored one of the main reasons why second liners organize and attend parades: to build and celebrate their communities. This chapter focuses an equally important reason, which is to access spirit. The Second Line's spiritual dimensions blossom from its roots as a funeral procession, connected to burial traditions of West and West Central Africa, the Caribbean, and African American Christian churches. The Second Line's spirituality is not limited to mortuary rites, however.[4] Like African diasporic dance more generally, the Second Line blurs boundaries between solemnity and celebration and between sacred and secular, so that sex, drugs, and spirit often conspire to generate ecstatic experiences achieved through bodily movement. Since Africanist epistemologies honor dance as a spiritual practice at the center of life, any dance can capture the spirit, no matter what the dance is about or where it takes place.[5] Whether following a miles-long processional route in the rain or sweating inside a compact nightclub, footwork carries second liners through the gates of spirit.

• • •

Reaching toward a spiritual plane of existence, writes the choreographer and scholar Kariamu Welsh, is basic to African aesthetics.[6] The first concept for understanding the manifestation of spirit in African cultures, as outlined by Welsh, is "Carry," or the rhythm's ability to take the body on a journey and then return it to its former state. As music carries participants, energy exchanged between dancers, musicians, and onlookers enables one's "Transformation" into a charged state of existence—Welsh's second concept.[7] Transformation may include but is not limited to "Transcendence," Welsh's third concept, a fully altered state of awareness in which the body is given over to the control of a particular energy, spirit, or deity.[8] Other kinds of transcendence occur in the Second Line, too. People transcend their everyday roles to become "performers," earning praise or at least recognition from onlookers, and, increasingly, from online comments that follow videos of fancy footwork posted to social media sites.[9] In transcending social roles by means of aesthetically heightened dance performances, second liners may also transcend their earthbound awareness. The Caribbean dance researcher Yvonne Daniel calls these moments of transcendence "suprahuman performances." She poetically describes the moment when dancers "reach for the extraordinary, [when] the overwhelming sensation of awe attains and their bodies (and those of some would-be 'viewers') experience transcendence—even for a few moments."[10]

The dancer's transformed state may become evident to others when she begins to execute more superbly nuanced or exceptionally exquisite dancing, or simply allows her inner experience to shine through her eyes. Big Seven member Terry "Squillee" Gable says he can tell when fellow second liners are having a spiritual experience by the expressions on their faces. "Their feelings come out in their dance and you can see it. Some of it be pain and some of it be laughter, they be happy.... It's a spiritual [thing]—it will get you. And certain songs, those church hymns, when the band goes to playing 'I'll Fly Away' ... It's deep."[11]

The Second Line's sacred roots are as multifaceted as the populations who have called New Orleans home. The dance historian and Grand Marshal Lenwood Sloan claims that the key to understanding second lining lies in the reverence for the dead that permeates the cultures of the West African and Caribbean peoples that built the city. "I think it is almost impossible to define the Second Line," he stated, "without defining its purpose and structure, which is to release sorrow."[12] The first line of the funeral-with-music procession is the family of the deceased; the third line, he says, is comprised of ghosts: the spirit of the person who has just passed and those of the ancestors who wish to come back to earth. The second line is comprised of the community whose job is to protect the living family from their deceased relatives and remind the ghosts that they are not of this world anymore. Drawing connections to West African and Caribbean traditions such as Egungun processions, charivari, and John Canoe, he sees the self-styled percussion section in a Second Line—who follow the band playing tambourines or bells and tapping on glass bottles—as a holdover from the ritual function of the community members to blow whistles, bang on cans, and shake rattles to break up evil.[13]

The historian Freddi Williams Evans's archival research bears out Sloan's conclusions. She claims that, although the term *Second Line* was not used to refer to dances or processions in antebellum New Orleans, eyewitness accounts recorded during that time period reveal characteristics of the present-day tradition, including the specific rhythms that characterize brass band music, the improvisational music-making techniques employed by musicians and chanting paraders, and the public setting of the performances.[14] Much like contemporary Second Line parades, the antebellum festivities in New Orleans's streets and squares retained their sacred connections. The religious studies scholar Richard Brent Turner goes so far as to say that Black New Orleanians "reinterpreted the sacred music and dances of Vodou in weekly public African festivals every Sunday until the Civil War."[15] Turner refers to the small but strong Vodou community that has been active in New Orleans ever since the early nineteenth century, when the Haitian revolution and Cuba's subsequent exile of Haitian refugees swelled the numbers of enslaved and free descendants of Africans in the city.[16] White observers used *voodoo* as a shorthand to sensationalize and demonize the sonic-kinetic expressions of African and diasporic dancers, but despite fallible accounts in print, very real sacred practices nourished public festivals.[17]

A primary location in which eyewitnesses recorded observations of African and diasporic dances, including so-called voodoo, was in Congo Square. In this grassy expanse just outside the colonial city limits (the present-day French Quarter), enslaved and free people of color gathered to sell handmade goods, speak their mother tongues, play music, and dance. The marketplace came alive on Sundays from the early eighteenth century until at least the 1850s.[18] Under French rule, the Code Noir of Louisiana designated Sunday as a non-workday for the colony, and local custom extended this privilege to the enslaved. The tradition continued under Spanish and American rule.[19]

The activity in Congo Square was heavily policed. As the dance historian Katrina Hazzard-Gordon declares, "Contrary to the interpretations of several historians of slavery, the establishment of Congo Square represents a restricting rather than an encouraging of slave dancing and culture."[20] In other words, city officials delimited the space in order to increase control over bodily expression, not to facilitate it. In fact, the mayor's designation of Congo Square as a sanctioned place for gatherings in 1817 may have been an attempt to contain the movement of enslaved persons during their free day and thus control threats of revolt. The city's perceived need to police the crowds grew as the performances attracted white visitors, who stood outside the area's fenced-off perimeter and consumed the city's already well-known Africanist culture.[21]

Despite surveillance and the exoticizing tourist gaze, it is still possible to imagine that dancers, musicians, and singers at antebellum Congo Square found pleasure. Inside fenced and policed circles, performers managed to subvert their oppression. There was always much more going on than onlookers realized.[22] Through rhythmic drumming and dancing, the people gathered inside Congo Square's fences could (re)create a psycho-spiritual space wherein "blacks were no longer 'slave' or 'subaltern,' but where they in fact called into being prior and new meanings of themselves."[23] Congo Square provided an arena for white consumption and constriction of Black expressive culture; at the same time, musicians, dancers, and artisans used this space to perform collectivities, experience joy, and access spirit in a body otherwise marked for possession and labor.[24]

In addition to festive celebrations and economic exchange, Congo Square also served as a burial ground, a ritual site for marking transitions from Earth to the afterlife.[25] In her history of African American mortuary rituals, Karla Holloway notes that mourning and dancing traditions of West Africa have "perhaps found their strongest corollary in twentieth-century black America in the jazz funerals of New Orleans."[26] She goes on to cite the funerary practices of enslaved Kongolese people in Louisiana as precursors to the drumming, tambourine playing, and dancing that characterize today's jazz funerals.[27] She does not draw simple continuous lines between such practices, but she recognizes that the "cultural continuity of these rituals is difficult to ignore."[28] Although Congo Square was not the only place where dances such as the bamboula, calenda, chica, and "the Congo dance"[29] were performed, it holds the distinction of being the longest-lasting designated location for enslaved and free Africans and people of African descent to drum and dance openly in North America.[30] As such, it served as an incubator for the development of creolized cultures based in Africa, and its impact, not only on New Orleans's dance and musical traditions but also on American culture at large, is significant.[31] Locally, second liners, community historians, and academics commonly claim that the Second Line tradition of dancing on Sunday afternoons can be traced to Sunday gatherings in Congo Square.

Several writers who witnessed such dancing at Congo Square noted that participants gathered in circles or rings.[32] Dancers on the circle's edge participated by singing, clapping, patting their bodies in rhythm, and stepping in place.[33] Perhaps the rings of musicians and singers encircling the dancers acted as a protective layer, cushioning the dancers from the violent control exerted outside the fence. The circular formation of dances at Congo Square connects them to the ring shout, a counterclockwise sacred circle dance practiced widely in North America among African American bondsmen and later among freedmen.[34] In his writing about burial ceremonies in Congo Square, the Black music theorist Samuel Floyd traces contemporary Second Lines back to the ring shout. He argues that, eventually, "the ring straightened itself to become the Second Line of funerals with music, in which the movements of the participants were identical to those of the participants in the ring—even to the point of individual counterclockwise movements by Second Line participants, where the ring was absent because of the necessity of the participants to move to a particular remote destination (the return to town from the burial ground)." Floyd stresses that the "integrity of the shout" remained intact, meaning that the marching, shuffling, grounded steps continued, and individual dancers still performed leaps and turns when inspired.[35] In addition, he suggests that the structure of the jazz funeral parallels the walk-to-shout structure of the ring shout, where "the slow and dignified measure of the 'walk' is followed by a double quick, tripping measure in the 'shout'."[36]

The ring shout predates African descendants' widespread conversation to Christianity in the United States but was later imported into Black Christian worship.[37] The shout and subsequent expressions that developed inside African American Christian churches in the late nineteenth and early twentieth centuries played an important role in shaping second lining's sonic-kinetic core. In his account of Louis Armstrong's New Orleans, Thomas Brothers reveals the tremendous influence of the Sanctified church on the development of jazz. Its worship structure retained the aesthetic values of the blues—aesthetic values honed in the ring shout—such as collective bodily movement, polyrhythm, percussive feet, improvised singing and dancing, and harmonic dissonance, all in service of direct experience with the Holy Spirit.[38] The Second Line brought out into the streets the aesthetic values of Sanctified church services, as well as the embodied worship of Spiritual churches.[39] Michael White suggests that, although Christian churches did not and still do not typically sponsor funeral processions from the altar to the cemetery (benevolent associations have typically organized them), nor host celebratory Second Lines, Protestant worshippers found that the same "emotionalism that caused them to shout, cry, and dance with the 'spirit' could be expressed in parades."[40] In the first half of the twentieth century, the parades' essential spiritual functions eventually spurred some Protestant congregations to hold their own Sunday school parades.[41]

Today's SAPCs still bury their members with music, but Sunday Second Lines (SAPCs' anniversary parades) have taken on their own significance in the community as independent and secular events.[42] Sacred elements, which are not uncommon in secular dance practices in the African diaspora, permeate these weekly celebrations. In fact, neglecting the ways in which threads of spirituality are woven into the fabric of social dances can seriously limit one's understanding of them.[43] Scholars of African diasporic dance dismiss the distinction between sacred and secular as a separation imposed in the West that has long precluded basic comprehension and substantial analysis of music and dance derived from Africa.[44] It should not be surprising, then, that second liners commonly describe transformational and transcendent experiences occurring while engaging in what some might consider the most profane or mundane activities: drinking alcohol, smoking marijuana, eating sandwiches, catching up with friends and family, flirting with a romantic interest, or showing off a new motorcycle. Their experiences are not anomalies but part of a geographical and historical pattern of danced events in the African diaspora in which divisions between Earth and spirit worlds remain fluid.

A concrete example of the ways in which spiritual elements imbue the secular Second Line can be found in the white handkerchief, which links contemporary paraders to spiritual practices past.[45] Waving this piece of cloth in the air is a potent visual signifier for the Second Line, so much so that tourists grab white napkins to "second line" at hotel bars.[46] One point of its origins can be found in Congo Square, where waving the handkerchief was meant to purify the air.[47] I have also been told that it evokes releasing doves at sacred ceremonies. Although many second liners today often discard the symbolic handkerchief in favor of the utilitarian sweat towel, this symbolic object continues to make appearances, as when Edward Buckner came out the door in 2014.

Was Buckner intentionally evoking centuries-old rituals? Maybe, maybe not, but it doesn't much matter. Second liners need not be devotees of West African or Caribbean religions to express both the cultural memory and subconscious knowledge of drumming, singing, and dancing in those religions.[48] Likewise, today's practitioners do not have to be devout Christians to catch the spirit at the parade. As the musicologist Guthrie Ramsey observes, the Second Line's ability to spark cultural memory, catharsis, or transcendence does not rely on practitioners' knowledge of the social, cultural, historical, and material grounding of the experience.[49] In other words, a history lesson is not required to experience the parade's spiritual effects.

• • •

The handkerchief is but one example; contemporary Second Lines are saturated with many other sacred elements, both in structure (the procession itself and funerals embedded within the celebration) and in individuals' danced experiences of Carry, Transformation, and Transcendence.

In her study of Second Lines, the dance scholar Jacqui Malone emphasizes the importance of the procession as a choreographic form. She quotes Rex Nettleford, artistic director of Jamaica's National Dance Theatre Company, who notes the kinesthetic quality and visual impact of "mobilizing masses of people in marches, with their feet keeping a basic rhythm while the upper parts of the body in polyrhythmic counterpoint carve myriad designs in space."[50] As they do in Jamaica, New Orleans's funeral processions spring in part from the Yoruba concept of rituals as transformative journeys.[51] When participants embark on a physical journey through space and time, they may also take a metaphysical one. Yanique Hume emphasizes this point in her analysis of the Jamaican mortuary cycle. In Kingston, street processions lead into public cemeteries, carrying the body and spirit of the recently deceased literally and figuratively to their final resting place. Simultaneously, "the community also marks the journey in their bodies as they dance alongside the corpses."[52] Whether occasioned by death or another significant event such as a religious holiday or festival celebration, a procession moves participants from a deliberately chosen departure point to an intentional site of arrival. The route taken and the stops made connect multiple locales, making meaning in linking them together. This all takes time, which is significant. Processions in the African diaspora socially mark the beginning of sacred time, so they have a spiritual function.⁵³ The durational quality of processions such as Second Lines allows time for participants to transition from one state to another and back again.

Not every second liner dances, but everyone moves forward. Whether walking, pushing a wheelchair, or riding in a float reserved for guests of honor, most second liners pulse in time with the beat (footfalls, shoulder shrugs, head nods), moving in concert with the collective. Many clap, sing, or chant as they go. Each person's movement, synced up with the group and the unifying rhythm, facilitates individuals' potential to reach transformed states in dancing. Like participants in the sacred Caribbean dances researched by Daniel, second liners access suprahuman performances by tapping into the crowd's energy to improvise movements within a choreographed structure.⁵⁴ As a result, second liners can participate in the parade in whatever way pleases them and, simultaneously, unwittingly, facilitate a fellow parader's spiritual experience. While not everyone experiences Transformation and Transcendence, those who do can affect the experiences of those around them. As Daniel explains, "Interested observers become enthralled participants; the dance becomes music as the music becomes dance; and a dance community comes into being."⁵⁵ Second liners' upward soaring simultaneously carries them away from *and* grounds them in the collective that supports their transformative experiences.

Social aid and pleasure clubs harness the processional form to allow for a range of spiritually inflected experiences, from mourning to healing to ecstasy. For example, during the Original Big Seven's 2013 re-do parade, the club returned to the site of the shooting that occurred a few weeks earlier at the intersection of Frenchmen and Villere Streets. As the Big Seven approached, just twenty minutes into the four-hour procession, Buckner turned to his fellow members: "Let's go bless this corner."⁵⁶ Each division paused in the middle of the intersection. They knelt, removed their hats, and prayed.⁵⁷ During this brief memorial the musicians did not switch to a dirge, the slow-tempo music reserved for funeral processions, but continued to play up-tempo dance music. The band was the To Be Continued Brass Band, the same band whose playing had been interrupted by gunshots on the preceding Mother's Day. As the final Big Seven division knelt, the band kept on playing their arrangement of Arrested Development's "Everyday People," one of their crowd pleasers. In response, the second liners who encircled the kneeling club pounded out furious, funky footwork on the sidewalks and stoops. The Big Seven members soon stood and joined in. Just as they rose, raindrops began to fall. One member, Oliver Hunter Jr., extended his palm to catch a few drops. "Holy water," he said, before executing his signature standing split. Next to him, Willie

Hall proved that his feet were as "good as new," despite taking a bullet in the ankle on Mother's Day, by jumping alongside Hunter.[58] While Hall found physical healing through dancing on the very piece of pavement where he was shot, others sought spiritual and psychological healing by dancing there, too.

A year later, the Big Seven's route approached the intersection from the opposite direction, and this time, the holy water came early: Rain poured as the procession left Buckner's house and headed toward Lake Pontchartrain on Elysian Fields Avenue. The reverse pathway taken in 2014 meant that we passed through the intersection of Frenchmen and Villere during the parade's final hour instead of its first. When we arrived, members of the governing division, led by Buckner, paused and arranged themselves in a loose circle facing the center of the intersection, moving from the sacred configuration of the procession to another sacred arrangement: the circle, cypher, or ring. They laid their feathered fans on the ground in the center. A few knelt on one knee.

The Big Seven's intersection circle calls up the crossroads as a potent symbol in African diasporic expressive culture, from Haitian Rara processions to Mississippi Delta blues.[59] In the 1930s, blues guitarist Robert Johnson sang about the ritual action of journeying to the crossroads and falling down on one's knees, channeling the spiritual forces that gather there.[60] Some scholars look to Kongolese cosmology as the origin of legends in the African diaspora about the crossroads.[61] Ritual space in Kongolese ceremonies is marked with a cross, wherein the horizontal line represents the boundary and the vertical line represents both the path leading across the boundary and the power linking above and below, the living and the dead, and Earth and the beyond. The initiate who kneels in the center situates himself "between life and death, and invokes the judgment of God and the dead upon himself."[62] The crossroads accrue a certain potency when music and dance open them up. By kneeling at the intersection of Frenchmen and Villere Streets, the Big Seven members invited all present to endow this crossroad with a memory of life and death, to give gratitude to the gods, to honor those who have passed on, and to rejoice in the fact that we all lived to dance another day. Their somber reflection only lasted a moment before the band switched to the up-tempo hymn "I'll Fly Away" (Gable's favorite) and escorted us out to Elysian Fields Avenue. We exited the space through the pathway that we used to enter it (twice) the previous year, high-stepping and singing, "I'll fly away, oh glory, I'll fly away. When I die, hallelujah by and by, I'll fly away." By carrying paraders through the crossroads in reverse, the Big Seven moved participants from one place to another and, as a result, from one state to another, transforming people and place alike. Bodies, spirits, and pavement were all blessed on that corner.

The procession, the crossroads, the circle, the hymn—so many threads of second lining's sacred roots crystallized in that moment in 2014 at the intersection of Frenchmen and Villere Streets. Though no one had died in the 2013 shooting, the club's memorializing pause reflected a larger practice of embedding brief memorials into celebratory parades. As alluded to above, funerals hold an important key to unlocking second lining's sacred dimensions. Although the Second Lines' influences include a panoply of Africanist festival forms, the benevolent association's burial with music is an important precursor. The early history of the Young Men Olympian Jr. Benevolent Association, established in 1884, provides a case study of how club-sponsored Second Lines became independent from funerals. Current president (at the time of writing) Norman Dixon Jr. explained that at least six years passed between the organization's founding and the establishment of an annual anniversary parade. At first, the association buried its musician members in the traditional manner: a burial with music. "Other members, who wasn't actually musicians, wanted the same thing," he said. "So the organization passed [a resolution] where every member that died would have a funeral procession, with a band." This went on for some time until "years went past, and nobody seemed to die. So they wasn't having a reason to have a parade until some of the members came together and brought it in front of the board that they actually have a annual parade that just celebrate no one dying and to celebrate anniversaries."[63] The association still holds two anniversary parades per year in addition to any necessary funerals.

The funeral's temporal unfolding carries the living through states of mourning and celebration. In the first half of a burial with music, now commonly known as a "jazz funeral," the Second Line of joiners follows the first line, consisting of the family, pallbearers, and casket. Mourners take weighted, measured steps in time with the brass band's slow dirges. However, after the pallbearers place the casket in the tomb—or into the hearse to be driven to a cemetery beyond walking distance—the deceased body is said to be "cut loose," and the living bodies cut loose, too. The band kicks into a series of up-tempo tunes, the signal for second liners to lift themselves out of weighty mourning and dance vigorously to a hall or home to share food and conversation.[64]

The funeral's structure reflects an ethos at the core of the entire Second Line tradition: the embrace of two seemingly incommensurate realities, such as dancing and death, at once. Francine Ott, a New York–based choreographer raised on New Orleans Second Lines, points to the opposing physical concepts of weight and lightness to explain the embrace of opposites in the jazz funeral tradition. The funeral honors the fact that death can be "weighted for some people," she said, even while it creates a space that is also "celebratory, which is the lift, the lightness."[65] Her description encapsulates what Robert Farris Thompson famously dubbed the "aesthetic of the cool," or the "ecstatic unions of sensuous pleasure and moral responsibility" present in many dances of the African diaspora.[66] Such an ecstatic union is on full display in the jazz funeral. Celebrants complexly interweave mourning and celebrating, responsibility and pleasure, weightedness and lightness.

Notably, Ott articulates how the funeral's temporal structure is mapped onto the individual body of the dancer, who moves in ways weighted and lifted, often simultaneously. While stepping to dirges, second liners move low and heavy on the half notes. Second liner Rodrick Davis calls this step the "dead man walk," which he learned from older members of the several SAPCs to which he belongs.[67] The step's name indicates that, historically, Black men have been honored by jazz funerals more than women have, especially since, as explained by Dixon above, the honor used to be reserved for jazz musicians, who have always been overwhelmingly male. Men often but not always do the official honoring as members of a benevolent society or as a grand marshal.[68] Regardless of the gender of the deceased or the mourners, the dead man walk embodies an experience of death as dignified yet mournful.

At least two versions of the dead man walk can be seen at contemporary funerals and in footage from the early 1960s.[69] In one version the mourner steps forward on the one-count and lingers in a wide-legged stance, rocking back slightly on the two-count, until stepping the back foot forward on three. Some exaggerate the rock so much that the weight shift takes on a triplet quality. In another version, mourners step-touch instead of rocking, digging one toe next to the weight-bearing foot on the two-count. Hands remain clasped behind the back or dangling at the sides. The knees bend with each step, which accentuates the body's release toward the ground. At the same time, a regally upright spine and open chest reflect a sober, honorable commemoration. The body sways side to side, zigzagging down the street, a choreography that Lenwood Sloan says can "trick the dead so they can't follow you back" (see video 3.2 on this book's web page).[70]

When the band shifts to a Second Line beat, dancers rearrange their relation to gravity. They dig into the bass drum's rhythms even while leaping and climbing over any obstacle in their way. They reach down to lift off into ecstatic performance. They become engrossed in lightning-fast footwork, locked in with the tuba's complex rhythm and sweating through some buckjumping—second liners' term for energetic, athletic dancing. The New Orleans poet, activist, and music critic Kalamu ya Salaam wrote an evocative account of dancing during the second half of a jazz funeral in 1982:

> Nowhere else in this country were people dancing in the streets after someone had died.... Nowhere else was death so pointedly belittled. One of us dying was only a small matter, an occasion for the rest of us to make music and dance. Nothing could kill us all. Nothing could keep us contained. With this spirit and this music in us, Black people would never die, never die, never.[71]

This passage, published in the local music journal *Wavelengths*, obliquely evokes the mortal threats facing African American New Orleanians in 1982, including rampant poverty and a violently corrupt police force. His meditations might also remind readers that the jazz funeral tradition emerged during the violent backlash that followed Reconstruction and the height of lynching. But if music and dance can resist the annihilation of Black life, it is much more than a response to racism. Pleasure pulls New Orleanians to Second Line. Salaam continues,

> We don't really know or understand how all of this hooks up, it's [sic] meaning. But we feel its importance and smile at it and go with it 'cause it's good. Dancing is good. Music is good. Shaking in the sun is good. Shouting and second lining together is good. So we go with it and are never disappointed by being together like this.[72]

Dancing after someone has died, especially when that death is caused by the direct or indirect violence of antiblack racism, grounds Salaam in his living communities and allows his spirit to link up with ancestral communities. Salaam acknowledges that dancers can feel its importance even if they "don't really know or understand how all of this hooks up." It doesn't matter. In the face of so much bad, dancing together is good.

Danced memorials not only enliven participants' memories of the deceased but also insist on a public recognition of those memories. By moving through multiple locations that mark significant people and events in the club's or neighborhood's history, Second Lines perform a local archive.[73] Writing about jazz funerals in particular, Helen A. Regis observes that individual lives of working-class men, whose names will never enter history books, are "forcefully inscribed into the landscape in massive celebrations that keep alive the memory of freedom, dignity, and community which these men embodied."[74] As memorializing rituals, Second Line funerals create a space for local African American counterhistories

Members of the Black Men of Labor SAPC doing the "dead man walk" during a funeral procession honoring Nelson Mandela on December 21, 2013. (Photo by Judy Cooper.)

to exist in an urban landscape that enshrines the city's Old World and old South past with statues, plaques, and preserved architecture.[75] In addition to full-fledged funerals, ceremonial stops embedded within weekly SAPC anniversary parades perform a similar function. Sunday Second Lines often stop at houses, workplaces, or hangouts significant to members (living or deceased) to mark points on a map of relationships, experiences, and memories that re-spatialize a neighborhood according to one club's history. During each stop, the club might simply pause and reflect, as did the Big Seven when it reached the site of the 2013 shooting. When passing the home or business of a deceased community member or the site of fatal violence, the club might ask the band to switch to a dirge so that it can move through the street with the dead man walk. Members might also pour libations or place a wreath of flowers at significant sites.[76] During funerals, or when a late member's life is honored as part of a weekly Second Line, participants often wear T-shirts emblazoned with commemorative text and a photographic image of the deceased. By honoring individual lives that are rarely celebrated in the city's monuments, second liners dance through their neighborhoods wearing cloth memorials, and their performances function as "moving monuments made of flesh and blood."[77]

Furthermore, some clubs hold funerals for prominent figures such as Michael Jackson and Nelson Mandela and in so doing connect local histories to global events. In 2013, Original Big Nine S&PC's founder Ronald W. Lewis's parade-day streamer (or sash) featured a "Mandela Forever" button, to honor Nelson Mandela's recent death. He affixed the button next to the streamer's embroidered statement, "I'm back," which proclaimed his return to the streets after an illness-induced absence.[78] Lewis's streamer provides an excellent example of the many ways in which second liners weave together the personal and the political, the hyperlocal and the global. Any parade can contain spiritual, social, and political purposes, simultaneously carrying participants into altered states of awareness, enacting a collective local memory, and performing a global present.

• • •

Within the sacred structure, individual second liners access spirit through music and dance in distinct moments of divine communion. For many, the parade *is* a kind of church, where people find fellowship, make new acquaintances, and catch the spirit—and it can occasionally interfere with *actual* church. Catina Braxton Robertson, president and CEO of the Ice Divas S&PC, recalls a time in her life when, she says, she "wouldn't miss a Second Line for nothing in the world. I go to church—some Sundays I wouldn't even go to church because I wanted to be at the Second Line for twelve o'clock!"[79] Although Braxton Robertson is certainly not alone in her church truancy, many second liners seamlessly move from church services to the parade, even if it means catching the parade en route. Several clubs begin their own parade days by attending services together. But for others, like Braxton Robertson, the life-sustaining experiences found at the Second Line pull them out of the pew and into the street. The dancing transports her to another realm of consciousness, to another physical location, and even into another body, much in the way that Kariamu Welsh would characterize Carry and Transformation. "You just become a whole new person when you're out [there] performing and dancing, and you hear the music," Braxton Robertson said. "You step out of your body into another body and you just enjoy yourself."[80] (Listen to the full interview on this book's web page.)

Her description aligns with that of Harry Jackson, another dedicated parader. When I asked him how he feels when he's second lining, he let out a big sigh.

> Man . . . it's a feeling that is unexplainable. It just *take* me. It just take you somewhere. I don't even know, it's just a feeling that you can't help. I mean, it's just crazy. Once you hear the music, . . . the *music* make you move. The music take your body in its own way. You can be standing there, and they can play a song that you like, and then your body just move to the song, and then the next thing you know, you're doing something else. You all over now. You way over there. The music just take you wherever . . . however you feeling. It's like. . . . that's all it is, man! I don't know man, it's just . . . unexplainable. It's explainable but it's not because it's only a feeling that you can have with the music.[81]

Jackson's transformative experiences occur alongside others who approach the parade as a purely social event, and the diversity of experiences presents neither contradiction nor hindrance to the parade's spiritual potential. Jackson explained,

> Some people say, "I'm going to the Second Line, I *know* they going to have those women out there. I know they going to be out there. They're going to be dressed up, looking nice." "I'm going out there to hear the band." "Man, they going to have those bikes out there. I know they going to be out there. Take some pictures for me." You know, they might have somebody that's incarcerated, that want you to go take pictures of the scenery, just to keep a look on how everything looking on the outside. I'm mean there's plenty of reasons why you go to Second Lines.[82]

As Kalamu ya Salaam describes it, in New Orleans, the streets remain a natural venue of spiritual expression, holding the profane and the sacred all at once.[83] Second liners mobilize a balance described by Brenda Dixon Gottschild as a "sensual, visceral connotation of connectedness with the earth" and all the earthly pleasures, "and, concomitantly, a reaching for the spirit."[84] Derrick Tabb, drummer for the Rebirth Brass Band, acknowledged that balance when he commented that, although many second liners compare their parading experiences to church, for him it feels "like an orgasm. It does. That's the best I could tell you. Find something better than an orgasm. A lot of people say it's like church. Church don't make me feel like that!"[85] During my interviews with dancers and musicians, several compared their second lining euphoria to other kinds of ecstasy such as drug use. "Junkie" and "addiction" were frequently referenced to describe an inability to resist the music. Even when dancers talk about extraordinary dance experiences as "getting in the zone," "letting go," and even just "gettin' it," they nod to a transformative charge that they access through rhythmic, energetic footwork.

Wellington Ratcliff Jr., better known as "Skelly" or "Skelly Well," describes his extraordinary dance experiences explicitly in terms of spirit.

Ratcliff is one of several second liners who parade in their wheelchairs. His signature dance style features dexterous maneuvers on wheels and pulsing rhythms in his upper body. When he is really feeling the spirit, he will even lift himself out of the chair and hang onto a pole or crawl on his hands. The Second Line community regularly acknowledges Ratcliff and other second liners on wheels as excellent. A local journalist testified to this fact when responding to Ratcliff's dancing: "He's one of several brothers in New Orleans confined to a wheelchair that rolls at all the Second Lines and even parades with a few clubs. Don't tell me he ain't got footwork!"[86] As this comment indicates, Ratcliff has expanded the cultural significance of the wheelchair from "a signal of the handicapped to a sign of embodiment";[87] in other words, he is widely recognized as a legend.

Before he was paralyzed by a gunshot wound in 1986 at age nineteen, Ratcliff competed as a b-boy with his neighborhood crew, Footloose Breakers, in amateur circuits around New Orleans. They also busked on sidewalks in the French Quarter for cash. Simultaneously, Ratcliff danced as an avid second liner who started parading with the Young Men Olympian Jr. Benevolent Association when he was twelve. After his injury, Ratcliff's rudimentary iron chair could not keep him from the parades. Today, he nimbly pushes his slim chair, compactly designed for wheelchair basketball (his other passion), for miles through the city streets in order to merely *arrive* at a parade. When he is moved, he dances hard, a signal that he is experiencing Carry, Transformation, and/or Transcendence. He describes it this way:

> I tell people, I could be out in a crowd of 1,500 people, but I don't see them people. All I hear and see is that band, and that's where I want to be: behind that band, listening, feeling that beat. . . . It's like that experience, some people say, "I had an out-of-body experience." My body could be right here but my spirit . . . you know what I'm saying? I'm flying above the whole Second Line. That's my spirit right there. And you see the expression on my face and say, "Boy, he going HAM [Hard As a Motherfucker]." People like, "Skelly, man, boy, he be cutting up!" And that's not just to be for show. That's how I be feeling. When I'm feeling the music, you're going to see me dance.[88]

Raticliff's narrative evokes paradoxes surrounding dance's relation to the material body and transcendence (listen to the full interview on this book's web page). The anthropologist and dancer Aimee Meredith Cox discusses the paradoxes, writing, "Exceptional dancers are able to give the impression that they are deeply in their bodies as they transcend [them]—carving stories, meanings, memories, and images in space that surely emanate from the physical being, but somehow appear to make the body irrelevant, despite its virtuosity."[89] Cox names the dual importance of being in the body and transcending it, but as the anthropologist Daniella Santoro points out, disabled dancers can be romanticized in ways that privilege the transcendent over the material. Writing of Second Lines in particular, she observes that stories of physically disabled or ill dancers who seem to overcome their limitations or ailments are sometimes proffered as proof of the parades' spiritual power. She gives the example of a participant tossing aside the cane before engaging in some dexterous footwork. Although such experiences do occur, and can rightly remind us of the sacred current flowing through a secular event, valorizing such moments of "transcending" physical limitations can reify an assumption that dancers are temporarily forgetting their disabilities and obscure the fact that dancers embrace their disabilities as creative assets for dance improvisation.[90] Ratcliff's testimony could be read, perhaps benignly, as a kind of forgetting. But Santoro prefers to privilege individuals' creative agency over the transcendental quality of music and dance, asserting that second liners' "public self-expression is built up *from* one's disability, not in spite of it." Referring to Raticliff, she continues: "Skelly need not mourn the loss of his dance capabilities along with the changes in his mobility; he is able to adapt, reincorporate, and rewrite new dance moves."[91] If moments of spiritual ecstasy manifest via the dancer's heightened self-expression (as Ratcliff put it, "When I'm feeling the music, you're going to see me dance"), then perspectives such as these are useful for understanding the connections between dance, embodiment, and transcendence (see video 3.3 on this book's web page).

The power of danced transcendence rests in the importance of not only situating oneself *within* tactile experience, but also creating worlds *beyond* it.[92] According to queer studies and performance studies scholar José Muñoz, the ability to conjure worlds beyond the immanent is what endows danced transcendence with political potential. When one enters what he calls "ecstatic time," an affective excess overflows the here and now and allows one to glimpse something beyond the everyday.[93] Ecstatic time, he says, is crucial for those living a life marginalized by white supremacy, those whose futurity is often limited by expectations of a too-early death, a death foretold by situational or environmental hazards.[94] Moments of ecstasy like those that Ratcliff experiences while second lining dare to imagine a past, present, and future freed from physical, environmental, and social limitations. As Santoro concludes, dance intervenes where discourses of disability, Blackness, and masculinity "have failed to adequately and equitably represent the lived experiences of disability" and its intersectionality with race, gender, and the tragic consequences of violence.[95]

Wellington "Skelly" Ratcliff Jr. coming out the door for the Uptown Swingers SAPC's Second Line parade on June 26, 2016. (Photo by Pableaux Johnson.)

Ecstatic time names the politics of divine pleasure experienced by dancers like Ratcliff, whose flights of spirit reimagine the social roles—and dance moves—scripted for him.

• • •

Wherever footwork travels, it brings its sacred roots along, not just into the streets but into barrooms and nightclubs as well. These establishments have long been important to the Second Line community because, in between Sundays (and when parades were less frequent than they are today), indoor brass band shows allow the community to gather and dance.

Some clubs also hold their regular meetings at their neighborhood bars, often honoring the business by planning a stop at the bar during their parade. In the early twenty-first century the Wednesday night set played by the To Be Continued brass band (TBC) at Celebration Hall on St. Bernard Avenue became a can't-miss event for dedicated second liners. The Wednesday night show functioned as a pep rally for whichever club was going to come out the door the following Sunday. To promote their upcoming parade, club members usually wore matching shirts, distributed route sheets, and sometimes decorated a table reserved for members and supporters. A television played footage from that club's previous parade. No matter which club was honored on a given Wednesday, a cadre of regulars packed the small dance floor. If second liners talk about the parade as church, then nightclubs deserve a similar accolade. For example, Don Robertson, a retired member of the Young Men Olympian Jr. Benevolent Association, remembers dancing to the Pinstripe Brass Band in an uptown nightclub decades ago. That was "where the holy ghost first hit me," he said, "in the club" (listen to the full interview on this book's web page).[96] Nightclubs such as Celebration Hall house similar spiritual experiences.

I walked into Celebration Hall at about 11:45 p.m. one steamy night in May 2014, just a week and a half after the Big Seven's parade in the rain. By the time I arrived, TBC was already in the middle of the first set. It was hot. Sweaty footwork artists maneuvered into every available space, drilling their feet into the floor, climbing a pole, spinning, crawling under each other's legs, squatting down, and jumping wide. One dancer playfully gyrated against someone sitting in a chair on the perimeter, who was receptive to the gesture. I saw two women in their early-to-mid-fifties tearing up the dance floor while encouraging and challenging younger dancers. They owned the space. At one point, they grabbed a small portion of the crowd and formed a circle. Holding hands, they walked around as one person at a time entered the center to improvise. I had just been reading Samuel Floyd's "Ring Shout!" that afternoon, so I smiled to see a praise house ring shout and Congo Square circle dance transported onto the linoleum floor of Celebration Hall. The entire scene affirmed what the performance studies scholar E. Patrick Johnson calls "feeling the spirit in the dark." In his discussion of Black church performance conventions in the Black gay male club, Johnson testifies to the experience of uniting flesh and spirit in the alternative "sanctuary" of the nightclub. "The space secularizes the whole notion of the 'shout' or the 'holy dance,'" he writes, and "in turn, a sexualized body is offered in praise of God. The result is that the dancer affirms both the sexual and the spiritual."[97] At Celebration Hall that night, a range of secularized shouts emerged on the dance floor, from the gyrating duo to the communal circle to individual expressions of rhythmic-driven ecstasy.

I recognized the women who led the circle dance as regulars at Second Line parades. During the band's first set break, I talked with them outside. I wished one a happy birthday, the occasion proclaimed by a stack of dollar bills pinned to her shirt, as is the New Orleans birthday tradition. We enjoyed the feeble breeze wicking away pearls of sweat as the self-described best friends reminisced about dancing to the Rebirth Brass Band until four o'clock in the morning at the Glass House, a tiny barroom located uptown in the Third Ward or Central City neighborhood. It was there that the Dirty Dozen Brass Band and later the Rebirth Brass Band played a weekly set from the late 1970s until the early 1990s. During its heyday, the Glass House was one of the most important locations in the city for those who counted themselves as members of the Second Line culture.

The first scene in local author Tom Dent's unpublished 1983 screenplay "Second Line" takes place at the Glass House. It frames the dancers' explosive energy in spiritual terms:

> All around, young men (and an occasional young woman) are whirling, dropping into sudden knee-bends, spinning other dancers at random, falling flat on their faces, flipping over and over in time to the music, imitating animals, *letting their bodies respond to whatever old and powerful spirit moves them.* . . . He [Leroy, the protagonist] grabs the backs of empty chairs, kicks up his feet behind him, and floats unsupported (except by the music) in mid-air—for as long as he wants to! He picks up another dancer (who keeps right on dancing), carries him across the floor, and puts him down. He brings one of his feet around, seeming to knock his knees out from under himself, and sinks to his knees as lightly as a feather![98]

Dent captures the thrill of full-body improvisation with other dancers, the physical environment, and the music at the Glass House. Dent's description, though fictionalized, documents how spirit moved people at the Glass House and suggests why it, and nightclubs that came before and after it, served as a joyful refuge from the economic, political, and social struggles that its Black patrons faced every other day of the week.

Standing outside Celebration Hall, the friends who had been two of those "occasional" young women at the Glass House wandered down memory lane, which took them across town and back a few decades. As they reminisced, they regarded the crowd that had spilled out of Celebration Hall and onto St. Bernard Avenue. People drank bottles of beer, rolled joints, and purchased food from a vendor who had set up shop outside the nightclub. *All these younger people,* they said, *they don't know the history. They might just think we're some old ladies, but they have no idea who we are. No idea.* No doubt that was true, at least in part, and yet, these "old ladies" were passing on their history—and, whether or not they intended it, much older histories, too—via their impromptu ring shout.

In New Orleans, social dancing and Christian worship (and, for a small community, Vodou ceremony) provide interconnected vehicles for transcendence and communal connection. Dirty Dozen saxophonist Roger Lewis sums up the close relationship between spiritual devotion and secular pleasure that animates the city's social and cultural life. "New Orleans is like real sexual along with religious. Because you got a barroom on the block and a church on the corner. That's in a lot of neighborhoods."[99] Close proximity between bar and church makes for quick transit between the two when necessary. Lewis recalled a club called Off Limits that did not open until three o'clock in the morning. "You come out of there, it be time to go to church. You know, New Orleans is like that."[100] And according to E. Patrick Johnson, in many southern Black communities, the musicians playing at the club would be the same ones providing music for the church service a few hours later.[101]

Sometimes the bar and the church resided in the same location. The Dirty Dozen's founder and bass drummer, Benny Jones Sr., grew up on the same block as Ruth's Cozy Corner in the Sixth Ward, or Tremé.[102] On most nights of the week Ruth's served as a barroom, but on Sunday mornings, Ruth Queen, known to her community as Mama Ruth, hung a sheet over the liquor and held a church service in the back. Once worship concluded, Mama Ruth removed the sheet so that congregants, including Jones's mother, could drink beer in the front.[103] Lewis's and Jones's memories affirm how bodily pleasures intertwine with, and even facilitate, religious devotion in African American social and cultural life. Notably, both mention the built environment—the proximity of barrooms to churches—to illustrate the point. The Glass House and Celebration Hall are no exceptions. The Glass House's neighbors included a large Catholic church that stood just around the corner, and several of the storefronts on the surrounding blocks served as Baptist churches over the decades.[104] As I stood outside Celebration Hall listening to remembrances of the Glass House, I could see Sacred Heart Catholic Church across the street.

Well, more precisely, I could see the building that once *was* Sacred Heart. By 2014 it had been converted into an apartment building.[105] Redevelopment is but one force that portends the disappearance of Black cultural sites. Today, Ruth's Cozy Corner and the Glass House no longer stand. At the time of writing, Celebration Hall is still in operation, but a fire and

COVID-19 physical distancing measures presented significant challenges, and other nightclubs have usurped its status as the favorite locale for footwork fanatics. As for the Glass House, an empty lot is all that remains in the spot where it once stood. Dancers who experienced it as a site of divine communion now lament younger generations' lack of knowledge about the place, its importance, and older generations' role in shaping that history. The disappearance of worship sites, whether churches or nightclubs, makes it even more difficult for Black cultural histories to endure. In the face of physical erasure (and there are many more examples), sonic and embodied connections to history such as second lining take on heightened significance.

After the Glass House closed its doors in 1991, Benny Jones felt its absence. The feeling was most poignant during uptown parades. By the late 1980s many SAPCs in the area had designated the Glass House as a parade stop, but after it closed, clubs rerouted their parades to stop elsewhere.[106] When its manager, Thelma "Tee" Jones, died several years after her club's closing, her life was honored with a large funeral led by the Dirty Dozen.[107] She was, at the time, one of the relatively few women to be recognized in this way for her contribution to Second Line culture. The honorific was well earned. In some ways Jones functioned like the holy women who have long guided religious communities in New Orleans, creating an alternative sanctuary for Black residents to touch psychic and spiritual freedom through ecstatic, transformational, suprahuman dancing.[108]

• • •

The spiritual functions of the Second Line are many. Footwork carries practitioners through myriad transformations, from individuals to a collective, from wounded to healed, from everyday worker to star performer, from earthbound to airborne. Although the New Orleans Police Department insists on a four-hour limit to the ritual, parade time remains flexible, bent to the service of spirit. The procession's duration presses paraders' exhausted bodies into states of surrender and allows time for transitions to altered states and back again. This is perhaps most apparent in the funeral's walk-to-shout structure but also holds during purely celebratory parades. The procession itself brackets parading activity within sacred time, no less potent because SAPCs' anniversary parades happen on Sundays, the traditional day of Christian rest and worship.[109] The parades happen *nearly every* Sunday and have crisscrossed virtually unchanged routes for generations. The same club traverses the same streets annually, even if it's repeating the route with a difference, like the Big Seven did when approaching the crossroads in reverse. As is the case in Black music and dance more broadly, repetition serves to heighten potency.[110] The cyclical nature of the parading calendar also aids Second Lines in marking spiritual time. When footwork carries second liners indoors, miles of syncopated marching accrue on compact patches of linoleum or tile. As dancers feel the spirit in the dark, they transport themselves and others around them into flashes of history.[111]

Spirit is central to the Second Line's pleasures, be it the exhilaration of transcendence, a healing release, or the groundedness of tapping into sacred histories. In the street or in the club, the politics of spiritual pleasure reach into past, present, and future. Black New Orleanians summon histories of their ancestors dancing in the face of annihilation from antebellum Congo Square to the earliest jazz funerals to more recent history made at the Glass House. Second liners' footwork enacts this archive of local histories, at once personal and political, local and global, sacred and secular. Simultaneously, second liners' journeys into ecstatic time dare to imagine a future unbound by the constraints of racism, poverty, and other interlocking forms of structural violence. The political potency of the Second Line's spiritual pleasure lies in its ability to carry dancers into untold histories and unwritten futures, to live, in the present, a more just, even divine, existence.

Gerald Platenburg, wearing a black leather suit in homage to the Black Panther Party, parading with Nine Times SAPC on November 20, 2016. (Photo by Pableaux Johnson.)

INTERLUDE

Gerald Platenburg

March 28, 2017

Gerald Platenburg is unmistakably recognizable at Second Line parades—just look for the man standing on his head in the middle of the street. Platenburg's history as a b-boy (or breakdancer, as Platenburg calls it) inflects his Second Line style. In the 1990s he and his breakdancing group, Grandmaster Showcase, won a talent show sponsored by a local radio station, which sent them on an all-expenses-paid trip to perform at the Apollo Theater in New York. His b-boy–inspired Second Line footwork has earned him trophies and cash prizes at footwork competitions in New Orleans and landed him a job as the grand marshal for the Kinfolk Brass Band. In addition to attending nearly every Sunday Second Line, Platenburg works ten to fifteen gigs per weekend with the band. During the week, he splits his days between the kitchens of two French Quarter establishments, a luxury hotel and a restaurant popular with tourists. We conducted our interview in the French Quarter offices of the Jazz and Heritage Foundation Archive since its location was convenient for him. He arrived still wearing his sauce-splattered uniform.

Platenburg grew up in the Desire public housing development in the Ninth Ward, home to both the New Orleans chapter of the Black Panther Party and the Nine Times Social Aid and Pleasure Club. Platenburg joined the Nine Times shortly after its inception.[1] In this excerpt he recounts the club's decision to don Black Panther–inspired apparel for its 2016 parade to protest the police killings of Black people. His reflections on the Nine Times's commitment to social aid links the sustaining work of SAPCs and Black freedom movements such as the Black Panthers.[2]

My name is Gerald Platenburg, born in New Orleans, Louisiana. I was born October the fourth, 1966.

The way I picked Second Line dancing up was in the Desire Projects, and, I want to say probably 1982. They had this group, back then they was called Nine Times Steppers, and I never was part of the club, but after watching it so long, I kinda fell in love with it. I always could dance, but never could second line.

RACHEL CARRICO: [*laughs*] What kind of dance, though?

GERALD PLATENBURG: Well, hip hop, breakdance. And when I seen the Second Line, it's kind of got my attention, so I said, "I'ma try that," and I been doing it ever since now for, I want to say, fifteen years now.

I mean, if you look at it, second lining, breakdancing, it almost the same thing, it's just not doing a lot of flipping. That's the difference between it. Second lining is more on your feet, breakdancing is whatever goes, whatever comes to your mind. On your head, on your back, but second lining's more on-your-feet dancing. . . . And breakdancing is kind of up-tempo. Second lining's a little upbeat, but breakdancing's an upper tempo music.

RC: Mm-hmm. I see you sometimes still, your history as a breakdancer is still evident in the—

GP: Yeah, yeah, yeah. It do, cause sometimes I get on my head, or I'll do a little split right quick, so you about right.

RC: Yeah, you'll do like a freeze on your head. [*laughs*]

GP: Yeah, that's my signature move, that's my "get out my way" move there.

Nine Times, Social Aid, and Pleasure

I joined Nine Times, it was founded in '92, I joined it I want to say in '95, after the founder got killed, . . . Louis Pierre. And I always promised him I was gonna join, I was gonna join, and sorry I didn't join before he got killed, but after he got killed, that was my first year in it. So it was like three years after the club started, I joined. . . . When I joined, it was like five, six members. Now it's grown to twenty-five.

RC: And was there a ladies' division back then?

GP: No, it was just the guys first; the ladies came maybe three years afterwards. . . . Yeah, '98 the ladies joined, and they been there ever since now.

RC: And, besides your annual parade, which is a big one, it's one people come to every year—besides the parade, what else do you all do as a club throughout the year?

GP: Well, we believe in kids and family first, we believe in that, so the first thing we have is a Mardi Gras where, you know, we do our big cookout on Dumaine and Claiborne. We been doing that for about

fifteen years now, and it's been a big draw. And we feed everybody, it don't matter where you from, who you is, come over, get something to eat, we feed everybody.... And our second event, which is coming up, for the kids, is an Easter egg hunt. We give a big Easter egg hunt on Sampson Park. We give baskets, we give candy, and we also interact with the kids—see where they're at in school, we discuss a lot of stuff with 'em. Counseling, in other words. And let 'em know, if you all want to be part of this, this what you got to do, and we just try to be positive, give 'em positive, lead 'em in a positive direction. And the next thing we do for kids is back to school. We have a back-to-school giveaway, we give 'em away book sacks, pencils, you know, we just do a lot, we just try to keep the community, not just a parade like some clubs, we try to bring the community together.
. . .

I feel the pleasure is what you pass on to people. What people get out of it. It's not selfish, because I mean, it would be selfish to have pleasure in yourself, so I think the pleasure is how people, how you perceive the people, how you take on the community. And I think that's the pleasure part, being appreciative and giving back to the community, that's our pleasure, the pleasure we get out of seeing kids happy.

Spiritual Movement

I couldn't describe it [dancing], but I got to tell you, it's a good feeling. Because I mean, I don't drink, I don't smoke, so that's a way of relieving a lot of anger within me, and that's how I express myself, in dancing. But it's a, I'ma tell you, once you get to love it, once you get to like it, you learn to love it.... I think it's very spiritual. You know, because I am, everybody, it's accepting your fear. And like I said, you can't teach second line dancing; either you got it, or you don't. 'Cause if you could teach it, I think I'd be the best teacher in the city, but I just can't see no kind of way to teach it. But I wish I could, but I think it is a spiritual movement, you know? . . .

RC: Do people come to you and ask [for lessons]?

GP: Always! . . . I'll try to show 'em, because I, like I told you, I'm not selfish, so I don't mind passing it on, because it was passed to me, but it wasn't taught to me. It was passed to me by watching it and seeing it. . . . I never really tried [teaching], so maybe I need to try it, and maybe I can teach, but I don't really think so.

2016 Parade: Black Panther Theme

Yearly, we [the Nine Times SAPC] sit at the table and we ask each member to have an idea [for that year's parade theme], because we believe everybody in the club have an opinion, and everybody have a voice. So we sit down, and, you know, we have like five choices to make. And with the murder rate and the senseless killing going on with the police, and the community killing the police and the police killing the community, senseless, we thought it would be a good idea to do the Black Panther theme, because I mean, they wasn't for violence, neither, they was just for what was right. And when the police did something wrong, the Black Panthers came together and stood up for it. So, we thought that would be a good idea to touch the community, to touch New Orleans, the city that we love that we are from. And we didn't say, Black lives matter, we said all lives. That mean white, Black or whatever race you was, it didn't matter, if you was mistreated, we was there for you, and so we thought that would be a good theme, and we thought that would get great attention in the city. On the crime. . . . That's where that theme came from, and that's why we used that.

RC: On each of your streamers you had the name of someone that had been, an unarmed Black person that had been killed by police.

GP: Yeah, yeah, we did it because we just wanted to let not only New Orleans, we wanted to let the world know that we in New Orleans, we do care about people, no matter who you from or where you're at. We do care about people, and we gave each member the option to pick who they choose to wear on their streamer, whether it's [someone from] New Orleans, wherever they from. And it was good to see a lot of people pick people from out of state, you know? But a lot of us had people locally. Because I mean, we do have a lot of, you know, we have trouble ourselves in the city we have to get under wraps.

CHAPTER 4

Freedom

Fights for Black freedom beat at the heart of second lining's history. Just ask Jerome Smith, founder of the youth educational program Tambourine and Fan Club. Created in the early 1970s, Tambourine and Fan teaches young people about New Orleans's Black cultural traditions such as brass band music, Mardi Gras Indian masking, and second lining. The pedagogy emphasizes the ways in which local cultural expressions are a part of worldwide struggles for Black liberation.[1]

In designing the Tambourine and Fan Club's parades, Smith has sought to leverage the Second Line's joyful power as a mechanism for protest. In Tambourine and Fan's early years, children carried fans emblazoned with messages about Nelson Mandela and civil rights workers killed by the Ku Klux Klan. Although these kinds of explicit political messages are uncommon in second lining's history, they are unsurprising coming from Jerome Smith. In the early 1960s, Smith co-founded the New Orleans chapter of the Congress of Racial Equality (CORE), a national civil rights organization responsible for tremendous social change in the United States. He saw his work with Tambourine and Fan as an extension of his activism, positing local parading traditions alongside sit-ins and Freedom Schools as tools for self-emancipation. "I just see myself as a community organizer, you know," he told the historian Kim Lacy Rogers in 1988. "In CORE, they called us a fieldworker. I'm a fieldworker. Then and now, that's how I see myself. No more, no less."[2] Smith continues his efforts as a fieldworker to this day, running youth programs at the Tremé Community Center.

Despite Smith's seamless movement between community organizing and cultural participation, he encountered limited reception to social justice issues when he integrated them into the Second Line parades. More than forty years after founding Tambourine and Fan, Smith lamented, "In the middle of everything we were doing at the parades, nobody in the audience seemed to pick that up. They'd compliment the kids' dancing. Come talking about their footwork. But they don't ever come talking about their fan that had some statement on it. That discouraged me, and made me want to do something else. I'm still thinking about it."[3]

Smith is not alone in his ambivalence about the efficacy of explicitly weaving activism into Second Line practice. Joe Stern, a Jewish member of the Second Line community who got involved through his movement work in the 1980s, expressed similar sentiments. Stern, who served as president of the Prince of Wales Social Aid and Pleasure Club from 2006 until his death in 2023 (and is featured in the final interlude of this book), sometimes felt frustrated that politics and pleasure *don't* overlap as much as he would have liked. "I've brought issues up to people, and I hand out fliers, and encourage people to come to demonstrations," he said, but he did not see nearly as many people from the Second Line community turn out for political marches as for pleasurable ones.[4] I spoke with one second liner who recounted a parade at which someone was handing out fliers for a political candidate or an upcoming demonstration (it might have been Stern!). She watched as people eagerly snatched the papers—and immediately repurposed them as fans without so much as reading a word.[5] It seemed to Stern that

> New Orleans is a hard place to get people motivated politically. Partially because they can always go out, and the frustration and the rage and all that that builds up over the week from being exploited, being misused, and having to endure all the bullshit, you can go out at the Second Line and, you know, drink a few beers and smoke a joint and dance for four hours, and see all these people that you see every Sunday.[6]

In one way, the Second Line's pleasure can discourage political action by providing a release valve. At the same time, and to quote author Ishmael Reed, "There's so much more to black pleasure than merely fun."[7] By drinking, eating, dancing, and communing on public streets, Black New Orleanians publicly insist on their right to ownership, mobility, collective memory, and joy. In other words, there is political force in that release valve.

And yet Stern's point stands. Recognizing the politics of pleasure does not nullify the need for direct action to effect change. Even if second lining can, as Randy Martin notes, "enlarge the sense of what is possible" in social life, a parade cannot, by itself, automatically cause changes in policy, economies, and oppressive social norms.[8] For that to happen, people must put their bodies on the line in other ways. But second lining has a role in that kind of politics, too. If, today, activism and second lining have largely drifted apart, the tradition's roots conjoin community organizing and partying.[9] As Stern summarized, "It's just in the nature of working-class people to organize and form their own organizations to meet some of their own needs. I mean, that was the original reason that social aid and pleasure clubs got together: to help each other out, as well as, just in New Orleans, they also had a parade."[10] Stern imagined that, if more people knew about Second Line parades' roots in organizing, they may be more eager to occasionally march for causes in addition to marching for enjoyment—two complementary paths to freedom.

This chapter answers calls like Stern's to know more about those roots.[11] For centuries, Black voluntary associations in New Orleans have leveraged their organizing power to marshal human and material resources in service of social justice movements. In one example considered below, activists *refused* to dance in the streets so that they could redirect money, time, and press coverage to movement organizations instead. Still today, Second Line parades share ground, literally and figuratively, with direct action protests in negotiating state power and insisting on the freedom of Black people to move. The intertwined histories of New Orleanians' cultural parades and activist demonstrations highlight the organizing power inherent in Black cultural traditions and, conversely, the ways in which New Orleanian activists' strategies have long been influenced by local cultural traditions. This chapter looks to the early 1960s, not to fetishize the period as the only moment in the city's history when Black-led activism mattered, but in order to understand how some of the better-known moments in New Orleans's social movements (Freedom Rides, school integration) emerged from a larger ecosystem wherein social movement organizing intertwined in meaningful ways with danced movement and cultures.

• • •

Before looking at the 1960s, it is important to understand the histories that activists and such culture bearers as Jerome Smith inherited. It is difficult if not impossible to locate second lining's precise origins, but a valuable place to begin the story is with the Emancipation Jubilee on June 11, 1864. The Civil War would not end for another ten months, but Louisiana had just re-entered the Union with a revised state constitution that outlawed slavery. Black benevolent associations and other community organizations assembled a committee to plan a parade commemorating the occasion.[12] Festivities began and ended at Congo Square, the open field adjacent to the French Quarter where Africans and people of African descent had created a festive marketplace on Sundays for many years. Congo Square also hosted political gatherings, union meetings, and campaign rallies. At the time the jubilee took place the area was designated as the Place d'Armes, signifying it as a location for Sunday military drills.[13] During the Emancipation Jubilee, two connotations of the term *march*, dancing and protesting, converged with its militaristic usage, revealing the influence of military parades on the Second Line tradition.[14]

Thousands assembled in Congo Square in the morning to hear speeches in both English and French, enjoy the singing of schoolchildren, and collectively celebrate the end of slavery in Louisiana. Afro-Creole New Orleanians, many of whom had long enjoyed free status, joined the newly freed. They made their way to the assembly in groups, first gathering at schools, churches, and society halls and then walking to Congo Square with banners and flags in hand, accompanied by mobile bands. According to the commemorative program, attendees dressed in "their holiday attire," festooned with national flags.[15] Shortly after noon, an orderly and lengthy procession filed onto Rampart Street. Each of four parading divisions was led by a grand marshal and his deputies, followed by military brass bands, federal troops, local regiments of free Black Union soldiers, city and state politicians, clergymen, public school students, and benevolent societies such as the Société d'Economie et d'Assistance Mutuelle, and United Brothers. Members of the Free State Committee, which had drafted the abolitionist constitution (yet stopped short of granting suffrage to Black male Louisianans), marched in the procession as well.[16] Much as SAPCs do today, the arrangements committee printed the route in local newspapers so that New Orleanians could watch it pass or even join; the fourth and final division was named "the Public in general."[17] The historian Eric Seiferth writes that, as local Black organizations joined with white abolitionist politicians and the United States military to march up and down city streets, they reclaimed "the South's largest and richest metropolis, a place which was thrown into secession by its ruling white elite only a few years prior, and where only weeks before, many Black Americans were legally held in slavery."[18] The parade evidences the long history of political organizing among New Orleans's Black parading communities.

A little more than a decade after the Emancipation Jubilee, Union forces left New Orleans and the period of Reconstruction came to an end. Across the South, white supremacist backlash against the Reconstruction-era gains for equality ushered in a new period of terror for African Americans. This was also the historical moment in which Second Line parades, as we know them today, began to take shape. As the number of lynchings rose, Black brass band processions unapologetically celebrated Black life. As legalized segregation ossified the urban landscape into "white" and "colored" areas, parades defiantly occupied public spaces.[19] White supremacists began erecting monuments to whiteness to further territorialize the city. In 1884 a group of powerful white New Orleanians unveiled a bronze statue of the confederate general Robert E. Lee, standing atop a sixty-foot marble column, in a prominent public square, Tivoli Circle. It came to be known as Lee Circle, proclaiming its status as one of the first southern monuments to the confederacy and an architectural centerpiece of the Cult of the Lost Cause.[20] As more such monuments appeared throughout the city, Black dance processions continued to serve as embodied memorials to Black New Orleanians' lives and struggles. During jazz funerals and celebratory parades, second liners marched (and continue to march) in the literal shadows of monuments glorifying the forces behind their premature deaths. With defiantly pleasurable footwork, turn-of-the-century second liners remapped the urban landscape according to Black geographies and histories.

As Jim Crow laws took hold of public space and public life, one of the city's most famous second line organizations emerged: the Zulu Social Aid and Pleasure Club. The club locates its own origins in 1909, when Black men belonging to an existing benevolent society attended a musical comedy at the Pythian Theater. The Smart Set, a traveling vaudeville group of Black performers, performed a skit titled "There Never Was and Never Will Be a King Like Me," which chronicled events of the Zulu tribe.[21] Inspired by the skit, the society members renamed their group the Zulus and planned a parade for the next Mardi Gras accordingly. William Story came out as their king, wearing a crown fashioned from a lard can and carrying a banana stalk scepter.[22] Zulu's debut performance has frequently been interpreted by scholars and fans alike as a parody of the white Carnival and specifically of King Rex, who symbolically rules over the city during Mardi Gras Day.[23] King Rex's reign is inaugurated each Mardi Gras Day when he docks his ship on the Mississippi River, welcomed by city police. William Story's King Zulu lampooned this ritual by arriving on the New Basin Canal on a tugboat, greeted by his waiting "warriors," the other Black men in the group, who wore grass skirts and blackface makeup. They escorted King Zulu through the city, tossing coconuts to bystanders.[24] The historian Jeroen Dewulf situates the Zulu's performance beyond parody, connecting it to ancient court traditions in the Kingdom of Kongo and its diaspora in the Americas. Because of the intense segregation and racist violence that characterized the early twentieth-century New Orleans Carnival, he argues, revivals of such Kongolese king parades were only possible with the carnivalesque smokescreen of self-parody.[25] Zulu's burlesque continues today, blackface and all, harnessing pleasure—in this case, humorous satire—to forward a vision of freedom.

Zulu has never ceased functioning as a benevolent society, hosting Sunday Second Lines and burying its members with music, in addition to its annual Mardi Gras parade. But most members are drawn to its prestige as a Carnival organization and exclusive private club.[26] Its Carnival parade holds a prime place on the festival calendar: mid-morning on Mardi Gras Day. Even today, catching a coconut remains a coveted rite for many Mardi Gras participants. The Zulu spectacle is a send-up rife with critique, but it can also reproduce the very stereotypes it mocks. The latter perspective characterized the reigning opinion of influential Black New Orleanians in the 1960s, when Zulu's membership reached an all-time low.[27] In 1961 the African American periodical *Louisiana Weekly* took no pleasure in the Zulu club's performance, blasting its members as "smiling and shuffling Uncle Toms." The accusation evoked the legacy of blackface minstrelsy as a performance tradition that can, for some viewers, cement racialized systems of oppression even as, for other viewers and participants, it can resist oppression.[28]

The damning article appeared when debates about Zulu commanded center stage in local politics. As a result, on Mardi Gras Day in 1961 the Zulu parade was, according to the *Louisiana Weekly*, the "shortest, most protected [by police] and less viewed in the Club's history."[29] It began ominously. A heavy fog settled over the banks of the Mississippi River as King Zulu made his way to shore from his royal barge (by 1961, the New Basin Canal had been filled, so King Zulu made the same approach as King Rex). The newspaper reported that a small watercraft carrying three white photographers had capsized and, at press time, only one had been recovered. But the parade continued on. That year's purported King Zulu, Henry Johnson (the person on the float kept his identity anonymous), rode guarded by police dogs, "not merrily on his way but hurriedly and worriedly." Queen Zulu's float rolled without a queen at all, her vacant throne flanked by four attendants who "nervously [tossed] their beads and other trinkets to the few spectators that happened along the way." The floats found Claiborne Avenue, the nerve center of Black Carnival, "practically deserted." The usual Second Line which follows the parade, led that year by the Eureka Brass Band, "was composed of more whites than Negroes."[30] Overall, the newspaper painted a distressing picture of a moribund parade, the absence of Black revelers brought into high relief by the presence of oblivious white paraders. Even the mainstream *Times-Picayune* noted the unusually calm and quiet Zulu parade.[31]

Zulu's lack of Black support in 1961 was not entirely owed to growing unease with the club's primitivist performance tropes. African Americans were also absent that day because of an organized boycott of the entirety of Mardi Gras. Zulu had, in effect, crossed the picket line. About two months before its parade, representatives from an array of African American Carnival organizations and other local activists gathered with NAACP members in a Catholic school auditorium on Christmas Eve. They were summoned there by Leonard Burns, co-founder of United Clubs, Inc. (UCI), formed in 1953 as an umbrella organization for parading clubs and the local musicians' union. Burns and his compatriots were drumming up support for a widespread boycott of Mardi Gras that season. They urged all organizations to cancel social activities during the winter of 1960–1961 and divert funds to civil rights organizations. Burns felt confident in his proposal; he had done it before. Taking inspiration from the bus boycott unfolding in neighboring Alabama, UCI had led Black New Orleanians in canceling their balls and parades during the 1956–1957 Mardi Gras season. They invested $60,000 of their dancing and parading budgets in the national NAACP.[32] The 1957 Mardi Gras Blackout harnessed a force made possible when people immobilize or withhold dancing. Elsewhere, I argue for the multiple ways in which Black New Orleanians dancing together on public streets *mobilizes* political forces to various ends: enacting self-possession, keeping records, staking a claim to city space, and more. But the Mardi Gras Blackouts invite a different consideration of dance's resistive potential: What happens when dancers refuse to move?[33]

Burns understood that immobilizing dancing enables communities to unite otherwise, diverting their human and material resources elsewhere. In 1960, UCI's call for a Carnival boycott responded to the bitter, violent struggle over school integration in New Orleans. November 14, 1960, marked the first day that public elementary schools were desegregated in the Deep South, and it happened at two schools in white working-class areas of New Orleans's Lower Ninth Ward. Ruby Bridges was the one African American student hand-picked by the school board to integrate the first grade at William Frantz School, made nationally famous by Norman Rockwell's illustration in a 1964 issue of *Look* magazine. Nearby, three African American first-graders were making the same walk as Bridges but received much less national attention. Leona Tate, Tessie Prevost, and Gail Etienne were escorted by U.S. Marshals through angry white protestors as they integrated McDonogh 19 Public School.[34] White mobs gathered outside the schools to harass the four African American students along with the white students and the parents who continued to send their children there. Protestors hurled threats, racial slurs, eggs, and rocks at the children and their escorts every day throughout November and December. Journalists' photos from these months show police officers present, but, according to Kim Lacy Rogers, Mayor de Lesseps Morrison would not order police to control the crowds.[35] Segregationists also made death threats to NAACP leaders, to the parents of all the children, and to the white activists in Save Our Schools who escorted the white children to integrated schools for the first four weeks. White Citizens' Councils, who organized opposition to integration in any form, intimidated white families into enforcing their boycott of the schools. They were so effective that, by the end of the first week of classes, only three white families continued to send their children to school with Ruby Bridges. Tate, Prevost, and Etienne attended McDonogh 19 alone for the remainder of the school year. White business leaders stayed silent for the first few months of what came to be known as the "school crisis."[36]

New Orleans's Black leaders increased organizational efforts to respond to the racist violence on the streets, assaults from the state legislature's continued attempts to overturn desegregation, and elected officials' complicity in it all. Coordinated response required Black leaders to unite across divides marked by generation, class, and culture within African American communities in 1960s New Orleans. These fragmentations informed and at times stalled civil rights movement work. Although crucial moments of solidarity led to hard-earned gains, divisions persisted between the city's formally educated Catholic Creole elites and the mostly working-class Protestant African Americans. Creoles of color had assumed positions of social and political leadership in New Orleans even before the Civil War. During the long civil rights movement, they became the movement's lawyers, NAACP leaders, and business negotiators. Eventually, the city's first Black mayor, Ernest "Dutch" Morial, would come from this community. Creoles of color were often political moderates who favored negotiation over confrontation. By contrast, many CORE members such as Jerome Smith and other youth activists came from working-class backgrounds, believed in CORE'S philosophy of nonviolent direct action, and tended to be united by Protestant ministers.[37]

Adam Fairclough concludes that the social gulf that separated New Orleans's NAACP leaders from the city's lower classes hurt the organization's ability to attract popular support. He points to the debate over the Zulu parade as an example, quoting a prominent NAACP lawyer, A. P. Tureaud: "Once we climbed the so-called ladder of middle-class America we ... felt that that was not a good image of middle-class life—to be parading and having the men and women in the streets carrying on these body gyrations, 'shaking,' as they'd say on the street."[38] Similarly, the civil rights lawyer Lolis Elie recalled that, when he was young, parading in the street was seen as the activity of the disrespectable, nonreligious, and unemployed.[39] At the same time, many Black New Orleanians of all classes celebrated Black cultural traditions that enriched their lives.[40] In her study of social dancing among African Americans in general, the dance historian Katrina Hazzard-Gordon names this paradox, in which dance has both solidified community and reified class distinctions, a phenomenon she traces from antebellum institutions to post-emancipation events to 1960s dance arenas.[41] If respectability politics divided opinion of bodies dancing in the streets, divisions also held regarding street protests. Afro-Creole leaders often opposed street protests and direct-action demonstrations for fear of violence, though the *threat* of violence, which would harm the city's tourist economy, was negotiators' most powerful form of leverage.[42] Regarding both forms of marching—parades and protests—middle-class Black movement leaders expressed ambivalence or outright derision while deriving some power and sustenance from them. In sum, centuries-old rifts between New Orleanians of African descent may have prevented the organization of large-scale civil unrest, but the communities' varied tactics combined to win considerable fights for racial equality. One such example can be found in the 1961 Mardi Gras Blackout.

Burns and other UCI members urged Black Carnival clubs to cancel all of the major balls that dotted the seasonal calendar and pledge money to national and local civil rights organizations.[43] United Clubs, Inc. publicized the campaign widely, holding other mass meetings like that of December 1960 and securing press coverage in the *Louisiana Weekly*. The group mobilized social infrastructure with a tried-and-true formula. It pledged time and money reserved for dancing to organized resistance instead. That Christmas Eve, Burns and other speakers cited three aims for a repeat Mardi Gras Blackout in 1961: to raise money for the long legal fight for integration, to promote awareness of the battles unfolding in Baton Rouge (Louisiana's capitol) and Washington, DC, and to put pressure on the city by harming its economy. In an uncommon show of intergenerational solidarity, students at Xavier University in New Orleans burst in during the speeches to parade through the auditorium. They chanted, "2, 4, 6, 8, we DO want to integrate!" and held signs that read, "To Dance or Not to Dance is No Question at All" and "Carnival Can Wait, But Not Human Dignity."[44]

As Mardi Gras Day drew nearer, the blackout campaign gained steam. By mid-January an estimated seventy-five clubs had canceled their balls or pledged to donate increasing amounts to the cause. By early February, Burns estimated that one hundred clubs had joined the protest. In addition, a local musicians' union made a financial contribution and several orchestras and halls extended contract dates by one year to organizations participating in the protest.⁴⁵ The spirit of collective ownership and wealth redistribution spread to several corners of the Mardi Gras economy. A group of flambeaux, African American men who carried lit torches to illuminate white krewes' parades, went on strike to demand a raise from $2 to $5 from the Knights of Gemini and the Krewe of Babylon.⁴⁶

Amid the enthusiasm for the boycott, the Zulu Social Aid and Pleasure Club remained a holdout. Two weeks before Mardi Gras Day, the club was undecided about whether to hold its forty-third annual parade. Opposition, including vocal disagreement by young people and withdrawals of endorsements by powerful groups such as the Tavern Owners of Greater New Orleans, Inc., mounted in Black communities. Financial support from white merchants also began to dwindle.⁴⁷ The crowned Zulu King, Henry Johnson, abdicated the throne for fear that he might lose his job at a produce company, since African Americans were threatening to boycott the company if Johnson paraded on Mardi Gras Day (hence the reason that whoever rode as king concealed his identity). Soon after, Zulu Queen Lucy Washington resigned, citing health conditions and potential boycott of her tavern. The loudest protest came from high school and college students who objected not only to the sheer fact of Zulu's participation in Mardi Gras during the boycott but also to the caricatures of uncivilized Blackness that Zulu displayed.⁴⁸

In the end, the Zulu parade rolled mostly as planned.⁴⁹ Burns claimed that a clandestine meeting with the mayor, who wanted to maintain an appearance of normalcy so that Mardi Gras tourist revenue remained unjeopardized, was the only reason the club went against the decision of its voting members to cancel. Because the usual sponsors had pulled their support, financing allegedly came from white business associations.⁵⁰ On Mardi Gras Day, Burns urged Black residents to stay away from the Zulu parade and off the streets in general, avoiding unnecessary clashes with "many expected revenge-seeking whites who are opposed to change." Instead, he suggested that Mardi Gras be "a day of prayerful reflection in the Negro community and not one of fun and frolic. Rejoicing can wait."⁵¹ If reports of Zulu's "practically deserted" parade are any indication, Burns's appeals were heeded and the Mardi Gras Blackout met its goals.⁵² It netted as much as $12,000 in donations distributed among the national and local chapters of the NAACP, the Urban League of Greater New Orleans, and other local civil rights organizations. Although the sum paled in comparison to the $60,000 raised in 1957, UCI still reported the blackout a success.⁵³ In addition to the cash collected, the effort exerted pressure on city officials and business elites to address entrenched segregation. By refusing to dance, Black New Orleanians reworked the politics of pleasure that has typically defined second lining and Mardi Gras—that is, the unapologetic display of Black pleasure in the streets. In this effort UCI leveraged the value of Black dance, which has sustained New Orleans's tourist economy since at least the days of Congo Square. In delaying their own "fun and frolic," and subsequently withholding the pleasure of consumption from would-be Carnival-goers, the Mardi Gras Blackout proved a powerful tactic by which Black New Orleanians pursued freedom.

In the fall of 1961, UCI's leaders drafted a letter to the officers and members. Burns and UCI president George Talbert praised the clubs' "magnificent and enthusiastic cooperation in protest" to "the trouble experienced by all in the City of New Orleans," acknowledging that their efforts had been reported around the world. They recognized the changes that had taken effect in the six months since the blackout, such as desegregation of schools without incident, segregation laws found unconstitutional, and city officials changing their attitudes toward their "constitutional obligations." Burns and Talbert also cited the selection of New Orleans for a multi-million-dollar Saturn rocket project as a sign that the city's tarnished reputation had not eliminated its ability to attract future investment. For all these reasons, UCI decided not to continue the Carnival boycott another year. Instead, it urged members to continue raising money for the cause, participate in voter registration drives, and to stop eating at lunch counters where CORE members picketed outside. Its final plea indicates that divisions persisted within Black New Orleanians' approaches to resistance and across generations, classes, and cultures more broadly. United Club's support for CORE was sincere, but it still preferred its activism at the ballot box and yearned for "the end to protests on the streets," hoping that, during the 1962 Carnival, it could cede the streets to dancing instead.[54]

• • •

Burns's and Talbert's calls for an end to street protests were not realized. The final weeks of 1961 saw an escalation of street protests and police violence against them. In the same year that New Orleans's mayor not only approved the permit needed for the Zulu SAPC to parade on Mardi Gras Day but also urged the club to do so, scores of civil rights protestors were arrested for parading without a permit or charged with similar offenses such as obstructing public passages. In New Orleans and across the South, local authorities weaponized the parade permit to squash demonstrations. In many cases, civil rights organizations denied parading permits proceeded with their marches anyway, knowing that arrests were inevitable. This was the case when Martin Luther King Jr. was arrested for obstructing the sidewalk and parading without a permit in Albany, Georgia, in December 1961. In New Orleans, on Canal Street alone, five Black CORE members were arrested in April 1961 while picketing stores there (the Louisiana Supreme Court overturned their convictions in 1962). In December, only a few days after King's arrest in Georgia, 290 Black marchers were arrested for violating a city ordinance by parading without a permit.[55] The state used the very juridical, political, and bureaucratic mechanisms that granted freedom of public expression and celebration to curtail freedom of public demands for rights.

As the Mardi Gras Blackout revealed, parading and protesting both engage in power struggles over public spaces. A major weapon in that struggle, as it unfolded in the twentieth-century United States, is the parade permit. According to theorists Peter Stallybrass and Allon White, the struggle over public spaces contains the political potential of Carnival writ large. In *The Politics and Poetics of Transgression*, the authors insist that any promise of political transformation achieved by means of carnivalesque performances hinges on revelers' abilities to challenge state and elite fiscal control of the physical sites of performance. The struggle over the streets during Carnival is what the authors call the politics of transgression.

Thinking about carnivalesque transgression from the perspective of material space departs from the Bakhtinian conceptions of the carnivalesque, which emphasize Carnival performances themselves as transgressive inversions of hierarchies.[56] Stallybrass and White dub such performative challenges to dominant codes of behavior as the "poetics of transgression," and although these kinds of transgressions matter to the authors, they matter far less than control of material resources. From the viewpoint of pleasure, a Bakhtinian approach would place the power of transgression in characters, events, and traditions that invert hierarchies—Zulu's burlesque, for example—and allow taboo delights to come out into the open, especially performances that flout sexual mores. The Baby Dolls, a Black women's masking tradition that celebrates female sexual pleasure, could certainly be seen that way.[57] However, thinking with Stallybrass and White, the greater power of carnivalesque transgressions lies in those performances' *locations*. Put simply, symbolic pleasurable transgressions become material and therefore political when they enter public space. Seen in this way, Carnival shares ground with direct-action protests, because both test the freedom to assemble and move.

As methods of public dissent, protest and Carnival have been shaped by three major infrastructures: the street, the role of policing, and the evolution of the law.[58] All three of these infrastructures converge in the parade permit. In New Orleans, permits for holding parades were first established by a 1930 ordinance.[59] Local laws such as New Orleans's gained federal protection in a landmark 1941 Supreme Court decision. The Court upheld the constitutionality of a New Hampshire law that required a license for any "parade or procession upon a public street."[60] The Court maintained that parades could be regulated both to ensure "good order" and to keep the streets free for traffic.[61] In 1956, New Orleans officials revised city ordinances to subject paraders to further restrictions.[62] Police officers and politicians leaned on laws regarding use of public space in order to justify arrests so that even "disruption of normal traffic patterns was often seen as unacceptable" and such peaceful civil disobedience "was equated with anarchy."[63] This seemed to be the case when, on one Saturday in August 1961, the Zulu SAPC buried its former king, Noel White. Police officers interrupted the procession, comprised of two brass bands and hundreds of second liners, to ask if Zulu had obtained a permit. When club members furnished no papers, the police ordered the procession to the sidewalk.[64] Though Zulu had curried favor with the mayor during Mardi Gras earlier that year, the mayor's esteem did not shield it from state intrusion on funerary practices.

In 1968 the NAACP appeared before the New Orleans City Council to oppose another proposed ordinance that would add a detailed application for parade permits to be filed with the police superintendent, a move that activists saw as aimed at curbing Black protest but would also affect cultural events such as Second Lines.[65] In the late 1970s the city intervened in Second Lines again, this time in response to gun violence breaking out during or near parades, by further policing the gatherings. The city altered SAPC parade routes, shortened the duration of parades, and increased mounted police patrols.[66] The history of policing Second Lines during the twentieth century followed a trajectory similar to that of policing protests, moving from escalated force to "negotiated management" with an elaborate permitting system at its core.[67] In either organized protest or carnivalesque festivities, permission to assemble must be granted by the state, explicitly or tacitly. In 1960s New Orleans, when the state granted such permission, it often came in the name of tradition, under the guise of tolerance, or in service of a narrative of racial exceptionalism, all of which ultimately facilitated profit from outside investments and revenue from tourism. The parade permit is a discursive site where the politics of transgression play out in battles over the material site of the street. One such battle unfolded between CORE activists and the NOPD in late 1961, just two months after Burns and Talbert celebrated the success of their 1961 Mardi Gras Blackout and expressed the wish that dancing would resume in the ensuing Carnival season.

Anxious to launch an assault on segregation throughout the city, in 1959 activists including Jerome Smith, Rudy Lombard, Ronnie Moore, Matt Suarez, and Oretha Castle joined picket lines organized by the Consumers' League of Greater New Orleans to boycott businesses on Dryades Street that refused to hire or serve African Americans.[68] The following year, this group of young Black residents, many of them students, joined an interracial group of activists to form the New Orleans chapter of CORE. The violence that attended school integration at first had a chilling effect, but before long the fight prompted solidarity, with the Mardi Gras Blackout as a prime example, and forced a national spotlight on New Orleans.[69] Throughout 1961 the New Orleans CORE chapter gained confidence and set the pace for Black protest. That year, CORE helped organize the Freedom Rides, in which activists risked their lives to test a Supreme Court decision prohibiting segregation in interstate travel facilities.[70] The Freedom Riders' buses left Washington, DC, and were intended to conclude their journey in New Orleans, but none made it further than Mississippi before white mobs attacked. Nonetheless, New Orleans CORE's central involvement in the Freedom Rides gave the chapter notoriety, unity, and energy.[71]

That energy no doubt enlivened a street march organized on a Monday afternoon in December 1961. At about 5:00 p.m., fifty NOPD officers accosted nearly three hundred marchers on Canal Street, a major business and tourist thoroughfare framing one end of the French Quarter that had seen much CORE activity. Beginning in 1960, activists picketed outside businesses that refused to hire and serve African Americans. In fact, Canal Street became one of CORE's three targeted zones.[72] This time, however, their goal was not the shopping district. The group met at a nearby African Methodist Episcopal church to march to the state office building, traversing Canal Street along the way but avoiding the commercial strip. They made it three blocks before police halted their peaceful protest and ushered marchers into patrol wagons. The police superintendent ordered the arrests because, though the marchers were on the sidewalk, he maintained that they were "violating a city ordinance by parading without a permit."[73] Of the 292 arrested, 290 were identified by the *Louisiana Weekly* as students at two of the city's historically Black universities, Dillard University and Southern University at New Orleans. The fact that the marchers were students is unsurprising, since their goal was to protest the arrests of university students days earlier in Baton Rouge, ninety miles away.[74] Reverend Avery Alexander, president of the Consumer's League of Greater New Orleans—who, with eleven others, was arrested separately on the same day—wired President Kennedy to inform him of the students' treatment. They were "run down and hunted by dogs like animals," he wrote, "while walking peacefully to a local state office building."[75] That night, Clarence "Chink" Henry, president of the New Orleans chapter of the International Longshoremen's Association, conferred with attorneys and had most of the arrested activists paroled. A week later, prominent CORE leader Oretha Castle told the *Louisiana Weekly* that CORE was planning a hunger strike in sympathy with student demonstrators in Baton Rouge who spent Christmas in jail.[76]

The events of 1961 in New Orleans exemplify performance studies scholar Harvey Young's insistence that the African diaspora is not purely about movement but is also characterized by stillness. Stillness, writes Young, can be either imposed as a technique of violence and domination (the ship's hold, the shackle, the solitary confinement cell) or harnessed as a tactic for resisting that domination (the sit-in, the strike, more mundane forms of refusal to move).[77] The Mardi Gras Blackout performed a refusal to dance in the streets, in response to white mobs blocking integration. This tactic was almost the inverse of picket lines and sit-ins, which occupy spaces not permitted by law or by custom, in that it refused to occupy space in ways condoned by the state and society. The blackout thus refused to serve the narrative of a multicultural city and ultimately the tourist economy. When CORE protesters and college students were arrested for parading without a permit on Canal Street, the event revealed the state's power to oblige, prevent, sanction, or criminalize bodies occupying public space. The actions coordinated by UCI, CORE, and others tested the freedom of Black people to march together, whether for politics or for pleasure. The blackout and CORE's direct-action protests also laid bare the racist ideologies and policies that determined access to the state's resources and flows of capital. In both cases, the state capriciously weaponized the permit, mobilizing Zulu's dancing when Black activists refused to move and stilling those who took to the streets in mourning, pleasure, and dissent. Two years later, in 1963, many of these same activists would strategically thread the needle between the types of assembly that the state condoned and those it suppressed. By appealing to the ambiguity of the term *march*—to walk in protest or dance with a brass band—activists were able to stage one of the largest protests in New Orleans's history.

∙ ∙ ∙

One of the processions sanctioned by the state during the years of CORE's intensive activism was the Independent Aid & Social Club's Second Line parade, accompanied by the Eureka Brass Band, in June 1963. Footage captured by white filmmaker Jules Cahn shows dozens of African American paraders, including members of the band and the club, the dozens of dancers who follow them, and one police escort. During a pause, they rest against the exterior walls of a building. Two signs hang above the door: "Athenaeum Club" and "White Only." In the next shot, second liners zigzag toward the camera, moving down the wide thoroughfare of St. Charles Avenue with a forward-rolling step-touch. Women in particular lean forward and rock side-to-side, proudly thrusting their hips behind them. Young men march with high knees and even steps, showcasing the legacy of military bands that lives on in the city's high school marching bands. Paraders accent their marching step with skip-jumps and rock steps, almost always keeping their elbows bent and arms close to the ribcage. The concrete and steel structure of the elevated Pontchartrain Expressway overpass looms in the background. Next shot: a close-up of the Robert E. Lee statue that towers above the paraders as they round the traffic circle, buoyantly stepping underneath Lee's frozen stance, seemingly indifferent to his looming presence.[78]

These brief clips, viewed in succession, reveal layers of historic, institutionalized violence through which second liners have maneuvered since the nineteenth century. By 1963 the integration of public schools had sent multitudes of white middle-class residents fleeing to the suburbs, taking their tax base with them and exacerbating class divisions along lines of race.[79] In the same year that Bridges, Tate, Prevost, and Etienne walked into two white elementary schools, the Louisiana state legislature sought to limit Black geographic and social mobility, passing forty-three new Jim Crow statutes and tightening eligibility limits for mothers receiving welfare.[80] In 1963 almost half of all African American families earned incomes well below the poverty line. Despite tremendous need, the city's social welfare services ranked among the worst in the nation. Violent crime, including police brutality, occurred at rates much higher than the national average.[81] The Independent Aid & Social Club strutted through the last vestiges of legalized segregation, high-stepped in the shadow of slavery, and grooved past urban renewal developments, such as freeway construction projects, that frequently displaced poor people of color. They second lined through, underneath, and around brick-and-mortar manifestations of racism, capitalism, and the structural violence that attends their articulations.

Black New Orleanians were not only dancing to survive and thrive within the entrenched racist power structures of the Jim Crow South; many were also actively working to demolish those structures. On August 12, 1963, just two months after the Independent Aid & Social Club paused its Second Line outside the whites-only Athenaeum Club, the city's Black leadership announced that they had reached an agreement with Mayor

Still from Jules Cahn's 1963 footage of the Independent Aid & Social Club's Second Line, with the Robert E. Lee statue looming in the background. (The Jules Cahn Collection at The Historic New Orleans Collection, acc. no. 2000.78.4.7.)

Victor Schiro. New Orleans's public buildings would no longer feature racial designation signs for restrooms, water fountains, and other facilities. The city government would "refrain from appealing" court orders that desegregated local institutions and quit harassing businessmen who desired to desegregate their operations. The city also promised to hire more African Americans in civil service positions. The agreement reflected several years of negotiations that city leaders held with Black and white Citizens' Committees (not to be confused with the all-white Citizens' Council, which directly opposed integration in all forms). The two Citizens' Committees had already managed to desegregate many lunch counters and obtain employment for African Americans in some previously whites-only jobs, all without the assistance of the mayor or City Council. Now, they asked the city to follow the lead of private businesses.[82]

Six weeks later, however, few of the mayor's promises had been fulfilled. In response, the Black Citizens' Committee organized the massive

Freedom March. It started in Shakespeare Park, a municipal park in the Central City neighborhood that also served as the launching pad for a brass band parade nearly every Sunday during the 1940s and 1950s.[83] Estimates of the number of participants range from eight thousand to fifteen thousand, including several hundred white marchers and scores of police officers dispatched to escort the march.[84] Organizer Don Hubbard recalled how the procession swelled during his four-mile trek:

> We started marching, along with maybe a dozen ministers and some representatives from the NAACP and what have you. Nobody else was marching, we were walking by ourselves. So we got from Third Street to Second Street, we looked back, the street was, you know, it might have had fifty people, and we just kept walking. By the time we got to Jackson Avenue and we looked back, the street was packed. By the time we got to Martin Luther King, which was Melpomene Street at that time, there must have been 5,000 people. By the time we got to city hall, when the buses started showing up from the Ninth Ward and from Algiers and what have you, there were 8,000 people at the march.[85]

The Citizens' Committee had representatives from half a dozen civil rights groups, including CORE and United Clubs, Inc. Its diverse makeup, which crossed generational, class, and cultural divides, made it at once a formidable force and a site for divisions to play out. For example, Hubbard recalls that CORE initiated the idea for the march on City Hall, inspired by the March on Washington in August 1963. It accepted the requests of ministers and older, more conservative activists to join. Hubbard landed on the Citizens Committee's payroll as a march organizer, and his home became planning headquarters. It was there that he persuaded Oretha Castle to speak at the march, since her voice would alone carry CORE's point of view. Castle threatened to back out because the ministers wanted to "hijack the march" and censor her speech, deleting the portion in which she pledged to sit at City Hall until all their demands were met. In the end, she delivered the censored speech alongside other prominent civil rights leaders in the city, all males (see video 4.1 on this book's web page).[86]

In addition to civil rights groups, march organizers enlisted the cooperation of benevolent societies, Carnival clubs, and civic and business associations.[87] Together, these groups published an open letter in the *Louisiana Weekly* calling on readers to join the demonstration and listing their demands, which included desegregating whites-only bars and music clubs such as those that the Independent Aid & Social Club members paraded past but could not enter. Schiro denounced the Freedom March, telling reporters that a better path forward would be to work out differences around a conference table. He referred to the recent church bombing in Birmingham, Alabama, to justify his tactics, claiming that he was only trying to avoid the kinds of violence that had plagued other cities.[88] Schiro declared his opposition to unruly "demonstrations" but conceded that "anyone has a legal right to stage a parade providing he complies with the city ordinance regarding parades"—which the organizers did.[89] Ordinances regarding parades would have been very familiar to the march's organizers and endorsers, many of them members of organizations such as Masonic lodges and SAPCs that regularly hosted parades. Furthermore, the savvy organizers stated in the full-page ad that "The Freedom March ... will not be a 'demonstration' in the strict sense of the word, but a peaceful protest to develop greater public awareness of the grievances of non-white Orleanians, for we have a permit to march."[90] The organizers signaled their awareness of the permit as a central weapon in the struggle over public space, declaring their permitted status lest it be refuted or revoked by the state at will. In designing the Freedom March, those who planned carnivalesque parades and political protest worked together—indeed, many of its organizers moved in both worlds—demonstrating the truth of Stallybrass and White's assertion that the power of carnivalesque transgression lies in the ability to take control of public space.

The printed exchange between the mayor and the marchers illuminates complex conceptions of race, rights, and popular dance in 1963 New Orleans. Whereas the mayor could publicly defend the legal right of "anyone," including Black residents, to "stage a parade," he could not as easily defend the demands of Freedom March organizers, such as access to equal job opportunities and adequate housing, the right to patronize businesses of their choosing, and the right to serve on city boards and commissions.[91] Schiro conflated the terms *march* and *parade* and cast both against "demonstration," thereby displacing the politically motivated march into the seemingly benign realm of culture. Thus, in defending the rights of Black New Orleanians to participate in the city's hallowed parading traditions, he gave the appearance of tolerance while simultaneously denying the outcomes demanded by activists. He protected the right of Black citizens to move through the city's segregated and unequal landscape in parades—if those parades did not seek to topple the very physical and ideological structures that framed their routes.

However, Schiro drew a false line between cultural parades (pleasure) and activist demonstrations (politics), and in so doing, he underestimated the organizing power inherent in Black cultural traditions, or the politics of pleasure. Attorney Revius O. Ortique Jr., a movement lawyer and featured speaker at the Freedom March, told the crowd of thousands that the

JOIN THE PEACEFUL PROTEST MARCH

To City Hall for FREEDOM and EQUAL JOB OPPORTUNITIES

The Freedom March on the New Orleans City Hall scheduled for September 30, 1963, will not be a "demonstration" in the strict sense of the word, but a peaceful protest to develop greater public awareness of the grievances of non-white Orleanians, for we have a permit to march. The march will be interracial and interfaith.

The high point of the march will be the presenting of a petition to city officials asking immediate corrective action on the following:

1. A statement from the Mayor and the City Council to the effect that they support democratic practices in employment and public accommodations, and that merchants who desegregate their businesses will have the city government support.

2. Abolishment of the dual system of classification in the City Civil Service so that qualified Negroes can be considered for jobs in other than Negro institutions, as well as jobs in all levels of city government.

3. The appointment of Negroes to various boards and commissions particularly to the Housing Authority of New Orleans where Negroes constitute a majority of the tenants.

4. The removal of racial signs from municipally owned buildings such as City Hall, Civil Courts Building, and the Municipal courts building.

5. Repeal of all city ordinances that require segregation of the races, particularly the ordinance requiring segregation in places serving alcoholic beverages, and that the Mayor will not veto the repeal of any such ordinances.

6. The end of racial discrimination at the Delgado Trade and Technical Institute.

7. That henceforth there will be no legal delaying tactics used by the city during the course of the suits once the courts have acted on desegregation.

As a person in a responsible position, we urge you to inform and urge your friends to participate in the MARCH for FREEDOM and JOB OPPORTUNITIES.

ASSEMBLE: SHAKESPEARE PARK
DATE: SEPTEMBER 30, 1963
TIME: 6 P.M.

FOR INFORMATION CALL HEADQUARTERS TW. 9–2519
ABOUT MARSHALS, SIGNS AND IDENTITY

Organizers printed a full-page notice in the September 28, 1963, issue of the *Louisiana Weekly*. (*Louisiana Weekly* collection, Amistad Research Center, New Orleans.)

march's purpose was to "have the patter of our feet ring out to the community, to our state, to the nation and to the world, in unison, carrying out, shouting out that we wish only for that liberty and the freedom which our constitution states should be for all Americans."[92] When the Independent Aid & Social Club second lined for pleasure and when protestors marched for rights, the patter of feet rung out wishes for, and embodiments of, freedom.

On the same day as the Freedom March, Leonard Burns (director of UCI and member of the Citizens Committee) and Gerald Thomas (president of UCI) wrote a letter to presidents of all Black social clubs to urge them, on behalf of "our militant Citizens Committee members," to meet in ten days' time. Carnival season was upon them, and it was time to decide if they "should dance in joy, while others of our race face jail terms for our welfare and all Negroes are denied human dignity."[93] Organizers still had much work to do, because the Freedom March had caused little change. A month after the march, Avery Alexander was refused service in the City Hall cafeteria and dragged, limp, from the building. Reverend A. L. Davis, who had been appointed in 1961 as the city's first director of race relations, was arrested when attempting to meet with Mayor Schiro in his office.[94] Ultimately, Black leaders decided not to pursue their goals by remounting the Mardi Gras Blackout in 1964 (or in any succeeding year). But their deliberations concerning "to dance or not to dance" raised questions of how to mobilize or immobilize pleasure with a view toward political gains in New Orleans's tightly woven cultural and activist communities.

• • •

This chapter's goal of illuminating some of second lining's roots in organizing resonates with the Black Men of Labor Social Aid and Pleasure Club's 2011 anniversary parade, which it dedicated to the New Orleans chapter of CORE. A couple of hours before the parade began, the Black Men of Labor (BMOL) hosted a ceremony to honor the Freedom Riders, including several from New Orleans CORE. About twenty BMOL members posed for pictures with eight civil rights activists in front of a large mural designed by Ayo Scott. The mural graced the side of Sweet Lorraine's Jazz Club in the Seventh Ward, the official home of BMOL, where its images educated passers-by about individuals and scenes of protests from the civil rights era. The center of the mural featured a scroll that read, "The Black Men of Labor salutes and pays tribute to the New Orleans Chapter of CORE, Congress of Racial Equality, & the 50th anniversary of the Freedom Riders."[95] The mural and the 2011 parade acted as two forms of public history, highlighting the significance of local actors for national events.

Photo from the Black Men of Labor Second Line parade on October 29, 2011. The group honored the Freedom Riders and members of New Orleans's CORE chapter, pictured here (Doratha Smith-Simmons, center) posing in front of the Ayo Scott mural depicting New Orleans civil rights activists. (Photo © 2011 OffBeat, Inc./Kim Welsh.)

The year 2011 marked BMOL's seventeenth anniversary parade. Since its founding in 1993, the club's mission, as stated on its website (https://thebmol.org), has been to maintain New Orleans's benevolent societies, which "not only provide financial support and a sense of community, they are a living testament to the cultures, traditions and ceremony that originated with their African ancestors." In an interview with the documentarians Rachel Breunlin and Bruce "Sunpie" Barnes, BMOL co-founder and president Fred Johnson Jr. explained that the club's name was chosen, in part, to combat stereotypes about "black men [who] always get a bad rap about how they don't take care of their business or their house."[96] The name, along with the club's chosen Labor Day parade date, also pays homage to the Longshoremen's Protective Union and Benevolent Association (an antecedent to the International Longshoremen's Association, which was responsible for bailing CORE members out of jail in 1961).[97] According to accounts that Johnson heard growing up, this powerful labor union's turn-of-the-century Labor Day parades were some of the biggest that the city had ever seen.[98] When BMOL came out the door for the first time in 1994, it wore overalls in honor of the Longshoremen's parading uniform. In subsequent years, BMOL became distinguished for parading in African-inspired attire such as Senegalese boubous and three-piece suits custom-made from kente cloth.[99] Mutual aid, musical tradition, and Black pride: BMOL's mission shares these values with civil rights organizations such as CORE.

In pre-parade photos, New Orleans CORE member Doratha "Dodie" Smith-Simmons stands in the center of the Freedom Riders, smiling broadly.[100] "Their parade meant more to me than going to the Freedom Rider convention in Mississippi where we were given an award shaped like a bus," she said, because it celebrated both the politics and pleasure at the roots of New Orleans's Black expressive cultures. "For me, my involvement in the civil rights movement led me to . . . a rich life in music. Their parade honors the same origins."[101] The organizing skills gained during her work with CORE equipped Smith-Simmons to turn her love for music into a career. In the 1960s her constant presence at Preservation Hall, a French Quarter music venue dedicated to traditional jazz, led to a job there. Soon after, she was drafted as one of the original organizers of the New Orleans Jazz and Heritage Festival, and she then went on to organize global brass band tours. For Smith-Simmons, her two passions, CORE and New Orleans brass band music, are inseparable. "If you know the history behind benevolent societies, you would see that that was done to help people, people who didn't have anything," she said. "They'd put in a nickel a week [to] pay into this society. They had benevolent societ[ies] [that] had dance halls; they had music. So what's the difference?"[102]

Smith-Simmons gave the example of benevolent societies that held sessions to teach African Americans how to pass required voting tests. She may have been recalling postwar voter registration drives organized by Black voluntary associations, arm-in-arm with activist and civic organizations such as the NAACP and the People's Defense League. Thanks to energetic campaigns, Black registration in Orleans Parish doubled between 1946 and 1948. In the early 1960s, when Smith-Simmons was involved in CORE, such registration efforts netted far less success.[103] But, despite the varied efficacy of these efforts, Smith-Simmons recalled the combined purposes of politics and pleasure as exemplified by benevolent associations' voting campaigns. When people showed up to learn how to access the ballot box, "there [was] music, food, there [was] socializing," she said. "So it's all intertwined."[104]

Smith-Simmons also recognized that New Orleanians' involvement in the civil rights movement would inevitably be imbued with the city's musical traditions because "music has always been a part of life in New

Orleans." Why would it disappear on the picket line? "We didn't have bands," she said, "but there was always singing." She thought of New Orleans CORE co-founder Jerome Smith, who, when they were both in high school, was already exercising his leadership skills as a drum major with the marching band.[105] Smith himself located the origins of his political consciousness not at a rally or a meeting but at a procession of Black Masking Indians, a tradition dating back to the late nineteenth century, that he witnessed as a child:

> When Black folks are doing something of excellence, the police would try to run us off the streets, our tribe [Yellow Pocahontas] off the street. But we wouldn't get off the street. Like one Mardi Gras Day they tried to run him [Chief Allison "Tootie" Montana] down. They tried to run him down because folks was saying how beautiful he was, they never seen nothing like that. So these police turned the corner and tried to run us out the street. My first encounter with police dogs wasn't in Mississippi or Baton Rouge. It was right here in New Orleans—on Mardi Gras Day! When the street was supposed to be wide open for Mardi Gras![106]

After resigning from CORE in the late 1960s, Jerome Smith, Dodie Smith-Simmons, and several other movement leaders turned to work in cultural fields instead of running for political office or going to law school. Smith-Simmons went to work for existing music organizations; Smith started Tambourine and Fan. Fred Johnson Jr., BMOL co-founder, also worked with Tambourine and Fan, and that experience came to bear on BMOL's 2011 parade. Speaking of the idea to dedicate the club's parade to CORE and the Freedom Riders, Johnson reflected,

> Since Rudy [Lombard, first chairman of New Orleans CORE] and Jerome used the methods of organizing they learned in New Orleans CORE in Tambourine and Fan, I've thought about the way we honor *the freedom to assemble and move through time and space together*. Fifty years ago, the group of people who come to our Second Line could have been arrested for spending an afternoon together, but because of the men and women who fought, bled, and died to make a way for equality, we are able to share it today.[107]

The parade made tangible, especially for a younger generation, the symbiotic relationship between community organizing and the street processions of the city's African diaspora. On picket lines and in Second Lines, Black New Orleanians have long insisted on, in Johnson's words, the freedom to move through time and space—together.

Terrylyn Dorsey dancing on Washington Avenue during the Single Men SAPC's Second Line parade on March 20, 2016. (Photo by Judy Cooper.)

INTERLUDE

Terrylyn Dorsey

March 24, 2017

Terrylyn Dorsey began second lining as a child in the early twenty-first century. She attended parades with her mother, Yarnell Dorsey, who was a member of the Single Ladies Social and Pleasure Club. Even at an early age, weekly parades were not enough for her, so she also spent evenings dancing to bands playing for tips on streets in the French Quarter before she was old enough to get into nightclubs where the same bands would play. As an adult she first joined an all-male SAPC because, in her opinion, men share her focus on footwork more than women do (since this interview was conducted, Dorsey has shifted to an all-female club, Versatile Ladies of Style, that meets her standards). Her obsession with footwork has paid off as she has crafted a dance career for herself, working in the grassroots way that many brass band musicians do. With the stage name Secondline Shorty, she graduated from audience to performer at those street-corner brass band shows, putting out her own box for tips. She began appearing as a featured performer at the annual Jazz and Heritage Festival and uses social media networks to book her services as a grand marshal for parties, weddings, funerals, promo videos, and more. In response to local demand, she also began offering biweekly Second Line dance classes at a studio in July 2021, charging a $35 per class. Although second lining has become a business for Dorsey, she's never lost her passion for it, which she describes as "feeling the music in my soul."

My name is Terrylyn, known as Secondline Shorty. I'm born April 3, 1995. . . .

RACHEL CARRICO: Ok, tell us how you started second lining. How did you get into this thing?

TERRYLYN DORSEY: Well, my mom was in the Single Ladies Social and Pleasure Club, and she started taking me to Second Lines with her, and once I got older, I started going on Bourbon [Street] on my own. . . . In front of, it used to be Foot Locker, but it's CVS now. Bourbon and Canal. . . . And, like, Toulouse Street. Bourbon and Toulouse.

. . . And once I heard the Second Line band, I'm like, you know, I'm feeling this. And I went every day, every day, and was watching . . . other people second line, and I just went out there and started second lining. . . . I was sixteen.

RC: So, what does it feel like when you're out there dancing and you're really in it, like in your element, what does it feel like?

TD: Phew. I be in whole 'nother zone. I feel the music, like, I be feeling the music in my soul to what, that's when I really get interested in, once I'm in my zone, I don't hear nobody, I don't see nobody. I just hear this music. . . . Well, a lot of folks be like, 'Shorty cutting up! Oh, Shorty at the Second Line! Shorty giving me life!' [*laughs*] You know? Everybody just be telling me how great I am.

. . .

That's how I release my stress. I'm not gonna say stress—problems. . . . The problems are gone. But eventually, you know, you get back to 'em. But at the moment, nothing but fun.

. . .

I just be like, you know, dancing, my eyes closed. Once my eyes close, then, when my eyes close, I be like, I'm really feeling it. Feeling it in my soul, like, for real. A lot of people might think, you know, you can't feel it, but for real, I really be feeling that music in my soul. [*laughs*] For real.

Straight Footwork

RC: And tell me about your decision to join the Single Men. I'm sure any social and pleasure club in the city would love to have you—

TD: Mm-hmm.

RC: why Single Men?

TD: Well, because they from uptown . . . Because that's where I'm from. [*laughs*] And, I like, you know, I can roll with men more than I can roll with women. So that's why I picked that club. . . . Because men will make you rock. Women, they do all that booty shaking, and, you know; men, straight footwork. You know? They make you have fun.

RC: Yeah. And that's what you're into, straight footwork.

TD: Straight footwork. Footwork and fun. . . . In my eyes, this is how I look at it, uptown is more like funky. You know? They dance more funky, more footworking. Or whatever. And downtown is like, traditional. That's, in my eyes. . . . Maybe somebody else would think different, but this is what I see.... Like, I guess it's like the, just a lot of sliding, you know.... The two stepping! [*laughs*] ... Yeah, and they do, like, jump, they be like jumping, you know, and stuff like that....

RC: How do you keep your energy up the whole time?

TD: Just keep dancing. [*laughs*]

RC: Just don't stop.

TD: Don't stop! [*laughs*]

RC: Do you have any special thing, do you eat or drink or anything, so like you don't get cramps, or any, like, tricks like that?

TD: I don't even drink water at the Second Line....

RC: You don't get dehydrated?

TD: Do I! But still. [*laughs*] I still don't drink water. I just second line, straight second line, just dance the whole four hours.

RC: You don't have time to stop and get a drink of water, mm-hmm.

TD: Might miss my part! [*laughs*]

RC: And where do you like to be in the parade, like, if you're not in the club, where do you like to be?

TD: On the side. My area is on the side of the band, on the side by the rope. Or sometimes, some clubs will let me get, like, in the front of the band, like right there by the little rope man.... On the right side, I'm always on the right side.... Because I can hear the music, and then I have a little, my own little space where I can do what I gotta do.... I listen for the tuba, the snare drum and the bass drum. Sometimes, if I like the trombone, or the trumpet, then, yeah, but it's mostly the bass drum, the snare drum and the tuba. And the cowbell.... And I like the little silver [thing], with the spoons?

RC: Oh yeah, the washboard!

TD: Yeah. I like that, too. Yeah, that.

RC: Yeah, so the rhythm section.

TD: Right, yeah.... Gets down! [*laughs*] ...

RC: And so, is Da Truth your favorite band right now?[1]

TD: Yes.

RC: Yeah, yeah. What do they do that you like?

TD: I just like the bass drum. [*laughs*] That's why they my favorite band. ... That's the honest truth, if you go on Facebook, everybody say, "That blue drum, that blue drum," yup, that blue drum.... Make me do things I never even did before! [*laughs*] I be crawling on the ground, everything! [*laughs*]

Role Models

RC: And who are some of your role models, or mentors, when you were first starting to, like, really master your footwork?

TD: Well, I think Trombone Shorty.[2]

RC: Yeah.

TD: Because it's like, you know, he doing the same thing I'm doing, but he just playing his horn, and like, I want to travel and experience, you know. And show my talent to other folks.

. . .

RC: What about people in terms of whose dance style you admire, or try to kind of—

TD: My mom. Yeah. We got a little battle going on . . . [*laughs*] And that's just how she be. "Oh yeah, I'ma catch my second wind."

Going Viral

TD: Well, the reason I went viral was because Itchy,[3] he was the cameraman every Sunday, and he just used to record, record, and like, one day, I guess Lil Boosie[4] just caught the video, and he just reposted, and once Lil Boosie reposted, like, a lot of folks started recognizing [me]. . . . I love making money doing what I love to do. . . . I post my business card on Instagram, Facebook, and like, folks get in touch with me with gigs. . . . Like, weddings, parties, Jazz Fest, videos, . . . commercials. . . . I did a workshop with a few girls in Lafayette. . . .

RC: So, what are your visions for your future in this?

TD: Like I say, I just, you know, I wanna do like Trombone Shorty doing, just exploring, making money off my feet. [*laughter*]

CHAPTER 5

Do Whatcha Wanna

Doratha "Dodie" Smith-Simmons has lived in New Orleans since 1945, when she was two years old. Raised downtown in the Ninth Ward, she was surrounded by live music played at local bars, fish fries, and rent parties, which, before jukeboxes were available, always featured a trio or at least a pianist. She recalls, "There was always music around. We would have a good time with music and dance." Occasionally, she followed a jazz funeral, or, when she was in high school, she and her classmates grooved in the schoolyard as a brass band paraded past. From these experiences, she learned to dance. When I asked Smith-Simmons how she began second lining, she replied with a chuckle, "Quite easily. . . . It's something that comes natural."[1]

I also asked Tamara Jackson Snowden, a leader in the Second Line community who is a generation younger than Smith-Simmons, how she recalled getting her footwork. Her response mirrored that of Smith-Simmons: "It was just natural. It was natural." She continued,

> It goes back to the Rebirth [Brass Band] song, 'Do Whatcha Wanna.' You just basically do what you want do, do what you feel. You know, second line—there's no particular way to second line. It's all about the individual's expression, and just following and keeping up with the rhythm and the beat. The beat of the drum, and the horns, and it just motivates you. It's eclectic, but everybody have they own style. Some people are really, really elaborate. And then there's others that just trot [. . .]. And *everything is OK*. Whatever style you choose, it's acceptable.[2]

Jackson Snowden invokes the Rebirth Brass Band's 1995 Carnival classic "Do Whatcha Wanna" to insist that any style of dance is acceptable at the Second Line. She's right. It's also true that second lining can be characterized as a coherent dance form with an identifiable aesthetic. While trying to perfect my footwork, I would occasionally approach second liners I admired and ask them for tips. Many would simply respond, "Just feel the music," "Just do you," or "Do whatcha wanna." Similarly, when in researcher mode and asking second liners how they learned to dance, some, like Smith-Simmons and Jackson Snowden, declared that the process was natural. At first, I found these responses perplexing. It was clear that if I did what I wanted to do, what came naturally to me, then I might have a good time, but I would not embody the specific movement vocabulary that characterizes second lining. Over time, I began to see that, much more that obfuscating the details of footwork technique or dismissing tedious researcher questions about something that's supposed to be fun, stances like Smith-Simmons's and Jackson Snowden's do a lot of important work (listen to the full Jackson Snowden interview, along Rebirth's "Do Whatcha Wanna," on this book's web page).

From conversations and experiences such as those briefly described above, I identified four research questions about Second Line knowledge transmission that guide this chapter. These questions do *not* include, "Which is it? Natural ability or technique?" but rather invite an interrogation of those concepts to explore the assumptions and cultural values that lie underneath. First, how do second liners gain dance skills and share their knowledge with others? Second, what histories, values, and sensibilities are imparted along with physical information? Third, what about Second Line embodiment has changed over the years and what has remained consistent? Finally, how do second liners receive outsider attempts to acquire embodied knowledge? Through first-hand participation, interviews, and archival research I have come to understand that Second Line communities collectively cultivate a balance between aesthetic continuity and innovation using informal but elaborate protocols for sharing dance knowledge. In the process, they also protect the cultural values embedded in the aesthetics, even when adapting those values to meet the moment.[3] When debates erupt about right and wrong ways to second line (and they do), they reveal divergent values among different generations, class positions, or gender identities. An important function of the do-whatcha-wanna ethos, which animates the circulation of second liners' embodied knowledge, is that it keeps practitioners focused on *why* they are dancing as opposed to *what steps* they are doing. It also supplies a ready response when second liners encounter outsider inquiries about their dancing—mine included—sufficient to redress an inevitable power imbalance in which knowledge is often appropriated without any material benefit to the dancer. Overall, doing what "comes natural" maintains some level of ownership of cultural knowledge within the community.

• • •

How do second liners gain dance skills and share their knowledge? A primary method is to observe others' movements, imitate them, and alter them to create unique styles. Tyree Smith, secretary of Family Ties SAPC, remembers when he first started second lining at the age of thirteen. For him, it did not come naturally:

> Oh my god [picking up footwork] was hard! It was real hard because at first I couldn't keep up with everybody. . . . I really was off beat. I felt unorthodox. So I started going on the regular . . . and I just started watching people. And I was like, "Oh, I got that move. Oh, I got that move. OK, I can do this, I can do that." So I just kind of put all that together and kind of created my own style with a little swag from this person, a little swag from that person. That's where I came from. That's what created me. From everybody else.[4]

Smith describes a strategy that has long been central to African American performance. Thomas DeFrantz names it "versioning," a term that indicates exactly what's happening: One person creates a new version of existing material.[5] Reusing, reworking, and extending others' stories, bass lines, or steps is a basic element of West African cultural practice that has continued in African American music and dance since at least the nineteenth century.[6] For example, in tap dance and Lindy Hop communities, dancers describe "stealing" others' steps as an affectionate process of communal learning.[7] The dance historian Anthea Kraut details why, in mid-century New York spaces such as the Hoofers' Club and the Savoy Ballroom, copying others was the way to learn. Few studios taught the Lindy Hop, and most tappers would never hold a novice's hand through a step. Imitation allowed dancers to improve, attract better dance partners, establish status, and have fun in friendly one-upmanship. As hoofers and Lindy Hoppers sought their own pleasure by reworking others' moves, something else was happening, too: The dances evolved. As Kraut puts it, "Imitation and innovation were the dual engines that propelled the dance forms forward."[8]

The musical concept of "borrowing," developed in the study of European written repertories, is less appropriate to Africanist traditions than the concept of "sharing."[9] Sharing, like versioning, avoids implications of ownership and acknowledges that, in vernacular traditions, there is often no distinct entity from which to borrow. This remains true across African and African diasporic music and dance forms generally, and fits within second lining's specific political economy. Sharing embodies a cultural value placed on common property, consistent with the Second Line's roots in mutual aid societies, wherein each member's economic contribution to the common pot becomes a collective asset. Decades ago, each dues-paying member contributed a prescribed monthly amount, available to anyone who needed medical, burial, or other services. Some organizations still subscribe to this model today, while other SAPCs use the same method to finance their annual parades. The time-honored technique of replicating steps is, in a way, a version of mutual aid, a community member's withdrawal from the shared account of intellectual property. Imitation, however, is just the beginning; the next, more crucial piece is to tailor those moves to fit one's unique style. One must make not only withdrawals, but contributions as well, in the form of copy-worthy embellishments.

Originality is one of the qualities that second liners prize most, so it follows that dancers devote hours of practice to styling a singular oeuvre. For example, Terrinika Smith, a dedicated second liner and a member of the Jazzy Ladies SAPC, works to cultivate a never-before-seen quality with her footwork. Smith can often be found second lining near her cousin Terrylyn Dorsey (whose interview excerpt precedes this chapter). Dorsey proclaimed, "When it's me and Terrinika, we tear the *floor up*." On Sundays, they tear the street up as well. When we talked in 2014, Smith had assumed the role of dance coach for her cousin. Dorsey recalled then, "Terrinika always be telling me, 'Uh uh! Don't be doing that! You can't be doing the same thing over! You got to do some new moves!'" Smith agreed: "Exactly. Shock them every time."[10] In the ensuing years, Dorsey went on to stake her claim as an accomplished second liner who's now coaching others. Smith shifted her tutelage to her son, who, at the time of writing, is commanding paraders' attention with his spectacular footwork. As is evident in her advice to Dorsey, Smith does not want to be seen as a mimic but as the one whom others try to emulate. She admires those who are "not trying to be somebody else. Because if you copy off of somebody else, they going to say, 'Man, they're doing what he doing.' But if you bring your own style, they going to say, 'Man I'm going to go home and try that!'"[11]

Smith's comments imply that second liners try out observed movements at home, a tactic that others described during my interviews with them. For example, Walter Kimble grew up dancing with his cousin Chester. "We'll be at his house just parading around," Kimble explained. That's how they perfected their "team second lining," where they would "do tricks together, like grab [each other's] arms and go like a rodeo, fall back, go under each other's legs and stuff." Being inside the house is key detail; they would not

Terrylyn Dorsey (left) and Terrinika Smith (right) encourage each other during the Single Men SAPC's Second Line parade, March 16, 2014. (Photo by Pableaux Johnson.)

go in the yard because they didn't "want to show nobody [their] moves," lest they be poached.[12] Second liners are not alone in their "go home and try that" approach. In her study of African American social dancing of the 1930s and 1940s, Marya Annette McQuirter notes the importance of dancing at home.[13] Then and now, dancers observe moves in public settings and then refine them in private with family members, in front of a mirror, or, today, while rewatching recorded performances on social media platforms. When second liners step out to perform perfected steps, they do not look like an exact copy of anyone else, since they flavor their footwork with a signature spice—or, in DeFrantz's terms, they "make the common personal."[14] The cycle of sharing and versioning continues, and with each display of creativity, dancers establish status within Second Line communities and the dance form evolves. As Terrinika Smith emphatically stated, no one wants to be seen as a mimic; to achieve respect, originality is key.

While observing, practicing at home, and trying new moves on the street, second liners occasionally find mentors, just as Dorsey found in her cousin. Tyree Smith recalls that an older friend would give him advice: "You're moving too fast. Pick your feet up. Slow down."[15] As a child, Rodrick Davis received similar tips from his uncles. "They would tell me, just pace myself sometimes, I don't have to always go fast. Stuff like that. I got all that told to me at a real early age." Davis was hungry for the information. "I wanted to learn," he remembers. "I was looking to see what I needed to do to make everything look like the moves were perfect."[16] Davis's decades of study were recognized when he was crowned champion of the first and second annual Big Easy Footwork Competitions in 2014 and 2015. As this honorific implies, Davis shifted away from his student role and now takes on mentees himself. The same is true for Tyree Smith, who started a division within Family Ties SAPC to welcome young men who love to second line but could not afford the dues attached to regular membership. Davis, in his early twenties at the time of our interview, reported receiving individual requests for tutelage. "Now, I mean, nobody tell me nothing, they come asking me. They come asking *me*. The same people that were older than me, [who] was telling me, [now they're] asking me. 'Show me how to do this! Show me how to do that! I got to learn this move!'"[17] He said that the wives of some male club members will ask him to come to their houses a week before their husbands' parades to show them a move or two. Davis told me that he is usually too busy working as a restaurant cook to take these requests, but he loves to coach children at the Second Line. He can often be seen with a train of young people following him, imitating his quick yet expansive steps (listen to full interviews with Smith and Davis on this book's web page).

Although important mentorship networks form at parades, many second liners' dance education begins at home. Wellington "Skelly" Ratcliff Jr., a veteran second liner who has belonged to several SAPCs for decades, recalls, "I really learned how to dance from my mom and them. My mom and them would get together, family gatherings, and they'd get in the house, put music on, and you'd be in the room, they'd come out: 'Come show me you know how to dance!'"[18] Others I spoke with remember their "home training" sessions as friendly competitions when the adults upped the ante by offering a meager cash prize for the child they deemed best.[19] As is the case in tap, breaking, and a host of other Black dance genres, competition has been instrumental in the development of second lining. Nadine George-Graves makes this assertion in her study of the Cakewalk. "Throughout American history," she writes, "black dancers engaged in one-upmanship to gain popularity, created signature styles when no copyright law would protect their intellectual property, and played up rivalries to increase the dramatic stakes behind their dance battles."[20] In these kitchen-floor competitions second liners improve their skills, refine their personal styles, and have fun with friendly challenges. In so doing, they also reinforce cultural values regarding excellence as something achieved by dialogic exchange and adjudicated according to community appraisal.[21]

For Terrinika Smith, who is Ratcliff's daughter, the influence of family has also been important. When she was a child, her mother paraded with a club called the Lady Sequence, and these women provided her earliest examples of second lining:

> I was five years old when Lady Sequence used to come out uptown on Dryades Street. That was my first Second Line. It was a group of women and they used to wear these hats with furs, and they used to come down the steps. I was like, "Man, I want to do *just* what they doing!" And I went home, and I was like, "Mom, look at me!" And I put her clothes on. ... I didn't put her pants on, I just put her little jacket on and her little hat, and her little gloves, ... and I was like, 'I'm coming out the door!' And she was like, 'Look at this girl, she know how to second line!' And I was like, "I be watching y'all, I be watching y'all."[22]

Smith's earliest experiences of "going home to try that" are evident in her intricate footwork today. As the anthropologist Margaret Drewal observes, when performers "have been trained from childhood in particular techniques," it enables them to "play spontaneously with learned, in-body formulas. This kind of mastery distinguishes a brilliant performer from a merely competent one."[23] As Smith's and others' experiences make evident, childhood training in Second Line vocabularies produces spectacularly skilled improvisers. Making moment-to-moment artistic choices in time with the rhythm, Smith crafts her own footwork style as she performs it.[24] Stories of informal mentorship reveal that dancers transmit knowledge, refine technique, and creatively assemble sequences from a shared movement vocabulary—in other words, they choreograph their second lining—under the gaze of friends and family or under the scrutiny of mentors. The intergenerational networks in which Second Line knowledge circulates adhere to cultural values placed on community, kinship, and respect for elders.

Second liners copy, style, mentor, improvise, and compete at every dance event, including Second Line parades. In fact, the inclusive structure and repetitive occurrence of parades disturb any neat divisions between performer and audience, rehearsal and performance, or "studio" and "stage." During each Second Line's four-hour duration, dancers encounter innumerable opportunities to repeat, and therefore perfect, their moves. One might seize a few choice moments to dance in obvious spotlights, such as atop a porch or in a truck bed, and at other times might hide amid the thick crowd while trying out a new step. Second lining's cyclical calendar, which promises a parade almost every Sunday and many other social events during the week, offers dancers regular opportunities to simultaneously practice and perform these choreographies.

Although it is not common, sometimes dance practice occurs in more dedicated rehearsal spaces organized by SAPCs. For example, the Young Men Olympian Jr. Benevolent Association (YMO) hosts rehearsals for its members. As the longest-running Second Line organization in the city, founded in 1884, YMO is known for maintaining more traditional aspects of the benevolent association tradition such as holding regular business meetings, requiring club members to attend the funeral of a deceased member, and holding practices before their parades. Although YMO is a bearer of tradition, it has also been the source of major innovations in the Second Line scene. Over the years, younger club members have formed new divisions within the large organization (which boasts more than one hundred members) that have been instrumental in developing new footwork styles and sartorial choices. Two of these innovative divisions, the Furious Five and the Mellow Fellows, were formed in the 1980s. Along with the Lady Buckjumpers, they were two of the earliest groups to parade with the musicians who were dramatically changing the sound of brass band music in the late twentieth century (discussed below). Although the Furious Five and the Mellow Fellows departed from YMO's traditional style of dress, trading in black-and-white suits for Technicolor ones, and dance—replacing upright, lateral step-touches with lightning-fast footwork and acrobatic feats—these groups maintained the organization's insistence on practice.

Skelly Ratcliff joined YMO in the late 1970s, when he was only twelve years old. Ratcliff's grandmother brought him to Second Lines when he was a child, and "more and more, she started [to see that] I liked to dance to the music." She approached a senior YMO member, Alfred "Bucket" Carter, and asked if her grandson could join. Ratcliff recalls that YMO "used to have Second Line practice just like Indian practice," referring to the gathering of Black Masking Indian tribes on Sunday evenings during the months before Mardi Gras to rehearse their signature forms of chanting, tambourine playing, and dancing. When I asked what exactly was taught during YMO practices, Ratcliff said that they drilled the formations. In all divisions of YMO members were assigned specific locations in the lineup. One person's role was to "lead the band," or to make sure that each member stayed in his designated location (and levy fines if he strayed). During practice, members rehearsed transitions into and out of various formations. "They come into one line," Ratcliff said. "Break down, put their fans down. All that was taught."[25] Practices helped these groups pass on knowledge of the more traditional aspects of parading with YMO, such as parade formations, even as they tested the boundaries of other traditional performance conventions such as attire, music, and footwork style (listen to the full interview with Ratcliff on this book's web page).

The Mellow Fellows' practices were reminiscent of a Second Line parade itself, with beer, music, and conversation. The party atmosphere did not, however, relieve members of hard work. The spirit of competition drove them to hone their craft, especially when they tried to out-dance a rival club, the Scene Boosters. Not ones to be shown up, the Mellow Fellows were determined to come out the door with their best. In order to earn the respect of their communities, clubs such as the Mellow Fellows must do more than march in crisp lines: Each member must display his or her self-styled repertoire of sophisticated footwork and/or daring stunts. Though improvised, footwork also requires preparation, but that preparation looks different from drilling formations. As Ratcliff put it, the club "taught you the formation, but you pick[ed] up your steps."[26] Multiple kinds of pleasure imbue SAPC practices: community bonding through trial and error, a leisurely approach to work, the thrill of friendly competition, and the satisfaction of knowing that all that practice will pay off with an impressive parade-day performance.

Parading clubs' labor is rewarded with verbal affirmations and encouragement from the sidelines: "Show me what you're working with!" "Footwork!" "Feetwork!" "Knock!" "Roll with it!" As Second Line performances become more and more common on social media networks, the comments sections have become another venue for expressing approval and, more often than in person, disapproval. Along with other modes of passing on dance knowledge, verbal (and now written) feedback is one way in which second liners simultaneously encourage innovation *and* guarantee the continuity of their improvised tradition.[27]

Second liners' descriptions of acquiring and sharing embodied knowledge resonate with Katrina Hazzard-Gordon's summary of learning to dance in Black cultural spaces. Dance ability, she writes, results from long-term "exposure to black working-class experiences at home and in the neighborhood." She goes on to say, "Training in this context is a matter of conditioning. It is informal, but it is training nevertheless. Because the training is so subtle, the outcome often seems like second nature."[28] From backyards to sidewalks to kitchen floors, second liners routinely observe, perfect, and share their dancing. Through mimicking, styling, mentoring, and competing, each generation shares second lining's signature steps, gestures, and rhythms with the next. Along the way, generations also impart the political power of pleasure—the comradery of kinship and friendship, thrill of showmanship, and satisfaction of mastery—that has sustained Black New Orleanians through centuries of struggle. All this and more comprises the nuance contained in Dodie Smith-Simmons' and Tamara Jackson Snowden's assertions that opened this chapter: that, for them, learning to dance was natural.

As should be clear by now, the openness of the do-whatcha-wanna approach doesn't necessarily mean that anything goes when it comes to second lining. Doing what you want leaves plenty of space for friction to arise between groups who hold opposing ideas about the boundaries of the dance form or what kind of embodiment is "right" or "wrong." Because second liners take seriously their collective responsibility to cultivate a balance between aesthetic continuity and innovation, those who alter the music or dance can encounter resistance. The following section looks at one such contentious period of transformation in second lining's long history.

• • •

By the mid-1970s the Second Line season had dwindled to a handful of parades between September and November. Changes in economic, social, and bureaucratic arenas combined to threaten the tradition. For one thing, increased access to medical and life insurance companies made membership in benevolent associations less imperative for Black New Orleanians, which decreased the number of Second Line parades hosted by those organizations.[29] Second, social attitudes toward brass band music were changing. As the promises and fervor of the civil rights movement faded, some African Americans associated traditional jazz with a subservient past that they would rather leave behind.[30] According to the music historian Mick Burns, by the mid-1970s, "The whole neighborhood parade scene was more or less moribund, and most people saw it as increasingly old fashioned and irrelevant."[31] Moreover, disco had taken over the city's prime tourism district, Bourbon Street, replacing live performances with recorded music. Without steady work, several bands broke up, and as older members died, fewer young people picked up a horn. "In just a few short years," writes the clarinetist and historian Michael White, "many bands and musicians who had been highly visible in community parades and funerals rapidly disappeared from the scene."[32] When bands did take to the streets, their music had lost some of its luster for seasoned second liners with their keen ears and rhythmic feet. New Orleans's growing tourism economy prompted musicians to narrow their repertoire to a short list of recognizable standards rather than push new sounds forward in dialogue with second liners on the street.[33] On top of these social and economic shifts, the city steadily increased its regulation, taxation, and policing of parades starting in the mid-1950s (see Chapter 4). Though the new ordinances may not have been uniformly enforced—people recall parades held well into the 1980s that operated without police escorts or time restrictions—the state's intrusion undoubtedly added to the economic and cultural factors that chipped away at a thriving cultural practice.

In response to two related crises—the dying of the brass band tradition and the lack of opportunity for youth—the jazz guitarist Danny Barker started a youth brass band in 1972. The Fairview Baptist Church Brass Band, and other youth bands spearheaded by Barker in the ensuing years, "made brass band music 'cool' for a generation of young people," writes Burns, "and made it commercially viable to have a band consisting mostly of teenagers."[34] At the same time, the civil rights leaders Jerome Smith and Rudy Lombard organized Tambourine and Fan, an organization for children to learn about New Orleans's cultural traditions with an emphasis on Black resistance. Tambourine and Fan's Second Line group, the Bucket Men, inspired a new generation of SAPCs. These two organizations laid the foundation for a movement that Burns has called the "brass band renaissance."[35]

The band almost universally credited for igniting the renaissance is the Dirty Dozen Brass Band, made up mostly of Fairview Brass Band alumni.[36] The Dirty Dozen put themselves on the map during their weekly sets at the Glass House, the small nightclub in New Orleans's uptown Third Ward, or Central City neighborhood. It was there that they, and later the Rebirth Brass Band, played every week for more than a decade. The sonic-kinetic innovations crafted by musicians and dancers at the Glass House from the late 1970s to the early 1990s amounted to a significant revolution in second lining's aesthetics and practice. According to one music producer, the venue was "a pivotal place for the whole new brass band sound to form, to come together."[37] I add that it was a pivotal place for a whole new dance style to form, as well. In fact, musicians and dancers pushed each other to experiment with the boundaries of Second Line music and dance, expanding the two forms interdependently. What has changed in how people second line and what has remained consistent? The Glass House is an appropriate place to pursue an answer to that question. On its tiny dance floor, Black New Orleanians molded Second Line aesthetics to match their experiences of a post–civil rights and late capitalist world but met the moment using enduring methods for creating and sharing embodied Second Line knowledge.

The scene inside the Glass House was recorded one night in 1982 by the folklorist Alan Lomax and his film crew.[38] While panning the crowd, the camera catches its first glimpse of Eddie "Sugar Slim" Durell, whose baby blue polo shirt boasts his name and club affiliation in iron-on letters: "Mellow Fellows" on the front of the shirt, and "Sugar Slim" on the back. Sugar Slim is a legend; musicians and second liners today still speak his name when they list the canon of great Second Line dancers, along with others, many known by their nicknames: Spiderman, Squirky Man,

Swinging Gate, Ice Cream, and Mr. Smith.[39] Oliver "Squirk" (or "Squirky Man") Hunter still attends Second Lines today, but many others are no longer on the scene because of death or incarceration.[40] Their biographies off the dance floor illustrate the enormous social and economic factors delimiting Black life in the 1970s and 1980s in New Orleans. When they were in motion on the dance floor, these men were immersed in a spiritual, pleasurable refuge from the struggles that awaited them outside the door.

In Lomax's footage, Sugar Slim is among the several dancers in full tilt. He shows off some one-footed hopping, constantly bouncing up and down instead of side-to-side. He jumps up and drops to the floor, rebounds to standing, crisscrosses his feet back and forth multiple times, then knocks his knees together in double time. When he returns to focus on footwork, he keeps his torso erect, unlike other men, who pitch their spines forward. When the Dirty Dozen plays "Lickey D Split," several women come into view, stepping on the downbeat, swinging their hips, fanning themselves, and waving a hand in the air—sometimes with a sweaty towel in it. The women, by and large, do not punch out rapid-fire footwork as Sugar Slim does, but there are exceptions. A short young woman wearing a yellow polo shirt, shorts, scrunched-up socks, and white tennis shoes dances next to him. The camera zooms in on her feet. She scoots them percussively, on the quarter notes, without lifting them off the ground. She glides her heel out to the side and back to the front on the eighth notes and finishes with a one-footed move that is still popular today: hopping on the weight-bearing foot and swinging the free leg back and forth, hinging from the knee (see video of dancing at the Glass House on this book's web page).[41]

A call-and-response style of competition drove innovation at the Glass House, where musicians and dancers infused their sonic-kinetic conversations with friendly dares. According to Dirty Dozen trumpeter and bandleader Gregory "Blodie" Davis, patrons challenged the band with their dancing:

> They'd do some steps, and we'd have to say, "OK, now you top this. We'll play something." The next week, we'd have something new for them to try and top what we were doing. It was a competitive kind of thing. So not only did the music change, but the style of second lining and buck jumping changed also, along with what we were doing. Now that I look back on it, I can see the development, whereas when I was in it, I wasn't really paying attention to what was happening.[42]

Responding to these challenges, dancers and musicians pushed each other to accelerate the tempo, punch up the energy, and take bolder risks. Their efforts resulted in at least two kinesthetic "developments," to use Davis's word. First, second lining's marching style of footwork sped up dramatically to emerge as an airborne heel-to-toe step. This change emerged in tandem with the music's increased tempo. Dirty Dozen saxophonist Roger Lewis related, "We slightly picked up the beat, which made people dance faster. Now if you come to a Second Line where the Dirty Dozen playing, make sure you have your tennis shoes on and your jogging suit because you going to get a good workout. I mean you going to sweat, we going to make you sweat!"[43] Speaking in 2020, Keep-N-It Real SAPC president Perry Franklin still remembered how fast he had to dance in order to keep up. 'We caught the bands at the Glass House. The Dirty Dozen wasn't nothing nice to play with. The dancers had to be fast. They'll cut you up if you come in there slow, jack."[44] Glass House dancers whipped up intricate footwork patterns in time with accelerated tempos, and in turn, challenged musicians to match the speed and rhythmic sophistication of their densely packed combinations. Over time, previous generations' grounded step-touch morphed into a jackhammer bounce. Roger Lewis referred to a dancer who went by the nickname Mr. Smith as an exemplar of this newer, faster footwork. It required an impressive mastery of a grounded-yet-lifted posture to divide one's upper and lower body. "Now if you look at him, he's standing up straight, right?" Lewis recalled. "And his body, this part of his body [torso] is just straight. But the other part of his body is moving. It really, I mean it was like really freaky!"[45]

The increased tempo supported the second kinesthetic innovation in second lining: The dance's emphasis on footwork, which makes sense for a processional form, became punctuated with full-body, athletic, even acrobatic moves referred to as *buckjumping*. The term's origins are contested but may have roots in nineteenth-century buck dancing, golden-age brass bands' competitions, which were known as bucking contests, or the equestrian term for a horse throwing off its rider, now used to express the dance's vitality and intensity.[46] *Buckjumping* is still used by second liners today to refer to a quality of heightened energy in dancing rather than to a particular step. Efrem Townes, another trumpeter with the Dirty Dozen, praised a group of Glass House dancers who

> used to do some dances with the music, and whoooo, their knees were parallel to their chin! It was a very physical form of dancing, but it was beautiful to watch because they coincided the dancing with everything we played. You were actually relating to someone, speaking to them, and they would respond to it by persuading their body to do different things.[47]

This "very physical form of dancing" came to be called buckjumping, and it provides a concrete example of versioning, especially in its alignment

Dancers move to the Dirty Dozen Brass Band at the Glass House. (Photograph by Michael P. Smith ©The Historic New Orleans Collection, acc. no. 2007.0103.4.330.)

with youthful innovation. "In terms of dance," DeFrantz writes, "new versions of existing forms typically offer heightened physical risk,"[48] as was the case with buckjumping at the Glass House.

Davis's and Townes's memories of dialoguing and competing with dancers suggest that the musicians and movers inside the Glass House made something new with very old tools, namely, call-and-response and competition. This venue provides a poignant example of what the scholar Paul Gilroy has called a "changing same." Challenging the way tradition is commonly seen, namely as a safeguard against change, Gilroy charts the ways in which traditions of the African diaspora are constantly remade (or versioned) according to the changing identities of participants. Furthermore, traditions themselves are instrumental in continually remaking individual and collective identities.[49] A new generation of musicians and dancers developed a version of their tradition that expressed their identities, especially as they differed from previous generations. Their lightning-fast footwork reflected the increased speed of capital exchange that came with the onset of late capitalism and globalization in the second half of the twentieth century. Their space-eating, in-your-face style of buckjumping eschewed tenets of respectable self-comportment that had been eroding since the late 1960s. Their intense uses of time and space captured, and were at times fueled by, the prevalence of synthetic drugs.[50] Changes in the local music and dance scene paralleled a wider cultural shift that gave rise to funk music and dance, since both styles offered an alternative to the assimilation-minded efforts of black pop music and traditional jazz.[51] Like funk, the new style of Second Line music and dance reflected "both the optimism and disillusionment of African Americans in the struggle for racial equality."[52]

As a changing same, the emerging version of second lining's practice indicated and even advanced shifts in social values and group identity occurring globally, nationally, and locally. The names of SAPCs established (or, in the case of the Money Wasters, re-established) during this time reflect evolving values—Men and Lady Buckjumpers (elaborate dance performance), Money Wasters (material extravagance)—and enduring ones—Avenue Steppers (ownership of the streets) and Sudan (Black pride).[53] New Orleans author James Borders IV links the reinvigoration expressed by buckjumpers to a feeling of political possibility in the city. "When [Ernest] Dutch Morial was elected" as the city's first Black mayor in 1977 "and the Dirty Dozen started hyping up the crowds outside the Glass House" that same year, "the new New Orleans was born," he writes. "There was good reason to dance in the streets again. It was a glorious moment."[54]

Not everyone shared Borders's enthusiasm. Some elders and others with an affinity for traditional music criticized the Dirty Dozen for sullying the brass band repertoire with bebop and popular music. Gregory Davis recalled an incident in which the band was playing a fundraising gig at the Sanger Theater in the French Quarter. Someone in the audience, a member of an SAPC (Davis doesn't recall which one), felt inspired to join them onstage, and while dancing, suffered a fatal heart attack. As Davis experienced it, this incident provided some Dirty Dozen critics with proof that their tempos were dangerously fast. "I would hope it was just his time to go on to glory," Davis reflected. "We've been given credit for sending him on, but I don't think that was our intent," he added with levity. "But it was that some of the people were saying, 'Oh that's too fast, you can't do this.'"[55] Pleas to slow down can be understood in more ways than one. The band's massive popularity threatened to overturn in a year what took a century to build.

Davis remembers that as late as the 1960s, second lining remained the provenance of older, more restrained dancers. "By the time I was seeing Second Lines as a five- or six-year-old kid [1962 or 1963]," he recalled, "it was people in at least their forties participating. They were a more reserved style of dancing, compared to what these guys were doing in the '70s at the Glass House."⁵⁶ Before buckjumpers took over the scene, second lining had been characterized as "stepping," which allowed dancers to move playfully yet gracefully in time with the moderate tempos of brass band songs that were popular in the first half of the twentieth century. In the 1940s and 1950s, jazz music was becoming detached from dance, broadly speaking, but it retained that connection in New Orleans, in part because of the Second Line tradition.⁵⁷ New Orleans's robust rhythm and blues industry, which produced multiple homegrown stars and hosted bands that toured on the Chitlin' Circuit, nourished mid-century parading practices with the flavor of popular styles.⁵⁸ Speaking of second lining during this period, Joe Glasper, a member of Jolly Bunch S&PC (established 1941), proclaimed, "We weren't 'buckers,' we were 'steppers' then. We could dance to any tunes they (the brass bands) would play without getting all sweaty."⁵⁹ Ronald W. Lewis, president of the Big Nine SAPC, concurred: "Back then, the movement of the people was more flowing. They had a suavey type of style to the dance."⁶⁰ Suavey stepping allowed dancers to incorporate innumerable social dances as they changed with the times, weaving the Bop and the Bunny Hop, for example, into a step-touch. Stepping relied on the feet, freeing up the hands to hold traditional props (known as "decorations" when featured in SAPC parade-day attire) such as umbrellas or handkerchiefs. Buckers prefer more functional terrycloth towels.

For Jerome Smith, a notable civil rights activist, the new sounds and moves erupting at the Glass House represented a kind of "dislinkage" (his word) between these aesthetics and the histories they carried. Concurrent with the Dirty Dozen's rise, Smith was spearheading the Tambourine and Fan Club (discussed in Chapter 4) to revive young people's interest in Black cultural traditions. Speaking in 2002, Smith expressed concern about the developments in dance that had taken place since advent of the Dirty Dozen. Smith saw the entire tradition as emanating from the Christian church's rituals and protocols, even when a Second Line was not directly connected to a funeral, church group, or religious function. As he witnessed the church become less central to the social fabric of younger generations, he also saw the form of Second Line dancing change, noting,

> The dancing changed because it's conditioned by another kind of social approach; there's been a rupture in the protocols. . . . Now, because youngsters are not church based, in terms of dealing with the rituals, that makes for a certain kind of emotional projection. So the dance has changed—it hasn't lost the energy but certain kind of grace and dignity.⁶¹

Smith noticed that the change in dance signaled a society that was changing and, from his point of view, not for the better. The "dignity" Smith no longer saw in 2002 might have been expressed in the upright, smooth, flowing footwork of steppers such as Joe Glasper and Ronald Lewis. The transition from stepping to bucking represented, for Smith, the breakdown of support institutions such as the church.

At the same time, as the institutions of Christian churches and secret society lodges became less central to the Second Line culture, so did patriarchal control. Beginning in the mid-to-late 1970s, women began carving out spaces for their own participation on the dance floor and in the procession. Before that time, women's participation in brass band parades consisted mainly of riding ceremoniously in cars as members of a male club's royal court or marching with children in church-organized Sunday school parades.[62] (The Ladies Zulu SAPC, established in 1933, stands out as an exception. Footage of their 1965 parade, which features several club members grinding and shaking, cautions against any totalizing statement about chaste dancing by women before the Dirty Dozen era.[63]) Women's groups began to form with the explicit purpose of dancing in the streets. Barbara Lacen Keller, who was active in SAPCs at the time, recalls that the Scene Boosters started a women's division called the Fun Lovers, and the Calliope Steppers introduced their women's division, the Jet Setters. But according to Lacen Keller (corroborated by fellow parader Lois Nelson), it was the Lady Money Wasters who first paraded independently.[64] "We wasn't attached to the men," she said, referring to the all-male Money Wasters SAPC. "A separate day. Separate permit, everything." Lacen Keller remembers that these new women's groups were supported by the established male SAPCs and the community at large.

> They [the women] knew how to dance, and they just wanted to dance! And the men, and the culture felt, "Ok, that's all right!" You know, because the Second Line is out here dancing, the women [are in the Second Line], so why not have a women's division [in the main line]? . . . Because it wasn't a thing where [the women] was challenging anyone.

When I asked Lacen Keller if the women's liberation movement influenced this development, she acknowledged the possibility but downplayed the movement's significance, implying its whiteness.

> But you gotta understand, especially in the African American community, it wasn't about women being liberated. I think it wasn't that, "Well, we gonna show 'em." And, because, as I told you, what's so unique about this culture is how we love each other, how we support each other. Case in point, I remember that same year, the Lady Money Wasters, when we had our first parade, we were late, we were behind in getting our stuff done. I remember that morning, how all these men came to my

house, and helping us getting everything together, for us to make it on the street. You know, so that was a sense of togetherness. [They said,] "Even though you're going out by yourself, we're still here, we're gonna help you. We gonna help you get on the street by yourself." So, I think it seems different to liberate.... I don't think in the culture that's what we were doing, I think what we wanted to do, even though we were part of it, we still wanted to show you we could do it on our own, too. In our own way.

Lacen Keller's position reflects a womanist (as opposed to feminist) point of view. *Womanist* was defined by Alice Walker as a Black woman "committed to survival and wholeness of entire people, male and female. Not a separatist."[65] The historian Janet Allured, in her history of second-wave feminism in Louisiana, observes that Black women who advocated feminist goals in the South "were not much interested in separatism of any kind, either racial or gender."[66] She goes on to note that, in Louisiana, Black women activists supported women's rights not by organizing explicitly on behalf of feminist causes but by working within community uplift or social service organizations such as churches, service-oriented sororities, and the Urban League; one could add SAPCs to that list.[67] When Lacen Keller insisted that Black women weren't looking to be liberated from the men and emphasized the support of Black men in their efforts to establish women's equality within the Money Wasters, she presented an example of the larger sociocultural landscape of Black feminism or womanism within Louisiana in the 1970s and 1980s.

Since the 1970s women have, more and more, claimed spaces for themselves in the shifting landscape of the Second Line scene. The importance of buckjumping for women in this era was reflected in the new SAPC that Lacen Keller joined shortly after its inception in 1984: the Original New Orleans Lady Buckjumpers, created in conjunction with the Original Men Buckjumpers. The fact that the club named itself after buckjumping signaled the rising prominence of a new form of second lining; more generally, it indicated that social standards for bodily comportment were changing. As female second liners such as the Lady Buckjumpers traded in their polite marching in Sunday school parades for vigorous footwork, they eschewed racialized and gendered standards for bodily behavior according to which African American women should perform "church-endorsed modesty and middle-class aesthetics."[68]

One aspect of the change that was afoot was evidenced by Glass House dancers' embrace of sweat as a positive attribute. When the Dirty Dozen's Roger Lewis promised that the band would "make you sweat," he nodded to sweat as an indication of success.⁶⁹ Today, all clubs are expected to "come out clean," but those who ascribe value to sweat praise a destroyed appearance at the end of the parade as evidence of having done it right. If you still have energy (not to mention clean clothes and intact shoes) at the end of the Second Line, then you haven't given it your all. Club members trade tips for replacing the sodium lost to sweat, such as drinking pickle juice to sustain themselves throughout a four-hour parade. Sweat indexes the communal values of endurance, virtuosity, a refusal to hold back, and a prioritization of physical exertion over appearance. Those who come to sweat prefer the up-tempo music influenced by the Dirty Dozen. The result is a flavor of footwork that remains popular with several generations of second liners today. Yet Glass House devotees' positive association with sweat clashed with members of previous generations of second liners, such as Joe Glasper, who boasted that he could dance to bands "without getting all sweaty."

Divergent appraisals of sweat give one example of the friction that can result when a new generation of practitioners tests the boundaries of a musical or dance form. As the anthropologist Anna Tsing explains, however, friction doesn't only limit progress by slowing it down. Friction also enables forward movement, much as friction on the road enables a wheel to turn (or, to borrow second-liners' parlance, to roll).⁷⁰ The productive friction between the traditionalists and innovators in this period produced a spectrum of approaches to second-lining, from preservationist to trendsetting, which ultimately invited a much broader range of Black New Orleanians to see themselves as part of it. As the ethnomusicologist Matt Sakakeeny writes, the arguments and alliances that erupt within diverse sets of musicians and SAPC members create the kind of productive friction that Tsing theorizes, ensuring that Second Line tradition remains relevant.⁷¹

A noticeable shift in embodied Second Line aesthetics certainly occurred during the 1970s and 1980s, and the lasting influence of movement that developed in tandem with the Dirty Dozen's sound can still be seen at every parade today. Even so, it is important not to claim that this period was the only era of invention in second lining's history. Another way to understand the story of the Dirty Dozen and the Glass House is to see the very fact of innovation as an enduring value held by the Second Line community. In 1960 the jazz trumpeter Punch Miller noted the similarities between the ratty dancing of the ragtime era ("guys squatting to the floor and coming up shaking") to what people did at parades in his time.⁷² Miller's recollection troubles a neat history of Second Line dancing that would trace it from the dignity of nineteenth-century racial uplift to the wild buckjumping of the post–civil rights era and reminds readers that, long before buckjumpers came on the scene, New Orleanians were already dropping and shaking to early forms of jazz. In second lining's nascent years, a range of movements and of cultural values was on display. A linear history of the shift from stepping to jumping is further complicated by the fact that heel-to-toe footwork styles bear a strong resemblance to descriptions of footwork executed by male dancers in Congo Square and harkens back to shuffling, jigging, and buck dancing of the nineteenth century.

Wynton Marsalis, one of New Orleans's best-known jazz musicians, describes the nonlinear temporality of continuity and change in the Second Line in this way: "Musicians are improvising, and dancers are improvising. And they're doing something they've been doing a long time. So they have to feel it, not only as this moment—here's something that never happened—it's a moment that's always happened."[73] In other words, second lining is neither an exact replication of codified steps nor something devoid of technique or history. Although each step "has never happened" before, it is recognizable to second liners because they have seen it many times before. The dance that has never happened is the moment of improvisation, in which the dancer gives shape to herself.[74] She reiterates the dance that has "always happened," calling on her experiences to do the moves she knows, but with her own approach, timing, and combination of steps.[75] The satisfaction, joy, and thrill of self-expression achieved by improvised footwork is so deeply felt precisely because the dance is the result of generations of transmission, connecting the dancer to place and history.

In a 2021 interview Jazz Henry, a trumpeter with the all-female Pinettes Brass Band and member of the Footwerk Family SAPC, described the dance that's never happened and has always happened in her own words:

> These moves that we doing today is recycled. Like, these people been doing these moves. My grandpa could do a split. I can't even do a split. And he's 70 years old! So you know, like, this stuff is not new. We just made it modern. Like, you know, we switched it up, gave it a little spice, funked it up a little bit, and you know, that's what it is. But it's not a competition.... It's about having fun and doing what you want to do![76]

Henry gives shape to a history and set of cultural values while putting her own spin on it all (literally). By expanding the boundaries of the tradition to make room for herself, with a reverence for those who came before her and a do-whatcha-wanna attitude, she ensures that its aesthetics, histories, and values endure.

• • •

In B-roll footage of Alan Lomax's night at the Glass House in 1982, the folklorist asks patrons about the dance they do, including the names of the steps (to which he gets responses that range from "the traditional Second Line" to "disco"). Perhaps trying to connect Second Line footwork to the ring shout, he asks one woman, "I heard that if you crossed your feet when dancing you'd get kicked out of church. Is that still true?" She smiles incredulously, "No, no, you just do what you feel. That's all."[77] Lomax got a do-whatcha-wanna response as he tried to dig up ethnographic details for his documentary film. When I saw this clip, I nodded in recognition. I had been there, too. Over time, I came to understand such responses to inquiries like Lomax's and my own as part of a discourse that privileges the dancing's function over its form, or the *why* over the *how*.[78] It indicates that practitioners value dancing as a vehicle for communing with others and for catching the spirit, not as a storehouse of aesthetic technique.

Precisely because this attitude keeps the focus on the why, it supplies an effective response to outsider inquiries into the how. As a white newcomer to the Second Line scene, my desire to learn the technique inevitably evoked histories of colonial theft. As I have discussed elsewhere, being told to do what I wanted in my quest for the how of second-lining can be understood as a form of anticolonial resistance against white people's assumptions that all cultures are theirs to know.[79] Although it is relatively easy for newcomers and tourists to join a parade, learning to perform the specific repertoire of steps is much harder. When asking for tips, a newcomer might be told, "Just do whatcha wanna"—and this is a powerful response. Even if I were able to master second lining's form, my practice would never be grounded in a lived experience of Black life, nor in an expression of generations-old community networks.

Do-whatcha-wanna discourses could be viewed as an expression of "opacity," a term developed by the Caribbean-born post-colonial poet and philosopher Édouard Glissant. According to Glissant, Europeans and Euro-Americans insist on a right to fully understand Afro-Caribbean cultures (Second Line culture falls under this banner) and do not accept that some cultural practices are complex enough that an outsider (or perhaps even an insider) could never grasp them in their totality. He writes,

> If we look at the process of "understanding" beings and ideas as it operates in western society, we find that it is founded on an insistence on this kind of transparency. In order to "understand" and therefore accept

you, I must reduce your density to this scale of conceptual measurement which gives me a basis for comparisons and perhaps for judgments.[80]

In a colonialist formulation, "understanding" constructs the Other as an object of knowledge and. In turn, a refusal to be known can function as resistance.[81] If viewed in its historical and political contexts, do-whatcha-wanna discourse appears as a gesture of opacity. When dance lessons remain on kitchen tile instead of studio Marley, and when documentarians' requests for descriptions are met with, "Just do what you feel," New Orleanians protect second lining's embodied expressions in a layer of opacity, refusing to Other their tradition by offering it up for analysis and consumption. That includes my own misguided attempts to get at the specifics of footwork technique with a Eurocentric, studio-trained approach. The second liners with whom I spoke were not necessarily being ungenerous or deceptive; their viewpoint is best understood not as a rationale for conscious individual actions but rather as a cultural philosophy that manifests in discourse and infrastructure.[82]

Do-whatcha-wanna remains a potent strategy to use in the post-Katrina and post–post-Katrina city, where more tourists and white or new residents than ever are joining weekly Second Line parades. In Katrina's wake, waves of newcomers, myself included, moved in and inflated the housing market. In 2015, ten years after the hurricane and floods, one hundred thousand African Americans remained displaced from New Orleans, without the resources to return even if they wanted to. As a result, the city became smaller, whiter, and wealthier than before the storm.[83] By espousing do-whatcha-wanna, paraders simultaneously retain the Second Line's ethos of inclusiveness and ground their practice in Black social and ritual spaces, even when non-Black dancers enter those spaces. They maintain ownership of cultural knowledge within the community and reinforce the importance of the informal settings where that knowledge is shared, from kitchen floors to nightclubs and neighborhood streets.

When second lining's embodied knowledge is transmitted and debated so are the social values and cultural identities attached to it. The ethnomusicologist Kyra D. Gaunt insists that "black identity has been specifically constituted through experience," namely embodied musical experience.[84] As illustrated by the stories above, the experiences that construct second-liners' identities extend well beyond each Sunday parade; they grow within a system of family, friends, and neighbors. Gaunt evokes such a network, going beyond identity to speak of belonging. "Musical blackness," she writes, "is an imagined 'home,' . . . a *learned* place of inhabitance; an *embodied* dwelling." Creating home via shared musical experiences within

Black social spaces is necessary, she argues, because African Americans perpetually confront "a kind of 'homelessness' in this so-called New World dominated by descendants of Europeans."[85] Gaunt is speaking figuratively, positing homelessness as a state that recalls African Americans' continual marginalization in the United States. But her figuration is powerful when considered in the more literal context of homelessness that resulted for African Americans after Katrina through displacement to other locales and the skyrocketing number of unhoused people within the city. By means of do-whatcha-wanna attitudes and discourse, Black New Orleanians construct home in the sense of belonging. Chapter 6 looks at the ways in which second liners not only leverage the politics of pleasure to create a felt sense of home but also fight for their material homes.

Nicole Lazard executes her signature high-heeled footwork while parading with the Single Men SAPC on March 19, 2017. (Photo by MJ Mastrogiovanni.)

INTERLUDE

Nicole Lazard

September 7, 2017

Nicole Lazard might hold the title for paying dues to the largest number of SAPCs at one time, parading with as many as six different clubs within the span of a few short years. Lazard's mother, one of the few women who scaled rooftops to dance above the crowd, a move usually performed by men, introduced her to second lining as a child in the 1970s, but her adult involvement had to wait until 2003, after she finished several tours with the army. While deployed overseas, she brought brass band music with her and taught her fellow soldiers a little footwork so that she could second line with a collective. Once she returned to New Orleans Lazard followed in her mother's footsteps, but with a twist: She limits her aerial moves to dancing in high-heeled shoes, a preference she developed after all those years of dancing in army boots.

My name is Nicole Lazard [On] 8/14/69, I was born in New Orleans, Louisiana....

[I got into second lining] through my mom and my . . . uncle. . . . They used to go every Sunday. And I used to be at church, so when I got out of church, [the parades] used to be passing in front of the church, and I wanted to go, but then my dad used to tell us, "No, you can't go, it's dangerous out there," stuff like that. So I'd just go back home, and then I'd hear the band sometimes on a Sunday when church wasn't let out, and me and my friend, we'll go dip out there and dance on the porch of the church and go back in. [*laughs*] That was uptown. So I don't know which parade it was, but every Sunday a parade would pass down Washington Avenue and stuff, but we'll be at the church, and we'll sneak out there and go. It was a Baptist church on Washington Avenue.

My Mom Used to Get on Top of Buildings

And I just danced at family functions and stuff; I would never go to the Second Lines when I was younger. Because of [what] my father said.
RACHEL CARRICO: Mm-hmm. And you said he said it's dangerous out there. . . .
NICOLE LAZARD: Only reason he said that is because my mom used to get on top of buildings and all of these things, and she fell one time, and she broke her wrist. So she came home holding her wrist, I remember this, and we had to go take her to the hospital. I remember this. Then, you know, the next Sunday, she went back out there, with the cast on.

"She's Dancing in Heels!"

RC: So, you belong to many social aid and pleasure clubs, currently, and have even more in the past.
NL: Yes.
RC: What was the first one that you joined?
NL: CTC [Cross the Canal] Steppers. . . . I joined them in 2003, yes. . . . Because my cousin actually belongs to that club. So I just was like, I joined that club but I didn't join that club. I just go to all they functions and things, but I didn't parade with them until 2006, actually. So I just—yes, the year after Katrina, I actually paraded with them.

The first parade I rolled as a maid [honorary royalty on a float], actually, but then the next year I hit the street with them. It was just beautiful, because I wore the pretty dress and everything as a maid, and I'm just sitting up there [on the float] and I'm just like, "I gotta get down, I gotta get down." So they was like, "You can't get down! You gotta look cute up there!" I was like, "I don't wanna look cute. I wanna be on the ground, I wanna be on the ground, cause I'm just feeling—" because they had the Stooges Brass Band playing behind me, and I'm like, "Oh, I'm ready to go, I'm ready to go!"[1] So then finally, like three blocks before the end, they let all the maids and the queen down, I raised that dress up and I'm working out, and it was like, "She's dancing in heels!" I'm like, "I'm not supposed to dance in heels?" So I'm just, like, rocking the heels, because that's what I was used to working and dancing in. It was like . . ."No, you can't be a maid, you can't be a queen; you have to be out there dancing." So the next year, that's how I paraded.

. . .

RC: Ok, so the next year, you were on the streets—
NL: Yes, I was on the street. And we actually wore burgundy that year, yes. We had on—because all the women couldn't wear heels. I wanted the heels, so at least I had to go with the majority. So we had some little box heels and things. And I broke the heel off, and it was a box

heel, I said, "How I don't break the stilettos but I break the box?" They said, "You were really working it."

...

I prefer heels. Because when I get off work, I put on heels, all the time. So I go out, I'm wearing heels. Flats hurt my feet. So it's like, I can dance in all type of shoes, but I feel more comfortable in heels, like I have more stability. I don't know why, people's like, that's crazy. I dance in the flip-flops. I figure with dancing, you have to be universal, be able to change costumes. And so, I prefer the heels. And I feel, you know when you put on heels, you got to be upright. So I just want to be upright. Cause tennis shoes, you know, like sitting at your desk, you be like, all grumpy. So, I just love the heels! It seem like I can do more in the heels. I test 'em out first. Have to test 'em out first. Yeah, you got to test them out. So I can only bounce on my heels a little bit, depends on how wide the heels are. But if I have on a wedge heel or something, I can get all the way on the heel, so you know when you change the shoes, your style of dancing changes.... You have about five people that I know that can get down, they can go from the heels to the tennis shoes, you can do the flip-flops—they gonna work 'em. And you'll see 'em work them heels even harder.

...

The next club [I joined] was VIP Ladies. So I paraded with them. So that was uptown! So I started from Cross the Canal, then I came uptown. And people's like, "You can't do that!" I'm like, "Why I can't do that?" They were like, "How you gonna go from Cross the Canal [to] uptown?" I said, "I was born and raised uptown." "Well, why you didn't start uptown?" "Because my cousin asked me to come downtown, so that's what I did." "When?" So it was like, when you can't—no, it was like, "It's my money; I'm gonna spend my money where I want to spend my money." And that's what I did. And I paraded with them for two years.

So now I'm currently with Single Ladies,.... I've been with [them] for the past four years. That's uptown. Then I went to Single Men, and that was where Richard Anderson called me up and asked me to come parade with him. So that was two years ago. So I paraded with him that year, he asked was I coming back the next year, and I paraded with him, because it's only one female, one young girl, Terrylyn Dorsey, she parades with them, and then myself. I'm the only other lady that parades with them.

So then I have Valley of Silent Men; I parade with them for the past years [since 2016]. I'm the first woman, they said I made history to parade with them. I'm the only woman. But I got involved with them because of Mr. Leon Anderson Sr. He's deceased now. He was part of YMO [Young Men Olympian Jr. Benevolent Association], and he told me, "Oh, I remember your uncle, and your mom, and all that." He said,

"Young lady, you gonna do great things in this Second Line world." I'm like, "I'm just having fun." He say, "That's the thing: have fun what you do." He said, "Block out everything else; just have fun." So when his son [Leon "Smurf" Anderson Jr. was] like, "You come and parade with me?" Right, yup. And they was just like, "Yes, yes!" Everybody just like, "My daddy smiling down on you, 'cause"—and I posted [on social media]—he said, "Now you work out and have fun, young lady," cause that's what he always tell me, every time I come out and parade he come out and see me, and that's what he tells me.

Bridging the Gap

So, my final club, that's in December, New Generation. So, he used to have a big group, I was their queen in 2008. So, then I always found, because I had a relative with them, so then, when he lost all his members, it was just him, they were calling him the one-man gang. I remember, the first person to parade by themselves, pay for the whole thing. So it was him. So, now it's him and I.

All those clubs are uptown, except CTC, mm-hmm. So when you see my thing, you always see "Uptown Girl" on the back [of my streamer]. When I paraded with CTC, I always had "Uptown Girl" on the back. They was like, "Hey, you can't wear that decoration," I'm like, "Yeah, I'm an uptown girl." So when I, my family did t-shirts, . . . I put on there, "Bridging the gap." So I had on there, UPT and CTC, and I had a bridge, and I had me splitting on it, on the t-shirt. [*Carrico laughs*] I was bridging the gap. Because people from uptown only wanna parade uptown, people from downtown only wanna parade—so, my money spends anywhere. So that's what I do.

CHAPTER 6

Home

Uptown Swingers. Pigeon Town Steppers. Calliope High Steppers. These three Second Line parading organizations proclaim their members' geographic affiliations within New Orleans's archipelago of fiercely proud neighborhoods. Specifically, these three SAPCs hail from uptown or upriver of Canal Street, a main thoroughfare bordering the French Quarter and slicing a route from the Mississippi River to Lake Pontchartrain. The name of the Calliope High Steppers, who stopped parading before Hurricane Katrina in 2005, signaled their home base in the now-extinct Calliope public housing development. Two clubs located downtown (downriver of Canal Street) also began in public housing developments: the Nine Times SAPC (Desire, Ninth Ward) and the Original Big Seven SAPC (St. Bernard, Seventh Ward, discussed in detail below). As these last two examples show, some clubs' names refer to their wards or districts. The Ninth Ward alone has given rise to the Big Nine and the retired Double Nine. The Cross the Canal Steppers specifically claim the Lower Ninth Ward, across the Industrial Canal. The Dumaine Street Gang places itself even more hyperlocally, on a main drag in the Sixth Ward, or Tremé, neighborhood. The Westbank Steppers' name lets everyone know that parades even roll across the Mississippi River, far from more well-trodden Second Line geographies.

When a club hosts its annual Second Line parade, the organization's name appears prominently embroidered on the banner carried at the front of the procession and on the finery worn and held by club members such as sashes (known as streamers) and feathered fans. Second liners proclaim their allegiances to New Orleans's geographies not only in club names but also via song and dance. As weekly parades wind through the streets, a familiar chant often ripples through the crowd: "Way-y-y-y-y uptown!"

if parading above Canal Street or "Way-y-y-y-y downtown!" if below. No matter which SAPC is parading or where its route takes the crowd, second liners often place individuals according to dancing style. Buckjumping is commonly associated with uptown dancers and intricate footwork with downtown, the Sixth Ward in particular. These associations shift depending on who is dancing, who is assessing, and which neighborhood or neighborhoods they call home. By means of naming practices, improvisational chanting, and dance choices, second liners produce a multidimensional sense of home during every parade.

Anthropologists and other scholars of the Second Line frequently remark on the parades' place-making function. Marginalized residents have, since the early twentieth century, harnessed Second Lines to stage democratic, public ownership of place.[1] Helen A. Regis argues that Second Lines transform the city from its quotidian order of spatial apartheid by musically altering the atmosphere to create an alternative social and moral order of conviviality, solidarity, and collective ownership.[2] Not all second liners own homes or businesses, but they all collectively own the streets for four hours a week. These "temporary claims of ownership," argues Joyce Marie Jackson, "offer a modicum of cultural power."[3] In a city (in a country, in a world) where being Black in public is often criminalized, policed by both law enforcement's mandate to stop and frisk and by middle-class opposition to public congregation in gentrifying neighborhoods, Second Lines refuse to comply with hegemonic uses of public urban space.[4] Regis and Rachel Breunlin suggest that Second Lines forward alternative notions of place value and land ownership rooted in cultural citizenship rather than private property.[5] As Zada Johnson and others have shown, competing definitions of ownership took on particular potency in a post-Katrina context. Second Line parades contested exclusionary policies that prevented African American residents from returning home.[6]

This chapter builds on previous scholarship to consider how second liners claim ownership of and belonging to New Orleans by making specific choices about where, how, and with whom to move. When they interact with the built environment, either during street parades or inside music venues, they engage in what the Black feminist geographer Katherine McKittrick calls "saying place." Saying place involves poetic, affective efforts to "own" a place, such as dancing in it. McKittrick suggests that, in order to imagine Black geographies, one must think outside the colonialist, capitalist value of material ownership and reimagine what it means to own and belong.[7] By saying place, second liners not only expand notions of land ownership beyond capitalist logics but also enact modes of belonging that exceed legal categories of citizenship. In the United States, where the legacy of chattel slavery long endured in laws that anchored property ownership to citizenship,[8] African Americans' poetic modes of material possession make possible creative modes of claiming full citizenship. Dance is a powerful tool for both. The dance scholar Yvonne Daniel writes that citizenship forms the social meaning of all African diasporic dance, that is, if citizenship is taken at its most essential meaning: the process of belonging to a group. By dancing together, in place, diasporic subjects negotiate belonging—a process that the anthropologist and dancer Aimee Meredith Cox calls "choreographing citizenship"—by solidifying community identity and showing concern about authority.[9] Second liners say place and choreograph citizenship, claiming New Orleans's streets and structures as their rightful ancestral and spiritual homes. Their footwork says, in effect, "This place belongs to me, and I belong here."

• • •

The procession itself is a way of saying place and choreographing citizenship. Related to its spiritual functions (discussed in Chapter 3), the procession is a mapping technology that links multiple locales together in a sonic-kinetic narrative. It enacts a ritual journey whose references can include local knowledge, such as one SAPC's annually repeated route, and can evoke larger histories of journeying, such as the forced migrations required by Hurricane Katrina and even the Middle Passage.[10] Along the parade route, each club chooses periodic stops in locations that honor and solidify living social connections between the club members and their networks. Many SAPCs will "give a stop" to a parading club at someone's house or business or even on a street corner. The club giving the stop provides food and drink to the parading SAPC members and musicians, frequently advertising its role by decorating the location with banners and flags and by wearing T-shirts bearing their club's insignia.[11] When the parade pauses at local establishments, especially barrooms, it honors long-term relationships between club members and business owners in the community.[12] Sometimes the place is owned by a club member, as is the case when Keep-N-It Real SAPC's Second Line concludes at President Perry Franklin's bar, Good Times II. Other pauses occur at the site of a fallen club member or other loved one to memorialize the person's life with a brief remembrance. After the procession concludes—horns laid down, ropes re-spooled—the experience of ritual journeying continues to impact the way physical landscapes are lived. Parades inhabit areas that have been abandoned because of government policies and economic investments, or where development plans have displaced African American residents. By inviting bodily performance, they transform these locales into sites of

Black pleasure: spiritual transcendence, community building, reverent remembrance, and joyful celebration.

Parade routes, including resting stops and memorial sites, accrue layers of meaning when the same streets are traversed and locations visited during multiple Second Lines throughout one season, and when repeated year after year. A map of all thirty-nine Second Line routes in the 2011–2012 season, published in *Unfathomable City: A New Orleans Atlas*, reveals that some streets, such as South Claiborne Avenue and Louisiana Avenue uptown and Broad Avenue and St. Bernard Avenue downtown, are repeatedly pounded with dancing feet.[13] Because most clubs retain the basic pathways of their routes from year to year, one can imagine that grooves might wear into the pavement, literally imprinting local memories into the landscape, were the streets and sidewalks not periodically resurfaced. Instead, repetition inscribes ritual pathways into the memories and bodies of second liners, re-spatializing imaginary if not immanent landscapes through repeated ritual performance.[14] Over time, second liners imprint experiences onto the social, cultural, and spiritual landscapes of their lives. Their footprints, in turn, re-spatialize New Orleans's working-class and working-poor neighborhoods as places worth celebrating and remembering by amplifying the community's ancestral, social, and spiritual attachments to them.

· · ·

One of the most dramatic ways in which second liners claim home is by dancing ten to twenty feet in the air. At nearly every Sunday Second Line, at least a few paraders dance atop buildings, balconies, parked vehicles, billboard trellises, or the shoulder of the raised interstate (see video of second liners dancing aloft in video 6.1 on this book's web page). Rooftop dancing has been a mainstay of Second Line choreographies since at least the 1970s. It was then that one adventurous second liner earned the moniker "Spiderman" for frequently scaling buildings. Alan Lomax's *Jazz Parades*, filmed in the early 1980s, features footage of Spiderman and other second liners dancing atop cars and clinging to telephone poles.[15] Some members of the Dirty Dozen Brass Band, who were playing many parades in that period, surmised that he was the first person to dance atop elevated structures during a parade.[16] Spiderman may not have been the first person to attempt such a feat—for example, footage from a 1975 Second Line depicts a teenager engrossed in some footwork on top of the wall that surrounds a cemetery—but he might have been the first to turn it into a signature stunt.[17] The novelty of the act gave rise to his nickname.

Beyond daredevil entertainment, second lining aloft taps into a long history of dancing in West Africa and the Caribbean that harnesses the power of vertical space. In the masquerade tradition of stilt dancing, for example, dancers move on impossibly tall poles, often at least one story high. Stilt dancing is said to symbolize the ancestors standing over the community physically as well as spiritually. The stilt dancer's height indicates the spiritual transformation of the act, transporting the human to higher earthly and spiritual planes. The acrobatic feat of stilt dancing "gives proof to the ability of the spirit to supersede the laws of physics and gravity which govern mortals."[18] Such ability has been enshrined in the legend of "the people who could fly," which tells of enslaved Africans who defied the whip to rise from the ground, arms outstretched, and disappear into the clouds, soaring back to Africa.[19] As second liners tap out athletic footwork on the impossibly thin railing of a highway overpass, they, too, demonstrate the spirit's ability to overcome earthly limitations.

In addition to its spiritual potential and links to the diaspora, second lining in the air must also be understood within the sociopolitical context of New Orleans's geography. About half of the city sits below sea level and has been sinking lower and lower since the early twentieth century,[20] a fact that the world beyond New Orleans realized during the media coverage of Hurricane Katrina and subsequent levee failures in 2005. The city's colonial founders built on the natural rise of the Mississippi River's banks. Further away from the river, "back-a-town" neighborhoods emerged in lower-lying land susceptible to flooding. For centuries, the city's topography took on "racial as well as socioeconomic significance" because back-a-town was occupied by "freed slaves, migrants, and later Southern and Eastern European immigrants denied other housing options."[21] In the twentieth century, pumping and draining technologies turned swamps into suburbs for middle- and working-class families of various racial and ethnic backgrounds. However, redlining, racial covenants, and other racist policies meant that more white than Black families were able to take advantage of the development boom.[22] As the historian Andy Horowitz summarizes, an irony occurred: White, middle-class New Orleanians lived in more valuable homes (with newer schools and newer streets) in drained-swamps-turned-suburbs, while many African Americans continued to live closer to the city center, on higher ground.[23] That is, unless they were displaced by "slum clearance" during the 1950s and 1960s. The back-a-town areas of the Ninth Ward and parts of New Orleans East, where working-class residential areas developed after World War II, remained some of the few areas available to Black home buyers, including those displaced from the city center.

The Ninth Ward and New Orleans East flooded catastrophically during the Katrina disaster because of several factors including low-lying land, levee failures, and man-made canals, which were built to facilitate industry but turned into storm surge superhighways.[24] News coverage positioned the Lower Ninth Ward as "a metaphor for poverty, race, and neglect," but despite the media's portrayal, Horowitz cautions that there are no simple correlations between land elevation, poverty, and race in New Orleans.[25] White-owned homes in the newer suburbs had water lines just as high as those in Black-owned homes in the Lower Ninth Ward. Public housing developments, overwhelming populated by African American residents, remained relatively unscathed. So why, then, did African American and poorer residents fare worse after the storm? Recovery policies nearly eliminated public housing and apportioned rebuilding funds according to the pre-storm value of the home instead of the actual cost of rebuilding. As Sarah Broom describes in her memoir *The Yellow House*, her family, like many other Black families, were left with no decision but to bulldoze her childhood home in New Orleans East. Recovery policies disproportionately benefited white property owners, many with homes on higher ground, but not all. Looking back on the Katrina disaster, Horowitz writes,

> Some observers thought it was natural that African Americans would be worse off. But in this case, as in others, Katrina provided an occasion for racial and economic inequalities to be sharpened and ordained by policy and practice, and only then observed—variously with sorrow or satisfaction—as if they were timeless features of the social landscape.[26]

He joins others in asserting an important point: Racial inequality, though historic and preexisting, was not an inevitable outcome of the recovery.[27] Decisions by power brokers made inequalities worse, and rhetoric made racial disparities seem as if they were so entrenched that nothing could be done. In her study of disaster tourism, Lynnell Thomas acknowledges that representations of Katrina temporarily made visible the long-standing disaster of racialized capital in New Orleans; but these representations also reinforced stereotypes of Black people and neighborhoods as inherent sites of disaster.[28]

All of this set the stage for the city to become smaller, whiter, and wealthier in the years following the storm—the very period in which I moved to New Orleans, part of a wave of mostly white outsider artists and educators drawn there by the promise of rebuilding a great American city through the arts. Our residential choices reinforced a settlement pattern described by the cultural geographer Richard Campanella as a "white teapot." The teapot's spout runs along the river, between Magazine Street

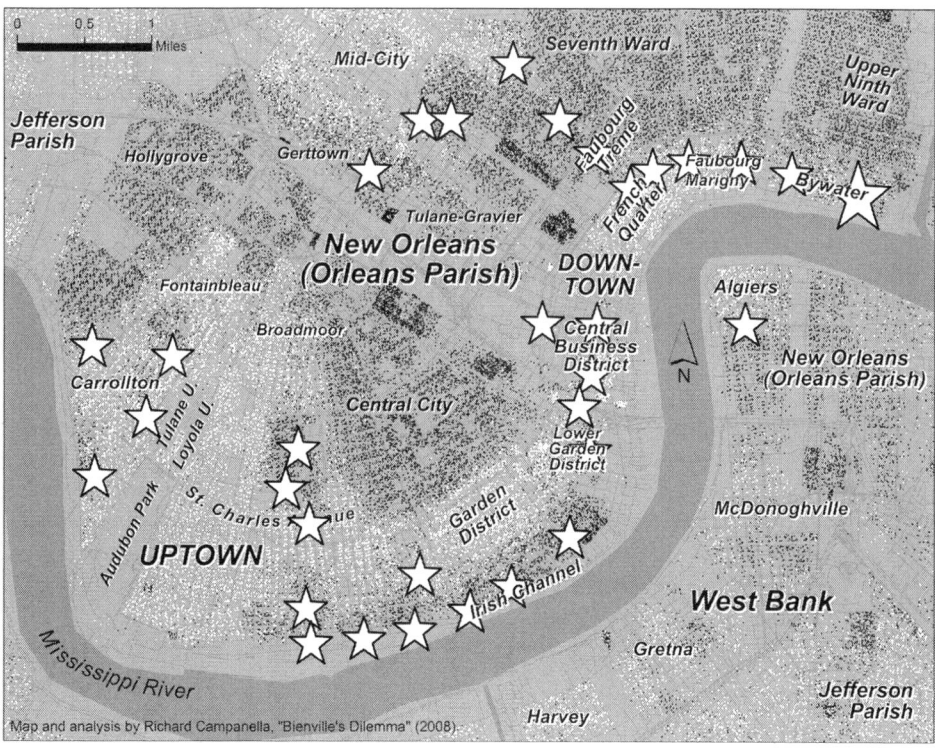

Dots represent populations at the block level of the 2000 Census; lighter-shaded dots represent white residents as well as smaller numbers of people of Asian ancestry and Hispanic ethnicity, and darker-shaded dots reflect members of the African American population. Stars indicate areas undergoing gentrification in the post-Katrina era. (Map and analysis by Richard Campanella, from *Bienville's Dilemma: A Historical Geography of New Orleans* [University of Louisiana Press, 2008].)

and St. Charles Avenue, on higher ground. Its "kettle" takes shape uptown, around Tulane and Loyola Universities. Given its stark boundaries, the teapot's impact is "dramatic." He writes:

> Crossing streets like St. Claude in Bywater (tip of the spout) or St. Charles/Carondelet in the Lower Garden District (trunk of the spout) takes a pedestrian across distinct race and class lines, and into strikingly different cityscapes. Guidebooks routinely warn tourists exploring the French Quarter not to exit the demographic pattern (though never so bluntly and not in those terms), while many African-Americans feel equally unwelcome and suspect upon entering it. So distinct are the urban characteristics within and beyond the white teapot that the two

areas almost seem like sub-cities, separate communities that happen to abut each other, but otherwise do not interact.[29]

The white teapot provides a stark example of the fact that race and space co-produce each other. In *How Racism Takes Place*, the African American studies scholar George Lipsitz argues, in deceptively simple terms, that it takes places for racism to take place. In his formulation, urban spaces in the United States are often dominated by two competing ideologies: the white spatial imaginary and the Black spatial imaginary. He argues that the white spatial imaginary, as the dominant one, does not have to name itself as white. It promotes space as primarily a locus for the generation of exchange value, being marked by a preference for private dwellings, private development, and the privatization of municipal services. Such approaches to city space may appear like race-neutral market choices, but they reinvest in whiteness and its accumulated privileges and immunities.[30] Since the end of legalized segregation in New Orleans, supposedly colorblind market choices have enabled white residents and those with more resources to occupy the most desirable areas, allowing the destruction of poor and Black neighborhoods in the name of progress and renewal.

In this context of historical, environmental, and structural racism, African American dancers find dance floors many feet above sea level. They perform a satirical inversion of history by saying place, claiming the highest available city space as their own. Their bravado radiates a feeling of accomplishment—they have, after all, scaled a structure and commanded the crowd's attention—but also, I suggest, of reaching the summit of a city space where his or her social and spatial mobility have been restricted.

Rodrick "Scubble" Davis is a self-professed "footwork junkie" who can be seen from below at nearly every Second Line parade, showing off his award-winning footwork skills atop roofs, bus shelters, and just about any surface he can manage.[31] Davis routinely scales predictable places such as a billboard on the corner of Orleans and Broad Avenues, where many parades pass. But his improvisation skills also allow him to take advantage of temporary stages such as the roof of a parked school bus. I asked Davis how he chooses his aerial dancing locations. Are they premeditated, spontaneous, or both? He replied,

> A lot of time it's pretty spontaneous, but if I'm uptown—I'm not from uptown, I'm from downtown—so when I go up there, I want them to know that we got the best footwork. This is where it originated from. Second Lines started downtown and I don't want them to forget it. Yes, they got a lot of good dancers uptown, but don't forget: downtown is where it started. So when I'm up on things uptown it's just to show

Rodrick "Scubble" Davis showing off his rooftop footwork during Tremé Sidewalk Steppers SAPC's twenty-fifth anniversary parade in downtown New Orleans on February 2, 2019. (Photo by Freddye Hill.)

off. It's to show off and provide more footwork for them. When I'm downtown, it just be happiness, joy, I'm home, I'm in my area. So it's just—everything I see I'm on. Everything I see I'm on.[32]

When Davis reflects on his chosen locations for aerial dancing, he is not thinking about colonial histories, environmental racism, or Hurricane Katrina. At least, not explicitly. According to this reflection, he's thinking more about pleasure than politics—friendly neighborhood rivalries and bragging rights. He takes pride in hailing from downtown, namely the Sixth Ward (or Tremé), as opposed to uptown, which, in Second Line geographies, usually refers to the Third Ward or Central City. The Sixth and Third Wards are only separated by a couple of miles, but for a long stretch of the city's history they were worlds apart. Tremé was home to Catholic Creoles—French, Spanish, and Creoles of color. Central City was home to Protestant Anglo and African American residents. When musicians and dancers crossed these boundaries at the turn of the twentieth century, their collaborative and competitive interactions were key to the birth of a musical form we now call jazz.[33] The development of Second

Line parades is an important part of that story, which continues to unfold on the streets of New Orleans every Sunday when second liners battle out claims to aesthetic superiority in thrilling one-upmanship.

Davis enters a century-old uptown-downtown dialogue each time he dances on top of a piece of the urban environment. Paying close attention to Davis's words reveals that he identifies *downtown* as both a geographical location and an imaginative space that holds a history of cultural practice. Davis brings downtown to uptown parades when he climbs atop uptown structures to "provide more footwork," downtown's signature dance contribution, "for them." Downtown, he both represents *and* produces his belonging by showcasing footwork atop the built environment. In other words, Davis's rooftop footwork celebrates neighborhood pride and makes an assertive claim to home. His associations between scaling buildings and place ownership suggest that he thinks of his performances as laying claim to—or *saying*—a place as his own.

Davis's story is exemplary for many reasons, including his gender identity. Dancing up high is performed almost exclusively by men. *Almost*. In the interlude that precedes this chapter, Nicole Lazard recalls that her mother danced on rooftops, but she was an exception. As the most visible second liners, those dancing above the crowd serve as a reminder that the Second Line tradition developed inside fraternal organizations. Although women have belonged to mutual aid societies since their inception, only since the late twentieth century have women regularly buckjumped on the street during Sunday Second Lines, as opposed to politely marching with church groups or riding ceremonially in vehicles.[34] In its gendered trends, too, dancing aloft evokes West African stilt dancing: Getting up high is understood as men's work.[35]

The relative absence of women on rooftops can also be understood within the historical context of U.S. city spaces, where dominant ideologies, social customs, and ordinances have excluded women of all races from the public realm, or included them in delimited roles, namely, the role of prostitute.[36] New Orleans is often considered distinct from other U.S. cities in this regard owing to its history of legalized sex work as a centerpiece of its tourism industry, and given the fact that multiple forms of street revelry have long provided sanctioned spaces for women to perform in public. Yet New Orleans is not exempt from the moral panics that can accompany women moving through urban spaces. For example, the city's most well-known red-light district, Storyville, emerged in the 1890s amid white middle class anxiety over spatially separating "respectable" women from those who were, as the Storyville ordinance put it, "notoriously abandoned to lewdness." A redistricting plan zoned all legal sex work into designated areas of the city.[37] This history is not unlike that of Congo Square (discussed in Chapter 2). In her book on Storyville, Alecia P. Long argues that, in the white mainstream imagination, sex workers shared ideological space with African Americans, both classes of people considered diseased and inherently sensual. As a result, ordinances segregated sex workers of all races and Black residents of all professions to the same handful of blocks.[38]

Like sex work, women's Carnival performances have repeatedly raised anxieties about gender, sex, race, and class. An example can be found in the Baby Dolls. As the story goes, in 1912 a group of women working in Black Storyville formed a social aid and pleasure club, the Million Dollar Baby Dolls, and emerged on Mardi Gras Day wearing short satin dresses, bonnets, and garters stuffed with cash. They strutted through the streets, combining sensual dancing with chanting and confrontational posturing (armed with ice picks just in case). In a tradition that continues today, the Baby Dolls flaunt and mock dominant ideas about Black women's place in the public sphere.[39] In her extensive study of the tradition, Kim Vaz-Deville argues that "reactions to women's masking can be considered an example of moral panic" as onlookers rebuked performances that challenged dominant values.[40]

Hazel Carby's pioneering work documents how Black women's migration into northern U.S. cities during the early twentieth century did not take them away from the harmful assumptions about race, class, and gender that permeated the urban South. They were met with alarm from northern middle-class urbanites who characterized Black women—especially southern, poor Black women—as sexually deviant and therefore socially dangerous.[41] This is an old story, but not a finished one. The anthropologist Aimee Meredith Cox argues that, still today, city streets can present "a troubling and contradictory space" where Black female bodies are normatively read as "undesirable, dangerous, captive, or out of place."[42] Cox cites the 2013 shooting of Renisha McBride as one example of the fact that Black women's movements through urban spaces still incite panic.[43]

Dance has long been a site in which powerful forces attempt to police Black women's bodies, even while the act of dancing has remained a powerful tactic for their self-determination, defiance, and pleasure. Dancing in public has historically attracted dangers for women and femmes of all races and ethnicities, since entertainers have also long been associated with sex work. Moreover, these dangers increase threefold for Black women performers because of associations between Blackness and sensuality on the part of the white middle class (the same associations that supported

1890s zoning ordinances in New Orleans).[44] According to Carby, early twentieth-century nightclubs and cabarets in such cities as Washington, D.C., were the places most feared and consequently policed by middle-class reformers, precisely because of the dancing done there.[45] Storyville, which was an important location for the emergence of jazz music and dance, attracted similar kinds of attention as city officials marshaled police to enforce the boundaries of the vice district.[46] Nevertheless, blues women utilized dancing and singing in U.S. urban spaces to access spatial mobility and financial gains that were unavailable to them by other means.[47] Their legacy lives on in twenty-first-century Detroit, where young Black women continue to dance in public, claiming their bodies and their city for themselves.[48] Cox writes about a performance in which dancers repurpose bus stops, which are sites of daily surveillance and struggle for them, as a stage for interactive performance. Like second liners, these Detroit street performers create new publics and remap streets as sites for joyful dance, networks of care, and spaces for open critique.[49]

Dancing atop elevated structures, including bus stop shelters, is one of second liners' most spectacular remapping strategies, inviting reconsiderations of mobility, urban space, and rights. But women at the Second Line rarely choose to choreograph citizenship on aerial structures. Instead, some choose another dangerous and impressive feat: doing footwork in high-heeled shoes. Nicole Lazard, for example, who parades with several clubs, follows her mother's footsteps, but with a crucial difference: she prefers to dance on the ground and elevate herself with her footwear. She likes how the shoes distribute her weight, allowing her to keep a constant bounce on the balls of her feet while giving her a little architecture to play with, especially balancing on the tips of the heels (see the interlude following Chapter 5).[50] I watched her do just that as she paraded with the Single Men SAPC in 2017 (as one of two female members, invited despite the club's name). In one impressive moment, she chugged forward on the balls of her feet four times before freezing in a dramatic heel balance. She recovered by dropping into a shallow squat before undulating backward into a rock step that propelled her forward into more footwork (see video 6.2 on this book's web page). High-heeled dancing such as Lazard's is another form of dancing aloft, one where female second liners grab attention through daredevil feats, if not on a rooftop, then on the narrow surface of their footwear. These dancers claim their bodies and their city for themselves, using their high heel-clad feet as tools for saying place.

Dancing up high, whether done on tall buildings or in tall shoes, can be seen as a form of choreographing citizenship as defined by Cox. "Choreography," she writes, "is concerned in a very fundamental sense with the ordering of bodies in space." In its most radical sense, choreography can discredit assumptions about who belongs in which places, about who is out of place, about who is a citizen and who is not.[51] By using dance as a tactic for claiming ownership of the city, second liners who rise above the street dissent against normative understandings of citizenship. As a way of saying place, to evoke McKittrick's term again, they defy the neoliberal logics of private ownership as a prerequisite for, and symbolic anchor of, citizenship in the white spatial imaginary. Instead, second liners' public performances articulate "alternative notions of value, land, and dwelling together in place."[52] Dancing on top of a building, transformer box, or overpass—or leveraging the height of one's shoes to dance a notch above the norm—proclaims, "I am from here. I am of this place. I belong here, this place belongs to me, and I can use it however I wish." The elevated performances of Rodrick Davis, Nicole Lazard, and other second liners articulate a form of ownership rooted in history, memory, and attachment to place. Such notions of place ownership and citizenship are, according to Breunlin and Regis, "routinely silenced in our naturalized understandings of private property denoting a singular relation to the land."[53]

Elevated second lining not only forwards an affective notion of ownership outside private property but also bucks regulations against trespassing, even if such laws seem to be suspended during the Second Line. Police officers escort every parade, and in tacitly allowing dancers to climb on any piece of residential or commercial property, officers selectively withhold constraints on movement. In these instances, second liners and police officers rehearse the tensions between legal and cultural citizenship, two interdependent forms of citizenship that often contradict one another. Rooftop footwork might be best described as a practice of dissenting citizenship, defined by Sunaina Maira as actions that critique the nation while still seeking inclusion in it.[54] When scaling structures in the presence of police escorts, second liners challenge the connections between land ownership and citizenship, creating a space where collective use of the cityscape is privileged over the state's protection of private property. Yet second liners simultaneously seek multicultural inclusion in the state by cooperating with police escorts and civic authorities to present a model of Black respectability that the state can condone.[55] By successfully gaining the permission and protection of the dominant society, second liners "enhance their own space and participation" within the social order, but find a way to do so according to the Second Line's own geographies, choreographies, and value systems.[56] By assuming the right to use the built environment in unusual and even illegal ways, dancers leverage the state's complicity with celebrations of difference in order to pursue their own agendas.[57] When dancing atop urban structures, second liners choreograph citizenship, including dissenting citizenship, by "map[ping] a different world" in which life "is not beholden to the state and controlled through capitalism."[58]

• • •

Dancing on elevated structures can only take place outdoors, but ironically, it may have started indoors. Reflecting on Spiderman's outdoor improvisations, Dirty Dozen musicians Benny Jones Sr. and Gregory Davis remembered him dancing inside the Glass House, the legendary nightclub where the Dirty Dozen played every week starting in 1977. There, a whole new style of Second Line music and dance took shape, and part of that aesthetic revolution involved improvisations with the physical space of the club (see Chapter 5). In the Glass House, Spiderman inspired dancers to find stages for footwork on the bar and chairs or by running up the wall.[59] Perhaps the choreography perfected inside the club found its way into the parades, or vice versa, stoking a shared passion for getting vertical inside and out. Jones's and Davis's conjectures about the possible relation between dancers' interactions with the built environment raise important questions about the physical layout of the club. How might the Glass House's architecture have shaped the characteristics of the changing dance form? What are the effects of saying place indoors as compared to on the streets? The following section takes on these questions with a focus on the Glass House.

My attention to the physical space of the Glass House follows the lead of New Orleans cultural critic Kalamu ya Salaam, who tracked the architectural layout of music venues in the development of jazz music. In a conversation with Gregory Davis, Salaam proposed that the reason the Dirty Dozen was able to create such an innovative sound was that the music remained connected to its community of listeners and dancers.[60] This was almost unavoidable at the Glass House because the small space left no room for physical separation. In the tiny club, with its six-inch-tall stage, dancers risked getting hit on the head with a trombone and musicians risked colliding with an acrobat's flying foot. At one point, the band placed chairs between themselves and the dance floor to offer a little physical protection, but the aesthetic and energetic connection between musicians and dancers remained strong.[61] A discerning, invested audience, Salaam said, "has been absent for much of the development of what is called modern jazz. Particularly in New York it was verboten to dance. They came in with the cabaret cars, all kinds of little things that separated dance from the music." Notice that Salaam appealed to the physical layout of New

York nightclubs when illustrating the experiential separation between jazz music and dance there. But in New Orleans, he said, the music "has always had an element of participation from the community and dance."[62] The communal participation in New Orleans jazz comes from the street parades, but that spirit migrates inside music venues such as the Glass House.

Salaam's comments resonate with dance scholar Susan Foster's suggestion that the material remains of architecture are more reliably accessed by the dance historian than are bodily movements. Foster writes that, in the past, bodies "rubbed up against or moved alongside geological and architectural constructions, music, clothing, interior decorations ... whose material remains leave further indications of those bodies' dispositions."[63] Her supposition stands to reason, following the logic of what Diana Taylor has influentially named the durable archive and ephemeral repertoire.[64] Typically, buildings last longer than bodies, and their material remains can give the dance historian some clues about how, when, and where bodies moved through them. Dance history lives on in the bodily archives of present-day dancers (as detailed in Chapter 5), but one can also get to the history of the dance and the dancers by means of an examination of the built environments through which they moved.[65]

The story of the Glass House, however, offers some complications to Foster's generalization. The venue closed in 1991. By that point, the Dirty Dozen had long since bestowed its weekly gig on the Rebirth Brass Band, but the place still held significance for Dirty Dozen musicians. Sometime in the early 1990s Gregory Davis took his children to see the site, but "by that time it was a toolshed. Somebody, whoever owned it, painted the whole thing a dark grey. I went up there and they had a fence around it, a chain-link fence."[66] Since then, the building has been demolished. All that remains of the Glass House is a vacant, grassy lot. Buildings are, like bodies, impermanent, and, like bodies, their life expectancies rely a great deal on economics, which in the United States is inextricably tied to race.

But long before it was a toolshed or a vacant lot, the Glass House was the place to be. Patrons' experience began long before walking through the door because the entire block filled with people and music. Salaam recalled, "You'd know you were near it because people would be all in the street. They kept the door open so you could hear the music, [and] that attracted more people."[67] After weaving through the dense crowd, dancers entered the Glass House through its swinging plate glass door. According to Benny Jones, a woman named Thelma (not to be confused with the manager, Thelma Jones, better known as Miss Tee) sat just inside collecting dollar bills. Next to her, a bouncer named Killroy adjudicated each

Glass House several years after it closed its doors. (Photograph by Mazza, courtesy of Jay Mazza; originally published in *Beat Street* magazine, 2003.)

person's entrance.[68] According to Salaam, "as soon as somebody came out, somebody came in. You had to get there early if you wanted to be inside."[69] That's because the Glass House was very compact. It occupied a single-story rectangular building at 2519 South Saratoga Street with a remarkably small footprint, comparable to a large living room. The modest structure was not originally intended to become a barroom when it was erected in about 1920 in the back of a lot that belonged to a double shotgun house around the corner on Third Street.[70] It served as a grocery and dry cleaners before becoming a tavern in the mid-1950s.[71] Once it became the Glass House, one of the most significant locations in the city's cultural scene, it exceeded its capacity by tenfold on a weekly basis. It seems a New Orleans miracle that so many people could flow in and out of this one-room club on a given night.

The squat, solid, and opaque building sat in the middle of the block in the Third Ward, and in many ways crystalized the economic and cultural histories of the neighborhood. The area was first settled after the Civil War by recently emancipated African Americans. It was originally the back-a-town swamp, so land and housing were cheap.[72] By the mid-twentieth century the neighborhood featured double shotgun houses and modest apartment complexes interspersed with locally owned businesses. The Dew Drop Inn, a fabled 1950s nightclub that hosted traveling Black musicians during the Jim Crow era, stood a two-minute walk from the building. Also nearby was Undertaker Lodge No. 2, an example of the vast networks of mutual aid societies that continue to stitch together the fabric of many Black New Orleans communities today.[73] Those societies regularly hosted brass band parades that departed from Shakespeare Park, just two blocks from the Glass House's front door.[74] Walking a few blocks in the other direction, one would find the corner of Second and Dryades Streets, an important meeting spot for uptown Black Masking Indian tribes.[75] The club at 2519 South Saratoga marked the epicenter of a rich cultural landscape in uptown New Orleans.

Entering dance history through the Glass House and its surroundings invites a consideration of second lining in its sociopolitical and cultural context. It also allows for a more thorough consideration of the role women have played in second lining's development, for the place was owned and run by women. The property on which the Glass House sat, which included two houses and the building which eventually became the nightclub, had been owned by Black women since 1957. During the club's heyday the lot was owned by Beatrice Braxton Lusk Moore and the business managed by the firm hand of Thelma Jones.[76] Women also staffed the bar and the door.[77] Like many women before and after them, Moore, Jones, and their staff contributed to the history of New Orleans jazz offstage and off the dance floor by ensuring that there was a stage and a dance floor to begin with.[78]

One can see these women at work in Alan Lomax's 1990 film *Jazz Parades*. In B-roll footage, the camera slowly scans crepe paper decorations in a mixture of Christmas and Mardi Gras colors hanging from the low, textured ceiling. Streamers of yellow, green, and purple hang in u-shaped formations, crisscrossed by ropes of gold tinsel and red bells dangling so low that some of the taller men graze the bells with their hair. As Dirty Dozen trumpeter Efrem Townes recalled, "At the Glass House, it was always Christmas time. Christmas year 'round, 365, seven days a week. The Christmas ornaments never came down."[79] As the crowd gathers and waits for the Dirty Dozen to take the stage, the camera pans the room to reveal wood-paneled walls covered with photographs, paintings, and prints, many featuring Black Masking Indians. Before the band plays one note, before anyone dances one step, those gathered in the bar are already dabbing sweat from their foreheads with terrycloth rags.

Benny Jones's bass drum sits onstage, displaying the words "Original 6th Ward Dirty Dozen" painted in block letters. Across from the stage a white marble bar stretches the length of the room, holding short glass bottles of 7-Up and full ashtrays. Neat stacks of liquor bottles line the wall behind the bar, where Margaret, Rosa Mary, and Cookie dish out Miss Tee's red beans in Styrofoam sectional plates and serve drinks in ice-filled plastic cups.[80] To the left of the stage, a jukebox stands against the wall. Interior concrete poles hold up the structure. Cigarette smoke hangs in the air. People stand around the bar, sit at the few small tables, or perch on the lip of the stage eating red beans. Almost everyone appears to be African American, save Lomax, his film crew, and one white woman with a long braid hanging down her back. Neon lights glint off the glass door as it swings open and shut, pushing into the dense crowd to let more people in.

That door, the sole opening puncturing the building's sided façade, led patrons directly into the space from the narrow sidewalk some six or eight feet from the curb. The club's name did not mean that the structure was transparent; it was derived from a decorative flourish of broken mirror shards affixed to one interior wall.[81] As the music writer Jay Mazza observed in 1990, when the Rebirth Brass Band was still holding weekly sets there, "The name the Glass House conjures up images of everything but what it is. The Glass House has no glass [save the plate glass door]; in fact, it has no windows at all"—at least, none that could open and let a little air in.[82] A single window air conditioning unit attempted to offer some relief from the tropical heat and humidity but was woefully insufficient.[83] But that didn't deter dancers and musicians from marathon sessions. Benny Jones Sr. remembered that the dancers would walk outside to take a break, but "before you know it, they're back in the club again dancing again. When they get going, oh them guys be soaking wet!"[84] According to Don Robertson, an avid footwork artist, it was not only the people who were sweating at the Glass House; even the wall perspired.

> It was crowded, hot. Right now, you don't even get the wall to sweat when you go see the bands now. The heat in there, the humidity.... You don't know nothing about humidity until you hit the Glass House. You wet, the people around you wet, even the guys who playing the horns: dripping wet. You know, it's like you just got out of the shower and put your clothes on and didn't even dry off. That's it! I'm telling you! If you lean on the wall, it's wet.[85]

Notably, Robertson's recollection that dancers caused the club's walls to sweat suggests that not only does the material environment shape the physical practice, but the physical practice also shapes the environment. In other words, dancing in the Glass House was a way of "saying place," in

McKittrick's terms, of molding cinder block walls by endowing them with meaning, memory, and sweat (listen to the full interview with Robertson on this book's web page).

It is important to recognize how Black New Orleanians in the 1970s claimed ownership of their physical and cultural spaces such as the Glass House and its neighboring sites because material structures played a critical role in the political and economic backlash against the gains made during the civil rights movement. The geographer Clyde Woods asserts that, following the end of de jure segregation in the mid-1960s, New Orleans's politicians and fiscal elites relied on the built environment to enforce de facto segregation. He details ten ways in which city officials and business leaders responded to legislative gains in racial equality by erecting a "massive resistance in concrete."[86] Redevelopment projects, urban renewal, gentrification, and interstate highway construction, along with other mechanisms, "created spatial barriers to social, economic, and cultural democratization" and "guaranteed the intensification of Black destitution."[87] The Glass House sat on the front line of this struggle owing to its location in the heart of the Third Ward, one of the Black neighborhoods suffering from "planned abandonment"[88] but also one that boasts a strong history of local cultural traditions and community organizing. New Orleans's "massive resistance in concrete" and Black organizers' resistance to it illustrate how racism and anti-racism take place.[89]

As important as the built environment is to material and cultural aspects of home, Black geographies cannot simply be mapped in terms of the presence or absence of structures. They must also be mapped in the ways the architecture is used, repurposed, and assigned meaning. The Glass House became a sanctuary for the musicians and dancers who came to sweat together inside its walls every week. Benny Jones remembers it as a place where "everybody knew everybody" and "everybody got along like a big family."[90] A similar analysis holds not only for the Glass House, but also for New Orleans's public housing developments, many of which served as incubators for developments in music and dance in the twentieth century. Like the Glass House, they no longer stand, but their impacts live on in cultural memory. The following section looks to the St. Bernard public housing development and its importance for the Original Big Seven SAPC as a final example of ways in which second liners claim home.

• • •

Most Big Seven parades leave from the home of the club's president, Edward Buckner, on Elysian Fields Avenue. The parades' ending points vary from year to year, but many end near the site of his former home and the birthplace of the club: the St. Bernard public housing development. This was the case during their June 1, 2013, parade.[91] The St. Bernard sits more than two miles from Buckner's house, so moving a large crowd that far in the summer heat required a feat of endurance. As we approached the end of the route, nearly four hours after departing, the cooler-pulling ambulatory vendors had run out of water. We had soaked through our clothes. Many paraders had left, but a dedicated pack of us continued, determined to see the procession through to its conclusion. We were buoyed by a second liner grooving on an overhead train trellis. In four hours and two miles, we had moved backward through the club's nearly twenty-year history, from its present-day headquarters on Elysian Fields Avenue to its birthplace in the St. Bernard.

In 1995 a group of St. Bernard residents, Buckner among them, founded a club called "Big Seven on the Other Side." After a year of meetings and fundraising, the group held its first parade in 1996; Buckner remembers that "the whole community came out." At first, the Big Seven was hosting "everyone's funeral in [the] neighborhood, until we realized that we couldn't afford to do everyone's funeral." They then instituted a rule that they would only bury club members who had been with the organization for at least two years. When Buckner became president around the year 2000, he changed the name to Original Big Seven SAPC. He has chosen several different locations throughout the large Seventh Ward for each parade's stops and end points, ensuring that the club continues to have the support of the entire Seventh Ward, in and beyond the St. Bernard.[92]

After Buckner moved out of the St. Bernard and purchased his own home in a different part of the Seventh Ward, he continued to choreograph the Big Seven's parade so that it would end there. He charts it as the site of the club's origin and a significant coordinate in the "spiritual grounds" of his own Seventh Ward upbringing, "the place where you can come and find out the roots about me and everything I've done."[93] The St. Bernard is personally important to other club members, as well. Terry "Squillee" Gable was not part of the founding cohort but his participation in the Big Seven also calls up the housing development. "My people was one of the first families . . . back there when it was still swamps and stuff," he said. "So I'm connected to the Seventh Ward like deep deep. When I dance and bring it on home, that's what I'm doing it for. I love going back there. Bringing it home."[94]

Former St. Bernard residents remember their home with Gable's fondness. For many of them, it felt like one big extended family. In fact, in some cases, one blood family *did* occupy an entire block. Neighbors watched each other's children so that parents could work. Children played in the courtyards until the streetlights came on: football in one courtyard, baseball in the next. Another courtyard hosted tops, marbles, water balloon fights, and dance-offs. Adults gathered in the courtyards, too, for birthday parties and cookouts. They'd slice a big cake, enjoy a DJ set up on one person's porch, and before it was all over, dance along with a brass band.[95] Resident Kyshun Webster remembered the safety and security of growing up in the densely populated St. Bernard. Contrary to "stereotypes that living in public housing may conjure up for some," he said, "we felt safe, we felt at home, and we felt like we were among community, and community that knew us, we knew them, and they all looked out for the children."[96] Recalling cultural events and community celebrations, housing activist and St. Bernard resident Sharon Jasper called the area "a big family."[97]

Children who grew up in the St. Bernard when Buckner did, in the 1960s and early 1970s, learned that New Orleans culture is a mechanism for building community and thriving inside it. The development was home to multiple generations of influential musicians such as pianist and producer Edwin Bocage, gospel singer Raymond Myles, and DJ Irv, whose sets in the St. Bernard courtyards helped give rise to bounce music, the city's unique style of hip hop. Second lining was also central to the residents' experience of home. In the 1970s the revered banjo player Danny Barker started the Fairview Baptist Church Brass Band around the corner from the St. Bernard and led Second Line parades through the property each Easter Sunday. The Fairview band galvanized a revival of brass band music (discussed in Chapter 5), with the Dirty Dozen Brass Band, which included St. Bernard resident Gregory Davis, being one of the new bands that emerged from among Fairview's alumni.[98] Brass bands came out for birthdays and other celebrations, as well. Resident Lilly Walker Woodfork recalled, "We had the band. Always had the band. You know they had to have a Second Line. Old people on walkers [said], 'Want to see me dance?' [I said,] 'No I don't want to see you fall.'"[99] Resident manager Lois Watson concluded that children who came out of St. Bernard learned about their culture "because we had community leaders who were interested" in sharing it with them.[100] Buckner's father, a musician, was one of them. He brought Buckner to Second Line parades when he was a child and played music at home so that he and his friends could dance. "My dad used to come home after drinking his wine at the Green Lounge on Basin St. and he'd play that Second Line. He'd be on the steps, we'd be singing 'Two Way Pocky Way' and dancing, and it would be two, three o'clock in the morning in the projects."[101] It is not hard to imagine how Buckner's and his fellow club members' upbringing in the development impacted the Big Seven's explicit values of culture, community, and youth (listen to an oral history with Edward Buckner and learn more about the St. Bernard's influential role in New Orleans's musical and cultural histories in video 6.3 on this book's web page).

The St. Bernard opened in 1942, in the era when the city's "big four" public housing developments were built to house African American residents, and the St. Thomas and Iberville were built for white families only.[102] Following the desegregation of public housing in the 1960s, white residents fled public housing and joined the mass flight to working-class suburbs. At the same time, urban renewal projects displaced thousands of Black residents from their homes, moving many into newly constructed public housing units. Within a few years, tens of thousands of poor African American residents became intensely consolidated within the ten developments, many of which were isolated and cut off from the street grid.[103] As federal, state, and city governments subsequently disinvested in public housing during the late twentieth century across the United States, densely populated housing developments became increasingly more impoverished and dangerous for residents. For example, epidemiological studies have linked the risk of homicide in New Orleans to the density of poverty as measured by how crowded the housing was.[104] Over time, public housing communities like the St. Bernard became centers of concentrated poverty and faced all the challenges and dangers that came with it.

In the late twentieth century local and federal officials cited public housing's ills as reasons for demolition, instead of owning their role in abandoning it. In 1992 the Department of Housing and Urban Development launched a new nationwide program called HOPE (Housing Opportunities for People Everywhere) VI to replace severely distressed public housing developments, occupied exclusively by poor families, with redesigned mixed-income housing. The program provided housing vouchers to enable some of the original residents to rent apartments in the private market.[105] In the early 2000s, HOPE VI came to New Orleans, enabling the city to bulldoze the St. Thomas development and build River Garden, which included only a fraction of the number of affordable housing units that the St. Thomas had offered.[106] When Hurricane Katrina made landfall four years later, most of New Orleans's public housing fared well in the storm and subsequent floods because they were sturdy structures built on relatively high ground. Nevertheless, the disaster provided the occasion that officials needed to accelerate existing plans to eradicate public housing. In the words of housing activist and St. Bernard resident Kawana Jasper, New Orleans officials "[used] a natural disaster to do their dirty work."[107] In the neoliberal environment of post-Katrina reconstruction, the public-private partnerships established before the storm sped up, and thousands of residents in New Orleans's housing developments were prevented from returning. Meanwhile, their undamaged homes, including those in the St. Bernard, were marked for demolition.[108]

Despite the challenges of displacement, resident activists sprang into action to protect their homes from the wrecking ball. Protestors assembled outside the St. Bernard in January 2007, marching, chanting, and singing their way through the chain-link gates and into the vacant apartments. They began a renegade cleanup effort and hung signs from balconies that read, "HUD [Housing and Urban Development] is CRUD," "HUD/HANO [Housing Authority of New Orleans] DISPLACED US, NOT KATRINA," and "Recovery means Everybody." Before long, the police arrived to shut down the effort. Afterward, HANO threatened to terminate rental assistance to residents who re-entered the property.[109] Ultimately, the St. Bernard was demolished, and its residents displaced. But they did not go without a fight.[110]

In place of the St. Bernard now stands Columbia Parc at the Bayou District, a planned community designed and built by an Atlanta-based development company, Columbia Residential. Instead of the St. Bernard's durable multi-apartment brick structures, separated by grassy common areas, Columbia Parc features townhomes and garden-style apartments adorned with colorful siding and ornamental balconies. Developers also outfitted the complex with an entertainment venue, lifestyle and management center, community health clinic, early learning center, and as of 2019, a K-8 charter school on the grounds.[111] Like River Garden and other HOPE VI redevelopment projects, Columbia Parc offers pathways to residency for public housing residents, including those of the former St. Bernard. According to a trade association that honored Columbia Parc with an award for excellence in public housing revitalization, Columbia Residential developers made good-faith efforts to get former St. Bernard residents into the new homes, even while they worked to attract "a significant number of new residents and market rate renters." Among other initiatives, Columbia Residential "made attempts to contact all 900 displaced families and offered a series of planning and informational meetings."[112] Yet no matter how successful the outreach, the fact remains that Columbia Parc contains a fraction of the public housing units once provided by the St. Bernard. The first phase of the development, which opened in 2010, replaced 963 public housing units with just 157 subsidized public housing apartments where rent is based on income. The remainder were market-rate apartments and affordable tax-credit units that targeted moderate-income households.[113] The result was that a small percentage of residents displaced by the St. Bernard's demolition were able to take advantage of the newly available amenities on the site of their former homes.[114]

This was where the Big Seven's parade on June 1, 2013, concluded: not at the St. Bernard but at Columbia Parc. By moving the club, three brass bands, and thousands of participants through the site of the club's original home, the Original Big Seven claimed that land for itself, if for only a moment, collectively owning the streets by dancing through them. The importance of the Big Seven's annual parade became even clearer in 2016, when the developers of Columbia Parc threatened to sue the Big Seven if the club paraded through their property. Despite the developers' concerns about property damage and residents' safety, the city of New Orleans maintained its approval of the Big Seven's parade route and the procession went on as planned.[115] In this struggle, the Big Seven's negotiation with the terms of dissenting citizenship ended in its favor. As was the case following a shooting that occurred during a parade several years earlier, the city's and the club's unified stance testified to years of organizing on the part of culture advocates.

Columbia Residential's efforts to stop the parade contrast starkly with those of the Big Seven and residents of the St. Bernard. The Big Seven, like other clubs, explicitly embraces its role in building a safe, resourced home for their communities. Their efforts go on year-round, but on parade day, SAPCs put those values in motion. Club members act as choreographers, in conjunction with musicians and police escorts, to move dancing bodies through areas of the city that are most impacted by structural and interpersonal violence to reclaim the streets from those forces. By enacting an alternative mode of moving through the white spatial imaginary, second liners challenge the structural violence of racial capitalism, which values private property more than Black humanity and limits the social mobility of the urban poor.[116] By assuming authoritative ownership of city streets that are feared as potentially dangerous, second liners challenge interpersonal violence as the only option for people living in these areas to establish power, authority, and credibility on the streets.[117]

Each week, when second liners high-step through New Orleans's African American neighborhoods (even when the buildings, such as the Glass House and the St. Bernard, no longer stand), they enact a way of being together in a place that values rhythm, sweat, and collectivity more than titles, deeds, and eminent domain. Dancing atop the built environment, balancing on high heels, sweating in nightclubs, and standing up to developers—each of these actions is crucial to charting Second Line geographies. Second liners' embodied acts of saying place and choreographing citizenship work against forces of dispossession and erasure to claim ownership of and belonging to home.

Joe Stern on the streets during the Prince of Wales SAPC's ninetieth anniversary parade, October 14, 2018. (Photo by Pableaux Johnson.)

INTERLUDE

Joe Stern

September 1, 2017

Joe Stern, who passed away in 2023 at the age of eighty-one, is known to those in the Second Line community as "White Boy Joe." When he joined the Prince of Wales Social Aid and Pleasure Club in 1988, he was one of the only non-Black members of any SAPC in the city. He wore the nickname proudly embroidered on his Prince of Wales shirts. Stern was a secular leftist Jew raised in Ohio; his involvement in the Second Line culture could be framed as continuous with a time in the city's history before the civil rights era, when Black and Jewish communities in New Orleans had closer relations.[1] Stern's involvement in parading was long and deep. His efforts were honored by his fellow Prince of Wales members when they unanimously elected him their president shortly after Hurricane Katrina. His role in organizing one of the first Second Line parades to hit the streets after the storm on December 18, 2005, as recounted below, played a role in that decision.[2]

Stern taught English courses for many years at Southern University at New Orleans, retiring in 2020, but it wasn't academia that had brought him to New Orleans; it was his first passion, community organizing. Until his death he continued to work with local activist efforts, often joining forces with the person who motivated his choice to come to New Orleans in the early 1980s, Malcolm Suber. Suber's decades of organizing became more widely known in 2015 because of his efforts with Take 'Em Down NOLA, which successfully pressured the New Orleans City Council to remove four Confederate statues. The skills that Stern drew on to plan the Prince of Wales's 2005 parade bore a strong resemblance to those honed through years of community organizing with Suber and others.

My name's Joseph M. Stern, or Joe Stern, as I prefer. I was born in Cleveland, Ohio, on July 11, 1942. I'm a longtime member of the Prince of Wales Social Aid and Pleasure Club, and I'm currently President. . . . I've been a member since 1988.

Joining the Prince of Wales

I actually came down here because I was working with, everybody knows Malcolm Suber, he's one of the leaders in the Take 'Em Down movement. Well, I came down here to work politically with him, in an organization, another organization that we were both in. It was a communist organization. A Marxist-Leninist organization. Yeah, so that's why I came down here.

. . .

After I moved to New Orleans, about 1980, about 1982, I moved into a neighborhood that's known in that neighborhood as the Twelfth Ward, which runs from Louisiana and Napoleon, Tchoupitoulas, mostly to Magazine, even though, like the neighborhood, the original Twelfth Ward actually goes all the way to Broad, where all those wards meet up.

And then I started meeting a lot of people who lived in the neighborhood, and made some friends, and was hanging out at a couple of barrooms. And this is how I know the date, and you can check, it might be a year off for all I know. But Owen Haynes, who was from the Twelfth Ward, was elected King of Zulu. So, he wanted the Prince of Wales to parade in the Zulu parade, like, because that's his roots and that's where he came from. So, at that time, the club had been inactive for, probably since the mid-1980s, like three or four years, maybe even six years.

But they were gonna organize and get back together. And a few months before—I had never been to a Second Line before—and a few months before, a longtime member, who had once been Grand Marshal of the club, had been murdered. . . . So they had a Second Line for him, and I went out there and I did that, and I had, like, a totally life-changing experience, I guess you'd say. And this was back in the time when you could just throw a Second Line for somebody, all you needed was a band. You didn't need police, and you didn't need this, and you didn't need all of that.

So, anyhow, when they said, the club is gonna get back together to parade in the Zulu parade with Owen, so they started, you know, getting together, and I said, "Well, hey, can I join?" And they said, "Sure!" So I joined. [*laughs*] And I did. So what happened was we paraded, and it was the year it was brutally cold for Mardi Gras. It probably didn't get, I know it didn't get above forty. I mean, because we paraded in tuxedos and then everybody bought long johns, and drank plenty of wine. But it was still really cold. And we really kind of stole the parade, because we were out there, and we had a band, and we were doing it right, and everybody else was so cold.

But everybody had such a good time, they decided that they might as well keep the club going, because they had like twenty, about twenty-five people do it. So they kept the club going, and we had a parade in August. We used to parade in August. August 12 is really our anniversary [even though the anniversary parade is now held in October].

I guess sometimes, you know, the culture thrives, and then it dies down, and thrives. Some of that has to do with economic conditions. I know, like when I moved to New Orleans in 1980, I couldn't find a place to live in New Orleans; I had to move to, I was living in Harvey. Because there were no affordable places, you know, in neighborhoods. And then after the oil bust, so I think, you know, maybe coming out of the oil bust, and people started working back again, . . . I guess the economy had got a little better or whatever. So, it didn't cost crazy money to parade back then.

. . .

It's just in the nature of working-class people to organize and form their own organizations to meet some of their own needs. I mean, that was the original reason that social aid and pleasure clubs got together: to help each other out, as well as, just in New Orleans, they also had a parade.

The First Post-Katrina Second Line

Given everything that had gone on [after Hurricane Katrina], I was very concerned, and also given the political thing that was going on, you could hear, you know, the obvious racism and everything that was going on, and destruction of Black communities, and why should we rebuild, and I was actually really concerned that if the culture didn't start back—I knew [Black Masking] Indians were gonna be Indians. You know, they were gonna come out regardless. Because Monk [Boudreaux, Chief of the Golden Eagles] was already sewing, right? And he was back. Everybody came back as soon as they could, a lot of people, right? So I was actually concerned that if we didn't parade, if the culture didn't start back up, then they would use that as an excuse—if we didn't do it right away, then they'd use it as an excuse to stop it, or to change it. I mean, for years, there had been rumors about, oh they only wanna have like four parades a year, or six parades a year, and they'll have, like, five or six clubs parade together, and blah, blah, blah.

. . .

So, you know, I was concerned. And it just happened to be five of my guys here, Alvin [Epps] was working, picking up old refrigerators, working for somebody [FEMA], throwing trash. I can't remember what Walter

[Andrews] was doing. Walter had a job somewhere doing something. Junior was here, and [so was] Little Bro—Sidney [Morris] who at that time does renovations and stuff like that. And I said, "Come on, we got to do this." You know, we need, I said, "Let's do it." Because unlike most places, our route basically was, a lot of it was still ok. Didn't flood! And even parts that did [flood] didn't flood as bad as some parts of the city.

. . .

And, because, we had, if you remember, when the hurricane was, right [August 29]? [Because we were supposed to parade in October,] we were getting [ready], we had already had all our clothes, and everything. We didn't have them, . . . but they were up on Chef, that little strip mall on Chef [Menteur Highway in New Orleans East] where the Wal-Mart is? Our clothes were there, but we also had money with Meyer [The Hatter], for hats.

RACHEL CARRICO: Oh, sure, right. French Quarter.

JOE STERN: So the clothes were gone, but we had money with Meyer. So I said, "Look, this is what we can do."

RC: Clothes were gone because that flooded.

JS: Buildings were practically gone, if I remember correctly. So I said, "Look, this is what we can do." Because people were working, people had money. You know. So I said, . . . "We'll rent tuxedos." First we tried to find clothes, we couldn't find any clothes. I said, "We'll rent tuxedos," we went to Meyer, I said, "Look, we got this money." I said, "Find us"—we wanted to use our colors, we wanted blue and white. So we rented tuxedos, and Meyer got us hats, and then my daughter [Lakisha] was living in Atlanta, my granddaughter's mother, they were living in Atlanta, and she found these cheap, these thirty-dollar shoes, royal blue shoes, in a shoe store in Atlanta, and bought them for us and sent them to us. And then Monk made us corsages, and that was it.

. . .

Ok. So then we went and put an application [for a parade permit]. . . . I wrote them [Putumayo Records], and I said, "Look, we're trying to do this." And they gave us a thousand dollars. And between that and I can't remember where the rest [came from], and then so we hired Rebirth, and I said, "Look, this is what we've got. And we're hustling. If we hustle more, we'll pay you more." So we did, we actually, think they said they'd do it for fifteen hundred, and we actually ended up giving them eighteen. Which wasn't, you know, but we were—I was just, I really thought it was a very, really important thing to do.

. . .

RC: Do you have several members of your family who are involved in the club?

JS: Yeah. My youngest daughter paraded one year, I think. . . . My grandchildren. [*Points at photograph*] Yeah, and that's my granddaughter. . . . She paraded after Katrina, too.

RC: Yeah?

JS: Mm-hmm. I'm so proud of that girl.

RC: How old was she then?

JS: How old was she then. . . . Nine.

RC: Nine. Wow. And what's her name?

JS: Maegan. But she was living in Georgia, she had just, it was, because it was so close to Christmas, there was Christmas break. And she was staying on the North Shore with her great-uncle's, at that time, wife, I guess you would call her. [*laughs*] And, what is it, she . . . was even late—and was so upset—to the parade. We started at Tipitina's, and then we went to the Rock Bottom. So she didn't show up until the Rock Bottom. Mad, because she wasn't in some of the first pictures. . . .

You know, I, it's funny, I don't remember whole lots about the day. I could talk about organizing, doing all of that. . . . I remember people coming up to me for months afterwards, thanking me. You know, and people telling me when the band started playing, they started crying. You know, it was really very emotional. . . . I mean, people—literally, for months, people would come up to me. "Man, thank you." I said, "You know, I did it for me! I needed it." [*laughs*] You know. I mean, a lot of people said, "You know, if this culture hadn't started back up, I wouldn't've come back." That's why they came back, because they couldn't live without the culture.

EPILOGUE

Social Aid and Pleasure in a Pandemic

On Thursday, March 6, 2020, I flew to New Orleans from Orlando, Florida. I was about six months into my first year as an assistant professor of dance studies at the University of Florida in Gainesville, and my spring break was dedicated to the Ice Divas Social and Pleasure Club. Nearly every one of my spring breaks had been reserved for the Divas since the club's founder and CEO, Catina Braxton Robertson, invited me to join in 2014. I accepted even though my academic career took me away from New Orleans and, for a time, kept me moving to a new location nearly every fall. No matter where I was teaching, I had flown back every March to hit the streets with the Ice Divas. In 2020 I was relieved to finally be back in the Gulf South region, with a relatively short flight away from New Orleans, for the foreseeable future.

Membership in the Ice Divas fluctuates from year to year, but a solid core of us have remained consistent. One of those women is Kristy Magner, a white transplant like me. By now, she is a longtime New Orleans resident. Each year she offers up her home, located near our parade's starting location, as our staging area. Our 2020 parade was no different. Early Sunday morning, all five of the Ice Divas participating that year met at Kristy's house. Once everyone arrived—hair pinned, nails painted—we sat around the dining room table and prayed over our breakfast (bacon, eggs, toast, grits, fruit, coffee, and mimosas). Catina asked God to bless the food and gave thanks for the sunny weather. Once fed, everybody quickly dispersed to dress, fixing streamers in place, fastening bow ties under collars, taping up toes, and sharing eyeliner and lip gloss. Kristy assumed her usual task of keeping an eye on the clock and ushering us into the backyard to take group pictures when the photographers arrived. This time, she also urged us to slip travel-sized bottles of hand sanitizer into our pants pockets. *There's this new virus making its way around the globe, and we should be careful,* she said. Her job in international education at Tulane University meant that she had been privy to the virus's lethal path long before any of us were. I thought she was overreacting when she ordered a batch of disposable contact lenses, just in case supply chains became disrupted. This sounded apocalyptic to me then. Everyone reading this knows that Kristy was right.

But on that beautiful Sunday, for those four glorious hours, we were blissfully unaware of the public health crisis bearing down on us. Our goldenrod suits reflected the luminous spring day, and our rhinestone-studded streamers and fans (handmade by fellow Diva Wynoka "Nokie" Boudreaux) glinted in the sunlight. The modest heels on our black-and-white ankle boots proved easier for me to dance in than I feared (although we did switch to flats after the first stop). The five of us and the second liners outside the ropes grooved to Da Truth Brass Band in between brief rests, and once we reached the disband site we reveled in an elated, relieved exhaustion. None of us (not even Kristy) knew that it would be the last time the City of New Orleans would grant a Second Line parade permit for fifteen months.

The day after our parade the *Wall Street Journal* published an opinion piece titled, "The Coronavirus Isn't Another Hurricane Katrina. It's Worse." Michael Gerson, who had served as President George W. Bush's policy adviser when Hurricane Katrina devastated the Gulf Coast in 2005, wrote that the coronavirus outbreak bore at least one similarity with Katrina: The problem was sure to be larger than the institutions built to deal with it. "All of the elements now exist for a swiftly unfolding emergency," he warned readers, "on a scale that dwarfs Katrina."[1] In the months to follow, other journalists echoed Gerson's comparison, especially when covering COVID-19's impact on southeast Louisiana. By the end of March 2020, just a few weeks after my fellow Divas and I had laughed off Kristy's plea to use hand sanitizer, Orleans Parish, the county in which the city of New Orleans is located, had reached the highest per capita death rate for the novel coronavirus among all U.S. counties. The county with the second highest rate lagged far behind, with a rate half that of New Orleans.[2] By then, Mayor LaToya Cantrell had implemented strict physical distancing measures that included the withdrawal of all parading permits.

In his insistence that the country learn the lessons of Katrina, Gerson did not recognize that the economic and social realities wrought by systemic racism mean that every disaster in New Orleans, like elsewhere, impacts African American residents the most. Inequalities in housing, education,

The Ice Divas S&PC line up before their Second Line parade on March 8, 2020. Left to right: Kristy Magner, Catina Braxton Robertson, Wynoka Boudreaux, Rachel Carrico, and Arielle Guice. (Photo by Freddye Hill.)

healthcare, and other basic needs impede Black residents' abilities to prepare for and recover from disaster; not surprisingly, this population felt the health and economic impacts of COVID-19 most acutely. By June 2021 the rate of African Americans dying from coronavirus tripled that of white residents.[3] Moreover, the pandemic worsened existing income disparity. According to 2010 census records, the median African American household in the city had an income of $25,000 per year, compared to the median white household income of $68,000.[4] Because of the city's heavy reliance on tourism, an industry that suffered from COVID-related travel restrictions, Moody Analytics deemed that New Orleans's economy was one of the "worst prepared" for the subsequent recession. Within the city's hospitality and entertainment economy, African American workers, overrepresented in low-wage positions and gig economy circuits, were most vulnerable to layoffs and event cancellations.[5] The city's silent streets and plywood-covered windows reminded trumpeter James Andrews of Hurricane Katrina, but with a crucial difference. "Where are you gonna run?" He said. "It's everywhere. It's bigger than Katrina."[6]

New Orleanians did not passively accept the situation. Activist groups such as Take 'Em Down NOLA took to the streets, objecting to, in their words, the "intensification of racism" made apparent "by the number of Black lives lost to Covid 19 and the forcing of Black, brown and low paid workers back to work despite the threat to their lives."[7] Their protests joined a wave of uprisings across the United States motivated by the pandemic and ignited by the deaths of Black people at the hands of police, especially George Floyd in Minneapolis and Breonna Taylor in Louisville. In a series of events that had become familiar to most Americans by 2020, a bystander captured Floyd's murder on video and made the recording publicly available online. Protests of Taylor's murder in Louisville included a viral social media campaign with the hashtag #SayHerName. But this time, many who had the privilege of looking away from the state-sanctioned murder of African Americans by police suddenly had fewer distractions. For those who were lucky enough to work or attend school remotely, like myself, physical distancing measures meant that we were often at home, glued to our screens. The events catalyzed a wave of uprisings across the country and the world condemning anti-Blackness and demanding police reform. Take 'Em Down NOLA called for an end to "the white supremacist capitalist system" that made it possible for Floyd, Taylor, and many others to be "gunned down for breathing while Black."[8] The group's statement named the ways in which racism and capitalism colluded to put Black and brown people most at risk of dying from COVID-19 and police violence.

In New Orleans, funerals—both the increased need for them and the inability to conduct them according to the city's musical tradition—came to represent a bellwether of the coronavirus's impact on the physical and social lives of Black communities. By June 2020 funeral parlors began scheduling back-to-back memorial services to keep up with the tripled demand. Funeral parlors' overbooked schedules, combined with restrictions on gatherings, meant that families and friends were unable to send off their loved ones in the communal, public, musical way that is such an important mechanism for healing. The clarinetist and historian Michael White, who has played many funerals in his long career, told local journalist Katy Reckdahl, "The thing I was wondering is what happens to all the souls that are restless and unable to completely transition. . . . It's like their soul is not being released by all of the community. It feels almost disrespectful. Of all of the hard things about the coronavirus, this is high on my list. It's just not right."[9] What's more, 2020 and 2021 saw the deaths of elders who were pillars of the cultural community such as Ronald W. Lewis (president of the Big Nine SAPC and director of the House of Dance and Feathers museum), Sylvester Francis (documentarian and director of the grassroots Backstreet Cultural Museum), Ellis Marsalis (pianist and beloved music teacher), Ezell Hines (president of the Uptown Swingers SAPC), Larry Hammond (King of Zulu SAPC's Mardi Gras parade in 2007), and Leona "Chine" Grandison (owner and proprietor of the Candlelight Lounge), to name but a few. Faced with such loss, Dow "Spy Boy" Edwards, a Black Masking Indian and leader within the cultural community, found it hard not to second line. "Now that we can't do that, it's painful," he said. "We start questioning, 'If we don't do this, will our loved one get to his rightful place?' It tears at the fiber of who we are."[10]

Edwards's words resonate with SAPC members, whose testimonies were captured by radio host Charles "Action" Jackson before his death from cancer in 2021. Known as "the voice of the Second Line community," Jackson was another cultural leader lost in a short period of time. Starting in 2011 he hosted on-air interviews with Black cultural leaders on community radio station WWOZ. During the Second Line season, he usually interviewed the president of whichever SAPC was about to hold its annual anniversary parade on the upcoming Sunday. He continued the practice during the pandemic shutdown, speaking with Second Line leaders by phone about the effects of COVID-19 on their clubs.[11] In November 2020 he asked a trio of SAPC presidents, "What mindset . . . would you have if we would never be able to second line again?" Raphael Parker of the Nine Times SAPC replied, after a sharp inhalation and an expletive, "I'm going to move. I think I'm going to leave New Orleans after that."[12] But, Parker quickly acknowledged, "'They're going to be trying to do something," recognizing second liners' unwillingness to forgo some kind of touchstone to the tradition that has sustained them for generations.

Parker was right. In response to multiple, overlapping needs brought on by the COVID-19 pandemic, New Orleanians got creative. Charbonnet Funeral Home in Tremé constructed a drive-through viewing chamber so that mourners could visit the body of the deceased, laid out behind plate glass. Musicians played virtual concerts, livestreamed on social media platforms for electronically transferred tips. The radio station WWOZ converted its daily "LiveWire" announcement of musical events to the "OnlineWire," promoting virtual concerts and encouraging listeners, as always, to "tip the musicians" through Venmo or CashApp. Action Jackson teamed up with Derrick Tabb of the Rebirth Brass Band and owner of the music venue Tremé Hideaway to bring virtual Second Lines into people's homes each Sunday. Jackson livestreamed footage of each club, captured by his friend Mr. C. From Mr. C's TV, on Tremé Hideaway's Facebook page from 1:00 to 3:00 p.m. on the date each club was supposed to parade.[13] The spirit of mutual aid, which is the wellspring of the Second Line tradition, motivated coordinated responses as well. A group of Baby Dolls, a Black Carnival masking tradition in which women parade in satin dresses, bonnets, and bloomers, began bringing lunch to funeral homes each Friday to make sure that overworked funeral directors were nourished.[14] Along with his son Traion, Travis Lyons, president of the Perfect Gentlemen SAPC, also shifted his services. As overseer of the Central City Youth Against Violence, he responded to restrictions on gathering in their center by coordinating outreach efforts to address young people's mental health through making music.[15] In an effort toward allyship, the white-run Mardi Gras group Krewe of Red Beans (named after one of the city's iconic dishes) organized "Feed the Secondline." The group partnered with SAPCs to organize weekly grocery runs for more than one hundred culture bearers and elders.[16] The project meant overcoming the considerable challenge of historical divisions and mistrust between white and Black parading organizations. Norman Dixon Jr. of the Young Men Olympian Jr. Benevolent Association was one of the many members of the Black cultural community willing to work with the Krewe of Red Beans because, as Dixon put it, "Our missions are the same."[17]

In addition to organizing mutual aid efforts, SAPCs continued to provide pleasure by practicing their culture in all the ways possible under gradually lifted restrictions. They hosted dances, coronation ceremonies, picnics, and, once venues began to open again, weekly brass band gigs. For example, on their parade day in November 2020, the Nine Times SAPC held a cookout and bike ride along the parade's traditional Ninth Ward route with the theme, "COVID Nine Times." Those who could not complete the ride but felt safe enough to gather outdoors celebrated at the cookout. According to Nine Times member Raphael Parker, "COVID Nine Times is a sickness too, because they're sick the parade is not going to be able to go. You got that COVID Nine Times? Come bike it or hike it and cure your mind in the Nine."[18] Another club that found ways to fulfill its pleasure-giving mission was the Original Big Seven SAPC, which held a party and what Big Seven president Edward Buckner called a "fake parade" on its regular date of Mother's Day in May 2021. It hired two bands so that each could lead a separate two-hour route and only attract the number of people that would allow the event to stay under the five-hundred-person limit. When I asked Buckner if he obtained a permit for this parade, he scoffed.

"They wouldn't give me a permit for that," he said. But he remained above reproach by inviting the public health department to offer COVID-19 vaccinations during the festivities.[19] Buckner's efforts to blend Second Line cultural practice with public health is but one example of his ongoing efforts to pair cultural leadership and civic activism—to weave politics with pleasure.

On May 26, 2021, New Orleans mayor LaToya Cantrell tweeted that the city would resume granting permits for Second Line parades. In addition to lifting other restrictions, she announced that "the COVID-related ban on second lines and parades will be removed and will be replaced by the traditional event permitting processes within the Department of Safety and Permits."[20] The tweet tore through second liners' social media networks, and soon enough, an ongoing text message thread among the Ice Divas created a rush of excitement. Catina let us know that we would hit the streets again in March 2022 with two words: "Let's roll." She immediately began soliciting ideas for suit and decoration colors.

A week after the mayor's announcement, I flew to New Orleans for the first time since the Divas' 2020 parade to attend a book launch for *Dancing in the Streets*, to which I had contributed an essay (alongside an essay by Action Jackson, quoted above), at the Historic New Orleans Collection.[21] The party attracted many paraders to the slick, monied French Quarter venue to see the book's companion exhibit, which featured dozens of contemporary second liners in photographs, ephemera, and oral histories, and to receive a free copy of the photo-filled book, which the HNOC offered to every SAPC member. Although the building and its surroundings stand far outside Second Line geographies in the city's Black working-class neighborhoods, the event offered an opportunity for second liners to convene with their broader community in ways that hadn't been as regularly available since the parade ban. Standing around in blue surgical and K-95 masks, club members chatted with each other and with documentarians such as myself, all speculating when the first official parade might roll. In an article posted to WWOZ's website, Tamara Jackson Snowden, president of the SAPC Task Force, reminded club presidents that, though the ban was lifted, restrictions remained. "The only restriction as it relates to us right now," she said, "is that we have to do the permitting process at least two weeks prior to the actual event. So the city is asking that we submit those applications timely with two weeks so NOPD has the opportunity to staff the parades."[22] Given the bureaucratic hurdles, and how late it was in the August–June season, Jackson Snowden logically assumed that parades would resume in August 2021, with the season's typical first parade by Valley of the Silent Men.

Since Jackson Snowden was not alone in her assumption, many were surprised that the first permitted "post-pandemic" Second Line was the Perfect Gentlemen Social and Pleasure Club's Father's Day parade on June 20. This club, founded in 1991, is one of the few organizations to hold two parades per year. Its full four-hour Second Line starts each calendar year on the first Sunday of January, and it holds a two-hour Father's Day celebration each June. Two weeks before Father's Day, the Instagram and Facebook accounts of SAPC members and brass band musicians circulated the news. "UPDATE PEOPLE," announced one post. "1ST SECONDLINE FATHERS DAY 6/20/21."

I decided to fly back for it, so I arrived in New Orleans for the second time in three weeks, after fifteen months away, on June 19, 2021. A tropical storm brewing in the Gulf of Mexico threatened to derail the parade, but I decided to risk it and boarded the plane anyway. The gamble paid off. Despite the forecast, the weekend unfolded with just a few sprinkles.

As I made my way toward New Orleans on Saturday, I learned that the Original Big Seven was also planning a march for the next day. Edward Buckner's Facebook post featured a flyer announcing its "Father's Day Celebration/Stop the Violence March" and urging New Orleanians to "celebrate life with a Secondline." Below the start time and location, the flyer promised, "Security in effect." I called Buckner while waiting for my flight to ask about the march and let him know I'd be there. He said that he wanted to take a stand against gun violence, which has always been a problem in New Orleans but had lessened as people remained inside during the months of physical restrictions. Now, as those restrictions loosened, rates of violence had begun to rise.[23] "It's touching our families," Buckner told me, explaining that his sister Deneen Buckner had found herself in the middle of a shootout while driving on the I-10 high rise on May 27 and had taken a bullet to her leg. Buckner emphasized that the Big Seven's march was not just about police violence, which had been the focus of recent nationwide protests. "It's not only the police," Buckner said. "We're killing each other and it's got to stop." He planned to issue his plea in a language that would speak directly to New Orleanians: brass band music and footwork.

So, on June 20, 2021, not one but two processions hosted by different SAPCs marked the city's emergence from the grip of COVID-19. The Perfect Gentlemen's Second Line was a humble but joyous affair. A handful of Perfect Gentlemen sported simple matching white T-shirts and pants, accented with white bandanas tied around their necks and white baseball caps with a yellow *P* embroidered on the front. They each carried a cane wrapped in white tape. The To Be Continued (TBC) Brass Band

Traion Lyons of the Perfect Gentlemen SAPC comes flying out the door at the start of the June 21, 2021, parade. (Photo by MJ Mastrogiovanni.)

arrived an hour after the advertised start time. Despite a sense of anticipation—as I walked up, I heard a woman with short hair exclaim to no one in particular, "I've been waiting so long for this!"—few seemed to mind the delay. It allowed a rare opportunity to mingle, check in, and catch up. People greeted each other with strong hugs, wide smiles, and expressions of gratitude for the cool breeze. The tropical storm had left behind cloud cover and lower temperatures, so communing felt more comfortable than could be expected during a New Orleans June day. We stood just outside A. L. Davis Park, formerly (and still locally known as) Shakespeare Park, where marchers gathered in 1963 for the Freedom March as well as innumerable pleasurable and political processions before and after. I wondered if this day would also be recorded in the history books (this one aside) as another momentous occasion on these very streets, themselves figuratively engraved with many important events in the city's Black history.

When the band finally arrived, the musicians catapulted the crowd into forward motion from the center of Washington Avenue and LaSalle Street. It led a crowd that grew over the course of the short route, which we had no trouble completing within the remaining permitted hour. Many regular second liners including Terrylyn "Secondline Shorty" Dorsey, Rodrick "Scubble" Davis, and Wellington "Skelly" Ratcliff Jr. went toe-to-toe (and wheel-to-toe, in Ratcliff's case) with Perfect Gentlemen club members and TBC musicians in energetic exchanges of music and footwork. On the periphery, friendly dance competitions emerged between graying men in seersucker suits and alligator shoes. Encouraging circles held young people who tried out new footwork skills (see video 7.1 on this book's web page). The intergenerational space of the Second Line resumed passing on physical know-how, cultural values, and love as seamlessly as if the practice had never stopped. Perhaps that's because it never completely did.

Before attending the Perfect Gentlemen's parade, I arrived at the starting point for the Big Seven's march on the other side of town. There, I also encountered a delay. I joined a huddle of Big Seven club members, who wore matching white shirts screen-printed with their club insignia and, on the sleeve, the names of all deceased members. Two photographers waited along with a smattering of supporters. The small crowd chatted for about thirty minutes until Buckner approached each cluster and explained the reason for the delay: The police escorts had not yet arrived. We had all assumed that the police cars that had pulled up earlier were there for the parade, but they had arrived to guard some construction equipment in an adjacent lot. Buckner, while waiting for a callback from NOPD, made the decision to go without them.

The NOPD's absence seemed suspicious to Buckner given his recent outspokenness against the city's role in managing the existence of New Orleans's grassroots Black cultural practices, especially Second Line parades. In an on-air interview with Action Jackson the previous month, Buckner countered Jackson's support of the mayor's physical distancing measures. As much as he supported vaccination efforts, he remained critical of the moratorium on Second Line permits, especially because the city found a way to provide opportunities for "alternative" Mardi Gras parades in 2021. In the end, he concluded, the Second Line culture "was never meant to be governed by the city."[24] Indeed, Second Lines had started crisscrossing New Orleans's streets long before politicians and police began to regulate them in the mid-twentieth century. Buckner named the delicate balance that SAPCs must strike. On one hand, they are forced to abide by legal ordinances and bureaucratic protocols so that the state will continue to permit, literally and figuratively, parades and other cultural practices to exist; on the other hand, the more that parades and other cultural expressions are domesticated by the state, the more they risk losing touch with the counter-hegemonic roots, sustenance networks, resources, and values that provide an alternative to, if not directly oppose, capitalist and white dominant cultures.

On Buckner's cue, the Young Fellaz Brass Band swung into action as a Big Seven member pulled Buckner's red pickup truck into the lake-bound lanes of Gentilly Boulevard. The truck carried Deneen Buckner, who hung a handmade sign out the window: "Gun Violence = Community Destruction." We filed in behind the truck, carrying signs proclaiming anti-violence messages while step-touching to the brass band's beats. Benjamin "BJ" Jones, the club's public relations manager, held a sign remembering his sons, both victims of gun violence. Cars lined up behind us, slowly and patiently crawling along. The only honks came from cars passing in the opposite direction, whose drivers waved in support. A couple of women emerged onto their porch and danced; one ran down the stairs and toward the procession. As the band passed an assisted living home, an elderly resident made her way to the sidewalk, leaned onto her walker, and grooved.

The route, which bordered Dillard University, was an unusual one for Second Line parades. In fact, it was not the intended route. Buckner wanted to begin at Columbia Parc, site of the former St. Bernard public housing development and the club's founding, where they might reach young people affected by systemic violence. However, he said, the NOPD required him to dramatically shorten the route, which eliminated Columbia Parc. Despite Buckner's having complied with the city's permitting processes, no NOPD officers ever arrived to escort the march. Twenty-four hours after the march, he had yet to receive word about their absence. The march marked another moment in Buckner's long history of negotiations with city hall and the police department in his efforts to keep his culture alive. When gun violence has erupted during or after the Big Seven's annual Second Line (as occurred in 2013, detailed in Chapter 2, and again in 2018), or when private developers have threatened to shut down the club's route through the site of the St. Bernard (2016, discussed in Chapter 6), Buckner and his club members' advocacy on and off the streets has asserted the need for, and power of, Second Line cultural practices. That power was not lost on me as I joined my first parade in more than a year. I felt a surge of happiness rise in my chest as I slipped into the street and strutted in syncopated time to the singular Second Line beat. At one point, I looked up and smiled to see that we were crossing Pleasure Street (see video 7.2 on this book's web page).

Both events on June 20, 2021, showcased the power of pleasure—the cross-generational nourishment, love, support, and connection—that was so needed as the city emerged from the devastation of COVID-19, grappled with the effects of structural and interpersonal violence, and reckoned, once again, with unabated police terror. The two marches also demonstrated Bucker's insistence that the Second Line culture "was never

The Original Big Seven SAPC crosses Pleasure Street as it leads a march against violence on June 21, 2021. (Photo by the author.)

meant to be governed by the city."[25] Yes, city-issued permits returned, allowing these events to occur, but the state's renewed permission is not the most significant benchmark in second liners' path through the pandemic's enduring hardships. Black New Orleanians have danced through the streets for centuries as one way to maneuver within and against structures of racist and economic violence: from enslavement to Jim Crow, from Reaganomics to the Katrina disaster. The coronavirus pandemic was no different. The SAPCs and cultural leaders stepped in to care for Black life where the state failed it, to affirm Black humanity in the face of dehumanization, and to meticulously, assiduously insist on the abundance of Black joy.

Notes

Chapter 1. Coming Out the Door

A portion of this chapter was previously published as "Catina Braxton: A Human Race of Second Liners," *Data News Weekly*, February 28–March 6, 2014, p. 4.

1. The term *Second Line* appears in print in a variety of ways: as one word, as two words, hyphenated, capitalized, and lowercase. I take my cues from Karen Celestan's directives regarding capitalization when writing about Second Lines, honoring the event, the collective, and the dance and musical forms as capitalized proper nouns. When the term appears as a verb, or is modified to "second liner," I do not capitalize. See Waters and Celestan, *Freedom's Dance*, xiii.

2. Sharpe, *In the Wake*, 104. When encountering the notion of hostile weather in the context of New Orleans, one might think of hurricanes, most notably Hurricane Katrina (2005). As many analysts have shown, it was the climate of antiblackness, not the rain and wind, that made the event a disaster for so many African American New Orleanians. See, e.g., Horowitz, *Katrina*.

3. Sharpe, *In the Wake*, 106.

4. "New Orleans and the Domestic Slave Trade Historical Marker," https://www.hmdb.org/m.asp?m=117438; W. Johnson, *Soul by Soul*; R. Johnson, *Slavery's Metropolis*.

5. Thomas, *Desire and Disaster in New Orleans*, 95, 101.

6. Arena, "Black and White." For more on public housing post-Katrina, see Chapter 6.

7. Sharpe, *In the Wake*, 12, 106.

8. Sharpe, *In the Wake*, 14.

9. Sakakeeny, "'Under the Bridge,'" 2–3.

10. Lipsitz, *How Racism Takes Place*, 224; Michna, "Hearing the Hurricane

Coming," 32–33; Kalamu ya Salaam, "Guarding the Flame of Life: The Funeral of Big Chief Donald Harrison Sr.," *Offbeat* (January 1999): 50–51.

11. Noah Bonaparte Pais, "An Original Passes," The Gambit, March 2, 2009, www.bestofneworleans.com/gambit/antoinette-kandmdashdoe/Content?oid =1255710. See also Carrico, "Reinvention: Miss Antoinette K-Doe and Her Baby Dolls."

12. Writing about "explicitly libidinal dance" in contemporary hip hop, Jasmine E. Johnson asks if we might move "toward an analytic in which pleasure is conjoined to pain—where power might be stolen, usurped, and reigned through the execution and mastery of flesh." Johnson, "Flesh Dance" (155). Writing about African American women dancing under enslavement and in jook joints in the early twentieth century, the historians Stephanie Camp and Tera Hunter (respectively) also argue that, for a person who has encountered oppression through the body, claiming one's body for one's self as a source of pleasure, pride, and expression can be powerful. Camp, *Closer to Freedom*, 62; Hunter, *To 'joy My Freedom*, 184.

13. Quoted in a. brown, *Pleasure Activism*, 271.

14. Prince of Wales SAPC, "Charter and By-Laws."

15. C. Jacobs, "Benevolent Societies of New Orleans Blacks," 21–33.

16. Solnit, "We Won't Bow Down."

17. Raeburn, "Dancing Hot and Sweet," 10.

18. Brothers, *Louis Armstrong's New Orleans*, 142.

19. Vaz-Deville, *"Baby Dolls,"* 30–37.

20. "The Atlantics," *New Orleans Republican*, January 19, 1872, 5; "Grand Military Ball," *New Orleans Republican*, January 23, 1873, 5.

21. Advertisement, *New Orleans Republican*, February 26, 1875.

22. "C.A. and P. Club Meets," *Louisiana Weekly*, November 17, 1928, 5; "Leisure Hour Pleasure and Embroidery Club," *Louisiana Weekly*, March 2, 1929, 5; "Zion City Sick and Friendship Club," *Louisiana Weekly*, March 2, 1929, 5.

23. Terrylyn Dorsey and Terrinika Smith, interview with the author, August 8, 2014.

24. Tamara Jackson Snowden, interview with the author, April 21, 2014.

25. Martin, *Critical Moves*, 3.

26. The historian Ned Sublette makes a similar assertion: "A second line is in effect a civil rights demonstration. Literally, demonstrating the civil right of the community to assemble in the street for peaceful purposes. Or, more simply, demonstrating the civil right of the community to exist." Sublette, email communication with Flaherty, quoted in Flaherty, *Floodlines*, 8.

27. Martin, *Critical Moves*, 25.

28. Martin, *Critical Moves*, 14.

29. A partial list includes C. Cooper, *Sound Clash*; Das, *Katherine Dunham*; Jasmine Johnson, "Flesh Dance"; Jones, "Can Rihanna Have Her Cake and Eat It Too?"; Lomax, "Black Bodies in Ecstasy"; Ophir, "Dancing to Transgress: Palestinian Dancer Sahar Damoni's Politics of Pleasure"; Monroe, "Oh No! Not This Lesbian Again!"; Nash, *Black Body in Ecstasy*; Schwadron, *Case of*

the Sexy Jewess; Warner, *Acts of Gaiety: LGBT Performance and the Politics of Pleasure*; Vaz-Deville, "Baby Dolls."

30. Reed, "Introduction: Black Pleasure," 169. The legal theorist Patricia J. Williams argued for the "much more" to Black pleasure in 1991 when she wrote, "The history of our [African Americans'] need is certainly moving enough to have been called poetry, oratory, epic entertainment—but it has never been portrayed by white institutions as the statement of a political priority. . . . Some of our greatest politicians have been forced to become ministers or blues singers." Williams, *Alchemy of Race and Rights*, 151.

31. Morgan, "Why We Get Off," 38. Morgan's work and that of others expands—and critiques—Audre Lorde's foundational 1984 essay on the erotic, which claims it as "an assertion of the lifeforce of women; of that creative energy empowered, the knowledge of which we are now reclaiming in our language, our history, our dancing, our loving, our work, our lives." Lorde, "Uses of the Erotic," 55.

32. Perry, "Racism Is Terrible."

33. For example, see Kleaver Cruz's "Black Joy Project" (https://kleavercruz.com/the-black-joy-project) and Cityline Canada's *How Celebrating Black Joy Online Became a Movement*. See also Tracey Micha'el Lewis-Giggetts's 2021 editorial for the *Washington Post*, "Perspective: My Daughter Reminded Me That Black Joy Is a Form of Resistance," which led to numerous podcast episodes, programming at the Smithsonian National Museum of African American History and Culture (Nichols, "Black Joy"), and a 2022 book by Lewis-Giggetts, *Black Joy*. Concurrently, and sometimes in conversation with Black joy but sometimes not, the "politics of pleasure" also entered mainstream parlance, as evidenced by the *Boston Review*'s 2022 issue of the same title. The issue included Black feminist and queer perspectives from such writers as adrienne maree brown, Jennifer Nash, and Jack Parlett, but also welcomed articles on topics as wide-ranging as "alternative hedonism" and nineteenth-century British designer William Morris (Chasman and Cohen, *Politics of Pleasure*). While some theorists draw distinctions between pleasure, joy, and ecstasy (see, e.g., Jennifer Nash's specific definitions for these terms in Nash, *Black Body in Ecstasy*, 54–58, 96–106, 147–151), I use *pleasure* in the way social aid and pleasure clubs do pleasure and discuss it, as a wide umbrella to encompass all manners of happiness, satisfaction, enjoyment, thrill, eroticism, and love.

34. Brown, *Pleasure Activism*, especially the introduction.

35. Cedric Robinson first used the term "racial capitalism" to describe the process by which capitalism's development and subsequent structures have been permeated, from the outset, by racialized hierarchies. Robinson, *Black Marxism: The Making of the Black Radical Tradition*. In her study of transnational Indian dancers, Priya Srinivasan reveals that thinking about dance as labor, even when dance is done for pleasure, can help illuminate the ways in which dancing is enmeshed within political economies. Srinivasan, *Sweating Saris*.

36. Browning, *Samba*; DeFrantz, "Black Beat Made Visible."
37. Hooks, *Black Looks*, 39.
38. Carrico and Tigner, "Close-Up."
39. E. Johnson, "'Quare' Studies," 7 (emphasis in original).
40. Regis, "Second Lines," 496.
41. In the twenty-first century, the Backstreet Cultural Museum began emailing a route sheet to its donors and subscribers each week. This is how I first began receiving route sheets. Since 2012 the community radio station WWOZ New Orleans 90.7 FM's blog and podcast, *Takin' It to the Streets*, has posted route sheets, along with audio interviews with SAPC members, for each week's upcoming parade (http://www.wwoz.org/new-orleans-community/inthestreet). J. Cooper, *Dancing in the Streets*, 128.
42. Thomas, *Desire and Disaster*, 172–173.
43. Tyree Smith, interview with the author, February 18, 2014.
44. Fischlin, Heble, and Lipsitz use the phrase "tactical mobility" to describe activism in New Orleans in *Fierce Urgency of Now*, 162. They evoke Michel de Certeau's formulation of *strategies* and *tactics*, used to describe power struggles over public space. De Certeau, *Practice of Everyday Life*.
45. Rebirth Brass Band, *Do Whatcha Wanna*.
46. Bowling and Carrico, "Lakeviews."
47. Carrico, "On Thieves."
48. For recent histories of Mardi Gras or Black Masking Indians in New Orleans, see Dewulf, *From the Kingdom of Kongo*, and Greene, "Aesthetics of Asé."
49. Since there were no available Sunday spots in 2013 for recently formed clubs to parade (and at the time of writing there still are none), the Ice Divas parade with the more established Keep-N-It Real Social & Pleasure Club as an autonomous but connected outfit each year.
50. Thank you to Nadine George-Graves for making this point clear to me.
51. Smith, "New Orleans' Hidden Carnival," 7.
52. Salaam, "Second Line," 31.
53. Drewal, "State of Research," 33–35. Helen A. Regis cites Drewal to reflect on her ethnographic research into this practice, "Second Lines," 482.
54. Coates, "My President Was Black."
55. My dancing ethnographer body might be described as what Francesca Castaldi calls the "corpo-real." The corpo-real body carries histories that reach back to previous generations of ethnographers and colonizers, constantly mediating between past and present, and between personal interactions and macropolitical processes. This introduction follows Castaldi's insistence that ethnographers insert their own bodies into the writing by relating them to the histories that shape the interactions between social subjects and the networks of power in which they participate. Castaldi, *Choreographies of African Identities*, 5.
56. Catina Braxton Robertson, interview with the author, April 14, 2014.
57. Catina Braxton Robertson, interview with the author, April 14, 2014.

58. Alghali and Falker-Obichigha, "Tipping Points."

59. I owe much of my education on this matter to Urban Bush Women's workshop "EBX: Entering, Building, and Exiting Community," which I took when attending the company's Summer Leadership Institutes in multiple years in New York and New Orleans. For more on the institute, see George-Graves, *Urban Bush Women*, 176–182; https://www.urbanbushwomen.org/summer-leadership.

60. Regis, "Second Lines," 482.

61. "Participation thus becomes an end in itself rather than a means of gathering closely observed data which will be subject to interpretation elsewhere *after the event*." Michael Jackson, *Paths Toward a Clearing*, 134–135, quoted in Drewal, "State of Research," 34.

62. Michna, "Hearing the Hurricane Coming"; Regis, "Blackness and the Politics of Memory"; Turner, *Jazz Religion*.

63. Breunlin and Regis, "Putting the Ninth Ward on the Map"; Z. Johnson, "Walking the Post-Disaster City"; Lipsitz, "Learning from New Orleans"; Lipsitz, *How Racism Takes Place*; Regis, "Second Lines"; Roach, "Mardi Gras Indians and Others."

64. Dinerstein, "Second Lining Post-Katrina."

65. Olsen, "Gift."

66. Raeburn, "They're Tryin' to Wash Us Away."

67. White, "New Orleans Brass Band," 78.

68. Sakakeeny, *Roll With It*, 34.

69. Stearns and Stearns, *Jazz Dance*; Emery, *Black Dance*.

70. Stearns and Stearns, *Jazz Dance;* Malone, *Steppin' on the Blues*, 183; Vaz-Deville, *"Baby Dolls,"* 38; Kalamu ya Salaam quoted in Breunlin, Lewis, and Regis, *House of Dance and Feathers*, 155. More extended discussions of dancing at the Second Line can be found in Roland Wingfield's 1959 essay for *Dance Magazine*, "New Orleans Marching Bands," and Greer Mendy's chapter on second lining in her 2018 book *Black Dance in Louisiana*.

71. Kyle DeCoste's MA thesis on the all-female Pinettes Brass Band documents a notable exception. DeCoste, "Street Queens."

72. The musicologist Inger Damsholt writes that "the relationship between music and dance has long been understood by means of a gendered metaphor, more specifically as a male/female relationship" (Damsholt, "Marriage of Music and Dance," 237–242). Throughout the nineteenth century and much of the twentieth in Europe, music was assigned an increasingly masculine role and dance a feminine one (music theory was founded on the hard science of acoustics; the Hegelian scheme of the arts reflected music as male/spirit and dance as female/body; and the ballet stage was filled with ballerinas while the orchestra pit held men). Writing of nineteenth-century Romantic ballet, the dance scholar Susan Leigh Foster similarly argues, "Other arts' capacity to edify and educate their audiences and to leave behind definitive documentation of their composition carried a masculine weight and authority that the pleasure-filled and ephemeral dance could not match." Foster, *Choreography*

and Narrative, 10. The dichotomy largely holds in literature concerning African American music but is complicated by social ideas about the mind/body split mapped onto gender *and* race. See Gaunt, *Games Black Girls Play*, 3–12.

73. Examples from the 1970s to 2020 include, in chronological order, Buerkle and Barker, *Bourbon Street Black*; W. Schafer, *Brass Bands*; Roach, "Mardi Gras Indians and Others"; White, "New Orleans Brass Band"; Burns, *Keeping the Beat on the Street*; Sakakeeny, *Roll With It*; Stooges Brass Band and DeCoste, *Can't Be Faded*. Kim Marie Vaz-Deville's recent scholarship on the Baby Dolls, an African American women's masking tradition, has broken open crucial conversations about intersectional analyses of race and gender in New Orleans's Black parading cultures. Vaz-Deville, *"Baby Dolls"*; Vaz-Deville, *Walking Raddy*.

74. Barnes and Breunlin, *Talk That Music Talk*, 73.

75. On the brass band renaissance see Burns, *Keeping the Beat on the Street*.

76. Woods, *Development Drowned and Reborn*, 181.

Interlude: Barbara Lacen Keller

This interview was conducted by the author as part of the oral history project "More Than Merely Fun: Dance, Politics and Pleasure at the New Orleans Second Line," funded by the New Orleans Jazz and Heritage Foundation Archive Fellowship (2016–2017). A recording and transcript of the full interview are housed at the New Orleans Jazz and Heritage Foundation Archive and available on this book's companion website.

1. For more on the founding of the Lady Money Wasters and the Lady Buckjumpers, see Jarrett Johnson et al., "Money Wasters," and Tapp, "Lady Buckjumpers."

Chapter 2. Community

1. Edward Buckner, interview with the author, July 30, 2013.

2. Nicole Lazard, interview with the author, September 7, 2017.

3. Although many newer clubs have updated their idea of what mutual aid means for their members, three of the earliest benevolent associations are still active and adhere to more traditional ideals: the Young Men Olympian Jr. Benevolent Society (established in 1884), Zulu Social Aid and Pleasure Club (1909), and Original Men's Prince of Wales (1928). Of the three, Young Men Olympian is most dedicated to the traditional style of a benevolent society. Their membership numbers are much higher than those of other clubs (more than one hundred, compared to under ten for many clubs), their oldest divisions still parade in traditional dress of black and white suits and hire brass bands to play traditional music, and their members still receive medical and burial assistance. Olsen, "Gift"; Wellington Ratcliff Jr., interview with the author and Daniella Santoro, March 26, 2014; Don Robertson, interview with the author, April 10, 2014.

4. The Norman Dixon Sr. Annual Second Line Parade fund, administered by the New Orleans Jazz and Heritage Foundation and managed by Norman Dixon Jr., financially supports a select number of SAPCs, usually in exchange for their performance at the organization's annual Jazz and Heritage Festival. Regis and Walton, "Producing the Folk," 411–416; C. Jackson, "Year Without Second Lines," 285. But even with additional assistance, club members and their families and friends regularly make financial sacrifices in order to participate.

5. Tyree Smith, interview with the author, February 18, 2014.

6. Gerald Platenburg, interview with the author, March 28, 2017.

7. Catina Braxton Robertson, interview with the author, April 14, 2014. These SAPC members' reflections give credence to Margaret Olsen's conclusion that the Second Line tradition operates as a gift economy, one that values welfare assistance, communal wealth, and the right of each community to own public space and that offers an alternative to individualistic neoliberal economies that value private wealth and accumulation. Olsen, "Gift."

8. Several times throughout our interview (September 5, 2017), Barbara Lacen Keller referred to the African American community as the group that she is accountable to as a cultural leader and community activist.

9. Tamara Jackson Snowden, interview with the author, April 21, 2014.

10. Julie Johnson, "Dancing Down the Floor," 161–162.

11. George-Graves, *Urban Bush Women*, 168–169. For another review of literature on community, see 167–170.

12. Amit and Rapport, *Trouble with Community*; Nancy, "Confronted Community"; Joseph, *Against the Romance of Community*.

13. Joseph, *Against the Romance of Community*, xxx–xxxiii.

14. Crehan, *Community Art*, 41, quoted in Julie Johnson, "Dancing Down the Floor," xvi.

15. Joseph, *Against the Romance of Community*, xxx–xxxiii.

16. Goldman, *I Want to Be Ready*.

17. Nancy, "Confronted Community," 31–32.

18. Johnson, "Dancing Down the Floor," 156.

19. In "Commonalities in African Dance," Kariamu Welsh (who published this essay as Kariamu Welsh Asante) names the following as key aesthetics of African dance: a curvilinear or circular quality in form, shape, and structure and a holistic sense, in which the whole is emphasized over the individual (75).

20. Edward Buckner, Terry Gable, and Leo Gorman, interview with the author, January 24, 2014.

21. Yvonne Daniel makes this same observation when watching ritual dancers in Haiti and Cuba: "Everyone inside was dancing and performing the identifying *oricha* gestures together, sensitively, above the changing but repetitive foot patterns. [In Cuba, just] like in Haiti, despite the densely crowded space, no one stepped on anyone's toes!" *Dancing Wisdom*, 20–21.

22. For example, in Cuba, African religious and cultural groups formed

nominally Catholic associations, or *cabildos*. In Brazil, people of African descent formed brotherhoods and sisterhoods called *irmandades*. Daniel, *Caribbean and Atlantic Diaspora Dance*, 133. For connections between Kongolese brotherhood groups and those in Latin America and New Orleans, see Dewulf, *From the Kingdom of Kongo*.

23. C. Jacobs, "Benevolent Societies," 22.

24. Logsdon and Bell, "Americanization of Black New Orleans," 233, 243.

25. Claude Jacobs notes that, in 1902, members of the Louisiana State Medical Society were told that pneumonia and tuberculosis would undoubtedly "solve the negro problem in the state" by killing off the Black population. Louisiana State Medical Society, *Transactions of the Louisiana State Medical Society* (1902), 130–131, quoted in Jacobs, "Benevolent Societies," 21.

26. Jacobs, "Benevolent Societies."

27. Arneson, "Learning the Lessons of Solidarity," 33. See also Buerkle and Barker, *Bourbon Street Black*, 9; Germany, *New Orleans After the Promises*, 248; Roach, *Cities of the Dead*, 179–237.

28. *Creole* is derived from the Portuguese *crioulo*, which in seventeenth-century Louisiana denoted a slave of African descent born in the New World. As the Louisiana historian Gwendolyn Midlo Hall writes, the word means "born here"—native, local. Over time the designations "Black" and "Creole" in New Orleans have become not interchangeable, nor historically bound, but "irreconcilable." Hall, *Africans in Colonial Louisiana*, 157–158. For a sample of the restrictions imposed on Afro-Creole New Orleanians in the early 1800s, including the prohibition of marriages between free people of color and whites, restricted access to public accommodations, and bans on entry, see Bell, *Revolution, Romanticism*, 75–81.

29. Emery, *Black Dance*, 149–154.

30. Hirsch and Logsdon, *Creole New Orleans*, esp. "Part III: Franco-Africans and African Americans," 189–319.

31. Shaik, *Economy Hall*, 236–240.

32. Logsdon and Bell, "Americanization of Black New Orleans," 233–234. For more on the Economy Society, see Shaik, *Economy Hall*. For more on the Prince Hall Masons, see Mitchell, Edwards, and Weldon, *Monumental*.

33. H. Walker, "Negro Benevolent Societies"; C. Jacobs, "Benevolent Societies."

34. Malone, *Steppin' on the Blues*, 168, 174–175.

35. W. Schafer, *Brass Bands*, 12; Hirsch, "Simply a Matter of Black and White," 266.

36. Buerkle and Barker, *Bourbon Street Black*, 10.

37. White, "New Orleans Brass Band," 77; Schafer, *Brass Bands*, 2; Buerkle and Barker, *Bourbon Street Black*, 17.

38. While many Black church leaders and congregants were opposed to Second Lines (and some still are), White claims that the parades' spiritual function is what eventually attracted Protestants to hold their own parades (and to join Second Lines and jazz funerals), for the same "emotionalism that

caused them to shout, cry, and dance with the 'spirit' could be expressed in parades." White, "New Orleans Brass Band," 80–81.

39. Sakakeeny, *Roll With It*, 18.

40. Schafer, *Brass Bands*, 21.

41. By the late nineteenth century, approximately four-fifths of New Orleanians of all races and ethnicities belonged to mutual aid societies, but Black residents continued to form these associations when they lost popularity with ethnic white residents, and even when membership declined within Black communities in the rest of the United States. Jacobs, "Benevolent Societies," 22.

42. H. Walker, "Negro Benevolent Societies," 43.

43. Malone, *Steppin' on the Blues*, 167 (emphasis in original).

44. Dewulf, *From the Kingdom of Kongo*.

45. Sakakeeny, *Roll With It*, 159–163. On the SilenceIsViolence march following Shavers's death, see 168–172.

46. Tamara Jackson Snowden, interview with the author, April 21, 2014.

47. Tamara Jackson Snowden, interview with the author, April 21, 2014. For more on SilenceIsViolence, see Watts and Porter, *New Orleans Suite*, 33–53.

48. Tamara Jackson Snowden, interview with the author, April 21, 2014.

49. Sakakeeny, *Roll With It*, 144–145.

50. Citing the anthropologist Phillipe Bourgois's study of Puerto Rican drug dealers in East Harlem, Sakakeeny observes the "crucial role that public displays of violence play in establishing credibility on the street." Bourgois, *In Search of Respect*, 171, quoted in Sakakeeny, *Roll With It*, 146.

51. Regis, "Second Lines," 486; Sakakeeny, *Roll With It*, 25; Michna, "Hearing the Hurricane Coming," 35.

52. Baker, *Turning South Again*. Dance scholar Danielle Goldman adopts Baker's term to discuss dance's connection to social and historical tight places. She explains that an improviser often "escapes confinement only to enter into or become aware of another set of strictures," and understanding the mover's ability to flexibly negotiate ever-changing constraints "is vital to understanding the political power of improvisation." Goldman, *I Want to Be Ready*, 4.

53. Campbell Robertson and Katy Reckdahl, "Celebrating, in Spite of the Risk," *The New York Times*, May 15, 2013, sec. U.S. https://www.nytimes.com/2013/05/15/us/new-orleans-parades-celebrating-in-spite-of-the-risk.html.

54. Thanos, "New Orleans Mother's Day Shooting."

55. Watts and Porter, *New Orleans Suite*, 50.

56. Sakakeeny, *Roll With It*, 127–130.

57. Tamara Jackson Snowden, interview with the author, April 21, 2014.

58. Katy Reckdahl, "The Price of Parading," *Offbeat*, November 1, 2006, https://www.offbeat.com/articles/the-price-of-parading/.

59. Watts and Porter, *New Orleans Suite*, 43.

60. Troeh, "Transcript: Second Line Fee Increase."

61. "Complaint," *Social Aid and Pleasure Club Task Force et al. v. City of New Orleans*, No. 06–10057 (E.D. La., Nov. 16, 2006), at 17.

62. Tamara Jackson Snowden, interview with the author, April 21, 2014; Katy Reckdahl, "Permit Fees Raining on Second-Line Parades," *Times-Picayune*, March 29, 2007, http://blog.nola.com/topnews/200Seven/03/permit_fees_raining_on_secondl.html. For more on the post-Katrina lawsuit regarding Second Line permitting fees, see Sakakeeny, *Roll With It*, 34–35; Watts and Porter, *New Orleans Suite*, 42–46.

63. In 2008 the task force and the ACLU once again brought legal action against the city when it threatened to revoke a parade permit it had previously granted for a Second Line on February 4, 2008, allegedly in favor of events hosted on the same day by two large Mardi Gras organizations. After the task force refused to move its parade, citing the large effort and expense that had already gone into organizing it, the NOPD began to apply "improper pressure" by making veiled assertions that the department would "deny permits to the Second Line organizations in the future for each organization's upcoming annual parade." Although the task force was successful in following through with its planned parade, some organizations succumbed to the pressure and withdrew from participation. Memorandum of Law in Support of Plaintiffs' Motion for a Temporary Restraining Order, *Social Aid and Pleasure Club Task Force v. City of New Orleans*, No. 08–803 (E.D. LA, 2008), at 5; Banks, "Post-Katrina Suppression."

64. Robertson and Reckdahl, "Celebrating."

65. Nola Martin, "Feds Indict 9 in Mother's Day Gang Shooting, Other Crimes," *Times-Picayune*, March 12, 2014, https://www.nola.com/news/crime_police/article_db2d246d-18ea-5c0e-8a1e-400c866c3bea.html. According to a 2016 press release from the U.S. Attorney's Office, the charges were later absorbed into a federal case against the Scott brothers and five other members of the Frenchmen/Derbigny gang on charges of racketeering, dealing in narcotics, and crimes of violence. Pursuant to plea agreements, all pled guilty to the charges; the Scott brothers pled guilty to the Mother's Day shooting and were sentenced to life in prison plus ten years. U.S. Attorney's Office, Eastern District of Louisiana, "FnD Gang Members Sentenced for Racketeering, Narcotics, and Violent Crimes, including the Mother's Day Shooting," press release, March 29, 2016,

https://www.justice.gov/usao-edla/pr/fnd-gang-members-sentenced-racketeering-narcotics-and-violent- crimes-including-mother- s#:~:text =SHAWN%20SCOTT%2C%20STANLEY%20SCOTT%2C%20and, 5%20 years%20of%20supervised%20release.

66. Edward Buckner, "Mother's Day Second Line Helps Nourish not Only the City's Culture but the Younger Generation," *Times-Picayune*, May 15, 2013, https://www.nola.com/opinions/article_3174a02e-b53c-5b72-8e6a-42a7e1730381.html.

67. Cotton's blog is no longer in operation, but, as of July 2021, her YouTube and Facebook pages were still viewable. Cotton, "BigRedCotton"; Cotton, "Big Red Cotton—Facebook."

68. Deborah "Big Red" Cotton, quoted in Katy Reckdahl, "Deborah Cotton, Writer Shot in 2013 Mother's Day Second-line Shooting, Dies at 52," *Times-Picayune*, May 2, 2017, https://www.nola.com/article_4daf1521-034c-502f-80f3-542ad93e5310.html.

69. Kevin Litten, "Deb 'Big Red' Cotton Remembered for Joy, Activism in Memorial Service," *Times-Picayune*, June 10, 2017, https://www.nola.com/news/crime_police/article_44a30387-cae1-5618-b983-eaf6ebad5f00.html.

70. Jarvis DeBerry, "Mother's Day Shooting in New Orleans Can't Put an End to Our Dance," *nola.com*, May 14, 2013, https://www.nola.com/opinions/article_8df9b50a-172b-5e4a-8229-a144564e839b.html.

71. Reflecting on Michelle Rosaldo's sudden death while doing research in the Philippines, the anthropologist Ruth Behar writes, "Yes, that was what had scared me the most: that you could die doing fieldwork, that the danger of dying was real, because fieldwork is about nothing more primitive than confronting, with our contemporaries, our own mortality." Behar, *Vulnerable Observer*, 172.

72. Imani Perry writes of "the spiritual majesty of joy in suffering" characteristic of Black culture and life in "Racism Is Terrible."

73. D'Amico-Samuels, "Undoing Fieldwork."

74. Regis, "Blackness and the Politics of Memory," 754.

75. Giroux, "Reading Hurricane Katrina." See also Butler, *Notes Toward a Performative Theory of Assembly*, esp. "Precarious Life and the Ethics of Cohabitation," 99–122.

76. Alex Woodward, "Sunday Bloody Sunday," *Gambit*, May 21, 2013, 7. See also Robertson and Reckdahl, "Celebrating."

77. Adam Nossiter, "Another Social Conflict Confronts New Orleans," *New York Times*, November 26, 2006, https://www.nytimes.com/2006/11/26/us/26parade.html.

78. "NOLA for Life Playbook," 17; see also Joshua Dubois, "Shutting Down America's Killing Fields," *Politico*, March 6, 2014, https://www.politico.com/magazine/story/2014/03/gun-violence-mayors-104389/.

79. Tamara Jackson Snowden, interview with the author, April 21, 2014.

80. In 1980, critical race theorist Derrick Bell Jr. coined the concept of "interest convergence," which holds that the "interest of blacks in achieving racial equality will be accommodated only when it converges with the interests of whites." See Bell, "Interest-Convergence Dilemma."

81. Tamara Jackson Snowden, interview with the author, April 21, 2014.

82. Salaam, "Spirit Family."

83. Salaam, "Spirit Family."

84. Salaam, "Spirit Family."

85. My analysis here is inspired by Rachel Harding's identification of the constellation of voluntary associations among Afro-Brazilians in Bahia. *Refuge in Thunder*, 1078.

86. Breunlin and Regis, "Putting the Ninth Ward on the Map."

87. Spillers, "Mama's Baby," 74.

88. Spillers, "Mama's Baby," 75. See also Mohanty, "Cartographies of Struggle," 64–71.
89. Tyree Smith, interview with the author, February 18, 2014; Sue Press, interview with the author, August 13, 2013. For more on the Ole N' Nu Style Fellas, see Carrico, "Sartorial Sundays."
90. Hooks, *All About Love*, 87–101.
91. Hooks, *All About Love*, 76.
92. Hooks, *All About Love*, 87.
93. Stockwell, "Radical Social Movements."
94. Sakakeeny, *Roll With It*, 150.
95. Buckner, "Mother's Day Second Line."

Interlude: Rodrick "Scubble" Davis

This interview was conducted by the author as part of the oral history project "More Than Merely Fun: Dance, Politics and Pleasure at the New Orleans Second Line," funded by the New Orleans Jazz and Heritage Foundation Archive Fellowship (2016–2017). A recording and transcript of the full interview are housed at the New Orleans Jazz and Heritage Foundation Archive and available on this book's companion website, where readers can also see video of Davis second lining.

Chapter 3. Spirit

Portions of this chapter appeared previously in "Flying High: Function and Form in New Orleans Second Line Dancing," co-authored with Esailama G. A. Diouf-Henry, in *Freedom's Dance: The Second Line in New Orleans* by Eric Waters and Karen Celestan (Baton Rouge: Louisiana State University Press, 2018), and "Wellington 'Skelly' Ratcliff, Jr.: Rolling and Flying High," *Data News Weekly*, February 14–20, 2014, p. 4.

1. Tamara Jackson Snowden, interview with the author, April 21, 2014.
2. For more details about the event, see Chapter 2.
3. Buckner, "Mother's Day Second Line."
4. Turner, *Jazz Religion*.
5. Gottschild, *Black Dancing Body*, 260.
6. Welsh, "'Gospel' of Memory," 84. I capitalize Carry, Transformation, and Transcendence when referring to Welsh's concepts specifically. Welsh's assertion resonates with Marta Morena Vega's claim that asé is the central creative impulse at the heart of all African and African diasporic dance. Vega, "Ancestral Sacred Creative Impulse."
7. Welsh, "'Gospel' of Memory," 84.
8. Welsh, "'Gospel' of Memory," 84–85.
9. Daniel, *Caribbean and Atlantic Diaspora Dance*, 190.
10. Daniel, *Caribbean and Atlantic Diaspora Dance*, 190.

11. Edward Buckner, Terry Gable, and Leo Gorman, interview with the author, January 24, 2014.

12. Lenwood Sloan, interview with the author, October 31, 2013.

13. Lenwood Sloan, interview with the author, October 31, 2013.

14. Evans, "Congo Square and the Roots of Second Line Parading," 24.

15. Turner, *Jazz Religion*, 3.

16. D. Walker, *No More, No More*, 7.

17. M. Gordon, "'Midnight Scenes and Orgies.'"

18. The exact dates during which this area was dedicated to the Sunday dance and music festivities of enslaved and free people of African descent have been estimated and debated by historians. These dates are taken from Evans, *Congo Square*, 23.

19. Evans, *Congo Square*, 1.

20. Hazzard-Gordon, *Jookin'*, 37–38.

21. Donaldson, "Window on Slave Culture," 66–67.

22. D. Walker, *No More, No More*, 18.

23. Harding, *Refuge in Thunder*, xv–xvi.

24. Camp, *Closer to Freedom*, 66–68, 91. On the psychological and emotional effects of Congo Square performances for the participants, see D. Walker, *No More, No More*, 57.

25. Evans, *Congo Square*, 19.

26. Holloway, *Passed On*, 174–175.

27. Historians suggest that the spot where African peoples gathered came to be called Congo Square because "Congo" became synonymous with "Africa" among Louisiana's colonists and Congo names for folk dances were common even among non-Congo Africans ("Slavery in Louisiana"; Evans, *Congo Square*, 6–7; Hall, *Africans in Colonial Louisiana*, 293–296). Recent scholarship disputes this explanation, claiming that Congo Square was named in order to recognize the heavy influence of Kongolese culture in New Orleans. See Dewulf, *From the Kingdom of Kongo*, xiv. The name may point to the retention of Bakongo/Kongolese cultures, but at the same time, Congo Square was also the site of many African cultures to endure and blend.

28. Holloway, *Passed On*, 174–175.

29. Lenwood Sloan, founder of the Louisiana Living History Project, claims, "Every time I see some kid second lining, and doing bamboula, chica, and calenda, the first three dances to arrive in the Americas from Africa, and not even knowing it, and not even caring, then I say, 'I'm standing on the history.'" Sloan, in Logsdon and Elie's film *Faubourg Treme*. See also Gerstin, "Allure of Origins," 127–130.

30. Evans, *Congo Square*, 24.

31. Robert Farris Thompson and Joseph Cornet single out Congo Square as the location where traditions derived from Kongo mixed with many other African and European dances and music to form "new creole styles which eventually reverberated all the way to Broadway and the entire world." Thompson

and Cornet, *Four Moments of the Sun*, 149. See also Estes, "Neo-African Vatican," 67; Gomez, *Exchanging Our Country Marks*, 57–58; Roberts, *Latin Jazz*, 7–8.

32. Evans, *Congo Square*, 89.
33. Evans, *Congo Square*, 68.
34. Hazzard-Donald, "Hoodoo Religion," 197.
35. Floyd, "Ring Shout!" 51.
36. Gordon, "Negro 'Shouts' from Georgia," 449, cited in Floyd, "Ring Shout!" 50.
37. Hazzard-Donald, "Hoodoo Religion," 197–199. Sakakeeny notes, "Until the 1840s slaves were permitted to congregate and sell goods on Sunday afternoons in Congo Square, a grassy expanse on the perimeter of the French Quarter, where they also sang and danced in the form of a ring shout." *Roll With It*, 18.
38. Brothers, *Louis Armstrong's New Orleans*, 38–44.
39. Brothers, *Louis Armstrong's New Orleans*, 21; C. Jacobs, "Spirit Guides and Possession," 46.
40. White, "New Orleans Brass Band," 80.
41. White, "New Orleans Brass Band," 80. Speaking of her 2006 work, *New Second Line*, choreographer Camille A. Brown defined second lining as "praise dance" and "a celebration of spirit." Her reference to praise dance, as well as the choreography of *New Second Line*, calls up associations with Christian concepts of transformation and transcendence such as catching the Holy Spirit or being moved by the Holy Ghost. Camille A. Brown, interview with the author, December 9, 2013. For more on *New Second Line*, see Carrico, "Second Line Choreographies."
42. Santoro, "Dancing Ground," 307.
43. Daniel, *Dancing Wisdom*, 54. The historian Sterling Stuckey writes that, throughout chattel slavery in the Americas, "slaveholders never understood that a form of spirituality almost indistinguishable from art was central to the cultures from which blacks came," in which distinctions between sacred and secular were rarely made. He goes on to explain, "Threads of spirituality—of art itself—were woven into the fabric of everyday life. In fact, dance was the principal means by which slaves, using its symbolism to evoke their spiritual view of the world, extended sacred observance throughout the week." Stuckey, "Christian Conversion," 55.
44. Daniel, *Caribbean and Atlantic Diaspora Dance*; Floyd, "Ring Shout!"; Hazzard-Donald, "Hoodoo Religion"; Hazzard-Gordon, *Jookin'*.
45. Thompson, "When the Saints," cited in Evans, "Congo Square," 25–26.
46. Another example of the white handkerchief's power as a visual signifier for the Second Line can be found in Urban Bush Women's 2009 work *Shelter*. When the choreographer Jawole Zollar restaged her 1980s classic to reflect on Hurricane Katrina, one of the few changes she made to the choreography was to give the dancers white handkerchiefs as they second lined off the stage. For more on *Shelter*, see Carrico, "Second Line Choreographies."

47. Thompson, "When the Saints," cited in Evans, "Congo Square," 25–26.
48. Turner, *Jazz Religion*, 104.
49. Ramsey, *Race Music*, 16.
50. Nettleford, "Implications for Caribbean Development," 186, quoted in Malone, *Steppin' on the Blues*, 184.
51. Turner, *Jazz Religion*, 97.
52. Hume, "Death and the Construction of Social Space," 123.
53. Daniel, *Caribbean and Atlantic Diaspora Dance*, 109.
54. Turner (*Jazz Religion*, 96–97) also uses Daniel's concept of the suprahuman to analyze Second Line dancing, although he limits his application to ecstatic dancing performed during a funeral procession. I expand my application of the term to describe ecstatic experiences that occur in parades that seem purely celebratory or secular.
55. Daniel references sacred dances in Trinidad, Haiti, and Cuba (*Caribbean and Atlantic Diaspora Dance*, 142, 190). Thomas Brothers makes a similar observation about collective dancing in New Orleans's Sanctified churches (*Louis Armstrong's New Orleans*, 40–41). While the dances described by Daniel and Brothers are intentionally done to facilitate spirit possession, the process of dancing to facilitate transcendence also applies to the secular Second Line, as described by those I have interviewed, including the interviewees quoted in this chapter.
56. Katy Reckdahl, "Dancing to Bless This Corner," *Advocate*, June 2, 2013.
57. Thanos, "New Orleans Mother's Day Shooting."
58. Reckdahl, "Dancing to Bless This Corner."
59. For an analysis of the crossroads as a unifying concept in Haitian Rara processions and New Orleans Second Lines, see Turner, *Jazz Religion*, 45–46.
60. Wald, *Escaping the Delta*; Anderson, *Brother Robert*.
61. Brothers, *Louis Armstrong's New Orleans*, 138; Turner, *Jazz Religion*, 46.
62. MacGaffey is quoted in Thompson, *Flash of the Spirit*, 108–110.
63. Dixon, interview with Rachel Breunlin, 2021.
64. For history and analysis of the jazz funeral tradition, see Brothers, *Louis Armstrong's New Orleans*; Sakakeeny, *Roll With It*; White, "New Orleans Brass Band"; Dewulf, *From the Kingdom of Kongo*.
65. Francine Ott, interview with the author, December 6, 2013.
66. Thompson, "Aesthetic of the Cool," 41–42.
67. Rodrick Davis, interview with the author, March 25, 2017.
68. Regis, "Second Lines," 488; Brothers, *Louis Armstrong's New Orleans*, 211. For more on gender and Second Line performance, see Carrico, "Dancing like a Man."
69. Various videos, Jules Cahn Collection at the Historic New Orleans Collection, New Orleans.
70. Lenwood Sloan, interview with the author, October 31, 2013.
71. Salaam, "Second Line," 28.
72. Salaam, "Second Line," 31.

73. Writing about British colonists' encounter with the Wampanoag American Indians, Foster notes that the Wampanoags preserved a memory of events by walking to the location where each event occurred and telling the story. "Their archive was maintained through the physical labor of traveling to the place where history was made. Events deemed of historical worth could not be separated from the land on which they were enacted." Foster, *Choreographing Empathy*, 32–33. Second Lines perform a similar function.

74. Regis, "Second Lines," 488.

75. Lynnell Thomas writes that New Orleans's predominant tourism narrative has long alternated between "constructions of Old World and old South memories and identities at the expense of the city's African and African American history and legacy." *Desire and Disaster in New Orleans*, 31.

76. Regis, "Blackness and the Politics of Memory," 763.

77. Regis, "Blackness and the Politics of Memory," 765.

78. Ronald Lewis's streamer was on view in the exhibition *Dancing in the Streets*, the Historic New Orleans Collection, February 25–June 13, 2021.

79. Catina Braxton Robertson, interview with the author, April 14, 2014.

80. Catina Braxton Robertson, interview with the author, April 14, 2014.

81. Harry Jackson, interview with the author, April 6, 2014.

82. Harry Jackson, interview with the author, April 6, 2014.

83. Salaam, "Spirit Family."

84. Gottschild, *Black Dancing Body*, 223, 234.

85. Derrick Tabb, interview with the author, April 15, 2014.

86. Cotton, "Videos from Old & Nu Style Fellas."

87. Albright, "Mining the Dance Field," 83.

88. Wellington Ratcliff Jr., interview with the author and Daniella Santoro, March 26, 2014.

89. Cox, *Shapeshifters*, 29.

90. Santoro, "Dancing Ground," 311.

91. Santoro, "Dancing Ground," 323.

92. The philosopher Gail Weiss asserts in her feminist critique of Merleau-Ponty and other body-focused phenomenologists that self-transformations achieved through bodily sensation (movement, color, texture, smell) bring pleasure precisely because they resituate oneself within one's existing, tactile condition. Weiss, *Body Images*, 59.

93. Muñoz, *Cruising Utopia*, 32.

94. King, "Which Way Is Down?" 28.

95. Santoro, "Dancing Ground," 314.

96. Don Robertson, interview with the author, April 10, 2014.

97. E. Johnson, "Feeling the Spirit," 410–413.

98. Second-Line Treatment By Tom Dent & Michael Goodwin. Coll. 117, Tom Dent Papers, Box No. 33, Folder #2: "Screen Play—Second-Line, 1983," Amistad Research Center, 11 (emphasis added).

99. Roger Lewis, interview with the author, May 26, 2020.

100. Roger Lewis, interview with the author, May 26, 2020.

101. E. Johnson, "Feeling the Spirit," 400.

102. For an extended analysis of Ruth's Cozy Corner, see Breunlin, "Papa Joe Glasper."

103. Benny Jones Sr., quoted in Barnes and Breunlin, *Talk That Music Talk*, 94; Benny Jones Sr., interview with the author, May 25, 2020.

104. Sanborn Map Company, "Sanborn Fire Insurance Map," 1909, vol. 4; Sanborn Map Company, "Sanborn Fire Insurance Map," 1952, vol. 4.

105. Sacred Heart church was converted into apartments by Columbia Residential, the Atlanta-based affordable housing firm discussed in Chapter 6 (https://www.columbiares.com/apartments-in-new-orleans/sacred-heart-at-st-bernard/).

106. Benny Jones Sr., interview with the author, May 25, 2020.

107. Gregory Davis, interview with the author, December 12, 2019; Roger Lewis, interview with the author, May 26, 2020; Benny Jones Sr., interview with the author, May 25, 2020.

108. Notable female spiritual leaders include Vodou priestess Marie Laveau and Mother Catherine Seals, leader of one of New Orleans's most prominent Spiritualist churches in the early twentieth century. C. Jacobs, "Spirit Guides and Possession"; Turner, *Jazz Religion*.

109. On bracketing, see Taylor, *Archive and the Repertoire*, 3.

110. Snead, "On Repetition."

111. Thompson, *Flash of the Spirit*.

Interlude: Gerald Platenburg

This interview was conducted by the author as part of the oral history project "More Than Merely Fun: Dance, Politics and Pleasure at the New Orleans Second Line," funded by the New Orleans Jazz and Heritage Foundation Archive Fellowship (2016–2017). A recording and transcript of the full interview are housed at the New Orleans Jazz and Heritage Foundation Archive and available on this book's companion website, where readers can also see video of Platenburg second lining.

1. For more on the Nine Times SAPC, see Nine Times Social and Pleasure Club, *Coming out the Door for the Ninth Ward*. For more on the Black Panther Party in New Orleans, see Germany, *New Orleans After the Promises*, 276–284; Moore, *Black Rage in New Orleans*, 70–95.

2. For more on the 2016 Nine Times parade, see MTV News's 2017 mini-documentary "Inside the New Orleans Nine Times Second Line Parade (Video Clip)," directed by Zac Manuel (https://www.mtv.com/video-clips/t2wzbk/inside-the-new-orleans-nine-times-second-line-parade).

Chapter 4. Freedom

A portion of this chapter was previously published as "'The Patter of Our Feet': Parading and Political Organizing in New Orleans," *Conversations Across the Field of Dance Studies* 38 (2018): 8–12.

1. Rogers, *Righteous Lives*, 184; Germany, *New Orleans After the Promises*, 101.
2. Rogers, *Righteous Lives*, 184.
3. Barnes and Breunlin, *Talk That Music Talk*, 30.
4. Joe Stern, interview with the author, September 1, 2017.
5. Latanya d. Tigner, interview with the author, May 15, 2015.
6. Joe Stern, interview with the author, September 1, 2017. Stern made these comments before the protests that swept the nation in 2020 following the murders of George Floyd and Breonna Taylor at the hands of police. I address protest in New Orleans during this period in the epilogue. Whether the suspension of Second Line permits during the 2020–2021 COVID-19 lockdown led to an increase in protest participation during that same period is an excellent area for further research.
7. Reed, "Introduction: Black Pleasure," 169; see also brown, *Pleasure Activism*.
8. Martin, *Critical Moves*, 14.
9. An important exception can be found in SilenceIsViolence, discussed in Chapter 2. This organization was founded by members of the Second Line community in response to a string of murders of musicians in 2006 and 2007. Among many other activities, they have combined musical processions with protest marches to demand that public officials address the city's violence epidemic. Watts and Porter, *New Orleans Suite*, 46–49; Sakakeeny, *Roll With It*, 169–172.
10. Joe Stern, interview with the author, September 1, 2017.
11. Stern's call echoes the desire of two anonymous second liners discussed in Chapter 3 who lament younger generations' lack of knowledge about the innovative dancers who came before them. Both instances articulate a desire for more widespread awareness of the tradition's history. However, unlike the spiritual dimension of the Second Line—which, I have argued, following others, one can experience without conscious knowledge of second lining's sacred roots—it is possible that more widespread awareness about second lining's histories of political activism might have an impact on how contemporary practitioners engage with it.
12. Seiferth, "Where Do Second Lines Come From?"
13. Evans, *Congo Square*, 19.
14. According to the jazz historian Jerry Brock, "the term 'second line' was propelled into American popular culture and New Orleans mainstream vernacular during World War I," when citizen support for the war effort "was encouraged as a 'second line' of battle or defense." Brock, "In Memory," 12.
15. Rogers, Boisdore, and Dove, "Grand celebration."

16. Rogers, Boisdore, and Dove, "Grand celebration." Free Black Union soldiers included the Louisiana Native Guards and Volunteers, which was a regiment consisting exclusively of "colored" men who offered their services to the governor to defend Louisiana at the outbreak of the Civil War. J. Schafer, *Becoming Free, Remaining Free*, 163–164. Caryn Cossé Bell's history of the Native Guards includes first-hand testimony of how free Black soldiers were threatened into enlisting for the Confederate cause. They later enlisted in the Union army once it occupied the city and could give protection. Bell, *Revolution, Romanticism*, 231–232.

17. Rogers, Boisdore, and Dove, "Grand celebration"; Seiferth, "Where Do Second Lines Come From?"

18. Seiferth, "Where Do Second Lines Come From?"

19. Sakakeeny, *Roll With It*, 18.

20. In 2015 the New Orleans City Council voted to remove four Confederate monuments, including the statue of Robert E. Lee, after a successful campaign led by Take 'Em Down NOLA (mentioned in Joe Stern's oral history interlude following Chapter 6). In 2022 the council changed the name from Lee Circle to Harmony Circle.

21. Malone, *Steppin' on the Blues*, 62–63.

22. Becknell, Price, and Short, "History."

23. Roach, "Carnival and the Law," 50.

24. Dewulf, *From the Kingdom of Kongo*, 138–139.

25. Dewulf, *From the Kingdom of Kongo*, 166–168.

26. Regis, "Second Lines," 498, n.4.

27. Regis, "Second Lines," 498; Becknell, Price, and Short, "History."

28. Fairclough, *Race and Democracy*, 278. Fairclough's view of Zulu resonates with studies of blackface more generally. For example, W. T. Lhamon claims that blackface minstrelsy in general is capable of simultaneously reinforcing and working against racial stereotyping (*Raising Cain*, 6, 134). When analyzing exchanges between Black performers and Black audiences in the early twentieth-century United States, Jayna Brown contends that Black performance is always multiply signifying, performing a "double operation" of exploiting racialisms and critiquing the absurdity of racialized depictions. In that doubling, Black laughter is a powerful form of criticism. She suggests that the same dance step can bring pleasure and self-making for the performer even as it reaffirms racist stereotypes (*Babylon Girls*, 5–15, 210).

29. "Mardi Gras 'Blackout' Isolates Zulus," *Louisiana Weekly*, February 18, 1961, 15–17.

30. "Mardi Gras 'Blackout' Isolates Zulus."

31. Vincent Randazzo, "Floats of Zulu Met by Cheers," *Times-Picayune*, February 15, 1961, sec. 1.

32. Fairclough, *Race and Democracy*, 208. In addition to the Blackouts, UCI also organized registration drives, fundraising, and protests against segregationist practices and laws. Rogers, *Righteous Lives*, 85.

33. Building on his influential theory of mobilization (Martin, *Critical Moves*), Randy Martin reflected on immobilization in the later stages of his career and life: "The counterintuitive part of dance is stillness. The political can be posed around the refusal to be moved by people. A refusal: Who is compelled to respond to movement—individual or social movement?" Kowal, Martin, and Siegmund, "Introduction," 7.

34. Germany, *New Orleans After the Promises*, 19, 24. Ruby Bridges integrated William Frantz Elementary School just two miles from the spot where Homer Plessy boarded a white train car seventy years earlier, leading to the Supreme Court decision that enshrined the principle of separate but equal into national law. Bridges, and, to a lesser degree, the "McDonogh Three," became the public face of integration after *Brown v. Board of Education* overturned the *Plessy* decision in 1954. For more on *Brown* and its lasting effects on institutional racism, see Harris, "Whiteness as Property."

35. Rogers, *Righteous Lives*, 71; "Save Our Schools," various newspaper clippings, Box 4, Folders 1 and 2, Amistad Research Center, New Orleans.

36. Fairclough, *Race and Democracy*, 234–264; Rogers, *Righteous Lives*, 71–74.

37. Rogers, *Righteous Lives*, 82, 115–127.

38. Joseph Logsdon interviewing A. P. Tureaud, numerous dates from 1968 to 1971, as quoted in Fairclough, *Race and Democracy*, 49.

39. Elie, "Niggertown Memories," quoted in Rogers, *Righteous Lives*, 7. In my interview with Barbara Lacen Keller (Interlude following Chapter 1), she refuted assumptions such as Elie's. In one of the earliest published studies of social aid and pleasure clubs (1990), the anthropologists William Jankowiak, Helen A. Regis, and Christina Turner point out that most researchers share this assumption but report that, instead, "The black social club is not exclusively a lower-class institution. . . . Our research indicated that more than half of the club members had incomes exceeding" that which would place them in the middle class. Jankowiak, Regis, and Turner, "Second-Line Marching Clubs," 669.

40. Rogers, *Righteous Lives*, 7.

41. Hazzard-Gordon, *Jookin'*, 47, 70, 162.

42. Rogers, *Righteous Lives*, 109.

43. "Dance 'Blackout' Includes 75 Clubs," *Louisiana Weekly*, January 14, 1961; "$12,000 Net Realized in 'Blackout,'" *Louisiana Weekly*, May 6, 1961; Rogers, *Righteous Lives*, 85; Fairclough, *Race and Democracy*, 278.

44. "Dance Clubs to Put Curb on Spending," *Louisana Weekly*, December 24, 1960.

45. "Dance 'Blackout' Includes 75 Clubs"; "Mardi Gras 'Blackout' Idea Gets Solid Backing," *Louisiana Weekly*, February 4, 1961.

46. "Troubles Plague Mardi Gras," *Chicago Daily Defender*, February 9, 1961.

47. "'Pressure' on Zulus to Cancel Parade," *Louisiana Weekly*, February 4, 1961.

48. "Mayor Blamed for Zulu 'Decision' to Parade," *Louisiana Weekly*, February 4, 1961.

49. Randazzo, "Floats of Zulu Met by Cheers."

50. "Mayor Blamed for Zulu 'Decision' to Parade"; "Mardi Gras 'Blackout' Isolates Zulus," *Louisiana Weekly*, February 18, 1961.

51. "'Pressure' on Zulus to Cancel Parade"; "Mayor Blamed for Zulu 'Decision' to Parade"; "Mardi Gras 'Blackout' Idea Gets Solid Backing"; William Giles, "Spirit of Mardi Gras High, but Integration Strife Cuts Tourism," *Wall Street Journal*, February 14, 1961.

52. "$12,000 Net Realized in 'Blackout.'"

53. "$12,000 Net Realized in 'Blackout.'"

54. George Talbert and Leonard Burns, letter to United Clubs officers and members, October 1961, Leonard Burns Collection, Amistad Research Center, New Orleans.

55. Robert F. Collins, Nils Douglas, and Lolis E. Elie, "Southern Justice," Box 2, Item 1: Bound personal papers, 1954–1968, Nils R. Douglas papers, 1893–1967, Amistad Research Center, New Orleans.

56. Bakhtin, *Rabelais and His World*.

57. Vaz-Deville, *"Baby Dolls."*

58. D. Mitchell and Staeheli, "Permitting Protest," 799.

59. According to the Synopsis of Ordinances 1841–1937 on the City Archives website, permits for holding parades were established by Ordinance 12524 CCS in 1930: http://archives.nolalibrary.org/~nopl/inv/synopsis/p.htm.

60. *Cox v. New Hampshire*, 312 U.S. 569 (1941), 570–571, as cited in D. Mitchell and Staeheli, "Permitting Protest," 801.

61. D. Mitchell and Staeheli, "Permitting Protest," 801.

62. J. Cooper, *Dancing in the Streets*, 41. Based on her conversation with Lieutenant Joe Valiente, who was in charge of the parades at the time, photographer Judy Cooper writes that a 1956 city ordinance forever changed the way clubs parade because it required a permit and subjected paraders to restrictions that remain until this day, including city approval, total number of hours, and total number of parading persons and vehicles. Cooper, personal correspondence with the author, June 14, 2021. When the city codified its ordinances in 1956, it required funerals, processions, and parades "containing two hundred or more persons or fifty or more vehicles" to obtain a permit from the Superintendent of Police. City of New Orleans, "The Code of the City," 501–502. The parading permit ordinance is still on the books: "Article XVI.—Parades, Code of Ordinances, New Orleans, LA, Municode Library."

63. McPhail, Schweingruber, and McCarthy, "Policing Protest," 52.

64. Howard Jacobs, "Pesky Police Punish Percolating Paraders," *Times-Picayune*, August 30, 1961.

65. "NAACP Plans to Oppose Parade Rule," *States-Item*, May 29, 1968.

66. White, "New Orleans Brass Band," 83.

67. McPhail, Schweingruber, and McCarthy, "Policing Protest," 54.

68. Rogers, *Righteous Lives*, 68–69, 110. Dryades Street is now named after one of CORE's prominent leaders, Oretha Castle Haley.

69. Fairclough, *Race and Democracy*, 276–277.

70. Chris Waddington, "Sweet Lorraine's Jazz Club Starting Point of Black Men of Labor Parade," *Times-Picayune*, September 1, 2011.

71. Fairclough, *Race and Democracy*, 78.

72. Fairclough, *Race and Democracy*, 272–275.

73. "No Resistance Is Offered by Marchers," *Louisiana Weekly*, December 23, 1963, 7A.

74. "No Resistance Is Offered by Marchers," 1, 7A.

75. "No Resistance Is Offered by Marchers," 7A.

76. "CORE Sit-Ins Harassed: Doused with Acid After New Technique," *Louisiana Weekly*, December 30, 1961, 2.

77. Young, *Embodying Black Experience*.

78. Jules Cahn Collection at the Historic New Orleans Collection, New Orleans, "Negro Marching," 16mm, color, silent, recorded June 1963.

79. As discussed in Chapter 6, New Orleans's racial geography ironically formed more segregated patterns in the early 2000s than it did in the early 1800s, following a slow transformation throughout the twentieth century that was shaped by metropolitanization of the city space, suburbanization of its environs, and the end of legalized segregation and racially defined patterns of mortgage lending. Campanella, *Bienville's Dilemma*, 183; Hirsch and Logsdon, *Creole New Orleans*, 198–199; Moore, *Black Rage in New Orleans*, 10; Thomas, *Desire and Disaster in New Orleans*, 19.

80. In addition to passing numerous new Jim Crow laws, the state legislature had by 1959 enacted a law that prohibited unmarried women from receiving benefits from the Aid to Dependent Children program if they had a child while receiving payments. When implemented in 1960, it purged more than twenty-two thousand children from the program (95 percent of whom were African American). Germany, *New Orleans After the Promises*, 228.

81. Germany, *New Orleans After the Promises*, 3, 32–38, 131.

82. Rogers, *Righteous Lives*, 91; "Mayor Schiro Calls for Responsible Leadership," *Louisiana Weekly*, September 21, 1963.

83. Gregg Stafford, interview with Mick Burns, October 2002, at his home on Second Street for the book *Keeping the Beat on the Street*, wave file (003.2002.008), New Orleans Jazz and Heritage Foundation Archive, New Orleans.

84. Rogers, *Righteous Lives*, 91–92; "Mayor Schiro Calls for Responsible Leadership"; Don Hubbard, oral history, September 18, 2017, MSS 936.7, Historic New Orleans Collection, New Orleans.

85. Don Hubbard, oral history, September 18, 2017.

86. Don Hubbard, oral history, September 18, 2017; "10,000 in 'Freedom March' on City Hall," *Louisiana Weekly*, October 5, 1963.

87. John E. Rousseau, "Peaceful Freedom March Gains Momentum," *Louisiana Weekly*, September 28, 1963, 4. In addition to spearheading UCI, Burns also

belonged to the Citizens' Committee. United Clubs, Inc. Collection, 1961–1964, Amistad Research Center, New Orleans.

88. "Mayor Schiro Calls for Responsible Leadership," 1.

89. Rousseau, "Peaceful Freedom March," 8.

90. Rousseau, "Peaceful Freedom March," 3.

91. Rousseau, "Peaceful Freedom March," 3–4.

92. "10,000 in 'Freedom March' on City Hall," 7.

93. Leonard Burns Collection, Amistad Research Center, New Orleans, Box 1, Correspondence: United Clubs, Inc., 1963.

94. Hirsch, "Simply a Matter of Black and White," 288.

95. Barnes and Breunlin, *Talk That Music Talk*, 73.

96. Barnes and Breunlin, *Talk That Music Talk*, 69.

97. Barnes and Breunlin, *Talk That Music Talk*, 69. In the post-Katrina years, BMOL moved its annual parading date from Labor Day to a Saturday in October because it was frequently threatened by hurricanes and tropical storms. Fred Johnson of BMOL blamed global warming for the increased frequency of late-season hurricanes and the subsequent need to move the parade date. Fred Johnson, interview with Charles "Action" Jackson, January 12, 2021. For more on the history of unionizing among Black dockworkers in New Orleans, including the emergence of the Longshoremen's Protective Union and Benevolent Association in 1872 and the ILA no. 1419 in 1936, see Northrup, "New Orleans Longshoremen."

98. For more on the Longshoremen's social events, see Arneson, "Learning the Lessons of Solidarity," 33.

99. Barnes and Breunlin, *Talk That Music Talk*, 69; Norman Dixon, interview with Rachel Breunlin, 2021. For an example of BMOL parading in kente cloth, see figure 7, Chapter 3.

100. Kim Welsh, Black Men of Labor 2011 parade, photo caption, *Offbeat*, October 19, 2011, https://www.flickr.com/photos/offbeatmagazine/6299071519/.

101. Smith-Simmons quoted in Barnes and Breunlin, *Talk That Music Talk*, 75.

102. Doratha Smith-Simmons and John Keith, interview with the author, November 8, 2013.

103. Between 1960 and 1962 the Louisiana legislature passed laws that increased the difficulty of voter registration for Black applicants. The acts made application forms even more bewildering (and intentionally confusing) than before and instituted a "citizenship test" that demanded the most arcane knowledge of the U.S. and Louisiana constitutions. Local organizations continued registration drives, teaching people how to fill out the forms and study for the test. But the shifting landscape of voter disenfranchisement, compounded by intimidation and humiliation heaped on applicants by registrars' offices, meant that even "well-organized and well-funded drives produced no overall increase" in Black voter registration in New Orleans in the early 1960s. Fairclough, *Race and Democracy*, 123, 309.

104. Doratha Smith-Simmons and John Keith Simmons, interview with the author, November 8, 2013.

105. Doratha Smith-Simmons and John Keith Simmons, interview with the author, November 8, 2013.

106. Tom Dent Papers, Amistad Research Center, New Orleans, Jerome Smith, interview with Tom Dent, September 23, 1983; Barnes and Breunlin, *Talk That Music Talk*, 23–24.

107. Barnes and Breunlin, *Talk That Music Talk*, 73 (emphasis added).

Interlude: Terrylyn Dorsey

This interview was conducted by the author as part of the oral history project "More Than Merely Fun: Dance, Politics and Pleasure at the New Orleans Second Line," funded by the New Orleans Jazz and Heritage Foundation Archive Fellowship (2016–2017). A recording and transcript of the full interview are housed at the New Orleans Jazz and Heritage Foundation Archive and available on the book's companion website.

1. Da Truth Brass Band, https://www.datruthbrassbandnola.com/.

2. Troy "Trombone Shorty" Andrews is one of New Orleans's best-known musicians of late, boasting Grammy nominations and a full international touring schedule, among other accolades. https://www.tromboneshorty.com/home.

3. Brandon Shelly, known to the Second Line community as "Itchy," is a documentarian who posts videos of each Second Line parade to his Instagram account, @Itchy_world. At the time of writing, Itchy's account was the most prominent virtual space for second liners to find their footwork memorialized and scrutinized.

4. Torrence Ivy Hatch Jr., better known by his stage name Boosie BadAzz or simply Boosie (formerly Lil Boosie), is a rapper from Baton Rouge. https://www.facebook.com/lilboosie/.

Chapter 5. Do Whatcha Wanna

This chapter is derived in part from an article published in 2016 in *TBS: The Black Scholar*, The Black World Foundation, available online at https//doi.org/10.1080/00064246.2015.1119536.

1. Doratha Smith-Simmons, interview with the author, November 8, 2013.

2. Tamara Jackson Snowden, interview with the author, April 21, 2014; Rebirth Brass Band, *Do Whatcha Wanna*.

3. My argument is informed by Imani Kai Johnson's reflections on training in breaking communities, in which she understands "training" in two ways: first, as "efforts to develop one's skills, or take direction from more experienced dancers"; second, and more important, as a gesture toward "Hip Hop cultural

imperatives or sensibilities embedded in that physical practice." I. Johnson, "(Home) Training in Breaking Culture," 51–52.

4. Tyree Smith, interview with the author, February 18, 2014.

5. DeFrantz builds on music theorist Dick Hebdige's concept of versioning in Caribbean popular music to apply the concept to African American dance. Hebdige, *Cut "n" Mix*, 12, cited in DeFrantz, *Dancing Revelations*, 82–84.

6. Burkholder, "Borrowing."

7. Kraut, "Stealing Steps," 180. See also Jonathan Jackson, "Improvisation in African-American Vernacular Dancing," and Hill, "Stepping, Stealing, Sharing, and Daring," 100.

8. Kraut, "Stealing Steps," 180.

9. Burkholder, "Borrowing."

10. Terrylyn Dorsey and Terrinika Smith, interview with the author, August 8, 2014.

11. Terrylyn Dorsey and Terrinika Smith, interview with the author, August 8, 2014.

12. Walter Kimble, interview with the author, May 27, 2014.

13. McQuirter, "Awkward Moves," 93–95.

14. DeFrantz, *Dancing Revelations*, 82.

15. Tyree Smith, interview with the author, February 18, 2014.

16. Rodrick Davis, interview with the author, January 16, 2014.

17. Rodrick Davis, interview with the author, January 16, 2014.

18. Wellington Ratcliff Jr., interview with the author and Daniella Santoro, March 26, 2014.

19. Johnson, "(Home) Training in Breaking Culture."

20. George-Graves, "Taking the Cake," 20.

21. For more on competition and second lining, see Carrico, "Dancing like a Man."

22. Terrylyn Dorsey and Terrinika Smith, interview with the author, August 8, 2014.

23. Drewal, *Yoruba Ritual*, 7.

24. Jonathan Jackson, "Improvisation."

25. Wellington Ratcliff Jr., interview with the author and Daniella Santoro, March 26, 2014.

26. Wellington Ratcliff Jr., interview with the author and Daniella Santoro, March 26, 2014.

27. Kraut, *Choreographing the Folk*, 131–132.

28. Hazzard-Gordon, *Jookin'*, 118, 28.

29. Gregory Stafford, quoted in Burns, *Keeping the Beat on the Street*, 46.

30. White, "New Orleans Brass Band," 87–89; Burns, *Keeping the Beat on the Street*, 5. The jazz historian and critic Jerry Brock recalls that the NAACP tried to stop the Second Lines: "They felt like it was a bit of a throwback, and it was time to move on. Harold Dejan and Danny Barker stood up to them and

said, 'This is valuable. This is a part of the history of our people.'" Jerry Brock, quoted in Burns, 102.

31. Burns, *Keeping the Beat on the Street*, 5. A major exception to the trend was Harold Dejan, who founded the Olympia Brass Band in 1960 and updated brass arrangements with the rhythm and blues sounds of the civil rights movement. Sakakeeny, *Roll With It*, 19.

32. White, "New Orleans Brass Band," 89.

33. White, "New Orleans Brass Band," 87–88.

34. Burns, *Keeping the Beat on the Street*, 6.

35. Burns points out that the concurrent emergence of several institutions—all spearheaded by white music fans—also supported, even generated, a renewed interest in brass band music. Tipitina's music venue opened, the local, listener-supported radio station WWOZ was founded, and the annual Jazz and Heritage Festival gained status as a world-renowned event. New local publications such as *Offbeat* magazine (and I would add the magazine *Wavelengths*) gave rise to comment and features on New Orleans music, whereas it attracted virtually no media coverage before the 1980s. These outlets allowed musicians to attain local celebrity status. Burns, *Keeping the Beat on the Street*, 8, 97–98.

36. Sakakeeny, *Roll With It*; Mazza, *Up Front and Center*.

37. Scott Billington, producer of Rounder Records, quoted in *Never a Dull Moment*.

38. This description is culled from a viewing of Alan Lomax's footage, filmed at the Glass House in 1982. Alan Lomax Video Collection, Hogan Jazz Archive, "Glass House 2" and "Glass House 9–15," DVDs 9–10, Tapes 44, 48–52, Odyssey Productions, Inc., The Association for Cultural Equity (New York).

39. George "Ice Cream" Dawson is mentioned in Robert Hare, "Brassy Traditions," *Times-Picayune*, December 9, 1988; Joseph "Joe Black" Baker remembers Charles Smith as a regular on the Glass House dance floor. Baker, "The Revolution." Gregory Davis, interview with the author, December 12, 2019; Roger Lewis, interview with the author, May 26, 2020; Benny Jones Sr., interview with the author, May 25, 2020.

40. Oliver "Squirky Man" Hunter is featured in a photo spread in Waters and Celestan, *Freedom's Dance*, 115–117.

41. Short clips of the dancing described here can be seen in Lomax, *Jazz Parades* (available online at https://www.folkstreams.net/films/jazz-parades-feet-don-t-fail-me-now) and in the Alan Lomax Archive's YouTube video "Dirty Dozen Brass Band at the Glass House: Bongo Beep (1982)," https://youtu.be/-jYB2bn74hc.

42. Davis is quoted in Burns, *Keeping the Beat on the Street*, 72.

43. Roger Lewis, interview with the author, May 26, 2020.

44. Franklin, "Keep'N It Real."

45. Roger Lewis, interview with the author, May 26, 2020.

46. DeFrantz, "Duke University Professor"; Hill, *Tap Dancing America*;

Bechet, *Treat It Gentle*, 67–68; Keber, *Buckjumping*; Waters and Celestan, "Glossary," 209.

47. Townes is quoted in Alex Rawls, "The Early Dirty Dozen," *Offbeat*, October 1, 2010.

48. DeFrantz, *Dancing Revelations*, 83.

49. Gilroy, *Black Atlantic*, 198.

50. Jay Mazza, interview with the author, December 13, 2019; Roger Lewis, interview with the author, May 26, 2020. My analysis here is informed by Novack, "Looking at Movement as Culture."

51. *Parallel* might not be the right word because funk itself has roots in the Second Line beat. Vincent, *Funk*; Doleac, "Strictly Second Line." Thomas DeFrantz ("Unchecked Popularity," 220) writes, "Funk emerged as an alternative to assimilation-minded efforts of black pop music; directed explicitly to black audiences, it offered a palpable genre of playful, expressive resistance."

52. Maultsby, "Funk," 311.

53. *Dancing in the Streets* exhibit wall text, 2021, Historic New Orleans Collection, New Orleans.

54. Borders, "New Orleans Negritude," 84.

55. Gregory Davis, interview with Kalamu ya Salaam, Glass House Reunion with the original members of the Dirty Dozen Brass Band, 2005, Allison Miner Music Heritage Stage Collection, New Orleans Jazz and Heritage Foundation Archive, New Orleans.

56. Gregory Davis, interview with the author, December 12, 2019.

57. Raeburn, "Dancing Hot and Sweet," 12–13.

58. WWOZ, "Dew Drop Inn."

59. Geraldine Wyckoff, "Jolly Bunch: A Venerable Social Aid and Pleasure Club Ready to Parade Again," *Gambit*, September 11, 2001.

60. Breunlin, Lewis, and Regis, *House of Dance and Feathers*, 154.

61. Burns, *Keeping the Beat on the Street*, 127.

62. Tamara Jackson Snowden, interview with the author, April 21, 2014; Johnson et al., "Money Wasters."

63. Jules Cahn collection at the Historic New Orleans Collection, Lady Zulu #1, September 1965, 16mm, color motion picture film, no sound, 2000.78.4.289.

64. Jarrett Johnson et al., "Money Wasters."

65. Walker, *In Search of Our Mothers' Gardens*, xi–xii.

66. Allured, *Remapping Second-Wave Feminism*, 10.

67. Allured, *Remapping Second-Wave Feminism*, 10–11.

68. Ford, *Liberated Threads*, 72.

69. Roger Lewis, interview with the author, May 26, 2020.

70. Tsing, *Friction*, 6.

71. Sakakeeny, *Roll With It*, 141.

72. Brothers, *Louis Armstrong's New Orleans*, 142.

73. Logsdon and Elie, *Faubourg Treme*.

74. Danielle Goldman defines improvised dance as "literally giving shape

to oneself by deciding how to move in relation to an unsteady landscape." *I Want to Be Ready*, 5.

75. Margaret Drewal adds that improvised dance is always reiteration, or repetition, with difference, which is a key concept in Black expressive culture. Each utterance is bracketed by quotation marks as it cites previous iterations of the utterance. Drewal, *Yoruba Ritual*, 3–5, 16–19.

76. Jazz Henry, interview with Rachel Breunlin, 2021, in *Dancing in the Streets*, online exhibition audio guide (https://artsandculture.google.com/story/dancing-in-the-streets/GgJi8icbIVkrIA).

77. Alan Lomax Video Collection, Hogan Jazz Archive, Tulane University, New Orleans, "Glass House 2," DVD 9, Tape 44, Odyssey Productions, Inc., The Association for Cultural Equity (New York).

78. Thomas DeFrantz considers non-Black dancers learning Black social dances outside of a Black social sphere, such as a studio classroom. He says that these dancers can copy the how's—the steps—but cannot so easily repeat the why's—tap into the dances' religiosity or their ability to generate action. DeFrantz, "Black Beat Made Visible," 76.

79. Carrico, "Un/Natural Disaster and Dancing."

80. Glissant, *Poétique de la Relation*, 204, translated by and quoted in Britton, *Edouard Glissant and Postcolonial Theory*, 19.

81. Britton, *Edouard Glissant and Postcolonial Theory*, 19–20.

82. In this way, "do watcha wanna" as a performance of opacity differs from "spectacular opacity" as discussed by Daphne Brooks. Brooks offers the phrase to illuminate how performers "create figurative sites for the reconfiguration of black and female bodies on display," confounding stable categories of race and gender by, paradoxically, revealing their bodies to a public gaze. While spectacular opacity resists "the 'dominant imposition of transparency'" willed onto Black bodies by white spectators through bodily performance, "do watch wanna" resists the imposition of transparency through discursive performances that contradict bodily ones. Brooks, *Bodies in Dissent*, 8.

83. Laura Bliss, "10 Years Later, There's So Much We Don't Know About Where Katrina Survivors Ended Up," *Atlantic: CityLab*, August 25, 2016, https://www.bloomberg.com/citylab; Maria Jackson, "Rebuilding."

84. Gaunt, *Games Black Girls Play*, 48.

85. Gaunt, *Games Black Girls Play*, 49 (emphasis in original).

Interlude: Nicole Lazard

This interview was conducted by the author as part of the oral history project "More Than Merely Fun: Dance, Politics and Pleasure at the New Orleans Second Line," funded by the New Orleans Jazz and Heritage Foundation Archive Fellowship (2016–2017). A recording and transcript of the full interview are housed at the New Orleans Jazz and Heritage Foundation Archive and available on the book's companion website.

1. For more on the Stooges Brass Band, see Stooges Brass Band and DeCoste, *Can't Be Faded*.

Chapter 6. Home

1. Michna, "Hearing the Hurricane Coming," 3–4; Sakakeeny, "'Under the Bridge'"; Brothers, *Louis Armstrong's New Orleans*, 21–22. Writing about Mardi Gras Indians, a related but distinct Black parading tradition in New Orleans, Joseph Roach argues that the tribes "claim the space through which they move," performing "a rite of territory repossessed, not to assert permanent ownership but temporary use." Roach, "Mardi Gras Indians and Others," 476.

2. Regis, "Second Lines"; Regis, "Blackness and the Politics of Memory."

3. Joyce Jackson, "Second Line Aesthetics," 13. This point of view regarding Second Lines, which are sometimes called moving block parties, resonates with Katrina Hazzard-Gordon's analysis of African American block parties, in which she identifies "claiming the street" as a "territorial triumph." Hazzard-Gordon, *Jookin'*, 160.

4. Regis, "Blackness and the Politics of Memory," 756–758.

5. Breunlin and Regis, "Putting the Ninth Ward on the Map," 14.

6. Z. Johnson, "Walking the Post-Disaster City"; Lipsitz, "Learning from New Orleans"; Raeburn, "They're Tryin' to Wash Us Away"; Spitzer, "Rebuilding the 'Land of Dreams,'" 320–322.

7. McKittrick, *Demonic Grounds*, xxiii, 3, 5.

8. Harris, "Whiteness as Property."

9. Daniel, *Caribbean and Atlantic Diaspora Dance*, 192–193; Cox, *Shapeshifters*.

10. Salaam, "New Orleans Mardi Gras Indians," quoted in Vaz-Deville, "*Baby Dolls*," 91; Gilroy, *Black Atlantic*, 111, 133.

11. Club leader Tamara Jackson Snowden recalls that this practice started after Hurricane Katrina, when bars and businesses were still closed. Jackson Snowden quoted in "VIP Ladies & Kids Second Line Parade." Nicole Lazard adds that stops on a street corner allow clubs to keep their routes similar if they can no longer stop at a relative's house because the person no longer lives in that location. Corner stops also appeal to clubs whose members do not drink alcohol, since they wouldn't be able to patronize a bar. Lazard, interview with the author, September 7, 2017.

12. Breunlin and Regis, "Putting the Ninth Ward on the Map," 755.

13. Solnit and Snedeker, *Unfathomable City*, 108–109.

14. Mazzocca, "Inscribing/Inscribed."

15. Lomax, *Jazz Parades*.

16. Gregory Davis, interview with the author, December 12, 2019; Benny Jones Sr., interview with the author, May 25, 2020.

17. Jules Cahn Collection, "Sister Eustis Funeral," 16mm, color, silent, recorded July 8 or 9, 1975.

18. Tom Dent Papers, Box 94, Folder 1: African and Caribbean Stilt Dance

Masquerade, 1986, undated (https://amistad-finding-aids.tulane.edu/repositories/2/archival_objects/67732). Tom Dent, New Orleans poet and playwright of the Black Arts movement, was asked to review an article by David Paul Robeson titled "African and Caribbean Stilt Dance Masquerade" (quotation is found on page 3). Dent wrote extensively about second lining, including an unpublished screenplay titled "Second Line," which he drafted in 1983, just as rooftop second lining was increasing on the streets of his city. Did Dent see a connection to stilt dance masquerade? Perhaps, perhaps not, but regardless, the appearance of Robeson's article in Dent's personal collection at the Amistad Research Center caused me to start thinking about possible connections between stilt dancing and aerial second lining. Alan Lomax also implies a connection by interspersing footage of Spiderman with footage of unnamed and unplaced stilt dancers in *Jazz Parades*.

19. In her recent tome about the American South, Imani Perry writes about the importance of the enduring story of flying Africans that has spread through oral history, children's books, and visual culture. In the historically recorded version, she explains, a group of enslaved Africans, ethnically Ibo, arrived in Savannah, Georgia, in 1803 and were quickly resold to planters on nearby St. Simons Island. On the ship transferring them to the island, the Ibo rebelled, drowned the captors, grounded the ship, and disembarked in a singing procession that led them into Dunbar Creek. They didn't walk back out. "Black folks said that some of them walked all the way across the ocean floor back to Africa" (Perry, *South to America*, 387.). The people of St. Simons, the Gullah Geechee, have kept the memory of the flying Ibo alive. For one recounting of the fictionalized version of the story, see Lester, "People Who Could Fly," 21–23.

20. Natural causes for the city's sinking have been compounded by interventions into the landscape, which have prevented the river's flooding and deposition of sediment. Metropolitan effects of subsidence, or sinking of land, include sunken cornerstones, buckled streets, and cracked and leaning buildings. Campanella, *Bienville's Dilemma*, 80, 327.

21. Campanella, *Geographies of New Orleans*, cited in Breunlin and Regis, "Putting the Ninth Ward on the Map," 749.

22. Breunlin and Regis, "Putting the Ninth Ward on the Map," 749; Horowitz, *Katrina*, 7–8.

23. Horowitz, *Katrina*, 7–8.

24. Breunlin and Regis, "Putting the Ninth Ward on the Map," 749–750. On New Orleans East, see Sarah Broom's memoir *The Yellow House*.

25. Breunlin and Regis, "Putting the Ninth Ward on the Map," 748; Horowitz, *Katrina*, 7.

26. Horowitz, *Katrina*, 140.

27. Lynnell Thomas states that the "racial disaster" of Katrina, in which the flooding and inequitable rebuilding disproportionately affected Black and poor residents, was an elongation and intensification of a long-standing racial disaster in New Orleans. Thomas, *Desire and Disaster in New Orleans*, 150.

28. Thomas, *Desire and Disaster in New Orleans*, esp. chap. 5.
29. Campanella, *Bienville's Dilemma*, 186–187.
30. Lipsitz, *How Racism Takes Place*, 30–35.
31. Rodrick Davis, interview with author, January 16, 2014.
32. Rodrick Davis, interview with author, January 16, 2014.
33. Sakakeeny, *Roll With It*, 18. Sakakeeny notes that there is debate as to whether historians and geographers have drawn too rigid a boundary between the downtown Creole and uptown African and Anglo-American neighborhoods of New Orleans. See also Campanella, "Ethnic Geography," 704–15.
34. On women's involvement in fraternal organizations, see Beito, *From Mutual Aid to the Welfare State*, 2–3. For more detail on women's participation in Second Lines, see Chapter 5 and Carrico, "Dancing Like a Man."
35. As David Paul Robeson wrote of stilt dancing, it is "performed only by men and the organizations responsible for it are composed only of men. While there are masquerades in Africa for women, the stilt dance is not one of them." Tom Dent Papers, Box 94, Folder 1: African and Caribbean Stilt Dance Masquerade, at 5.
36. Ruddick, "Constructing Difference," 135–136.
37. Tucker, "Feminist Perspective," 59; Vaz-Deville, *"Baby Dolls,"* 66–67.
38. Long, *Great Southern Babylon*, 129–130, 136–137.
39. Vaz-Deville, *"Baby Dolls,"* 1, 68–69.
40. Vaz-Deville, *"Baby Dolls,"* 55.
41. Carby, "Policing the Black Woman's Body."
42. Cox, *Shapeshifters*, 28–29.
43. McBride, a nineteen-year-old African American woman, was shot dead in the suburbs of Detroit when she knocked on a stranger's door seeking help with her stalled car (Cox, *Shapeshifters*, 25).
44. Tucker, "Feminist Perspective," 56–59; Long, *Great Southern Babylon*, 130.
45. Carby writes, "The moral panic about the lack of control over the sexual behavior of black women had become absorbed into the fundamental assumptions of the sociological analysis of urban black culture, which thus designated many of its forms of entertainment and leisure 'pathological' and in need of greater institutional control" ("Policing the Black Woman's Body," 751).
46. Long, *Great Southern Babylon*, 142–143, 216–217.
47. Carby, "Policing the Black Woman's Body," 755; Tucker, "Feminist Perspective," 60; Vaz-Deville, *"Baby Dolls,"* 68–69.
48. On the legacy of blues women in twenty-first-century Black women's performances of femininity, see I. Johnson, "From Blues Women to B-Girls."
49. Cox, *Shapeshifters*, 234.
50. Nicole Lazard, interview with the author, September 7, 2017.
51. Cox, *Shapeshifters*, 28–29.
52. Breunlin and Regis, "Putting the Ninth Ward on the Map," 745–746.
53. Breunlin and Regis, "Putting the Ninth Ward on the Map," 757.
54. Maira, *Missing*, 201.

55. Regis notes that, for many SAPC members, their role in the Second Line community signifies "an active stance against the forces of disorder and lawlessness." For this reason the city can appropriate the Second Line as a cultural icon of palatable, positive, and respectable Black culture to market its own image. Meanwhile, the city taxes clubs, blacks out certain dates, and otherwise presents obstacles to staging Second Line parades. Regis, "Second Lines," 483, 496. On the politics of respectability and the differing approaches of SAPCs to self-representation, see Sakakeeny, "Representational Power."

56. Rachel E. Harding makes a similar point in her analysis of candomblé in nineteenth-century Bahia, Brazil. She writes, "Blacks used institutions of the dominant society—such as *irmandades* and traditions of patronage—to enhance their own space and participation within the larger Brazilian society" (*Refuge in Thunder*, 125).

57. Maira, *Missing*, 248.

58. Cox, *Shapeshifters*, 146.

59. Gregory Davis, interview with the author, December 12, 2019; Benny Jones Sr., interview with the author, May 25, 2020.

60. Gregory Davis, interview with Kalamu ya Salaam, Glass House Reunion with the original members of the Dirty Dozen Brass Band, 2005.

61. Gregory Davis, Roger Lewis, and Kevin Harris, interview with Karen Celestan, 2009.

62. Gregory Davis, interview with Kalamu ya Salaam.

63. Foster, *Choreographing History*, 5.

64. Taylor, *Archive and the Repertoire*, esp. chap. 1.

65. On the "bodily archive," see Srinivasan, *Sweating Saris*, 17, and Lepecki, "Body as Archive."

66. Gregory Davis, interview with the author, December 12, 2019.

67. Gregory Davis, interview with Kalamu ya Salaam.

68. Benny Jones Sr., interview with the author, May 25, 2020.

69. Gregory Davis, interview with Kalamu ya Salaam.

70. The structure does not appear on a fire insurance map from 1909 but does make an appearance in the 1927 city directory as a grocery owned by Normand Braxton. Sanborn Map Company, "Sanborn Fire Insurance Map," vol. 1909; "New Orleans, Louisiana, City Directory, 1927," 187.

71. "New Orleans, Louisiana, City Directory, 1927," 187; "Polk's New Orleans City Directory, 1938," 261; "Polk's New Orleans City Directory, 1945–46," 736; "Polk's New Orleans City Directory, 1956," 1031; "Polk's New Orleans City Directory, 1960," 131.

72. Campanella, *Bienville's Dilemma*, 186.

73. Sanborn Map Company, "Sanborn Fire Insurance Map," vol. 1909, 400.

74. Gregg Stafford, interview with Mick Burns, October 2002; Mazza, *Up Front and Center*, 92. Shakespeare Park was renamed A. L. Davis Park, after the civil rights leader and first African American city council member, in 1979.

75. The cultural significance of these two locations is evidenced by their

frequent appearance in song lyrics. Even after its name change, Shakespeare Park has recurred regularly in songs such as Dr. John's 2004 "Marie Laveau" (Mazza, *Up Front and Center*, 92). Second and Dryades, or "Second and D," is referenced in numerous Mardi Gras Indian songs and New Orleans hip hop and funk lyrics, including the funk band Galactic's 2007 track featuring Mardi Gras Indian chief Monk Boudreaux, "Second and Dryades."

76. Robert Hare, "Brassy Traditions," *Times-Picayune*, December 9, 1988, 118. The property, which included a home and the structure that eventually housed the Glass House, was left to Moore and another family member in 1957. Moore acquired full ownership in 1958 and retained ownership until she sold the property in 1994. Chasey, "Judgment of Possession"; Simoneaux and Notary Public, "Sale of Property"; Newman and Notary Public, "Cash Sale."

77. Alan Lomax Video Collection, "Glass House 9–15," B-roll footage, Odyssey Productions, Inc., The Association for Cultural Equity (New York), DVD, Tapes 48–52; Benny Jones Sr., interview with the author, May 25, 2020.

78. For more on women's behind-the-scenes roles in the development of early New Orleans jazz, see Tucker, "Feminist Perspective." The importance of women bar owners, managers, and bartenders in the more recent history of New Orleans's music and dance cultures deserves more research. For example, Leona "Chine" Grandison, who died of COVID-19 in April 2020, owned and managed the Candlelight Lounge in Tremé, an important locale for brass band music and social aid and pleasure club activities, for thirty-five years.

79. Alex Rawls, "The Early Dirty Dozen Brass Band," *Offbeat*, October 1, 2010, https://www.offbeat.com/articles/the-early-dirty-dozen-brass-band/.

80. The bartenders and cook introduce themselves as Lomax interviews them on camera.

81. Roger Lewis, interview with the author, May 26, 2020.

82. Mazza, "Getting Loose."

83. Gregory Davis, interview with the author, December 12, 2019; Mazza, *Up Front and Center*, 93.

84. Benny Jones Sr., interview with the author, May 25, 2020.

85. Don Robertson, interview with the author, December 9, 2015.

86. Woods, *Development Drowned*, 181. Woods's terminology riffs on the "massive resistance" to integration encountered by New Orleanians a decade earlier (see Chapter 4).

87. Woods, *Development Drowned*, 201–202.

88. Woods, *Development Drowned*, 203.

89. Lipsitz, *How Racism Takes Place*.

90. Benny Jones Sr., interview with the author, May 25, 2020.

91. The June 1, 2013, parade was a re-do after the regularly scheduled May parade was halted by gunfire. For more on both events, see Chapters 2 and 3.

92. Edward Buckner, Terry Gable, and Leo Gorman, interview with the author, January 24, 2014.

93. Edward Buckner, Terry Gable, and Leo Gorman, interview with the author, January 24, 2014.

94. Edward Buckner, Terry Gable, and Leo Gorman, interview with the author, January 24, 2014.

95. Dennis, *Spirit of the St. Bernard*.

96. Dennis, *Spirit of the St. Bernard*.

97. Dantas, *Land of Opportunity*.

98. WWOZ, "St. Bernard Public Housing Development."

99. Dennis, *Spirit of the St. Bernard*.

100. Dennis, *Spirit of the St. Bernard*.

101. Edward Buckner, Terry Gable, and Leo Gorman, interview with the author, January 24, 2014.

102. The "big four" were the St. Bernard, B. W. Cooper, C. J. Peete (known as Magnolia), and Lafitte.

103. While New Orleans's public housing developments were densely populated compared to the rest of the city, they were not nearly as densely populated as similar developments in other U.S. cities. They were only a few stories tall, built on a modest scale, and featured airy verandas and shady courtyards. Campanella, *Bienville's Dilemma*, 183.

104. Regis, "Second Lines," 476.

105. Popkin et al., "A Decade of HOPE VI."

106. Flaherty, *Floodlines*, 196.

107. Dantas, *Land of Opportunity*.

108. Dantas, *Land of Opportunity*; Eckstein, *Sustaining New Orleans*, 175–210; Arena, "Black and White."

109. Dantas, *Land of Opportunity*.

110. For more on public housing activism after Katrina, see Arena, "Black and White."

111. As seen on the website for the Bayou District Foundation, an organization that partners with Columbia Residential to create the area's "Purpose Built Community" (https://bayoudistrictfoundation.com/our-story/).

112. This is how the Affordable Housing Tax Credit Coalition described Columbia Parc on its website when announcing that it had chosen Columbia Parc to receive the 2011 Charles L. Edson Tax Credit Excellence Award in the Public Housing Revitalization category (https://www.taxcreditcoalition.org/gallery/columbia-parc-at-the-bayou-district/).

113. WWL Staff, "Mixed-income Housing Development Replaces St. Bernard Projects," *WWL*, April 12, 2010, https://www.wwltv.com/article/news/mixed-income-housing-development-replaces-st-bernard-projects/289-347606844.

114. The history of public housing in New Orleans and elsewhere provides a stark example of Black and Third World feminists' observations that home is not necessarily a sanctuary apart from institutional and state policies. Chandra Talpade Mohanty explains that home can only remain a private domain under conditions of economic privilege. Institutional and state policies disrupt the

public-private divide for working-class and poor families. Mohanty, "Cartographies of Struggle," 53–54, 71–74. Although Mohanty explores the dissolution of the distinction between public and private in late capitalism in the context of the Third World, this type of analysis is equally central to U.S. Black feminist thinking regarding familial relations beginning with colonialism and slavery. See also Davis, *Women, Race and Class*; Spillers, "Mama's Baby"; Collins, *Black Feminist Thought*.

115. Katy Reckdahl, "Despite Complaints, Original Big 7 Club to Follow Traditional Route for Mother's Day Second-Line," *Advocate*, May 16, 2016, http://www.theadvocate.com/new_orleans/news/article_a6dc7351-2512-54f0-8899-9ec5a1dd66ab.html. A Facebook user, identified only as a manager of Columbia Parc, posted Reckdahl's article to Columbia Parc's Facebook page on Mother's Day in 2016 with a comment indicating that efforts to re-route the parade were spurred by resident requests, not top-down decisions: "Columbia Residential respects, celebrates and welcomes the Big 7 tradition and appreciates the Big 7 Social Aid and Pleasure Club. We also have respect for Mother's Day and its traditions. As manager of Columbia Parc, our first responsibility is to our residents and their concerns. The request we made to change route was for that sole purpose on behalf of our residents and their activities and privacy today. We respect the City's decision and look forward to a safe and festive Mothers Day!" Columbia Parc, "Columbia Residential respects, celebrates and welcomes the Big 7," Facebook, May 8, 2016, https://www.facebook.com/ColumbiaParcAtTheBayouDistrict/.

116. Lipsitz, *How Racism Takes Place*, 225, 234; Sakakeeny, *Roll With It*, 150.

117. Sakakeeny, *Roll With It*, 146; Bourgois, *In Search of Respect*.

Interlude: Joe Stern

This interview was conducted by the author as part of the oral history project "More Than Merely Fun: Dance, Politics and Pleasure at the New Orleans Second Line," funded by the New Orleans Jazz and Heritage Foundation Archive Fellowship (2016–2017). A recording and transcript of the full interview are housed at the New Orleans Jazz and Heritage Foundation Archive and available on the book's companion website.

1. Ariella Cohen, "In Big Easy, 'White Boy' Stern Makes Brass History," *Forward*, October 31, 2007, https://forward.com/news/11933/in-big-easy-white-boy-stern-makes-brass-his-00719/.

2. The Black Men of Labor hosted a Second Line parade between the storm and the Prince of Wales's December 2005 event, but Joel Dinerstein, an American studies scholar and Prince of Wales member, counts the Prince of Wales as the first major post-Katrina Second Line because the club organized it and ran it as it had in other years. In contrast, Black Men of Labor's parade purportedly was bankrolled by Spike Lee to generate footage for his documentary series *When the Levees Broke*. For a first-person account of the Prince of Wales' post-Katrina parade, see Dinerstein, "Second Lining Post-Katrina."

Epilogue

A portion of this chapter was previously published as "Second Line Organizations 'Return' to the Streets," *Data News Weekly*, June 26–July 2, 2021, pp. 2–3.

1. Michael Gerson, "The Coronavirus Isn't Another Hurricane Katrina. It's Worse." *Washington Post*, March 9, 2020, sec. Opinion. https://www.washingtonpost.com/opinions/coronavirus-isnt-another-hurricane-katrina-its-worse/2020/03/09/25c302f2-6224-11ea-acca-80c22bbee96f_story.html.

2. Gordon Russell, "Orleans Parish Has Highest Per-Capita Coronavirus Death Rate of American Counties—by Far," *Times-Picayune/Advocate*, March 26, 2020, https://www.nola.com/news/coronavirus/orleans-parish-has-highest-per-capita-coronavirus-death-rate-of-american-counties—/article_907e7d92-6fa3-11ea-9fcd-f3c3cf974ef1.html.

3. Statistics are taken from the Orleans Parish COVID-19 Dashboard at https://experience.arcgis.com/experience/746f03e88d204a2b82a7b958ea744bba/

4. David Benoit, "Coronavirus Devastates Black New Orleans: 'This Is Bigger Than Katrina'," *Wall Street Journal*, May 23, 2020, sec. Finance, https://www.wsj.com/articles/coronavirus-is-a-medical-and-financial-disaster-for-blacks-in-new-orleans-11590226200.

5. Benoit, "Coronavirus Devastates Black New Orleans."

6. Andrew J. Yawn, Maria Clark, and Todd A. Price, "Jazz Funerals Silenced: How New Orleans Grieves amid Coronavirus," *Tennessean*, April 23, 2020, https://www.tennessean.com/story/news/american-south/2020/04/23/coronavirus-how-new-orleans-grieves-jazz-funerals-silenced-covid-19/5123946002/.

7. Take 'Em Down NOLA published its full statement on its website, takeemdownnola.org (no longer active at the time of writing). It was reprinted in Ashley Dean, "Protests Are Planned for Every Night This Week in New Orleans," *WWNO*, June 1, 2020, sec. News, https://www.wwno.org/latest-news/2020-06-01/protests-are-planned-for-every-night-this-week-in-new-orleans. The group's name points to its purpose, which was to take down all Confederate monuments and other memorials to white supremacy in New Orleans. It successfully pressured city council to remove four of these statues in 2015. For a fuller account of the group's actions for monument removal and its connection to second lining, see Carrico, "The Patter of Our Feet."

8. The statement appeared on the organization's website, takeemdownola.org, which was no longer active at the time of writing. However, the statement has been preserved by the Library of Congress. "Take 'Em Down NOLA," Protests Against Racism Web Archive, Library of Congress, Washington, DC, https://www.loc.gov/item/lcwaN0033436/.

9. Katy Reckdahl, "Stripped of Its Cultural Rites, New Orleans Is at a Loss

for How to Mourn Covid-19 Deaths," *Vox*, June 5, 2020, https://www.vox.com/2020/6/5/21275105/new-orleans-funerals-covid-19-pandemic.

10. Reckdahl, "Stripped of Its Cultural Rites."

11. Jackson recorded weekly interviews called "Takin' It to the Streets" in WWOZ's studio and shared them publicly as audio files, along with the interviewed club's upcoming route sheets and photos of previous parades, on the station's website, https://www.wwoz.org/. After Jackson's death from cancer in 2021, India Sever continued the practice for the radio station.

12. C. Jackson, "Year Without Second Lines," 268.

13. C. Jackson, "Year Without Second Lines," 262.

14. Reckdahl, "Stripped of Its Cultural Rites."

15. Travis Lyons, interview with Charles "Action" Jackson, January 31, 2021, "Takin It To the Streets," WWOZ New Orleans 90.7 FM, https://www.wwoz.org/.

16. As of June 2021 Feed the Secondline reported that it had purchased more than $200,000 in groceries, delivered them to more than 128 culture bearers, and paid nearly half a million dollars in wages to musicians and artists. The group established itself as a 501(c)(3) nonprofit organization and continued its work even as pandemic restrictions eased (https://www.feedthesecondline.org/what-we-do).

17. Dixon, quoted in C. Jackson, "Year Without Second Lines," 286.

18. C. Jackson, "Year Without Second Lines," 283–284.

19. Edward Buckner, phone conversation with the author, June 19, 2021.

20. Mayor LaToya Cantrell, @mayorcantrell, Twitter, May 26, 2021, 5:04 p.m. CST, https://twitter.com/mayorcantrell/status/1397675108655931393?s=20.

21. Cooper, *Dancing in the Streets*.

22. Jackson Snowden, quoted in Carrie Booher, "Second Lines Return to New Orleans," WWOZ, May 28, 2021, https://www.wwoz.org/blog/653976.

23. Ramon Antonio Vargas and Jeff Adelson, "In New Orleans, Carjackings the Worst They've Been in a Decade: 'This Is Not a Safe Place'," *Nola.com*, June 19, 2021, https://www.nola.com/news/crime_police/article_bfd122d8-d047-11eb-ac36-13666e9f5007.html.

24. Edward Buckner, interview with Charles "Action" Jackson, June 1, 2021, "Takin It to the Streets," WWOZ New Orleans 90.7 FM, https://www.wwoz.org/blog/655731.

25. Edward Buckner, interview with Charles "Action" Jackson, June 1, 2021.

Bibliography

Archival Materials and Collections

Alan Lomax Video Collection, Hogan Jazz Archive, Tulane University, New Orleans.

Chasey, Paul E., Judge. "Judgment of Possession." Civil District Court for the Parish of Orleans, January 3, 1957. New Orleans Notarial Archives.

Collins, Robert F., Nils Douglas, and Lolis E. Elie. "Southern Justice," Box 2, Item 1: Bound personal papers, 1954–1968, Nils R. Douglas papers, 1893–1967, Amistad Research Center, New Orleans.

Dancing in the Streets, exhibition and Mobile Visitor Guide (audio recordings), February 25–June 13, 2021; and virtual exhibition, https://artsandculture.google.com/story/dancing-in-the-streets/GgJi8icbIVkrIA. Historic New Orleans Collection in collaboration with the Neighborhood Story Project, New Orleans.

Jules Cahn Collection at the Historic New Orleans Collection, New Orleans.

Leonard Burns Collection, Amistad Research Center, New Orleans.

Newman, Carol A., and Notary Public. "Cash Sale," June 30, 1994. New Orleans Notarial Archives.

New Orleans Imprints at the Historic New Orleans Collection, New Orleans.

New Orleans Jazz and Heritage Foundation Archive, New Orleans.

"New Orleans, Louisiana, City Directory, 1927, Vol. LIV." Soards Directory Co., Ltd., 1927, New Orleans Public Library.

Polk's New Orleans City Directories, various years. R. L. Polk and Co., Publishers. New Orleans Public Library.

Rogers, S. W., Francis Boisdore, and W. A. Dove, "Grand celebration in honor of the passage of the Ordinance of emancipation, by the Free State Convention, on the eleventh day of May, 1864, held in the Place d'Armes, New-Orleans, June 11th, with the programme, proceedings, speeches by Rev. Dr.

Rogers, Francis Boisdore, Rev. W. A. Dove &c. &c.: also the Proceedings of the American Arts Association of New Orleans, and the distribution of prizes, held first August, 1864," pamphlets, New Orleans Imprints at the Historic New Orleans Collection, New Orleans, 76-781-RL.

Sanborn Map Company. "Sanborn Fire Insurance Map from New Orleans, Orleans Parish, Louisiana." Vols. 1909 and 1952. New Orleans Public Library.

"Save Our Schools," Amistad Research Center, New Orleans.

Simoneaux, Moseman R., and Notary Public. "Sale of Property." City of New Orleans, March 5, 1958. New Orleans Notarial Archives.

Tom Dent Papers, Amistad Research Center, New Orleans.

United Clubs, Inc. Collection, 1961–1964, Amistad Research Center, New Orleans.

Secondary Sources

Albright, Ann Cooper. "Mining the Dance Field: Feminist Theory and Contemporary Dance." In *Choreographing Difference: The Body and Identity in Contemporary Dance*, 1–27. Middletown, CT: Wesleyan University Press, 1997.

Alghali, Ajara, and Erin Falker-Obichigha. "Interrogating Tipping Points: When Black Spaces Become White." Paper presented at the Biannual Meeting of the Collegium of African Diaspora Dance, Durham, NC/Zoom, 2022.

Allured, Janet. *Remapping Second-Wave Feminism: The Long Women's Rights Movement in Louisiana, 1950–1997*. Athens: University of Georgia Press, 2016.

Amit, Vered, and Nigel Rapport. *The Trouble with Community: Anthropological Reflections on Movement, Identity and Collectivity*. London: Pluto, 2002. https://doi.org/10.2307/j.ctt18mvnx3.

Anderson, Annye C. *Brother Robert: Growing up with Robert Johnson*. New York: Da Capo, 2020.

Arena, John. "Black and White, Unite and Fight? Identity Politics and New Orleans's Post-Katrina Public Housing Movement." In *The Neoliberal Deluge: Hurricane Katrina, Late Capitalism, and the Remaking of New Orleans*, edited by Cedric Johnson, 152–184. Minneapolis: University of Minnesota Press, 2011.

Arneson, Eric. "Learning the Lessons of Solidarity: Work Rules and Race Relations on the New Orleans Waterfront, 1880–1901." *Labor's Heritage* 1, no. 1 (January 1989): 26–45.

Asante, Kariamu Welsh. "Commonalities in African Dance." In *African Culture: The Rhythms of Unity*, edited by Molefi Kete Asante and Kariamu Welsh Asante, 71–82. Westport, CT: Greenwood, 1985.

Baker, Houston. *Turning South Again: Re-Thinking Modernism/Re-Reading Booker T*. Durham, NC: Duke University Press, 2001.

Bakhtin, Mikhail Mikhailovich. *Rabelais and His World*. Translated by Hélène Iswolsky. Bloominton: Indiana University Press, (1968) 1984.

Banks, Taunya L. "Post-Katrina Suppression of Black Working-Class Political

Expression." *Journal of Public Management and Social Policy* 22, no. 2 (2015): article 2.

Barnes, Bruce Sunpie, and Rachel Breunlin, eds. *Talk That Music Talk: Passing on Brass Band Music in New Orleans the Traditional Way*. New Orleans: Neighborhood Story Project and University of New Orleans Press, 2014.

Bechet, Sidney. *Treat It Gentle: An Autobiography*. London: Twayne, 1960.

Becknell, Clarence A., Thomas Price, and Don Short. "History of the Zulu Social Aid & Pleasure Club." Zulu Social Aid and Pleasure Club. http://www.kreweofzulu.com/history.

Behar, Ruth. *The Vulnerable Observer: Anthropology That Breaks Your Heart*. Boston: Beacon, 1996.

Beito, David T. *From Mutual Aid to the Welfare State: Fraternal Societies and Social Services, 1890–1967*. Chapel Hill: University of North Carolina Press, 2000.

Bell, Caryn Cossé. *Revolution, Romanticism, and the Afro-Creole Protest Tradition in Louisiana, 1718–1868*. Baton Rouge: Louisiana State University Press, 2004.

Bell, Derrick A. "*Brown v. Board of Education* and the Interest-Convergence Dilemma." *Harvard Law Review* 93, no. 3 (1980): 518–533.

Booher, Carrie. "Second Lines Return to New Orleans." WWOZ New Orleans 90.7 FM, May 28, 2021. https://www.wwoz.org/blog/653976.

Borders, James, IV. "New Orleans Negritude and the Second Line: Stankness, Stupidity, and Doofus Overload in the Streets of the Big Easy." In *Freedom's Dance: Social Aid and Pleasure Clubs in New Orleans*, by Eric Waters and Karen Celestan, 81–93. Baton Rouge: Louisiana State University Press, 2018.

Bourgois, Philippe I. *In Search of Respect: Selling Crack in El Barrio*. Structural Analysis in the Social Sciences. New York: Cambridge University Press, 1995.

Bowling, William, and Rachel Carrico. "Lakeviews: A Bus Tour as a Vehicle for Regrowth in New Orleans." *TDR/The Drama Review* 52, no. 1 (Spring 2008): 190–196.

Breunlin, Rachel. "Papa Joe Glasper and Joe's Cozy Corner: Downtown Development, Displacement, and the Creation of Community." MA thesis, University of New Orleans, 2004.

Breunlin, Rachel, Ronald W. Lewis, and Helen A. Regis. *The House of Dance and Feathers: A Museum by Ronald W. Lewis*. New Orleans: Neighborhood Story Project and University of New Orleans Press, 2009.

Breunlin, Rachel, and Helen A. Regis. "Putting the Ninth Ward on the Map: Race, Place, and Transformation in Desire, New Orleans." *American Anthropologist* 108, no. 4 (2006): 744–764.

Britton, Celia. *Édouard Glissant and Postcolonial Theory: Strategies of Language and Resistance*. Charlottesville: University of Virginia Press, 1999.

Brock, Jerry. "In Memory: Uncle Lionel Batiste[,] February 11, 1932–July 8, 2012[.] 'Colorful In Life—Rich In Spirit.'" *Jazz Archivist* 27 (2014): 3–17.

Brooks, Daphne. *Bodies in Dissent: Spectacular Performances of Race and Freedom, 1850–1910*. Durham, NC: Duke University Press, 2006.
Broom, Sarah M. *The Yellow House*. New York: Grove, 2019.
Brothers, Thomas David. *Louis Armstrong's New Orleans*. New York: Norton, 2007.
Brown, adrienne m. *Pleasure Activism: The Politics of Feeling Good*. Chico, CA: AK Press, 2019.
Brown, Charlie, dir. *Never a Dull Moment: 20 Years of the Rebirth Brass Band*. New Orleans: Mojotooth Productions, 2005.
Brown, Jayna. *Babylon Girls: Black Women Performers and the Shaping of the Modern*. Durham, NC: Duke University Press, 2008.
Browning, Barbara. *Samba: Resistance in Motion*. Bloomington: Indiana University Press, 1995.
Buerkle, Jack V., and Danny Barker. *Bourbon Street Black: The New Orleans Black Jazzman*. New York: Oxford University Press, 1973.
Burkholder, J. Peter. "Borrowing." *Grove Music Online*, 2001. https://doi.org/10.1093/gmo/9781561592630.article.52918.
Burns, Mick. *Keeping the Beat on the Street: The New Orleans Brass Band Renaissance*. Baton Rouge: Louisiana State University Press, 2008.
Butler, Judith. *Notes Toward a Performative Theory of Assembly*. Cambridge, MA: Harvard University Press, 2015.
Camp, Stephanie M. H. *Closer to Freedom: Enslaved Women and Everyday Resistance in the Plantation South*. Chapel Hill: University of North Carolina Press, 2004.
Campanella, Richard. *Bienville's Dilemma: A Historical Geography of New Orleans*. Lafayette: University of Louisiana at Lafayette Press, 2008.
Campanella, Richard. "An Ethnic Geography of New Orleans." *Journal of American History* 94, no. 3 (2007): 704–715. https://doi.org/10.2307/25095131.
Campanella, Richard. *Geographies of New Orleans: Urban Fabrics Before the Storm*. Lafayette: Center for Louisiana Studies, 2006.
Carby, Hazel V. "Policing the Black Woman's Body in an Urban Context." *Critical Inquiry* 18, no. 4 (1992): 738–755.
Carrico, Rachel, and Latanya d. Tigner. "Close Up: Step-Touch in New Orleans Popular Dance." In *Dance in US Popular Culture*, edited by Jennifer Atkins, 254–265. New York: Routledge, 2023.
Carrico, Rachel. "Dancing Like a Man: Competition and Gender in the New Orleans Second Line." In *The Oxford Handbook of Dance and Competition*, edited by Sherril Dodds, 572–596. Oxford: Oxford University Press, 2019. https://doi.org/10.1093/oxfordhb/9780190639082.013.25.
Carrico, Rachel. "On Thieves, Spiritless Bodies, and Creole Soul: Dancing Through the Streets of New Orleans." *TDR/The Drama Review* 57, no. 1 (Spring 2013): 70–87. https://doi.org/10.1162/DRAM_a_00235.
Carrico, Rachel. "Reinvention: Miss Antoinette K-Doe and Her Baby Dolls." In *Walking Raddy: The Baby Dolls of New Orleans*, edited by Kim Marie Vaz-Deville, 203–212. Jackson: University Press of Mississippi, 2018.

Carrico, Rachel. "Second Line Choreographies in and Beyond New Orleans." In *Futures of Dance Studies*, edited by Janice Ross, Susan Manning, and Rebecca Schneider, 191–208. Madison: University of Wisconsin Press, 2020.

Carrico, Rachel. "'The Patter of Our Feet': Parading and Political Organizing in New Orleans." *Conversations Across the Field of Dance Studies* 38 (2018): 8–12.

Carrico, Rachel. "Un/Natural Disaster and Dancing: Hurricane Katrina and Second Lining in New Orleans." *The Black Scholar* 46, no. 1 (2016): 27–36. https://doi.org/10.1080/00064246.2015.1119636.

Castaldi, Francesca. *Choreographies of African Identities: Négritude, Dance, and the National Ballet of Senegal*. Urbana: University of Illinois Press, 2006.

Certeau, Michel de. *The Practice of Everyday Life*. Los Angeles: University of California Press, 1984.

"Charter and By-Laws of the Prince of Wales Social Club," May 1, 1929. Personal papers, Joseph M. Stern.

Chasman, Deborah, and Joshua Cohen, eds. *The Politics of Pleasure: Boston Review Forum* no. 23 (Summer 2022).

Cityline Canada: *How Celebrating Black Joy Online Became a Movement*. Toronto, Ontario, Canada: Cityline, 2021. https://www.cityline.tv/video/how-celebrating-black-joy-online-became-a-movement/.

City of New Orleans Public Health Department. "The NOLA For Life Playbook: A Strategic Plan to Prevent Youth Violence in New Orleans." City of New Orleans Health Department, Fall 2013. https://nola.gov/getattachment/Health/Data-and-Publications/NOLA-FOR-LIFE-PLAYbook_for-web-9-2-14.pdf/.

Coates, Ta-Nehisi. "My President Was Black." *Atlantic*, February 2017. https://www.theatlantic.com/magazine/archive/2017/01/my-president-was-black/508793/.

Cohen, Ariella. "In Big Easy, 'White Boy' Stern Makes Brass History." *Forward*, October 31, 2007. https://forward.com/news/11933/in-big-easy-white-boy-stern-makes-brass-his-00719/.

Collins, Patricia Hill. *Black Feminist Thought: Knowledge, Consciousness, and the Politics of Empowerment*. 2nd ed. Routledge Classics. New York: Routledge, 2009.

Cooper, Carolyn. *Sound Clash: Jamaican Dancehall Culture at Large*. New York: Palgrave Macmillan, 2004.

Cooper, Judy. *Dancing in the Streets: Social Aid and Pleasure Clubs of New Orleans*. New Orleans: Historic New Orleans Collection, 2021.

Cotton, Deborah. "Big Red Cotton—Facebook." Facebook. https://www.facebook.com/BigRedCotton/.

Cotton, Deborah. "BigRedCotton—YouTube." YouTube. https://www.youtube.com/user/BigRedCotton.

Cotton, Deborah. "Videos from Old & Nu Style Fellas Second Line." *New Orleans Good Good* (blog), April 22, 2013. http://www.neworleansgoodgood.com.

Cox, Aimee Meredith. *Shapeshifters: Black Girls and the Choreography of Citizenship*. Durham, NC: Duke University Press, 2015.

Crehan, Kate. *Community Art: An Anthropological Perspective*. New York: Berg, 2011.

D'Amico-Samuels, Deborah. "Undoing Fieldwork: Personal, Political, Theoretical and Methodological Implications." In *Decolonizing Anthropology: Moving Toward an Anthropology for Liberation*, 3rd ed., edited by Faye V. Harrison, 68–87. Arlington, VA: American Anthropological Association, 2010.

Damsholt, Inger. "The Marriage of Music and Dance: Understanding the World of Choreomusical Relations Through a Gendered Metaphor." In *Of Another World: Dancing Between Dream and Reality*, edited by Monna Dithmer and Inger Damsholt, U.K. ed., 237–250. Copenhagen: Museum Tusculanum Press, 2002.

Daniel, Yvonne. *Caribbean and Atlantic Diaspora Dance: Igniting Citizenship*. Urbana: University of Illinois Press, 2011.

Daniel, Yvonne. *Dancing Wisdom: Embodied Knowledge in Haitian Vodou, Cuban Yoruba, and Bahian Candomblé*. Urbana: University of Illinois Press, 2005.

Dantas, Luisa, dir. *Land of Opportunity*. DVD. New Orleans: JoLu Productions, 2010.

Das, Joanna Dee. *Katherine Dunham: Dance and the African Diaspora*. New York: Oxford University Press, 2017.

Davis, Angela Y. *Women, Race and Class*. New York: Vintage, 1983.

DeCoste, Kyle. "Street Queens: The Original Pinettes and Black Feminism in New Orleans Brass Bands." MA Thesis, Tulane University, 2015.

DeFrantz, Thomas F. "The Black Beat Made Visible: Hip Hop Dance and Body Power." In *Of the Presence of the Body: Essays on Dance and Performance Theory*, edited by André Lepecki, 64–81. Middletown, CT: Wesleyan University Press, 2004.

DeFrantz, Thomas F. *Dancing Revelations: Alvin Ailey's Embodiment of African American Culture*. New York: Oxford University Press, 2004.

DeFrantz, Thomas F. "Duke University Professor Thomas F. DeFrantz: Buck, Wing and Jig." YouTube, March 26, 2012. https://www.youtube.com/watch?v=A34OD4eA17o.

DeFrantz, Thomas F. "Unchecked Popularity: Neoliberal Circulations of Black Social Dance." In *Neoliberalism and Global Theatres: Performance Permutations*, edited by Lara D. Nielsen and Patricia Ybarra, 128–142. New York: Palgrave Macmillan, 2012.

Dennis, Lloyd, dir. *Spirit of the St. Bernard: Recollections from the Lives of the People Who Lived There*. Columbia Residential, 2010. https://vimeo.com/16778834.

Dewulf, Jeroen. *From the Kingdom of Kongo to Congo Square: Kongo Dances and the Origins of the Mardi Gras Indians*. Lafayette: University of Louisiana at Lafayette Press, 2017.

Dinerstein, Joel. "Second Lining Post-Katrina: Learning Community from the Prince of Wales Social Aid and Pleasure Club." *American Quarterly* 61, no. 3 (2009): 615–637.

Doleac, Benjamin. "Strictly Second Line: Funk, Jazz, and the New Orleans Beat." *Ethnomusicology Review* 18 (2017): n.p. https://ethnomusicologyreview.ucla.edu/journal/volume/18/piece/699.

Donaldson, Gary A. "A Window on Slave Culture: Dances at Congo Square in New Orleans, 1800–1862." *Journal of Negro History* 69, no. 2 (1984): 63–72. https://doi.org/10.2307/2717598.

Drewal, Margaret Thompson. "The State of Research on Performance in Africa." *African Studies Review* 23 (1991): 1–64.

Drewal, Margaret Thompson. *Yoruba Ritual: Performers, Play, Agency*. Bloomington: Indiana University Press, 1992.

Eckstein, Barbara J. *Sustaining New Orleans: Literature, Local Memory, and the Fate of a City*. New York: Routledge, 2006.

Emery, Lynne F. *Black Dance in the United States from 1619–1970*. Palo Alto, CA: National Press Books, 1972.

Estes, David E. "The Neo-African Vatican: Zora Neale Hurston's New Orleans." In *Literary New Orleans in the Modern World*, edited by Richard S. Kennedy, 66–82. Baton Rouge: Louisiana State University Press, 1998.

Evans, Freddi Williams. *Congo Square: African Roots in New Orleans*. Lafayette: University of Louisiana at Lafayette Press, 2011.

Evans, Freddi Williams. "Congo Square and the Roots of Second Line Parading." In *Dancing in the Streets*, by Judy Cooper, 23–29. New Orleans: Historic New Orleans Collection, 2021.

Fairclough, Adam. *Race and Democracy: The Civil Rights Struggle in Louisiana, 1915–1972*. Athens: University of Georgia Press, 2008.

Fischlin, Daniel, Ajay Heble, and George Lipsitz. *The Fierce Urgency of Now: Improvisation, Rights, and the Ethics of Cocreation*. Durham, NC: Duke University Press, 2013.

Flaherty, Jordan. *Floodlines: Community and Resistance from Katrina to the Jena Six*. Chicago: Haymarket, 2010.

Floyd, Samuel A. "Ring Shout! Literary Studies, Historical Studies, and Black Music Inquiry." *Black Music Research Journal* 11, no. 2 (1991): 265–287. https://doi.org/10.2307/779269.

Ford, Tanisha C. *Liberated Threads: Black Women, Style, and the Global Politics of Soul*. Chapel Hill: University of North Carolina Press, 2015.

Foster, Susan Leigh. *Choreographing Empathy: Kinesthesia in Performance*. New York: Routledge, 2010.

Foster, Susan Leigh, ed. *Choreographing History*. Bloomington: Indiana University Press, 1995.

Foster, Susan Leigh. *Choreography and Narrative*. Bloomington: Indiana University Press, 1996.

Gaunt, Kyra D. *The Games Black Girls Play: Learning the Ropes from Double-Dutch to Hip-Hop*. New York: New York University Press, 2006.

George-Graves, Nadine. "Taking the Cake: Black Dance, Competition, and Value." In *The Oxford Handbook of Dance and Competition*, edited by Sherill Dodds, 17–39. New York: Oxford University Press, 2019.

George-Graves, Nadine. *Urban Bush Women: Twenty Years of African American Dance Theater, Community Engagement, and Working It Out*. Madison: University of Wisconsin Press, 2010.

Germany, Kent B. *New Orleans After the Promises: Poverty, Citizenship, and the Search for the Great Society*. Athens: University of Georgia Press, 2007.

Gerstin, Julian. "The Allure of Origins: Neo-African Dances in the French Caribbean and the Southern United States." In *Just Below South: Intercultural Performance in the Caribbean and the U.S. South*, edited by Jessica Adams, Michael P. Bibler, and Cécile Accilien, 127–130. Charlottesville: University of Virginia Press, 2007.

Gilroy, Paul. *The Black Atlantic: Modernity and Double Consciousness*. Cambridge, MA: Harvard University Press, 1993.

Giroux, Henry A. "Reading Hurricane Katrina: Race, Class, and the Biopolitics of Disposability." *College Literature* 33, no. 3 (Summer 2006): 171–196.

Glissant, Édouard. *Poétique de la Relation*. Paris: Gallimard, 1990.

Goldman, Danielle. *I Want to Be Ready: Improvised Dance as a Practice of Freedom*. Ann Arbor: University of Michigan Press, 2010.

Gomez, Michael A. *Exchanging Our Country Marks: The Transformation of African Identities in the Colonial and Antebellum South*. Chapel Hill: University of North Carolina Press, 2000.

Gordon, Michelle Y. "'Midnight Scenes and Orgies': Public Narratives of Voodoo in New Orleans and Nineteenth-Century Discourses of White Supremacy." *American Quarterly* 64, no. 4 (2012): 767–786. https://doi.org/10.1353/aq.2012.0060.

Gordon, Robert Winslow. "Negro 'Shouts' from Georgia." In *Mother Wit from the Laughing Barrel: Readings in the Interpretation of Afro-American Folklore*, edited by Alan Dundes, reprint, with addendum, 445–451. New York: Garland, 1981.

Gottschild, Brenda Dixon. *The Black Dancing Body: A Geography from Coon to Cool*. New York: Palgrave Macmillan, 2003.

Greene, Oliver N. "The Aesthetics of Asé in the Black Masking Indians of New Orleans: Musical Africanisms and Orisa Manifestiations in the Big Chief." *Fire!!* 6, no. 2 (Summer 2020): 73–127.

Hall, Gwendolyn Midlo. *Africans in Colonial Louisiana: The Development of Afro-Creole Culture in the Eighteenth Century*. Baton Rouge: Louisiana State University Press, 1992.

Harding, Rachel E. *A Refuge in Thunder: Candomblé and Alternative Spaces of Blackness*. Bloomington: Indiana University Press, 2003.

Harris, Cheryl I. "Whiteness as Property." *Harvard Law Review* 106, no. 8 (1993): 1707–1791. https://doi.org/10.2307/1341787.

Hazzard-Donald, Katrina. "Hoodoo Religion and American Dance Traditions:

Rethinking the Ring Shout." *Journal of Pan African Studies* 4, no. 6 (2011): 194–213.

Hazzard-Gordon, Katrina. *Jookin': The Rise of Social Dance Formations in African-American Culture*. Philadelphia: Temple University Press, 1990. http://www.jstor.org/stable/j.ctt14bt80j.5.

Hebdige, Dick. *Cut "n" Mix: Culture, Identity and Caribbean Music*. Digital printing. A Comedia Book. London: Routledge, 2010.

Hill, Constance Valis. "Stepping, Stealing, Sharing, and Daring: Improvisation and the Tap Dance Challenge." In *Taken by Surprise: A Dance Improvisation Reader*, edited by Ann Cooper Albright and David Gere, 89–104. Middletown, CT: Wesleyan University Press, 2003.

Hill, Constance Valis. *Tap Dancing America: A Cultural History*. Oxford: Oxford University Press, 2015.

Hirsch, Arnold R. "Simply a Matter of Black and White: The Transformation of Race and Politics in Twentieth-Century New Orleans." In *Creole New Orleans: Race and Americanization*, edited by Arnold R. Hirsch and Joseph Logsdon, 262–319. Baton Rouge: Louisiana State University Press, 1992.

Hirsch, Arnold R., and Joseph Logsdon. *Creole New Orleans: Race and Americanization*. Baton Rouge: Louisiana State University Press, 1992.

Holloway, Karla F. C. *Passed On: African American Mourning Stories; A Memorial*. Durham, NC: Duke University Press, 2002.

Hooks, bell. *All About Love: New Visions*. New York: HarperCollins, 2000.

Hooks, bell. *Black Looks: Race and Representation*. Boston: South End, 1992.

Horowitz, Andy. *Katrina: A History, 1915–2015*. Cambridge, MA: Harvard University Press, 2020.

Hume, Yanique. "Death and the Construction of Social Space: Land, Kinship, and Identity in the Jamaican Mortuary Cycle." In *Passages and Afterworlds*, edited by Maarit Forde and Yanique Hume, 109–138. Durham, NC: Duke University Press, 2018. https://doi.org/10.1215/9781478002130-006.

Hunter, Tera W. *To 'joy My Freedom: Southern Black Women's Lives and Labors After the Civil War*. Cambridge, MA: Harvard University Press, 1997.

Jackson, Charles. "The Year Without Second Lines." In *Dancing in the Streets: Social Aid and Pleasure Clubs of New Orleans*, by Judy Cooper, 281–289. New Orleans: Historic New Orleans Collection, 2021.

Jackson, Jonathan David. "Improvisation in African-American Vernacular Dancing." *Dance Research Journal* 33, no. 2 (2001): 40–53. https://doi.org/10.2307/1477803.

Jackson, Joyce Marie. "New Orleans Second Line Aesthetics and Identity." In *Freedom's Dance: Social Aid and Pleasure Clubs in New Orleans*, by Eric Waters and Karen Celestan, 3–21. Baton Rouge: Louisiana State University Press, 2018.

Jackson, Maria Rosario. "Rebuilding the Cultural Vitality of New Orleans." Washington, DC: Urban Institute, 2006. https://www.urban.org/research/publication/rebuilding-cultural-vitality-new-orleans.

Jackson, Michael. *Paths Toward a Clearing: Radical Empiricism and Ethnographic Inquiry*. Bloomington: Indiana University Press, 1989.

Jacobs, Claude F. "Benevolent Societies of New Orleans Blacks During the Late Nineteenth and Early Twentieth Centuries." *Louisiana History* 29, no. 1 (1988): 21–33.

Jacobs, Claude F. "Spirit Guides and Possession in the New Orleans Black Spiritual Churches." *Journal of American Folklore* 102, no. 403 (1989): 45–67. https://doi.org/10.2307/540080.

Jankowiak, William, Helen A. Regis, and Christina Turner. "Second-Line Marching Clubs: Inside New Orleans' Black Social Aid and Pleasure Clubs." *The World and I* 5 (1990): 665–673.

Johnson, E. Patrick. "Feeling the Spirit in the Dark: Expanding Notions of the Sacred in the African-American Gay Community." *Callaloo* 21, no. 2 (1998): 399–416.

Johnson, E. Patrick. "'Quare' Studies, or (Almost) Everything I Know About Queer Studies I Learned from My Grandmother." *Text and Performance Quarterly* 21, no. 1 (2001): 1–25. https://doi.org/10.1080/10462930128119.

Johnson, Imani Kai. "From Blues Women to B-Girls: Performing Badass Femininity." *Women and Performance* 24, no. 1 (2014): 15–28. https://doi.org/10.1080/0740770X.2014.902649.

Johnson, Imani Kai. "(Home) Training in Breaking Culture." *Conversations Across the Field of Dance Studies* 40 (2020): 51–53.

Johnson, Jasmine Elizabeth. "Flesh Dance: Black Women from Behind." In *Futures of Dance Studies*, edited by Susan Manning, Janice Ross, and Rebecca Schneider, 154–169. Madison: University of Wisconsin Press, 2020.

Johnson, Julie B. "Dancing Down the Floor: Experiences of a 'Community' in a 'West African' Dance Class in Philadelphia." PhD diss., Temple University, 2016.

Johnson, Rashauna. *Slavery's Metropolis: Unfree Labor in New Orleans During the Age of Revolutions*. Cambridge Studies on the African Diaspora. New York: Cambridge University Press, 2016.

Johnson, Walter. *Soul by Soul: Life Inside the Antebellum Slave Market*. Cambridge, MA: Harvard University Press, 1999.

Johnson, Zada. "Walking the Post-Disaster City: Race, Space and the Politics of Tradition in the African-American Parading Practices of Post-Katrina New Orleans." PhD diss., University of Chicago, 2010.

Jones, Adanna. "Can Rihanna Have Her Cake and Eat It Too? A Schizophrenic Search for Resistance Within the Screened Spectacles of a Winin' Fatale." In *The Oxford Handbook of Screendance Studies*, edited by Douglas Rosenberg, 676–694. Oxford: Oxford University Press, 2016. https://doi.org/10.1093/oxfordhb/9780199981601.013.32.

Joseph, Miranda. *Against the Romance of Community*. Minneapolis: University of Minnesota Press, 2002.

Keber, Lily, dir. *Buckjumping*. Color. New Orleans: Mairzy Doats Productions, 2018.

King, Jason. "Which Way Is Down? Improvisations on Black Mobility." *Women and Performance* 14, no. 1 (2004): 25–45. https://doi.org/10.1080/07407700408571439.

Kowal, Rebekah, Randy Martin, and Gerald Siegmund. Introduction to *The Oxford Handbook of Dance and Politics*, edited by Rebekah Kowal, Randy Martin, and Gerald Siegmund, 1–24. New York: Oxford University Press, 2017.

Kraut, Anthea. *Choreographing the Folk: The Dance Stagings of Zora Neale Hurston*. Minneapolis: University of Minnesota Press, 2008.

Kraut, Anthea. "'Stealing Steps' and Signature Moves: Embodied Theories of Dance as Intellectual Property." *Theatre Journal* 62, no. 2 (2010): 173–189.

Lepecki, André. "The Body as Archive: Will to Re-Enact and the Afterlives of Dances." *Dance Research Journal* 42, no. 2 (2010): 28–48.

Lester, Julius. "People Who Could Fly." In *Toni Morrison's Song of Solomon: A Casebook*, edited by Jan Furman, 21–23. New York: Oxford University Press, 2003.

Lewis-Giggetts, Tracey M. *Black Joy: A Strategy for Resistance, Resilience, and Restoration*. New York: Gallery, 2022.

Lhamon, W. T. *Raising Cain: Blackface Performance from Jim Crow to Hip Hop*. Cambridge, MA: Harvard University Press, 2000.

Lipsitz, George. *How Racism Takes Place*. Philadelphia: Temple University Press, 2011.

Lipsitz, George. "Learning from New Orleans: The Social Warrant of Hostile Privatism and Competitive Consumer Citizenship." *Cultural Anthropology* 21, no. 3 (2006): 451–468.

Logsdon, Dawn, and Lolis Eric Elie, dirs. *Faubourg Treme: The Untold Story of Black New Orleans*. San Francisco: Serendipity Films, LLC, 2007.

Logsdon, Joseph, and Caryn Cossé Bell. "The Americanization of Black New Orleans." In *Creole New Orleans*, edited by Arnold R. Hirsh and Joseph Logsdon, 201–261. Baton Rouge: Louisiana State University Press, 1992.

Lomax, Alan. *Jazz Parades: Feet Don't Fail Me Now*. 3/4 inch videotape. U-matic. New York: Association for Cultural Equity, 1990. http://www.folkstreams.net/film-detail.php?id=126.

Lomax, Tamura. "Black Bodies in Ecstasy: Black Women, the Black Church, and the Politics of Pleasure: An Introduction." *Black Theology* 16, no. 3 (2018): 189–194. https://doi.org/10.1080/14769948.2018.1492298.

Long, Alecia P. *The Great Southern Babylon: Sex, Race, and Respectability in New Orleans, 1865–1920*. Rev. ed. Baton Rouge: Louisiana State University Press, 2005.

Lorde, Audre. "Uses of the Erotic: The Erotic as Power." In *Sister Outsider: Essays and Speeches*, 53–39. Berkeley, CA: Crossing, [c. 2007].

Maira, Sunaina. *Missing: Youth, Citizenship, and Empire After 9/11*. Durham, NC: Duke University Press, 2009.

Malone, Jacqui. *Steppin' on the Blues: The Visible Rhythms of African American Dance*. Folklore and Society. Urbana: University of Illinois Press, 1996.

Manuel, Zac. "Inside the New Orleans Nine Times Second Line Parade (Video Clip)." mtv.com, February 28, 2017. https://www.mtv.com/video-clips/t2wzbk/inside-the-new-orleans-nine-times-second-line-parade.

Martin, Randy. *Critical Moves: Dance Studies in Theory and Politics*. Durham, NC: Duke University Press, 1998.

Maultsby, Portia K. "Funk." In *African American Music: An Introduction*, 293–314. New York: Routledge, 2006.

Mazza, Jay. "Getting Loose at the Glass House." *Beat Street* 1, no. 5 (1990): 50–51.

Mazza, Jay. *Up Front and Center: New Orleans Music at the End of the 20th Century*. New Orleans: Threadhead, 2012.

Mazzocca, Ann. "Inscribing/Inscribed: Bodies and Landscape in the Ritual of Embodied Remembrance at Souvenance Mystique." Paper presented at the Annual Meeting of the Society of Dance History Scholars and the Congress of Research on Dance, Iowa City, IA, 2014.

McKittrick, Katherine. *Demonic Grounds: Black Women and the Cartographies of Struggle*. Minneapolis: University of Minnesota Press, 2006.

McPhail, Clark, David Schweingruber, and John McCarthy. "Policing Protest in the United States: 1960–1995." In *Policing Protest: The Control of Mass Demonstrations in Western Democracies*, edited by Donatella della Porta and Herbert Reiter, 49–69. Minneapolis: University of Minnesota Press, 1998.

McQuirter, Marya Annette. "Awkward Moves: Dance Lessons from the 1940s." In *Dancing Many Drums: Excavations in African American Dance*, 81–103. Madison: University of Wisconsin Press, 2002.

Mendy, Greer E. *Black Dance in Louisiana: Guardian of a Cutlure*. New Orleans: Tekrema Center for African Diasporic Literacy, 2018.

Michna, Catherine. "Hearing the Hurricane Coming: Storytelling, Second-Line Knowledges, and the Struggle for Democracy in New Orleans." PhD diss., Boston College, 2011. https://www.academia.edu/27416432/Hearing_the_Hurricane_Coming_Storytelling_Second_Line_Knowledges_and_the_Struggle_for_Democracy_in_New_Orleans.

Mitchell, Brian K., Barrington S. Edwards, and Nick Weldon. *Monumental: Oscar Dunn and His Radical Fight in Reconstruction Louisiana*. New Orleans: Historic New Orleans Collection, 2021.

Mitchell, Don, and Lynn A. Staeheli. "Permitting Protest: Parsing the Fine Geography of Dissent in America." *International Journal of Urban and Regional Research* 29, no. 4 (2005): 796–813. https://doi.org/10.1111/j.1468-2427.2005.00622.x.

Mohanty, Chandra Talpade. "Cartographies of Struggle: Third World Women and the Politics of Feminism." In *Feminism Without Borders: Decolonizing Theory, Practicing Solidarity*, 43–84. Durham, NC: Duke University Press, 2003. https://doi.org/10.1215/9780822384649-003.

Monroe, Raquel L. "Oh No! Not This Lesbian Again! The Punany Poets Queer the Pimp-Ho Aesthetics." In *Queer Dance: Meanings and Makings*, edited by Clare Croft, 243–262. New York: Oxford University Press, 2017.

Moore, Leonard N. *Black Rage in New Orleans: Police Brutality and African American Activism from World War II to Hurricane Katrina*. Baton Rouge: Louisiana State University Press, 2010.

Morgan, Joan. "Why We Get Off: Moving Towards a Black Feminist Politics of Pleasure." *Black Scholar* 45, no. 4 (2015): 36–46. https://doi.org/10.1080/00064246.2015.1080915.

Muñoz, José Esteban. *Cruising Utopia: The Then and There of Queer Futurity*. New York: New York University Press, 2009.

Nancy, Jean-Luc. "The Confronted Community." *Postcolonial Studies* 6, no. 1 (2003): 23–36. https://doi.org/10.1080/13688790308110.

Nash, Jennifer C. *The Black Body in Ecstasy: Reading Race, Reading Pornography*. Durham, NC: Duke University Press, 2014.

Nettleford, Rex. "Implications for Caribbean Development." In *Caribbean Festival Arts*, edited by John W. Nunley and Judith Bettleheim, 183–197. Seattle: University of Washington Press, 1988.

"New Orleans and the Domestic Slave Trade Historical Marker." The Historical Marker Database. https://www.hmdb.org/m.asp?m=117438.

Nichols, Elaine. "Black Joy: Resistance, Resilience and Reclamation." National Museum of African American History and Culture. https://nmaahc.si.edu/explore/stories/black-joy-resistance-resilience-and-reclamation.

Nine Times Social and Pleasure Club. *Coming out the Door for the Ninth Ward*. New Orleans: Neighborhood Story Project and the University of New Orleans Press, 2009.

Northrup, Herbert R. "The New Orleans Longshoremen." *Political Science Quarterly* 57, no. 4 (1942): 526–544. https://doi.org/10.2307/2144755.

Novack, Cynthia J. "Looking at Movement as Culture: Contact Improvisation to Disco." *TDR/The Drama Review* 32, no. 4 (1988): 102–119. https://doi.org/10.2307/1145892.

Olsen, Margaret M. "The Gift of the New Orleans Second Line." In *Neoliberalism and Global Theatres: Performance Permutations*, edited by Lara D. Nielsen and Patricia Ybarra, 176–188. New York: Palgrave Macmillan, 2012.

Ophir, Hodel. "Dancing to Transgress: Palestinian Dancer Sahar Damoni's Politics of Pleasure." *Dance Research Journal* 53, no. 3 (2021): 25–45. https://doi.org/10.1017/S0149767721000401.

Perry, Imani. "Racism Is Terrible. Blackness Is Not." *Atlantic*, June 15, 2020. https://www.theatlantic.com/ideas/archive/2020/06/racism-terrible-blackness-not/613039/.

Perry, Imani. *South to America: A Journey Below the Mason-Dixon to Understand the Soul of a Nation*. New York: Ecco, 2022.

Popkin, Susan J., Bruce Katz, Mary K. Cunningham, Karen D. Brown, Jeremy Gustafson, and Margery Austin Turner. "A Decade of HOPE VI: Research Findings and Policy Challenges." Washington, DC: Urban Institute, May 18, 2004. https://www.urban.org/research/publication/decade-hope-vi.

Purcell, Mark. "Possible Worlds: Henri Lefebvre and the Right to the City."

Journal of Urban Affairs 36, no. 1 (2014): 141–154. https://doi.org/10.1111/juaf.12034.

Raeburn, Bruce Boyd. "Dancing Hot and Sweet: New Orleans Jazz in the 1920s." *The Jazz Archivist* 8, no. 1–2 (1992): 10–13.

Raeburn, Bruce Boyd. "'They're Tryin' to Wash Us Away': New Orleans Musicians Surviving Katrina." *Journal of American History* 94, no. 3 (2007): 812–819. https://doi.org/10.2307/25095143.

Ramsey, Guthrie P. *Race Music: Black Cultures from Bebop to Hip-Hop*. Berkeley: University of California Press, 2004.

Rebirth Brass Band. *Do Whatcha Wanna*. New Orleans: Mardi Gras Records, 1991.

Reed, Ishmael. "Introduction: Black Pleasure—An Oxymoron." In *Soul: Black Power, Politics, and Pleasure*, edited by Monique Guillory and Richard C. Green, 169–171. New York: New York University Press, 1998.

Regis, Helen A. "Blackness and the Politics of Memory in the New Orleans Second Line." *American Ethnologist* 28, no. 4 (2001): 752–777.

Regis, Helen A. "Second Lines, Minstrelsy, and the Contested Landscapes of New Orleans Afro-Creole Festivals." *Cultural Anthropology* 14, no. 4 (1999): 472–504.

Regis, Helen A., and Shana Walton. "Producing the Folk at the New Orleans Jazz and Heritage Festival." *Journal of American Folklore* 121, no. 482 (2008): 400–440.

Roach, Joseph R. "Carnival and the Law in New Orleans." *TDR/The Drama Review* 37, no. 3 (1993): 42–75. https://doi.org/10.2307/1146310.

Roach, Joseph R. *Cities of the Dead: Circum-Atlantic Performance*. New York: Columbia University Press, 1996.

Roach, Joseph R. "Mardi Gras Indians and Others: Genealogies of American Performance." *Theatre Journal* 44, no. 4 (1992): 461–483. https://doi.org/10.2307/3208769.

Roberts, John Storm. *Latin Jazz: The First of the Fusions, 1880s to Today*. New York: Schirmer, 1999.

Robinson, Cedric. *Black Marxism: The Making of the Black Radical Tradition*. Chapel Hill: University of North Carolina Press, 1983.

Rogers, Kim Lacy. *Righteous Lives: Narratives of the New Orleans Civil Rights Movement*. New York: New York University Press, 1995.

Ruddick, Susan. "Constructing Difference in Public Spaces: Race, Class, and Gender as Interlocking Systems." *Urban Geography* 17, no. 2 (1996): 135–136.

Sakakeeny, Matt. "The Representational Power of New Orleans Brass Bands." In *Brass Bands of the World: Militarism, Colonial Legacies, and Local Music Making*, edited by Suzel Ana Reily and Katherine Brucher, 123–138. Surrey: Ashgate, 2013.

Sakakeeny, Matt. *Roll With It: Brass Bands in the Streets of New Orleans*. Durham, NC: Duke University Press, 2013. https://doi.org/10.1515/9780822377207.

Sakakeeny, Matt. "'Under the Bridge': An Orientation to Soundscapes in New Orleans." *Ethnomusicology* 54, no. 1 (2010): 1–27.

Salaam, Kalamu ya. "He's the Prettiest: A Tribute to Big Chief Allison 'Tootie' Montana's 50 Years of Mardi Gras Indian Suiting." *Louisiana Folklife: Louisiana's Living Traditions*. 1997. Baton Rouge: Louisiana Division of the Arts, n.p. https://www.louisianafolklife.org/LT/Virtual_Books/Hes_Prettiest/hes_the_prettiest_tootie_montana.html.

Salaam, Kalamu ya. "Second Line: Cutting the Body Loose." *Wavelengths*, July 1982, 27–31.

Salaam, Kalamu ya. "The Spirit Family of the Streets." *WordUp: Kalamu's Words* (blog), May 28, 2010. https://wordup.posthaven.com/essay-spirit-family-of-the-streets.

Santoro, Daniella. "The Dancing Ground: Embodied Knowledge, Disability, and Visibility in New Orleans Second Lines." In *The Oxford Handbook of Music and Disability Studies*, edited by Blake Howe, Stephanie Jensen-Moulton, Neil Lerner, and Joseph Straus, 305–326. Oxford: Oxford University Press, 2016.

Schafer, Judith Kelleher. *Becoming Free, Remaining Free: Manumission and Enslavement in New Orleans, 1846–1862*. Baton Rouge: Louisiana State University Press, 2003.

Schafer, William John. *Brass Bands and New Orleans Jazz*. Baton Rouge: Louisiana State University Press, 1977.

Schwadron, Hannah. *The Case of the Sexy Jewess: Dance, Gender, and Jewish Joke-Work in U.S. Pop Culture*. New York: Oxford University Press, 2018.

Seiferth, Eric. "Where Do Second Lines Come From? The Origins Go Back More Than 200 Years." *First Draft: Stories from the Historic New Orleans Collection*. New Orleans: Historic New Orleans Collection, February 24, 2021. https://www.hnoc.org/publications/first-draft/symposium-2021/where-do-second-lines-come-origins-go-back-more-200-years.

Shaik, Fatima. *Economy Hall: The Hidden History of a Free Black Brotherhood*. New Orleans: Historic New Orleans Collection, 2022.

Sharpe, Christina Elizabeth. *In the Wake: On Blackness and Being*. Durham, NC: Duke University Press, 2016.

Smith, Michael P. "New Orleans' Hidden Carnival: Traditional African-American Freedom Celebrations in Urban New Orleans." *Cultural Vistas*, Autumn 1990, 4–23.

Snead, James A. "On Repetition in Black Culture." *Black American Literature Forum* 15, no. 4 (1981): 146–154. https://doi.org/10.2307/2904326.

Solnit, Rebecca. "We Won't Bow Down." *Yes*, February 15, 2010. www.yesmagazine.org/people-power/we-wont-bow-down.

Solnit, Rebecca, and Rebecca Snedeker. *Unfathomable City: A New Orleans Atlas*. Berkeley: University of California Press, 2013.

Spillers, Hortense J. "Mama's Baby, Papa's Maybe: An American Grammar Book." *Diacritics* 17, no. 2 (1987): 65–81. https://doi.org/10.2307/464747.

Spitzer, Nick. "Rebuilding the 'Land of Dreams' with Music." In *Rebuilding Urban Places After Disaster*, edited by Eugenie L. Birch and Susan M. Wachter, 305–328. Philadelphia: University of Pennsylvania Press, 2013.

Srinivasan, Priya. *Sweating Saris: Indian Dance as Transnational Labor*. Philadelphia: Temple University Press, 2011.

Stearns, Marshall Winslow, and Jean Stearns. *Jazz Dance: The Story of American Vernacular Dance*. New York: Da Capo, 1994.

Stockwell, Norman. "Radical Social Movements as Love Letters: An Interview with Robin D. G. Kelley." *Progressive*, August 22, 2017. https://progressive.org/magazine/interview-robin-d-g-kelley-stockwell/.

Stooges Brass Band and Kyle DeCoste, eds. *Can't Be Faded: Twenty Years in the New Orleans Brass Band Game*. American Made Music. Jackson: University Press of Mississippi, 2020.

Stuckey, Sterling. "Christian Conversion and the Challenge of Dance." In *Choreographing History*, edited by Susan Leigh Foster, 54–68. Bloomington: Indiana University Press, 1995.

Taylor, Diana. *The Archive and the Repertoire: Performing Cultural Memory in the Americas*. Durham, NC: Duke University Press, 2003.

Thanos, Nikki. "The New Orleans Mother's Day Shooting Was Like a Mass Shooting at a Church." *Bridge The Gulf Project* (blog), May 31, 2013. https://bridgethegulfproject.org/blog/2013/new-orleans-mother%E2%80%99s-day-shooting-was-mass-shooting-church.

Thomas, Lynnell L. *Desire and Disaster in New Orleans: Tourism, Race, and Historical Memory*. Durham, NC: Duke University Press, 2014.

Thompson, Robert Farris. "An Aesthetic of the Cool." *African Arts* 7, no. 1 (1973): 41–91. https://doi.org/10.2307/3334749.

Thompson, Robert Farris. *Flash of the Spirit: African & Afro-American Art & Philosophy*. Ann Arbor: University of Michigan Press, 1984.

Thompson, Robert Farris. "When the Saints Go Marching In: Kongo Louisiana, Kongo New Orleans." In *Resonance from the Past: African Sculpture from the New Orleans Museum of Art*, edited by Frank Herreman, 136–143. New York: Museum for African Art, 2005.

Thompson, Robert Farris, and Joseph Cornet. *The Four Moments of the Sun: Kongo Art in Two Worlds*. Washington, DC: National Gallery of Art, 1981.

Troeh, Eve. "Transcript: Second Line Fee Increase." *WWOZ Street Talk* (blog), April 1, 2006. http://wwozstreettalk.blogspot.com/2006_05_02_archive.html.

Tsing, Anna Lowenhaupt. *Friction: An Ethnography of Global Connection*. Princeton, NJ: Princeton University Press, 2005.

Tucker, Sherrie. "A Feminist Perspective on New Orleans Jazzwomen." New Orleans Jazz National Historical Park, September 30, 2004. https://www.nps.gov/jazz/learn/historyculture/upload/new_orleans_jazzwomen_rs-2.pdf.

Turner, Richard Brent. *Jazz Religion, the Second Line, and Black New Orleans*. Bloomington: Indiana University Press, 2009.

Urban Bush Women. "Summer Leadership Institute: Urban Bush Women." https://www.urbanbushwomen.org/summer-leadership.

Vaz-Deville, Kim Marie. *The "Baby Dolls": Breaking the Race and Gender Barriers of the New Orleans Mardi Gras Tradition*. Baton Rouge: Louisiana State University Press, 2013.

Vaz-Deville, Kim Marie, ed. *Walking Raddy: The Baby Dolls of New Orleans*. Jackson: University Press of Mississippi, 2018.

Vega, Marta Moreno. "The Ancestral Sacred Creative Impulse of Africa and the African Diaspora: Àse, the Nexus of the Black Global Aesthetic." *Lenox Avenue* 5 (1999): 45–57. https://doi.org/10.2307/4177077.

Vincent, Rickey. *Funk: The Music, the People, and the Rhythm of the One*. New York: St. Martin's Griffin, 1996.

"VIP Ladies & Kids Second Line Parade." WWOZ New Orleans 90.7 FM, March 6, 2022. https://www.wwoz.org/events/716411.

Wald, Elijah. *Escaping the Delta: Robert Johnson and the Invention of the Blues*. New York: HarperCollins, 2005.

Walker, Alice. *In Search of Our Mothers' Gardens: Womanist Prose*. New York: Harcourt Brace Jovanovich, 1983.

Walker, Daniel E. *No More, No More: Slavery and Cultural Resistance in Havana and New Orleans*. Minneapolis: University of Minnesota Press, 2004.

Walker, Harry J. "Negro Benevolent Societies in New Orleans: A Study of Their Structure, Function, and Membership." MA thesis, Fisk University, 1937.

Warner, Sara. *Acts of Gaiety: LGBT Performance and the Politics of Pleasure*. Triangulations: Lesbian/Gay/Queer Theater/Drama/Performance. Ann Arbor: University of Michigan Press, 2013.

Waters, Eric, and Karen Celestan. *Freedom's Dance: Social Aid and Pleasure Clubs in New Orleans*. Baton Rouge: Louisiana State University Press, 2018.

Waters, Eric, and Karen Celestan. "Glossary." In *Freedom's Dance: The Second Line in New Orleans*. Baton Rouge: Louisiana State University Press, 2018.

Watts, Lewis, and Eric Porter. *New Orleans Suite: Music and Culture in Transition*. Berkeley: University of California Press, 2013.

Weiss, Gail. *Body Images: Embodiment as Intercorporeality*. New York: Routledge, 1999.

Welsh, Kariamu. "The 'Gospel' of Memory: Inscribed Bodies in the African Diaspora." In *Hot Feet and Social Change: African Dance and Diaspora Communities*, edited by Kariamu Welsh, Esailama G .A. Diouf, and Yvonne Daniel, 84–103. Urbana: University of Illinois Press, 2019. https://doi.org/10.5406/j.ctvswx837.10.

White, Michael. "The New Orleans Brass Band: A Cultural Tradition." In *The Triumph of the Soul: Cultural and Psychological Aspects of African American Music*, edited by Ferdinand Jones and Arthur C. Jones, 69–96. Westport, CT: Praeger, 2001.

Whitney Plantation. "Slavery In Louisiana." https://www.whitneyplantation.org/history/slavery-in-louisiana/.

Williams, Patricia J. *The Alchemy of Race and Rights*. Cambridge, MA: Harvard University Press, 1991.

Wingfield, Roland. "New Orleans Marching Bands: A Choreographer's Delight." *Dance Magazine*, 1959.
Woods, Clyde A. *Development Drowned and Reborn: The Blues and Bourbon Restorations in Post-Katrina New Orleans*. Geographies of Social Justice and Social Transformation. Athens: University of Georgia Press, 2017.
WWOZ. "Dew Drop Inn." New Orleans Music Map, 2023. https://acloserwalknola.com/places/dew-drop-inn/.
WWOZ. "St. Bernard Public Housing Development." New Orleans Music Map, 2023. https://acloserwalknola.com/places/st-bernard-public-housing-development/.
Young, Harvey. *Embodying Black Experience: Stillness, Critical Memory, and the Black Body*. Theater: Theory/Text/Performance. Ann Arbor: University of Michigan Press, 2010.

Recorded Interviews (Not by the Author)

Baker, Joe. "The Revolution." Interview by Rachel Breunlin. Historic New Orleans Collection. https://www.hnoc.org/dits-club-narratives/revolution.
Buckner, Edward. Interview with Charles "Action" Jackson. June 1, 2021. "Takin It to the Streets," WWOZ New Orleans 90.7 FM. https://www.wwoz.org/blog/655731
Davis, Gregory. Interview with Kalamu ya Salaam. 2005. Allison Miner Music Heritage Stage Collection, New Orleans Jazz and Heritage Foundation Archive, New Orleans, LA.
Davis, Gregory, Roger Lewis, and Kevin Harris. Interview with Karen Celestan. 2009. DVD, New Orleans Jazz and Heritage Foundation Archive, New Orleans.
Dixon, Norman Jr. Interview with Rachel Breunlin. 2021. In *Dancing in the Streets*, online exhibition audio guide, https://artsandculture.google.com/story/dancing-in-the-streets/GgJi8icbIVkrIA.
Franklin, Perry. "Keep'N It Real." Interview by Rachel Breunlin. December 1, 2020. Historic New Orleans Collection. https://www.hnoc.org/dits-club-narratives/keepn-it-real-0.
Henry, Jazz. Interview with Rachel Breunlin. 2021. In *Dancing in the Streets*, online exhibition audio guide, https://artsandculture.google.com/story/dancing-in-the-streets/GgJi8icbIVkrIA.
Hubbard, Don, oral history, September 18, 2017, for NOLA Resistance, MSS 936, Williams Research Center, Historic New Orleans Collection.
Jackson Snowden, Tamara. Interview with Rachel Breunlin. 2021. In *Dancing in the Streets*, online exhibition audio guide, https://artsandculture.google.com/story/dancing-in-the-streets/GgJi8icbIVkrIA.
Johnson, Fred. Interview with Charles "Action" Jackson. January 12, 2021. "Takin It to the Streets," WWOZ New Orleans 90.7 FM. https://www.wwoz.org/blog/641756.
Johnson, Jarrett, Ada Robertson, Nelson Lois, and Kasey Batiste. "Money

Wasters." Interview by Rachel Breunlin, December 2, 2020. Historic New Orleans Collection. https://www.hnoc.org/dits-club-narratives/money-wasters-0.

Lyons, Travis. Interview with Charles "Action" Jackson. January 31, 2021. "Takin It to the Streets," WWOZ New Orleans 90.7 FM. https://www.wwoz.org/.

Nelson, Lois. Interview with Rachel Breunlin. In *Dancing in the Streets*, online exhibition audio guide. https://artsandculture.google.com/story/dancing-in-the-streets/GgJi8icbIVkrIA.

Smith, Jerome. Interview with Mick Burns. October 2002. At the Tremé Community Center for the book *Keeping the Beat on the Street*. Wave file (003.2002.007), New Orleans Jazz and Heritage Foundation Archive, New Orleans.

Smith, Jerome. Interview with Tom Dent. September 23, 1983. Tom Dent Papers, Amistad Research Center, New Orleans.

Stafford, Gregg. Interview with Mick Burns. October 2002. At his home for the book *Keeping the Beat on the Street*. Wave file (003.2002.008), New Orleans Jazz and Heritage Foundation Archive, New Orleans.

Tapp, Linda. "Lady Buckjumpers." Interview by Rachel Breunlin, November 5, 2020. Historic New Orleans Collection. https://www.hnoc.org/dits-club-narratives/lady-buckjumpers.

Tureaud, A. P. Interview with Joseph Logsdon. Numerous dates 1968–1971, as quoted in Fairclough, *Race and Democracy*, 49.

Interviews by the Author

Braxton Robertson, Catina. Interview with the author. April 14, 2014.
Brown, Camille A. Interview with the author. December 9, 2013.
Buckner, Edward. Interview with the author. July 30, 2013.
Buckner, Edward. Phone conversation with the author. June 19, 2021.
Buckner, Edward, Terry Gable, and Leo Gorman. Interview with the author. January 24, 2014.
Davis, Gregory. Interview with the author. December 12, 2019.
Davis, Rodrick. Interview with the author. January 16, 2014.
Davis, Rodrick. Interview with the author. March 25, 2017.
Dorsey, Terrylyn, and Terrinika Smith. Interview with the author. August 8, 2014.
Jackson, Harry. Interview with the author. April 6, 2014.
Jackson Snowden, Tamara. Interview with the author. April 21, 2014.
Jones, Benny, Sr. Interview with the author. May 25, 2020.
Kimble, Walter. Interview with the author, May 27, 2014.
Lacen Keller, Barbara. Interview with the author. September 5, 2017.
Lazard, Nicole. Interview with the author. September 7, 2017.
Lewis, Roger. Interview with the author. May 26, 2020.
Mazza, Jay. Interview with the author. December 13, 2019.

Ott, Francine. Interview with the author. December 6, 2013.
Platenburg, Gerald. Interview with the author. March 28, 2017.
Press, Sue. Interview with the author. August 13, 2013.
Ratcliff, Wellington, Jr. Interview with the author and Daniella Santoro. March 26, 2014.
Robertson, Don. Interview with the author. April 10, 2014.
Robertson, Don. Interview with the author. December 9, 2015.
Sloan, Lenwood. Interview with the author. October 31, 2013.
Smith, Tyree. Interview with the author. February 18, 2014.
Smith-Simmons, Doratha, and John Keith Simmons. Interview with the author. November 8, 2013.
Stern, Joe. Interview with the author. September 1, 2017.
Tabb, Derrick. Interview with the author. April 15, 2014.
Tigner, Latanya d. Interview with the author. May 15, 2015.

Index

Page numbers in *italics* refer to figures.

activism, 37, 44, 89–91, 99, 185, 194n44. *See also* SilenceIsViolence; social aid and pleasure clubs (SAPCs): aid and activism of
activists, 10–11, 17, 20, 71, 134, 136, 197n8, 208n11; and CORE, 95–96, 101–3, 106–7, 109–11; housing, 167–69; and Take 'Em Down NOLA, 173, 184
aesthetics, 14–15, 44, 61, 134, 197n19; aesthetic revolution, 39, 160; Second Line, 20–23, 65, 120, 128–29, 136–39, 156
Affordable Housing Tax Credit Coalition, 224n112
Africa, 29, 40, 151, 203n27, 203n29, 221n35
African Americans, 24, 46, 94–98, 111, 168, 193n30, 197n8, 206n75, 212n80, 222n74; and churches, 23, 29, 60, 64, 80, 102; and COVID-19, 180–82; and dance, 21, 192n12, 215n5; and jazz, 63, 128; neighborhoods of, 6, 9, 32, 42, 127–29, 151–55, 165, 170, 221n33; and nightlife, 162, 164; and New Orleans, 1, 6, 18, 28, 39, 42, 49, 71, 170, 191n2, 221n33; and performance, 121, 123, 196n72; and second lining, 17, 32, 40, 51, 92, 103–5, 133, 140–41, 148–49, 157; women, 135–36, 192n12, 196n73, 221n43
African American studies, 11
African dance, 11, 21, 30, 33, 61–62, 64–65, 70, 122, 197n19, 202n6, 221n35; West African, 33, 151, 156
African diaspora, 21, 65–66, 68, 70, 93, 103, 112, 132, 149, 151; and dance, 33, 61–62, 122, 202n6
Africanisms, 61, 63, 69, 121
African Methodist Episcopal church, 102
Africans, 11, 16, 37–38, 91, 198n22, 198n28, 203n18, 206n75, 220n19; and culture, 62–64, 110–11
Afro-Caribbeans, 23, 139
Afro-Creole New Orleanians, 1, 38–39, 92, 96–97, 155, 198n28
Afrofuturism, 7
Aid to Dependent Children program, 212n80
Alabama, 95, 107
Albany, Ga., 100
A. L. Davis Park, 106, 163, 187, 222n74, 223n75
Alexander, Avery, 102, 109
Alghali, Ajara, 19
All-Star Second Line, 44–45, 49
Allured, Janet, 136

allyship, 48, 184
American Civil Liberties Union (ACLU), 45, 200n63
Amos, Rodney, 56
ancestral memories, 21, 28, 40
ancestry, 38–40, 62, 71, 82, 110, 149–51, 153
Anderson, Leon, Sr., 145
Anderson, Leon "Smurf," Jr., 146
Anderson, Richard, 145
Andrews, James, 182
Andrews, Troy "Trombone Shorty," 117–18, 214n2
Andrews, Walter, 176
antebellum period, 5, 11, 38, 53, 62–63, 97
anthropology, 12, 18, 75–76, 125, 137, 148–49, 157, 199n50, 201n71, 210n39
antiblackness, 5, 7, 11, 24, 49, 50, 71, 182, 191n2. *See also* racism
Apollo Theater, 85
Armstrong, Louis, 64
Athenaeum Club, 104
Avenue Steppers Social Aid and Pleasure Club, 133

Baby Dolls, 7, 33, 100, 157, 184, 196n73
Backstreet Cultural Museum, 183, 194n41
Bakhtin, Mikhail, 100
ballet, 15, 195n72
Baptist churches, 5, 80, 129, 143, 167
Barker, Danny, 129, 167, 215n30
Barnes, Bruce "Sunpie," 110
Baton Rouge, 97, 102–3, 112
Bayou Steppers Social Aid and Pleasure Club, 40
Bayou St. John, 1
b-boys, 75, 85. *See also* breakdance
Behar, Ruth, 201n71
Bell, Caryn Cossé, 209n16
Bell, Derrick, Jr., 201n80
belly rub (dance), 8
belonging, sense of, 22, 24, 43, 140–41, 148–49, 156, 170
benevolent associations, 29, 37–39, 42, 65, 70, 91–94, 106, 110–11, 126–28, 196n3. *See also individual benevolent associations*
Beyoncé, 12
Big Easy Footwork Competitions, 124
Big Freedia, 12
Birmingham, Ala., 107
Black Citizens' Committee, 105–6, 109
Black excellence, 11, 112, 124
Black expressive culture, 6, 63, 68, 111, 218n75
blackface, 93–94, 209n28
Black feminism, 11, 136, 148, 193n33, 224n114, 225n114. *See also* womanism
Black humanity, 11, 170, 190
Black joy, 7, 11, 18, 49, 190, 193n33
Black liberation, 11, 22, 89, 135–36
Black Lives Matter movement, 11, 88
Black Masking Indians, 16, 33, 50, 112, 126, 163, 175, 183. *See also* Mardi Gras Indians
Black Men of Labor Social Aid and Pleasure Club (BMOL), 23, 44, *72*, 109–12, 213n97, 225n2
Black middle class, 6, 96–97, 136, 151, 210n39
Blackness, 11, 44, 76, 98, 140, 157
Black New Orleanians. *See* African Americans
Black Panther Party, *84*, 85, 87–88, 207n1
Black secret societies, 37, 39–40, 135
Black studies, 5
Black voluntary associations, 7–8, 37–40, 43, 91, 111. *See also* benevolent associations; Black secret societies; burial associations; social aid and pleasure clubs (SAPCs)
blues, 52, 65, 68, 134, 158, 193n30, 216n31, 221n48
Bocage, Edwine, 167
Boudreau, Wynoka "Nokie," 180–*81*
Boudreaux, Monk, 175, 176
bounce (music genre), 2, 12, 167
Bourgois, Phillipe, 199n50
brass band music, 20–23, 37, 43, 126, 143, 167, 170, 184, 186; competitions, 131–32; indoor, 77–79; and jazz,

29, 39, 69, 111, 115, 119, 128, 133–35, 216n35, 223n78; processional, 1–2, 8–9, 50, 62, 92, 101, 103, 106, 163, 189; youth, 45, 89, 129. *See also individual brass bands*
Braxton, Norman, 222n70
Braxton Robertson, Catina, 16, 32, 73, 179, *181*
Brazil, 198n22, 201n85, 222n56
breakdance, 85–86. *See also* b-boys
Breunlin, Rachel, 148, 159
Bridges, Ruby, 95–96, 104, 210n34
Brock, Jerry, 208n14, 215n30
Brooks, Daphne, 218n82
Brooks, Michael, Jr., 29
Broom, Sarah, 152
Brothers, Thomas, 64, 205n55
brown, adrienne maree, 11, 193n33
Brown, Camille A., 204n41
Brown, Jayna, 209n28
Bucket Men Social Aid and Pleasure Club, 129
buckjumping (dance), 14–15, 71, 131–34, 136, 138, 148, 156
Buckner, Deneen, 186, 189
Buckner, Edward, 16, 31, 45–48, 52, 59–60, 66–68, 165–67, 184–89
burial associations, 37
Burns, Leonard, 95, 97–99, 101, 109
Burns, Mick, 128–29
Bush, George W., 180

Cahn, Jules, 103, *105*
Cakewalk (dance), 124
call-and-response competitions, 23, 130, 132
Calliope High Steppers Social Aid and Pleasure Club, 135, 147
Calliope public housing development, 147
Camp, Stephanie, 192n12
Campanella, Richard, 152
Candlelight Lounge, 183, 223n78
Cantrell, LaToya, 27, 180, 185
capitalism, 7, 13, 24, 33, 104, 148, 160, 182, 188; late, 129, 132, 225n114; racial, 11, 152, 170, 193n35
Carby, Hazel, 157–58, 221n45

Caribbean, the, 11, 37, 60–62, 66–67, 139, 151, 215n5
Carnival, 1, 16, 93–95, 97, 99–101, 106, 109, 119, 157; masking traditions of, 1, 184. *See also* Baby Dolls; Black Masking Indians; krewes' parades; Mardi Gras; Mardi Gras Indians; *individual Krewes*
carnivalesque, the, 23, 94, 100–101, 107
carry, concept of, 61, 66, 68, 73, 75, 82, 202n6
Carter, Alfred "Bucket," 126
Castaldi, Francesca, 194n55
Castle, Oretha, 102–3, 106
Catholicism, 5, 38, 80, 95–96, 155, 198n22
Celebration Hall, 20, 78–80
Celestan, Karen, 191n1
Central City Youth Against Violence, 184
Certeau, Michel de, 194n44
chanting, 2, 6, 11, 62, 67, 97, 126, 147–48, 157, 169
charivari, 62
Chitlin' Circuit, 134
choreography, 12, 36, 53, 61, 70, 125, 150, 166, 204n41, 204n46; of citizenship, 149, 158–60, 170; structure of, 2–3, 22, 66–67
Chosen Few Social and Pleasure Club, 5
Christianity, 5, 15, 60, 64–65, 80–81, 134–35, 204n41. *See also* Baptist churches; Catholicism; Protestantism; Sanctified church
citizenship, 24, 38, 107, 148, 213n103; choreographing, 149, 158–60, 170
civil rights era, 24, 89, 95–99, 106, 109–11, 128, 134, 165, 192n26, 216n31; post-, 129, 138; pre-, 15, 173
Civil War, 37–39, 62, 91, 96, 162, 209n16
class, 7, 13, 28, 38, 96–99, 104, 106, 120, 153, 157. *See also* Black middle class; poverty; working class
Coates, Ta-Nehisi, 18
Code Noir of Louisiana, 63
collectives, 8, 15, 35–36, 51, 143

Index

collectivity, 8, 50–52, 92, 120, 128, 132, 143, 170, 191n1; and dancing, 2, 4, 6, 10, 20, 22, 34–36, 53, 65, 67, 205n55; and memory, 73, 90; and ownership, 13, 23, 53, 98, 122, 148, 159; and pride, 9–10, 42. *See also* benevolent associations; mutual aid; spirit family
colonialism, 18, 38, 62–63, 148, 151, 155, 194n55, 203n27, 206n73, 225n114; European, 40, 139–40. *See also* imperialism
colorism, 38
Columbia Parc housing development, 169–70, 189, 224n112, 225n115
Columbia Residential, 169–70, 189, 207n105, 224n111, 225n115
communism, 174
community building, 21, 44, 150, 167
competition, 75, 85, 124–25, 127, 130–32, 155, 188. *See also* call-and-response competitions
Confederacy, 93, 173, 209n16, 209n20, 226n7
Congo Square, 12, 21, 62, 65, 78, 82, 99, 138, 157, 203n31; and histories of slavery, 11, 63–64, 91–92, 203n27, 204n37
Congress of Racial Equality (CORE), 89, 96, 99–103, 106, 109–12
Consumers' League of Greater New Orleans, 102
Cooper, Judy, 211n62
Cornet, Joseph, 203n31
Cotton, Deborah "Big Red," 47, 200n67
counter-histories, 21, 71
COVID-19 pandemic, 24, 37, 81, 179–90, 208n6, 223n78
Cox, Aimee Meredith, 75–76, 149, 157–58
Crehan, Kate, 33
Creole identity, 38, 96, 155, 198n28, 221n33
criminalization, 103, 148
Cross the Canal Steppers Social Aid and Pleasure Club (CTC), 144, 146–47

Cuba, 62, 197n21, 197nn22–23, 205n55
Cult of the Lost Cause, 93

Damsholt, Inger, 195n72
dancing-with, 34, 51–53
Daniel, Yvonne, 61, 67, 149, 197n21, 205n55
Da Truth Brass Band, 180
Davis, A. L., 109
Davis, Gregory "Blodie," 130, 132–33, 160–61, 167
Davis, Rodrick "Scubble," 54–58, 70, 123–24, 154–56, 159, 188
Davis, Sandra, 56
dead man walk, 57, 70, 72
DeBerry, Jarvis, 47
DeFrantz, Thomas, 121, 123, 132, 215n5, 218n78
Dejan, Harold, 215n30, 216n31
Dent, Tom, 79, 220n18
Desire public housing development, 85–86, 147
Detroit, 158, 221n43
Dew Drop Inn, 163
Dewulf, Jeroen, 40, 93
dignity, 37, 49, 70–71, 109, 134, 138
Dillard University, 102, 189
Dinerstein, Joel, 225n2
dirge (music), 67, 69–70, 72
Dirty Dozen Brass Band, 56, 79–81, 121–37, 150, 160–61, 163, 167
Dirty Dozen Social Aid and Pleasure Club, 51
disability, 75–77
Divine Ladies, 2
Dixon, Norman, Jr., 69–70, 184, 197n4
Dixon Gottschild, Brenda, 74
DJ Irv, 167
Dorsey, Terrylyn, 57, *114*, 115–18, 122–23, *123*, 145, 188
Dorsey, Yarnell, 115
Double Nine Social Aid and Pleasure Club, 147
Drewal, Margaret, 18–19, 125, 218n75
drugs, 11, 42–43, 53, 61, 74, 133, 199n50
Dumaine Street Gang Social Aid and Pleasure Club, 56, 147
Durell, Eddie "Sugar Slim," 129

ecstasy, 10, 23, 61, 67, 70, 74, 76–79, 81–82, 193n33, 205n54
ecstatic time, 76–77, 82
Edwards, Dow "Spy Boy," 183
Egungun processions, 62
elders, 18, 23, 29, 125, 133, 183–84, 189
elected officials, 10, 50, 96
Elie, Lolis, 97, 210n39
Emancipation Jubilee, 91–92
embodiment, 47, 70–71, 75–76, 81, 93, 109, 137, 170; of knowledge, 120, 127–29, 140; of values, 22, 65, 122
Epps, Alvin, 175
ethnography, 17–19, 24, 48, 139, 194n55
ethnomusicology, 17, 21, 39, 42, 137, 140
Etienne, Gail, 95–96, 104
Eureka Brass Band, 94, 103
Europe, 15, 22, 39, 40, 121, 139–41, 151, 195, 203n31
Evans, Freddi Williams, 62

Facebook, 46–47, 117–18, 185–86, 225n115
Fairclough, Adam, 96, 209n28
Fairview Baptist Church Brass Band, 129, 167
Falker-Obichigha, Erin, 19
Family Ties Social Aid and Pleasure Club, 13, 31–32, 51, 121, 124
Feed the Secondline, 184, 227n16
femininity, 22, 195, 201n71
feminism, 136, 206n92, 224n114; Black feminism, 11, 136, 148, 193n33, 224n114, 225n114. *See also* womanism
fieldwork (research), 16, 18, 20, 201n71
first line, 2, 15, 62, 69
Fischlin, Daniel, 194n44
flambeaux, 98
flooding, 6, 140, 151–52, 168, 176, 220n20, 220n27
Floyd, George, 11, 24, 182, 208n6
Floyd, Samuel, 64, 78
Footloose Breakers, 75
Footwerk Family Social Aid and Pleasure Club, 51, 138
footwork (dance), 9, 20, 34–36, 46, 59, 90, 130–32, 135–40, 164, 214n3; acquisition of, 119–27; competitions, 85, 188; and downtown, 14–15; elevated, 23, *142*, 143, 148–51, 154–55, 158–60, 220n18; and funerals, 43, 81–82; improvised, 1–2, 5, 9, 13, 16–17; and Rodrick "Scubble" Davis, 55, 154–56; and Terrylyn Dorsey, 115–17; transformative power of, 61, 67–68, 70, 74–78, 93, 186
Foster, Susan Leigh, 161, 195, 195n72, 206n73
Fox, Antoinette Dorsey Kador, 7
Francis, Sylvester, 183
Franklin, Brandon, 42
Franklin, Perry, 131, 149
freedom, 34, 45, 53, 71, 81, 85, 89, 94, 99, 109; to assemble, 23, 91, 100, 103, 112
Freedom March, 23, 106–7, 109, 187
Freedom Rider Convention, 111
Freedom Riders, 102, 109–12
Freedom Rides, 91, 102
Freedom Schools, 89
Free State Committee, 92
French Quarter, 5, 75, 111, 115, 133, 147, 176, 185; and Congo Square, 63, 91, 204n37; and tourism, 12, 85, 102, 153
friction, 59, 128, 137
funerals, 2, 17, 20, 60, 115, 126, 128, 134, 166, 211n62; and COVID-19, 182–84; as ecstatic, 23, 56–57, 81, 205n54; expense of, 37, 42; jazz, 39, 55, 62–67, 69–73, 82, 93, 119, 199n38
Funky Butt (dance), 8
Fun Lovers, 135
Furious Five, 126

Gable, Terry "Squillee," 36, 61, 68, 166
Gaunt, Kyra, 140–41
gender, 7, 13–15, 20–22, 70, 76, 120, 136, 156–57, 195–96n72, 218n82. *See also* femininity; masculinity
generations, 10, 15, 20, 23, 127, 131–32, 139, 154, 183, 194; cross-generational, 45–46, 81, 96–97, 99, 106, 125, 167, 188–89; new, 8, 36, 112, 119–20, 129, 134, 137, 208n11

gentrification, 148, *153*, 165
geographies, 7, 34, 43, 65, 155–56, 159, 170, 185; Black, 104, 147–48, 151–52, 165, 212n79. *See also* white teapot
George-Graves, Nadine, 33, 124
Georgia, 100
Gerson, Michael, 180
Gilroy, Paul, 132
Glasper, Joe, 134–35, 137
Glass House, 79–82, 129–34, 136–37, 139, 160–65, 170, 216n39, 223n118
Glissant, Édouard, 139
Goldman, Danielle, 34, 199n52, 217n74
Good Times II, 149
Gorman, Leo, 60
Grandison, Leona "Chine," 183, 223n78
Grandmaster Showcase, 85
grassroots movements, 5, 12, 47, 49, 115, 183, 188
Green Lounge, 167

Haitian Rara processions, 68
Haitian revolution, 62
Haley, Oretha Castle. *See* Castle, Haley
Hall, Willie, 67–68
Hammond, Larry, 183
Harding, Rachel, 201n85, 222n56
Haynes, Owen, 174
Hazzard-Gordon, Katrina, 63, 97, 127, 219n3
Head, Stacey, 27
healthcare, 24, 27, 37, 53, 181
Heble, Ajay, 194n44
Henry, Clarence "Chink," 103
Henry, Jazz, 138
Hines, Ezell, 183
hip hop, 12, 44, 86, 167, 192n12, 223n75. *See also* bounce (music genre)
Historic New Orleans Collection, 185
Holloway, Karla, 63
holy dance. *See* ring shout
Holy Spirit, 65, 78, 204n41
homelessness, 31, 141
hoofers, 121
Hoofers' Club, 121

hooks, bell, 12, 52–53
Horowitz, Andy, 151–52
Hot 8 Brass Band, 40, 42
House of Dance and Feathers Museum, 183
Housing Opportunities for People Everywhere (HOPE) VI, 168–69
Hubbard, Don, 106
Hume, Yanique, 66
Hunter, Oliver "Squirk," Jr., 67–68, 130
Hunter, Tera, 192n12
Hurricane Katrina, 15, 18, 155, 173, 180, 182, 190, 191n2, 204n46; displacement caused by, 44–45, 140–41, 169; post-, 4–6, 24, 27, 46, 144, 148–49, 168–69, 213n97, 219n11; Second Line parades after, 175–77, 220n27, 225n2; and tourism, 13, 140–41, 151–53

Iberville public housing development, 6, 168
Ice Divas Social and Pleasure Club, 5, 16–19, 32, 73, 179, *181*, 185, 194n49
imitation, 121–22, 124
imperialism, 18. *See also* colonialism
improvisation, 20, 36, 43, 62, 65, 67, 78–79, 125, 148, 160; of dance, 34, 76, 199n52, 217n74, 218n75; of footwork, 1–2, 5, 8, 13, 17, 127, 138, 154
incarceration, 42–43, 74, 130. *See also* prison-industrial complex
Independent Aid and Social Club, 103–6, 109
individualism, 13, 53, 197n7
integration, 91, 95–97, 102–5, 210n34, 223n86
intellectual property, 122, 124
International Longshoremen's Association, 103, 110–11. *See also* Longshoremen's Protective Union and Benevolent Association
interviews, 18–20, 27, 40, 73–75, 78, 85, 110, 115, 120, 122–26, 138, 165; informal, 13, 17; on-air, 183, 188, 194n41. *See also individual interviews*

Jackson, Charles "Action," 183–85, 188
Jackson, Harry, 73–74

Jackson, Joyce Marie, 148
Jackson, Michael, 73
Jackson Snowden, Tamara, 9–10, 27, 32, 40–45, 49–50, 53, 119–20, 127, 186, 219n11, 227n11
Jacobs, Claude, 198n25
Jamaica, 66
Jankowiak, William, 210n39
Jasper, Kawana, 168
Jasper, Sharon, 167
jazz, 8, 15, 39, 65, 111, 128–29, 133–34, 137–38, 155, 158; dance, 21, 160–61, 163
Jazz and Heritage Festival, 55, 111, 115, 197n4, 216n35
Jazz and Heritage Foundation Archive, 85
Jazz Fest, 1, 58, 118
jazz funeral. *See* funerals: jazz
Jazzy Ladies Social Aid and Pleasure Club, 122
Jim Crow laws, 5, 39, 104, 163, 190, 212n80
John Canoe, 62
Johnson, E. Patrick, 12, 78, 80
Johnson, Fred, Jr., 23, 110, 112, 213n97
Johnson, Henry, 94, 98
Johnson, Imani Kai, 214n3
Johnson, Jasmine E., 192n12
Johnson, Julie, 33–34
Johnson, Robert, 68
Johnson, Zada, 148
Jolly Bunch Social and Pleasure Club, 28, 134
Jones, Benjamin "BJ," 189
Jones, Benny, Sr., 80–81, 160–61, 163–65
Jones, Thelma "Miss Tee," 81, 161, 163
Joseph, Miranda, 33
Juvenile Justice Project of Louisiana, 40

K-Doe, Antoinette. *See* Fox, Antoinette Dorsey Kador
Keep-N-It-Real Social & Pleasure Club, 1–2, *4*, 5, 8, 16, 131, 149, 194n49
Kelley, Robin D. G., 53
Kennedy, John F., 102

Kimble, Walter, 122
kinesthetics, 66, 130–31
Kinfolk Brass Band, 85
King, Martin Luther, Jr., 99–100, 106
Kingdom of Kongo, 40, 63, 68, 93, 203n27
Kingston, Jamaica, 66
kinship, 10, 22, 51, 125, 127
Knights of Gemini, 98
Knowles Carter, Beyoncé. *See* Beyoncé
Kraut, Anthea, 121
Krewe of Babylon, 98
Krewe of Red Beans, 184. *See also* Feed the Secondline
krewes' parades, 98
Ku Klux Klan, 89

labor, 11, 29, 63, 127, 193n35
Labor Day parades, 110, 213n97
Lacen, Anthony "Tuba Fats," 27
Lacen Keller, Barbara, *26*–30, 135–36, 197n8, 210n39
Ladies' Charity, Aid, and Pleasure Club, 8–9
Ladies Zulu Social Aid and Pleasure Club, 135
Lady Jolly Bunch Social and Pleasure Club, 28
Lady Money Wasters Social Aid and Pleasure Club, 27–28, 135–36
Lady Sequence Social Aid and Pleasure Club, 125
LaFleur, Ingrid, 7
Lake Pontchartrain, 68
Landrieu, Mitch, 49
Latin America, 37
Laveau, Marie, 207n108, 223n75
Lazard, Nicole, 31, *142*, 143–46, 156, 158–59, 219n11
Lee, Robert E., 93, 104, *105*, 209n20
Lee, Spike, 225n2
Lee Circle. *See* Tivoli Circle
Leisure Hour Pleasure and Embroidery Club, 9
levees, 151–52
Lewis, Augustine Germaine, 28
Lewis, Roger, 80, 131, 136

256 Index

Lewis, Ronald W., 73, 134–35, 183
LGBTQ people, 11
Lindy Hop (dance), 121
Lipsitz, George, 154, 194n44
lodges, 37, 135; Masonic, 38, 107
Lomax, Alan, 129–30, 139, 150, 163–64, 220n18
Lombard, Rudy, 102, 112, 129
Long, Alecia P., 157
Longshoremen's Protective Union and Benevolent Association, 110–11, 213n97. *See also* International Longshoremen's Association
Look (magazine), 95
Louisiana, 63, 91, 104, 136, 180, 203n27, 209n16, 213n103; antebellum, 38 (*see also* New Orleans, neighborhoods in); Baton Rouge, 97, 102–3, 112; Orleans Parish (county), 111, 180; slavery in, 40, 92
Louisiana Native Guards and Volunteers, 209n16
Louisiana State Medical Society, 198n25
Louisiana Supreme Court, 100
Louisiana Weekly, 94, 97, 102–3, *108*
Louisville, Ky., 24, 182
Loyola University, 153
lynching, 5, 71, 92
Lyons, Traion, 184, *187*
Lyons, Travis, 184

Magner, Kristy, 19, 179, *181*
Maira, Sunaina, 159
Malone, Jacqui, 39–40, 66
Mama Ruth. *See* Queen, Ruth
Mandela, Nelson, 72–73, 89
mapping, 34, 70, 72, 160, 165; re-, 49, 93, 158; technology, 149–50
Mardi Gras, 1, 5, 7, 50, 86, 112, 126, 157, 163; permits for, 184, 188, 200n63; and the Zulu parade, 93–94, 95, 97–101, 174, 183. *See also* Baby Dolls; Black Masking Indians; Carnival; Mardi Gras Indians; Skull and Bones gangs
Mardi Gras Blackout, 23, 95, 97–103

Mardi Gras Indians, 16, 27–28, 89, 219n1. *See also* Black Masking Indians
Marsalis, Ellis, 183
Marsalis, Wynton, 138
Martin, Randy, 10, 22, 90, 210n33
Marxism-Leninism, 174
masculinity, 15, 76, 195
masking, 7, 33, 89, 100, 157, 184, 196n73. *See also* Baby Dolls; Black Masking Indians; Mardi Gras Indians; Skull and Bones gangs
Mazza, Jay, 164
McBride, Renisha, 157, 221n43
McDonogh 19 Public School, 95–96
McKittrick, Katherine, 148, 159, 165
McQuirter, Marya Annette, 123
Mellow Fellows, 126–27, 129
mentorship, 23, 117, 123–25, 127
methodology of the book, 7, 10–11, 13–24. *See also* ethnography; fieldwork (research); interviews
Midlo Hall, Gwendolyn, 198n28
Miller, Punch, 137
Million Dollar Baby Dolls, 157
mimicking, 122–23, 127
Minneapolis, 24, 182
Miss Antoinette. *See* Fox, Antoinette Dorsey Kador
Mississippi, 102, 111–12
Mississippi Delta blues, 68
Mississippi River, 6, 93–94, 147, 151
modern dance, 15, 160
Mohanty, Chandra Talpade, 224n114
Money Wasters Social Aid and Pleasure Club, 28, 133, 135–36
Monotones, 52
Montana, Allison "Tootie," 112
Moody Analytics, 181
Moore, Beatrice Braxton, 163, 223n76
Moore, Ronnie, 102
Morgan, Joan, 11, 193n31
Morial, Ernest "Dutch," 96, 133
Morris, Sidney, 176
Morris, William, 193n33
Morrison, deLesseps Story, 96
mortuary rites, 23, 60, 63, 66

Mother In Law Lounge, 7
Mother's Day parades, 16, 45–47, 184, 225n115
Mother's Day shooting, 46–47, 49, 67–68, 200n65
Mr. C's TV, 184
Muñoz, José Esteban, 76
mutual aid, 7, 27
mutual aid societies. *See* benevolent associations; Black voluntary associations
Myles, Raymond, 167

Nancy, Jean-Luc, 34
Nash, Jennifer, 193n33
National Association for the Advancement of Colored People (NAACP), 95–96, 98, 101, 106, 111, 215n30
National Dance Theatre Company of Jamaica, 66
Nelson, Lois, 135
Nettleford, Rex, 66
New Basin Canal, 93–94
New Generation Social Aid and Pleasure Club, 146
New Hampshire, 101
New Orleans, neighborhoods in: Bayou District, 169; Central City, 27, 40, 79, 106, 129, 155, 184; Lower Ninth Ward, 95, 147, 152; New Orleans East, 151–52, 176; Ninth Ward, 85, 106, 119, 147, 151–52, 184; Seventh Ward, 16, 109, 147, 166; Sixth Ward/Tremé, 6, 28, 55, 80, 147–48, 155, 183, 223n78; Storyville, 156–58; Third Ward, 79, 129, 155, 162, 165; Twelfth Ward, 174. *See also* French Quarter
New Orleans City Hall, 27, 106, 109, 189
New Orleans Department of Housing and Urban Development, 168
New Orleans Department of Safety and Permits, 185
New Orleans Jazz and Heritage Festival, 55, 111, 115, 197n4, 216n35
New Orleans Police Department (NOPD), 20, 44–45, 49, 50, 81, 101–2, 185, 188–89, 200n63

New Orleans Republican, 8
New Orleans Social Aid and Pleasure Club Task Force, 27, 40, 44–46, 49, 185, 200n63
New York City, 15, 69, 85, 121, 160–61, 195n59
New York Times, 11
nightclubs, 7–8, 23–24, 61, 77–81, 115, 129, 140, 158, 160–63, 170. *See also individual nightclubs*
Nine Times Social Aid and Pleasure Club, 32, *84,* 84–87, 147, 183–84
NOLA for Life (mayoral initiative), 49
Norman Dixon Sr. Annual Second Line Parade fund, 197n4

Ole N Nu Style Fellas Social Aid and Pleasure Club, 51
Olsen, Margaret, 197n7
Olympia Brass Band, 216n31
opacity, 139–40, 218n82
oppression, 7, 10, 19, 53, 60, 63, 90, 94, 192n12. *See also* racism; slavery; violence
Original Big Nine Social and Pleasure Club, 73, 134, 147, 183
Original Big Seven Culture and Heritage, 45
Original Big Seven Junior Steppers, 59
Original Big Seven Social and Pleasure Club, 22, 24, 36–37, 51–53, 72, 78, 81, 147, 170, *190*; and Edward Buckner, 16, 31, 45–49, 59–61, 67–68, 165–67, 184, 186, 188–89
Original Men Buckjumpers Social Aid and Pleasure Club, 133, 136
Original Men's Prince of Whales, 196n3
Original New Orleans Lady Buckjumpers Social Aid and Pleasure Club, 2, 27–29, 126, 133, 136
Ortique, Revius O., Jr., 107
Ott, Francine, 69–70
ownership of place, 10, 22–24, 133, 156, 219n1; collective, 90, 121, 148, 159, 165, 170. *See also* place, concept of

Parker, Raphael, 183–84
Parlett, Jack, 193n33
People's Defense League, 111
Perfect Gentlemen Social Aid and Pleasure Club, 184–85, *187*–188
Perry, Imani, 11, 48, 201n72, 220n19
Philadelphia, 33
Pierre, Louis, 86
Pigeon Town Steppers Social Aid and Pleasure Club, 147
place, concept of, 12, 22–24, 46, 138, 149, 154, 161, 165, 170. *See also* ownership of place; saying place; tight places; white spatial imaginary
plaçage matches, 38
Platenburg, Gerald, 32, *84*–88
pleasure, definitions of, 7–8
poetics of transgression, 100–101, 107
police, 20, 45–46, 63, 93, 96, 101, 158, 169, 174; brutality, 24, 42, 57, 71, 85, 88, 99, 104, 112, 148, 182, 186, 188–89, 208n6; dogs, 94, 102, 112; escorts, 2–3, 13, 60, 106, 128, 159, 170, 188–89. *See also* New Orleans Police Department
politics of pleasure, definition of, 7
Pontchartrain Expressway, 104
Porch, The, 16
Porter, Eric, 44
poverty, 6, 39, 43, 71, 82, 104, 152, 168
Powell, Shannon, *26*
Preservation Hall, 111
Prevost, Tessie, 95–96, 104
Prince Hall Masonic Lodge, 38
Prince of Wales Social Aid and Pleasure Club, 7–9, 42, 90, *172*, 173–74
prison-industrial complex, 43
Progressive Era, 8
property, 24, 51; intellectual, 122, 124; ownership of, 10, 149, 152; private, 23, 148, 159, 170
Protestantism, 38, 65, 96, 155, 198n38
public housing, 6, 147, 152, 165, 167–69. *See also individual public housing developments*
public schools, 6, 92, 95, 99, 104. *See also* integration; segregation

public spaces, 1, 10, 93, 100–101, 107, 148, 194n44, 197n7
Putumayo Records, 176
Pythian Theater, 93

Quadroon balls, 21, 38
Queen, Ruth, 80
queerness, 11, 78, 193

race, 7, 13, 20–21, 37–38, 49, 76, 88, 94, 156–57, 161; and de/segregation, 95–96, 101–2, 104–5, 212n79; and Freedom March, 107, 109; and Hurricane Katrina, 18, 151–54, 220n27; racial capitalism, 11, 170, 193n35; racial equality, 97, 133, 165, 201n80; racial uplift, 136, 138
racism, 18, 53, 82, 103–4, 151, 154–55, 165, 175, 182, 209n28; antiblack, 49–50, 71; institutional, 8, 180, 220n34; structural, 24, 190; violent, 93, 96. *See also* antiblackness; Ku Klux Klan; white supremacy
Ramsey, Guthrie, 66
Rankins, Julius, 28
Rankins, Lawrence, Sr., 28
Rankins, Leroy, 28
Ratcliff, Wellington "Skelly," Jr., 74–77, 124–27, 188
ratty dancing, 8, 137
Reaganomics, 190
Rebirth Brass Band, 14, 74, 79, 119–20, 129, 161, 164, 176, 183
Reckdahl, Katy, 182, 225n115
Reconstruction era, 37–39, 71, 92
record keeping (dance as), 12, 95
redevelopment, 165, 169
Red Flame Hunters, 16
redlining, 151
Reed, Ishmael, 11, 90
Regis, Helen A., 12, 19, 49, 71, 148, 159, 210n39, 222n55
rehearsals, 122, 125–27
resistance, 7, 11–13, 21, 23–24, 60, 94–99, 103, 128–29, 139–40, 165
reverence, 5, 62, 138, 150, 167
ring shout, 64–65, 78, 80, 139

River Garden housing development, 168–69
Roach, Joseph, 219n1
Robertson, Don, 78, 164–65
Robeson, David Paul, 220n18, 221n35
Robinson, Cedric, 193n35
Rock Bottom, 177
Rockwell, Norman, 95
Rogers, Kim Lacy, 89, 96
rolling (dance), 14, 56, 104
rooftops, 13, 23–24, 143, 150, *155*, 156, 158–59, 220n18
Rosaldo, Michelle, 201n71
Ruth's Cozy Corner, 80

Sacred Heart Catholic Church, 80, 207n105
Sakakeeny, Matt, 21, 39, 42–44, 137, 199n49, 204n37, 221n33
Salaam, Kalamu ya, 17–18, 50–53, 71, 74, 160–62
Sanctified church, 65, 205n55
Sanger Theater, 133
Santoro, Daniella, 76
Save Our Schools, 96
Savoy Ballroom, 121
#SayHerName, 182
saying place, 148–49, 154, 156, 159–60, 164, 170
Scene Boosters Social Aid and Pleasure Club, 29, 127, 135
Schiro, Victor, 105–7, 109
Scott, Aekin, 46–47, 200n65
Scott, Ayo, 109, *110*
Scott, Shawn, 46–47, 200n65
Scubble. *See* Davis, Rodrick "Scubble"
Seals, Catherine, 207n108
Second Line Cultural Tradition Task Force. *See* New Orleans Social Aid and Pleasure Club Task Force
Secondline Shorty. *See* Dorsey, Terrylyn
segregation, 15, 39, 93, 104, 154, 165, 212n79; desegregation, 95–96, 99, 105–6, 168; protests against, 98, 102, 107, 209n32. *See also* Jim Crow laws
Seiferth, Eric, 92

self-expression, 23, 76, 138
self-reliance, 37
sexuality, 8, 78, 80, 100, 157, 221n45
sex work, 8, 156–57
Shakespeare Park. *See* A. L. Davis Park
Sharpe, Christina, 5–6
Shavers, Dinerral, 40–41
Shelly, Brandon "Itchy," 214n3
showmanship, 6, 127
sideliners, 35–36, 127
SilenceIsViolence, 22, 40–41, 44, 208n9
Single Ladies Social and Pleasure Club, 115–16, 145
Single Men Social and Pleasure Club, *114*, 116, *123*, *142*, 145, 158
Skelly Well. *See* Ratcliff, Wellington "Skelly," Jr.
Skull and Bones gangs, 50
slavery, 38, 40, 50–51, 151, 190, 192, 198, 208n18, 220n19, 225n114; chattel, 149, 204n37; and Congo Square, 11, 62–64, 91–92; legacy of, 5–6, 104
Sloan, Lenwood, 62, 70, 203n29
Smart Set. *See* Zulu Social Aid and Pleasure Club
Smith, Jerome, 89–91, 96, 102, 112, 129–31, 134–35
Smith, Michael P., 17
Smith, Terrinika, 9–10, 122–23, 125
Smith, Tyree, 13, 15, 32, 35, 121, 123–24
Smith-Simmons, Doratha "Dodie," *110*, 111–12, 119–20, 127
social aid and pleasure clubs (SAPCs), 27–28, 31, 40, 56, 67, 91, 144, 175, 193n33, 210n39; aid and activism of, 7–9, 37, 42–45. *See also individual SAPCs*
social and pleasure clubs (S&PCs). *See* social aid and pleasure clubs (SAPCs)
social dances, 21, 65, 134, 218n78
social mobility, 53, 104, 154, 170
social welfare, 104, 109, 197n7
Société d'Économie et d'Assistance Mutuelle (Economy Society), 38

Solnit, Rebecca, 8
sonic-kinetics, 2, 62, 64, 129–30, 149
Sons of Jazz, 29
Southern University at New Orleans, 102, 173
spatial mobility, 154, 158
Spiderman, moniker of, 129, 150, 160, 220n18
Spillers, Hortense, 51, 53
spirit, 3, 8, 21–23, 60, 71, 77–80, 166, 198–99n38, 204n43, 208n11; catching the, 14, 44–45, 66, 73, 139, 204n41; of the deceased, 29–30, 62–63, 66; spiritual movement, 87; and transcendence, 61, 65–67, 73–76, 81–82, 149–51, 205n55. *See also* transcendence, concept of; transformation, concept of
spirit family, 50–51, 53
Srinivasan, Priya, 193n35
Stallybrass, Peter, 100, 107
St. Bernard public housing development, 24, 47, 147, 165–70, 189
stepping (dance), 14–15, 68, 70, 104, 117, 130, 134–35, 138
Stern, Joe, 90–91, *172*–177, 208n6, 208n11
stilt dancing, 151, 156, 220n18, 221n35
St. Louis, 15
Stooges Brass Band, 144
Story, William, 93
strutting (dance), 2, 6, 8, 14–15, 42, 45, 60, 104, 157, 189
St. Thomas housing development, 168
Stuckey, Sterling, 204n43
styling (dance), 23, 122, 127
Suarez, Matt, 102
subaltern, 63
Suber, Malcom, 173–74
Sublette, Ned, 192n26
suffrage, 38, 92
Sunday school parades, 65, 135–36
Sweet Lorraine's Jazz Club, 109

Tabb, Derrick, 74, 183
Take 'Em Down NOLA movement, 173–74, 182, 209n20, 226n7
Takin' It to the Streets, 194n41, 227n11
Talbert, George, 99, 101
Tambourine and Fan Club, 89–90, 112, 129, 134
tap dance, 15, 121, 124
Tate, Leona, 95–96, 104
Tavern Owners of Greater New Orleans, Inc, 98
Taylor, Breonna, 24, 182, 208n6
Taylor, Diana, 161
Thanos, Nikki, 60
third line, 17, 62
Thomas, Gerald, 109
Thomas, Lynnell, 152, 206n75, 220n27
Thompson, Robert Farris, 70, 203n31
tight places, 43, 199n52
Times-Picayune, 47, 94
Tivoli Circle, 93, 209n20
To Be Continued Brass Band (TBC), 20, 42, 45–47, 67, 78, 186–88
tourism, 1, 6, 12, 36, 63, 65, 85, 111, 156, 206n75; disaster, 13, 152–53; economy from, 6, 50, 97–99, 101–3, 128, 181; and tourists joining parades, 139–40
Townes, Efrem, 131–32, 163
transcendence, concept of, 19, 38, 44, 60–61, 65–67, 73–76, 81–82, 149–51, 202n6, 204n41, 205n55
transformation, concept of, 61, 66–67, 69, 73–75, 81, 128, 151, 202n6
Treme (TV series), 13
Tremé Community Center, 89
Tremé Hideaway, 184
Tremé Sidewalk Steppers, *3, 54, 155*
Trombone Shorty. *See* Andrews, Troy "Trombone Shorty"
Tsing, Anna, 137
Tucka, 52
Tulane University, 153, 180
Tureaud, A. P., 96
Turner, Christina, 210n39
Turner, Richard Brent, 62

Undertaker Lodge No. 2, 163
unions, 37, 43, 92, 95, 97, 110, 213n97

United Brothers, 92
United Clubs, Inc. (UCI), 95, 97–99, 103, 106, 109, 209n32, 212n87
University of Florida, 179
un/survival, 6, 21, 50, 104, 136
Uptown Swingers Social Aid and Pleasure Club, 77, 147, 183
Urban Bush Women, 33, 195n59, 204n46
Urban League of Greater New Orleans, 98, 136
U.S. Army, 143
U.S. Gulf Coast, 180
U.S. Supreme Court, 101–2, 210n34

Valiente, Joe, 211n62
Valley of Silent Men Social Aid and Pleasure Club, 145, 185
Vaz-Deville, Kim Marie, 157, 196n73
Vega, Marta Morena, 202n6
Venmo, 183
Versatile Ladies of Style Social Aid and Pleasure Club, 115
vertical space, 23, 36, 51, 150–51, 158–60
violence, 17, 40, 44, 55, 64, 77, 107, 184, 199n50, 200n65; epidemic of, 49, 208n9; gun, 42–43, 45–48, 60, 72, 101, 186, 189; interpersonal, 22, 45–48, 53, 60, 170, 189; police, 24, 42, 57, 71, 85, 88, 99, 104, 112, 148, 182, 186, 188–89, 208n6; racial, 71, 93, 95–97, 102–4, 190; structural, 22, 43, 53, 60, 82, 85, 189. *See also* Mother's Day shooing; oppression; police; racism; SilenceIsViolence
VIP Ladies and Kids Social Aid and Pleasure Club, 9, 35, 40–42, 44, 145
Vodou, 62, 80, 207n108
voodoo, 62
voting, 10, 38, 92, 99, 111, 213n103

wake work, 6
Walker, Alice, 136
Walker, Harry J., 39
Walker, Lilly, 167

walking, in parades, 2, 15, 36, 56, 67
Wall Street Journal, 180
Wampanoag American Indians, 206n73
Washington, DC, 97, 102, 158
Washington, Lucy, 98
Watts, Lewis, 44
Wavelengths, 71, 216n35
weather (ontological), 5, 7, 191n2
Webster, Kyshun, 167
Weiss, Gail, 206n92
Welsh, Kariamu, 61, 73, 197n19, 202n6
we-ness, 19
West Africa, 18, 60, 62–63, 66, 121; and Christianity, 23, 60; and dance, 33, 151, 156
Westbank Steppers Social Aid and Pleasure Club, 147
West Central Africa, 60
"We Wrote the Book of Love" (theme), 52
White, Allon, 100
White, Michael G., 21, 39
White, Noel, 101
White Boy Joe. *See* Stern, Joe
White Citizens' Councils, 96
white spatial imaginary, 154, 159, 170
white supremacy, 76, 92–93, 182, 226n7. *See also* Ku Klux Klan
white teapot, 152–54
William Frantz Elementary School, 95, 210n34
Williams, Patricia J., 192n30
womanism, 136
women of color, 11, 38
Woodfork, Lilly Walker, 167
Woods, Clyde, 165, 223n86
Woods, Shelbra, 56
working class, 71, 91, 95–96, 127, 168, 175; neighborhoods, 9, 44, 150–51, 185, 225n114
Wright, Kobin, 4
WWOZ (radio station), 183, 185, 194n41, 216n35, 227n11

Young, Harvey, 103
Young Fellaz Brass Band, 189

Young Men Olympian Jr. Benevolent Association (YMO), 69, 75, 78, 126, 145, 184, 196n3. *See also* Furious Five; Mellow Fellows

youth programs, 16, 50, 89, 129. *See also individual youth organizations*

Zion City Sick and Friendship Club, 9

Zollar, Jawole Willa Jo, 205n46

Zulu Social Aid and Pleasure Club, 93–96, 98–101, 103, 174, 183, 196n3, 209n28

Zulu tribe, 93

RACHEL CARRICO is an assistant professor of dance studies at the University of Florida.

The University of Illinois Press
is a founding member of the
Association of University Presses.

———————————————

University of Illinois Press
1325 South Oak Street
Champaign, IL 61820-6903
www.press.uillinois.edu